2-17

EASTERN EUROPE
BETWEEN THE WARS
1918–1941

*the text of this book is printed
on 100% recycled paper*

EASTERN EUROPE
BETWEEN THE WARS
1918-1941

By

HUGH SETON-WATSON

THIRD EDITION, REVISED

Harper & Row, Publishers
New York, Evanston, and London

EASTERN EUROPE BETWEEN THE WARS,
1918-1941

Printed in the United States of America.

All rights reserved.

This book was originally published in 1945 by Cambridge University Press, with a second edition in 1946, and a third edition in 1962. It is here reprinted by arrangement with Cambridge University Press. The third edition was published in the United States by Archon Books, Hamden, Connecticut.

First HARPER PAPERBACK edition published 1967 by Harper & Row, Publishers, Inc., 10 East 53 rd Street, New York, N.Y. 10022.

CONTENTS

full restoration—Recovery of territory from Axis—Hungarian ruling class and Hungarian Imperialism—Vojvodina, Crisana and Ruthenia.

Balkan Imperialisms. Aims of Greek, Bulgarian and Serbian Imperialisms— Italian and Turkish aims in the Balkans—Serbo-Bulgarian relations—Greek attitude to Southern Slavs—Greece as maritime and continental Power—The Aegean coast—The Albanian problem—The Straits—Balkan Federation as a solution to Balkan problems.

CONTENTS

MAPS

PREFACE TO THE FIRST EDITION

THIS BOOK is the result of five years of intermittent study, of which the first three were spent in Eastern Europe and the last two in circumstances which allowed occasional leisure to sort out material and finally to write the book.

My interest in Eastern Europe does not date from five years, for I had met many, and got to know some, citizens of Eastern Europe, thus acquiring some knowledge of its background, before I ever tried to study special problems on the spot.

The original aim was to write a scientific work, based on all available sources. Even before the outbreak of war the volume and unreliability of the material led me to doubt whether this could be done. Now it is impossible, not only for the period of German occupation but for the future, for many records will have been destroyed before the enemy is finally expelled. All that remained possible was to make the best use of my own limited experiences, observations and reading.

My sources have mainly been people. Conversations with men and women of each nation, of various political views and social origin, give one in some ways a better picture than study of documents. The danger is that the opinions of individuals are always fallible and often insincere, and that time, labour and good luck, not always simultaneously available, are required to check them against each other.

A second source has been mere travel. I have visited for varying periods all the countries under review in this book, and in some of them I have spent considerable time. It is not essential to go to a country in order to learn about its politics, for one can discover much from nationals abroad. Nevertheless even a glimpse of the landscape and of a few towns can be of great help. He who uses his eyes and ears can sometimes find in an unexpected moment the key to a problem that has puzzled him for long.

The third source has been books. A few standard works in English, French and German are useful, but for much of the material the only written source is in local newspapers, which cannot be quoted in footnotes or bibliography because one throws them away as soon as one has read them. My task has been easier because I have fair reading knowledge of most, and good speaking knowledge of some, of the Eastern European languages. The most useful books which this has opened to me have been some serious studies of the condition of the peasantry in Hungarian, Roumanian and Serbo-Croat.

I have tried to treat the subject of Eastern Europe as a whole, seeking especially to avoid partisanship for any one national group at the expense of another.

I fear that no 'Integral Nationalist' of any Eastern European country would concede me the merit of 'objectivity', for to such men 'objectivity' means the total acceptance of their opinions.

There is another type, commoner in Britain than in Eastern Europe, who on different grounds will deny me any semblance of 'objectivity'. This is the man who considers the truth always to lie half-way between any pair of extremes. On no account must any 'objective' person agree on any point with any 'extremist'. This view is also sometimes combined with the British intellectual's dislike of simple ideas. Any political idea, especially one which can be grasped at once by the ordinary citizen, must be unsound, for it does less than due honour to intellects created to deal with subtleties.

Widespread though they are, these are surely misconceptions. An objective student of a problem is a man who does his best to consult all sources, human and documentary, which his time and his resources bring within his reach, and then, having carefully reflected, draws his own conclusions. The conclusions, which cannot claim infallibility, are his own, the product of his judgment combined with his material. He will not have to change them because he finds that they coincide in certain respects with those of any other individual or group.

To those friends in Eastern Europe whose help before the

war made this work possible, I hope to be able one day to acknowledge my debt. My greatest debt has been to my father, who not only provided the Appendix on 'Racial and Religious Statistics', and saw the MS. through the Press during my absence on service overseas, but in a more general way from earliest years aroused and maintained my interest in the subject.

H. S.-W.

November 1943

PREFACE TO THE THIRD EDITION

THIS BOOK was written in Capetown and Cairo during the late summer of 1942 and the winter of 1942–43. This was the critical period of the Second World War, in which the forces of Britain and of the Soviet Union were strained to their utmost, and when the vast resources of the United States had not yet made themselves fully felt. It was a time of enthusiasm in Britain for the Soviet ally. It was a time when Hitler's Reich was tremendously powerful, but the victory of the Allies was beginning to assume more concrete shape. It was a time when the hope, not only of ultimate victory but of a new and better world, in which Britain and Russia would play a leading part, together with their great American ally, was widespread in Britain. The book reflects the mood of those times, in which its author fully shared. The hopes have long since proved illusory, but I see no reason to feel ashamed, or to conceal the fact, that I shared them.

Eastern Europe was then under the yoke of Hitler. This yoke was replaced, not by liberty but by the new yoke of Soviet imperialism, from which only Greece, Austria and Yugoslavia were removed, at different times and in different ways, and with results of which different opinions may be held. My own views of these later events, for what they are worth, have been expressed in books written in more recent years.

A thorough study of Eastern Europe between the wars has yet to be written. To-day it would be impossible to produce a complete and balanced history, based on the principal documentary sources, since these would mostly not be available. But a book based on systematic study of secondary sources in East European languages, together with some fragmentary primary sources, could be written. Unfortunately my own preoccupations in recent years have been in a different direction, and I can only hope that some Western scholar, or group of scholars, will perform this difficult but valuable task in the next years. Meanwhile, in the absence of more scholarly surveys, my own book of twenty years ago seems worth reproducing, and I welcome the opportunity to present it again.

The last chapter of the original book, which concerned the relations of the Great Powers with regard to Eastern Europe, and pointed towards the future as I saw it then, has been removed, as it has been completely outdated by subsequent events. The rest of the book is produced exactly as it was, without change. My judgment of many of these events and problems has changed. But my judgment of 1942, which was that of many East Europeans whom I knew, is a small part of the history of the time, and should be respected as such, at least by me. I should like here to make only a few brief comments from the standpoint of the early 1960's.

The picture I presented of the political system is, I think, basically true. But I am now more aware than I was of the difficulty of reforming abuses and injustices. The corruption, inefficiency and injustice were due less than I thought to the wickedness of the political leaders of the 1930's, and more to the conditions which they had inherited. If I were writing the book to-day, I should lay stress on the chauvinist spirit which permeated the educational system of Eastern Europe, and pay greater tribute to those positive achievements which were made, despite all faults. The educational record of the small Balkan states between 1900 and 1940 certainly compares very favourably with that of Imperial Russia between 1800 and 1917, and it remains to be seen whether the new states of Asia and Africa will do better. The failure of the Balkan states after 1918 to put reality into the constitutional frameworks of democracy, which they constructed in the era of Wilsonian liberalism, has already been tragically paralleled by a number of independent Asian and African states.

The picture I presented of the appeal of communist ideas to

the educated young generations, and to a lesser extent to the masses, in a large part of Eastern Europe, was also true at the time I wrote it. The years after 1945 brought not a New Deal of liberty and social justice but a totalitarian tyranny and colonial subjection to the Soviet Empire. Yet in the 1940's many East Europeans had great hopes of true liberation from the East, and regarded the communist parties as brave champions of liberty and justice. They were wrong, and I who sympathised with them was wrong, but their illusions and mine are a part of history.

I wrote in 1943 that I could not then express my gratitude to those who had explained their country's problems to me, since they were living in Hitler's empire. To-day many of them are living in the Soviet empire, and the same considera- tion applies. But at least I can acknowledge my debt to the dead. One of my best Roumanian friends and informants was Anton Golopenţia, an outstanding expert on the social problems of Roumanian agriculture and indeed on the history, beliefs and customs of the peasantry of the whole Danube Basin. He died in a communist prison. One of the best of my Jugoslav friends and informants, Vasa Srzentic, after a life spent in and out of prison as a communist and ex-communist, led a migratory existence between communist Jugoslavia, the United States, France and communist Czechoslovakia, ended up in a refugee camp in Western Germany and died shortly after emerging from it. Of these two men—humane, intelligent, cultured and objective observers of their own countries and loyal friends—I can only express my useless but sincere gratitude that I was able to know them.

London, *December* 1961

INTRODUCTION

BETWEEN GERMANY and Russia live a hundred million people. A few hundred miles separate them from the shores of Britain, but to the British people, which is aware of the existence of Zulus and Malays, Maoris and Afridis, they are unknown. They have unpronounceable names, and live in plains and forests, on mountains and by rivers which might be in another world. When Mr Chamberlain spoke of the Czechoslovaks as 'people of whom we know nothing', he was telling the truth and he was speaking for the British people.

It is true that two World Wars have started in Eastern Europe, and that both have taken a heavy toll of British lives. It is true that the names of Eastern European places and politicians have begun in recent years to fill the British Press, and that an increasing number of books has appeared on the subject. It is true that recurrent crises in Eastern Europe have forced themselves on the attention of British statesmen. Yet knowledge of Eastern Europe is still uncommon in Britain, and it is probable that few are convinced that it is sufficiently important to deserve study.

Although both World Wars started in Eastern Europe, it would be absurd to claim that they were primarily caused by Eastern European problems. Both were the result of a combination of political, social and economic conflicts which governed the relations of the Imperialist Great Powers. Yet Eastern Europe, as a battle-ground of rival Imperialisms, had an important part to play in the origin of both. The Balkan ambitions of Imperial Russia on the one hand, and of Austria-Hungary supported by Germany on the other, were one of the principal factors in world politics in 1914, and it was the swift expansion of Germany towards Eastern Europe in 1938–39 that finally convinced the people and Government of Britain of the necessity of war. German expansion has deeper causes, which it is the task of the political scientist to explore. At the end of this war the establishment of peace for a reasonable period of time depends on the careful study of these causes and upon the adoption by statesmen of measures calculated to deal with the menace of German Imperialism. But it would be unfortunate if these statesmen were to ignore the field in which for fifty years German Imperialism has asserted itself, threatening the interests of Britain, Russia and France. That field is Eastern Europe.

The subject of this book is the region lying between Germany and Russia, and particularly the States of Czechoslovakia, Poland, Hungary, Roumania, Jugoslavia and Bulgaria. Reference will be made in the chapters dealing with foreign policy to Greece, Turkey, Albania and Lithuania, but during the greater part of the work only the first six countries will be considered.

It is unfortunate that no single expression exists which satisfactorily describes the area in question. German publicists have invented a convenient word 'Zwischeneuropa', which does not lend itself to translation. Some British writers have begun to speak of the 'Middle Zone', but this expression has acquired a particular political connotation. 'Central Europe' usually means the Danube Basin, while 'South-Eastern Europe' describes the Balkan Peninsula. For lack of any better phrase, I have used in this book 'Eastern Europe'. If Britain and Russia, both marginal Powers vitally interested in the Continent yet not belonging to it, are put aside, then the countries considered in this book may truly be described as 'Eastern Europe', since they constitute the eastern half of the European Continent in its strictest sense.

Individual Eastern countries offer interesting fields of study to the specialist, but are of small importance in world politics. But the Eastern European Problem, the problem of the hundred millions, is one of the major problems of our age. Its significance can only be understood if it is treated as a whole.

It is most important that the subject be approached without preconceived ideas. Arbitrary notions of 'powder-magazines', 'no-man's lands', 'cordons sanitaires', 'bulwarks', 'blocks' and 'buffers' must be put aside, and an attempt be made to examine the facts. The many solutions and remedies, the ingenious international permutations and combinations, that are discussed with so much interest and enthusiasm, would be more clearly understood if more were known of the problems with which it is proposed to deal.

The hundred millions of Eastern Europe are important to

the two Allied European Great Powers, Britain and Russia. They are important to Britain as a source of European unrest and as the field in which German expansion has made itself felt. They are important to Russia as populating her Western frontier, the security of which has preoccupied her for centuries. They present one of the problems that will affect the execution of the Anglo-Soviet Treaty, which must be one of the dominant factors in Europe during the next generation.

The hundred millions are important, but their importance can also be exaggerated. They have shown themselves weak, divided and inexperienced. Each of the peoples of Eastern Europe must enjoy liberty and self-government if unrest is to be avoided. But it is unrealistic to suppose that mere numbers make strength. The hundred millions cannot become overnight an united Great Power. They cannot do without the help and protection of Britain, America, and their great neighbour the Soviet Union, which are together fighting to save them from German tyranny.

Eastern Europe cannot be separated arbitrarily from the rest of the Continent, for the problems of the part are indissolubly connected with those of the whole. Yet the local factors must be understood if the position of Eastern Europe in the world is to be clear. This necessitates study not only of the interests of the Great Powers in Eastern Europe but of the relations of the Eastern European States with each other. This is impossible without knowledge of the internal political life of the States. This in turn requires a brief survey of their social problems, and especially of the relations of the peasantry with the recently formed bourgeoisie and industrial working-class. Moreover, the necessary minimum understanding of the character and aspirations of the Eastern European nations can be obtained only by reference to their history, which obliges the student to burrow far into the past in order to recognise the origin of forces still operative to-day. Finally, the economic and strategic facts of to-day must be briefly examined by a description, with the help of maps, of the main geographical features and economic resources of Eastern Europe.

In the following pages these points are considered in turn, beginning from the geographical facts and ending with the relation of Eastern Europe to the Great Powers.

CHAPTER ONE

GEOGRAPHICAL BACKGROUND

'EASTERN EUROPE' AND ITS BOUNDARIES

The area reviewed in this book is not a natural geographical unit. It is contained within political frontiers, which in many places do not coincide with natural or geographical landmarks. Nevertheless the area possesses certain geographical characteristics which it is necessary briefly to describe.

It is bounded on the north by the Baltic Sea, on the south by the Mediterranean—on the south-east by the Black Sea and the Aegean, and on the south-west by the Adriatic. The western and eastern borders of its northern section are less clearly marked.

The western line, starting from the eastern corner of the Alps, crosses the western fringe of the Central European plain to the Danube, beyond which it strikes the mountains of Bohemia. These form for 500 miles a natural barrier in the shape of a rough horse-shoe. From the junction of the former German, Polish and Czechoslovak frontiers in Silesia to the Baltic coast stretches a flat plain which offers no natural boundary to separate Poles from Germans.

The eastern line is still less satisfactory. The Dniestr and Prut rivers have served at different times as a frontier between Russia and Roumania, but neither is an effective obstacle to invasion from one side or the other. The same is true of the Russo-Polish frontier, which was for centuries the subject of inconclusive wars and remains an unsolved problem. In the extreme north-east are the Baltic States, equally devoid of natural boundaries and inhabited by three small peoples, of whom the Esthonians are related to the Finns, while the Lithuanians and Letts are distinct in character and language from their neighbours. All boundaries in this region must be arbitrary. In this book we shall take as the limit of our subject the post-1918 eastern frontiers of Poland and Roumania. Reference will be made at times to the Baltic States in connection with Polish policy, but they should be considered as being outside the scope of the book and the competence of the author.

Within the area defined above are three distinct regions, which we shall call the Baltic, the Danubian and the Balkan.

THE BALTIC REGION

The Baltic Region lies between the Baltic Sea and the Carpathian Mountains. It is a plain, broken by forests and marshes, especially in the Polish province of Polesia, and intersected by a number of big rivers. Of these far the most important is the Vistula, on which lie both Warsaw and Cracow, and which enters the sea at Danzig, the port of historical Poland. This broad and impressive stream is the greatest trade route in the country, and is fed by a number of large tributaries.

The Baltic Region is predominantly agricultural, producing rye, potatoes and wheat. The soil is not rich, save in Eastern Galicia, its south-eastern corner. Livestock and dairy-farming were developing on promising lines in Poland in the last years before the war, and Polish bacon was already filling the British market. The chief industrial areas are Silesia, whose rich coal mines made Poland an exporter of coal, and Lódz, the centre of an important textile industry and a city of 800,000 inhabitants. Eastern Galicia has important petroleum wells. A new industrial area was planned by the Polish State in the centre of the country, between Cracow, Sandomierz and Przemysl. Some progress had been made here with heavy industry before the German invasion. The only ports possessed by the modern Polish Republic were Danzig and Gdynia.

Between the Baltic Region and the Danube Basin lie Bohemia and Moravia. Their rivers run both north, into the Oder and the Elbe, and thence into the Baltic and North Seas, and south, into the Danube. They are surrounded on north, west and south by mountains, which in places are easily traversed but in others provide a formidable barrier. On the east minor hill ranges separate Moravia from the northern fringe of the Central European plain. The interior of Bohemia and Moravia consists of rolling country and plain, interrupted by hills. The land is fertile, and agriculture is prosperous, including cereals, livestock and dairy produce. The country is highly industrialised, the most important centres being Prague, Pilsen, Brno, Moravská Ostrava. Heavy industry is very strong, especially armaments. Textiles played a big part under the Czechoslovak Republic, and the specialised glass industry of Northern Bohemia once had markets all over the world.

THE DANUBIAN BASIN

The Danubian Basin is cut in two by the Carpathians, which after forming the northern boundary towards Poland turn south between Ruthenia and Bukovina, follow this direction for 250 miles, then run west from Braşov for 200 miles and finally turn south to meet the Danube at the Iron Gates, whose southern side is formed by the mountains of Eastern Serbia. This formidable barrier can be crossed without trouble by a number of passes, of which the most important are formed by the valleys of the Prahova, Olt, Bistritsa and Jiu. Northwest of these mountains is the contested province of Transylvania, consisting of barren mountains, forests, cultivable uplands and a few river valleys of fertile soil. Its natural boundary in the west is the lower range of the Ore Mountains, which run from north to south and connect the Carpathians of Ruthenia with those of the Banat.

On either side of these mountains are open, fertile plains. The western plain is the Pannonia of Roman times, now mostly included in the modern Hungary. Its centre is the Middle Danube, and its circumference is washed by the great tributaries, Drava and Sava in the south and Tisza in the east. Its natural boundaries are the Moravian hills and the Carpathians in the north, the foothills of the Alps in the west and the uplands of Croatia and Bosnia in the south. For our present purpose we will take as its limits in the west the Austro-Hungarian frontier, which since the Middle Ages has been advanced some 20 to 50 miles into the plain, and in the south the Sava to its junction with the Danube, and the latter as far as the Iron Gates.

The eastern plain stretches from the Danube northwards to merge in the steppes of the Ukraine. At the north-east bend of the Danube two rivers, Siret and Prut, enter it with a short interval between them. At this point the distance between Danube and Carpathians is small, and the lower course of the Siret, widened by a series of lakes and marshes, forms a moderately effective barrier between the strictly Danubian plain of Wallachia and the steppe-lands of Moldavia and Bessarabia. Between the last stretch of the Danube, here flowing from south to north, and the Black Sea, is the province called Dobrudja, an undulating country separated from that of Wallachia by the great river but divided by no natural boundary from Bulgaria.

This whole region is mainly agricultural, and in its agriculture cereals prevail over livestock and dairy produce. The latter flourish mainly in the neighbourhood of big cities, such as Budapest, Bucarest and Zagreb. In the uplands fruit and sheep-farming are important, for instance in Transylvania. The geese of Slovakia deserve special mention: their feathers fill the pillows of middle-class beds in Vienna. The most important mineral wealth of the region is the petrol wells of Roumania, centred in Ploeşti and the Prahova valley. There are appreciable quantities of gold in the Ore Mountains of Transylvania. Coal is mined near Pécs and Dorog in Hungary and at Petroşani in Southern Transylvania. Ruthenia, Transylvania and Moldavia are rich in timber. Manufacturing industry is highly developed in the Budapest region. Transylvania and the Bucarest district have made notable progress in industrialisation during the last twenty years. The only important seaport of this region is Constantsa. A good deal of trade passes in normal times through the Danube ports of Budapest, Bratislava, Giurgiu, Braila and Galaţ.

THE BALKAN PENINSULA

The Balkan Peninsula may be considered for our present purposes as bounded in the north-west by the Alps, in the north by the Sava and lower Danube and on all other sides by the sea. The only point left doubtful by this definition is the Dobrudja which, although on the Balkan side of the Danube, belongs rather to the Danubian Basin than to the Peninsula.

This region is mostly of mountainous character. In the west the coastal strip of Dalmatia is cut off from the interior by a wall of bare mountains, behind which are the less inhabitable lands of Croatia and Bosnia. Western Croatia and Slovenia are hilly and plentifully wooded. They stretch from the Alps and the coastal barrier to the Central European plain washed by Drava and Sava. Bosnia is a land of hills, woods and valleys, with small areas of good cultivable lands. It has high mountains in the south-east. Its main river is the Drina, which forms its frontier with Serbia and flows into the Sava, itself the boundary between Bosnia and Croatia. Hercegovina is

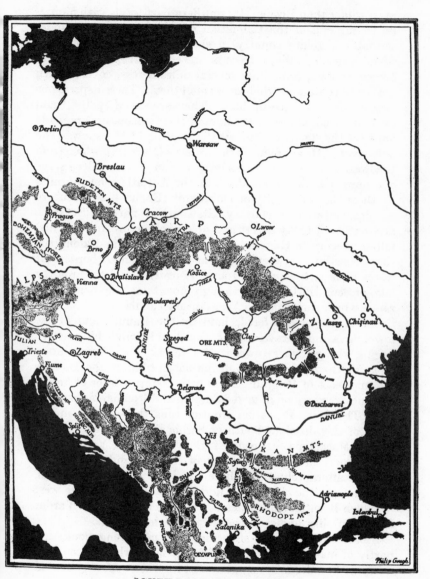

SOUTH-EASTERN EUROPE
(PHYSICAL FEATURES)

even wilder than Bosnia. Its southern part forms with Monte-negro the end of the Dalmatian coastal barrier. It is inde-scribably desolate country, a shapeless wilderness of rock, without peaks, valleys, trees or water, interrupted by unex-pected hollows, sometimes several miles across, covered with grass and containing villages or small towns. These depressions are the sites of dried-up lakes. They are called 'polje',[1] and are cultivated, although the lives of their cultivators are made hard by the floods caused by the melting of the snows. The only river of Hercegovina is the Neretva (Narenta), which from the Bosnian mountains forces its way through a long, deep gorge overhung by fantastic cliffs into the Adriatic some 40 miles north of the walled city of Dubrovnik (Ragusa). Montenegro is a desperately poor country. Its southern part has the same alternation of rocky desert and green hollows as Hercegovina, falling steeply to the sea in the bay of Kotor and along the short coastline between Kotor and the Albanian border. It has a little fertile ground round Podgorica and towards the lake of Scutari. In the north high mountains rise, part of the range which runs through Western Macedonia.

Serbia proper has fertile land by the Danube and in the lower Sava and Morava valleys. South of Belgrade hill country begins, rising higher towards Macedonia. The Morava flows from south to north through Serbia and enters the Danube 30 miles east of Belgrade. The north-eastern corner of Serbia is a backward region of mixed Serbian and Roumanian popula-tion. The Serbo-Bulgarian frontier runs through the moun-tains of this district. South of Serbia lies the much-coveted land of Macedonia. Its centre is the valley of the Vardar. This river flows through the towns of Skoplje and Veles, and, passing alternately through fertile land and rocky defiles, emerges into the open plain north of Salonica, 10 miles west of which it enters the Aegean. On either side of the Vardar are mountains, higher in the west than in the east.

Albania has a coastal strip some 270 miles long, consisting partly of marshes and partly of fertile land, which extends as many as 40 miles into the interior at its widest points. Behind it rise the mountains, stretching back into Macedonia. On the north-east of Albania, in Serbian territory, is the plateau

[1] This word, which in Slav languages means 'field', has also this local significance.

of Kosovo Polje, the scene of the most famous battle in Serbian history, which has besides Serbs a large Albanian population. In the south-east the lake of Ohrid was until 1941 divided between Albania and Jugoslavia. From this lake rises the main Albanian river, the Drin, which, running first north and then south-west into the Adriatic, cuts its way through the Albanian mountains from the main range of Western Macedonia.

Greece is essentially a mountainous country. Olympos, the Pindus and the ranges of the Peloponnese rise to over 7000 ft. There are small fertile plains in Attica, Boeotia, Thessaly and Macedonia. East of Salonica Greece held from 1919 a narrow strip of coast extending beyond the port of Alexandroupolis (Dedeagach) to the Turkish frontier on the Maritsa, cutting off Bulgaria from the sea. Besides the peninsula Greece included Crete, the Ionian and the greater part of the Aegean Islands. Exceptions were the Dodecanese, acquired by Italy in 1910, and the islands of Imbros and Tenedos, at the mouth of the Dardanelles, which belong to Turkey.

Bulgaria has a strip of fertile plain in the north along the Danube. South of this rise the foothills of the Balkan Mountains, which stretch from west to east across the full length of the country. From this range the whole peninsula takes its name. Bounded by the Balkan Mountains in the north and by the ranges of the Serbian frontier district in the west is a cultivable plateau on which is situated the capital, Sofia. South of this are the mountains of the Rila massif, the highest in the country, which reach more than 9000 ft. The south-western corner of Bulgaria is formed by the Struma valley, and is reckoned a part of Macedonia. Fifty miles south-east of Sofia begins the valley of the Maritsa, Bulgaria's main river, which flows 160 miles south-east before turning abruptly south to form the Greco-Turkish frontier and to emerge in the Aegean near Alexandroupolis. Between the Maritsa valley and the sea is the Rhodope range, which runs eastwards 150 miles, sending foothills into Turkish territory. The Black Sea coast of Bulgaria consists of low-lying country broken by hills.

The south-eastern extremity of Europe is Turkish Thrace, rolling country with some fairly high hills, very sparsely populated.

The Balkan Peninsula is predominantly agricultural. Cereals are grown on a big scale only in the rare fertile districts such as Northern Bulgaria and the valley of the Sava. Small quantities of maize and wheat are produced in many parts of the Peninsula on peasant holdings for the consumption of the family only, but with the exception of Bulgaria the Peninsula does not normally export cereals. Livestock farming flourishes in some parts, as for instance in Serbia, whose pigs are famous, and in Central Croatia. Vegetable farming is a Bulgarian speciality. Until recent years Bulgaria exported skilled market gardeners to Central Europe, but this has become less frequent lately. Fruit is produced in large quantities. Especially important are Bosnian plums, Bulgarian strawberries and Greek grapes. Special mention should be made of the 'rose-water industry' of the 'valley of roses' near Kazanlik in Bulgaria, from which the perfume 'attar of roses' is exported to the whole world. Vines are grown in most parts of the Balkans, and many of their wines are excellent, those of Dalmatia being perhaps the best of all. Tobacco is grown mainly in the valleys of the Vardar and Maritsa and along the Greek Aegean coast. The main centres for tobacco are Plovdiv, Kavala and Skoplje. A good deal of Turkey's tobacco is grown in her portion of Thrace. Another important crop in the Vardar valley is the opium poppy, the amount of which used to be regulated by treaty between Jugoslavia and Turkey in accordance with the League of Nations' opium policy. Timber is one of the chief products of Slovenia, Croatia and Bosnia, which once had a flourishing trade with Italy. Olives and olive oil are among the principal exports of Greece.

The Peninsula is rich in mines. Among the most important may be mentioned the copper of Bor in Eastern Serbia, the lead of Trepča near the plain of Kosovo, the Central European mines in Slovenia, the coal of Pernik in Bulgaria and the bauxite of Dalmatia. Manufacturing industry is not much developed. There are textile and other factories in Croatia which date from before 1914, and various factories have grown up in recent years in such centres as Belgrade, Athens, Sofia and Salonica. Mention should be made of the metallurgical works at Zenica in Bosnia and Kragujevac in Central Serbia. Kavala and Plovdiv have factories employing a large number of workers in connection with the tobacco industry. One of the most important branches of the Balkan economy is the Greek merchant fleet, which in peace time traded on all the seas of the world, and gave employment to thousands of Greeks both on its ships and in the docks of the Piraeus and other Greek harbours. The merchant fleets of Jugoslavia and Bulgaria were only beginning to develop in the period between the two wars. The principal ports of the Balkan Peninsula are Piraeus, Salonica and Kavala on the Aegean; Istanbul on the Bosphorus; Burgas and Varna on the Black Sea; Patras on the Gulf of Corinth; and Sušak, Split, Durazzo and Valona on the Adriatic. The chief Danube ports on the southern side of the river are Belgrade and Ruse (Ruščuk).

HISTORICAL, CULTURAL AND ETHNICAL BOUNDARIES

The natural lines of communication and the natural barriers indicated above have often served in the history of Eastern Europe as routes for invasions and frontiers for Kingdoms and Empires. Especially important in the first respect have been the valleys of the Vardar and the Maritsa, and the passes of Predeal and the Red Tower in the Carpathians and the Shipka in the Balkan Mountains. The most ancient natural frontiers have been the Bohemian Mountains, the Sava and the Carpathians. The Danube has been throughout known history a line of invasion, a commercial thoroughfare and a frontier line.

There is another line of division for our area which might appear more natural than that given above. This would distinguish between Central Europe, the Balkans and North-Eastern Europe. The first would consist of the Middle Danube plain, bounded by Alps, Carpathians and Serbian and Bosnian mountains. The second would comprise the Peninsula south and south-west of the plain. To the third would belong Poland and part of Trans-Carpathian Roumania, which, separated by no effective boundary from the Ukraine, may be regarded as a westward extension of the Russian steppes.

Such a division would correspond to the main cultural divisions in our area. 'Central Europe', as defined above, was once included within the Austro-Hungarian Monarchy, and shared in the common culture whose centre was Vienna. To-day the difference separating 'Central Europeans' from 'Balkanites' or 'Orientals' is still strongly marked, and the former insist, sometimes with little justification and much tactlessness, on their immense superiority to the latter. Although in my opinion the division between Baltic, Danubian and Balkan is more important than that between Central, South-Eastern and North-Eastern, the reader should not fail to bear in mind both lines of division.

The principal natural barriers in Eastern Europe have often formed frontiers of States, but they have seldom corresponded with ethnical boundaries. It is true that it is generally possible to associate certain Eastern European nations with certain geographical regions. Thus it can be said that the home of the Hungarians is the Middle Danube plain; of the Serbs the hilly country between the three rivers Danube, Drina and Morava; of the Bulgarians the Balkan Mountains and the Maritsa valley. But the exceptions to such rules are too numerous for them to have great value.

The Peace Settlement of 1919 was based on the principle of Nationality. It attempted for the first time in human history to erect States on an ethnical foundation. It is important to note that its frontiers cut across the geographical boundaries described above. Czechoslovakia from the north, Jugoslavia from the south and Great Roumania from the east all extended well into the Danubian plain. Roumania acquired the whole Dobrudja. The northern frontier of Greece ran across the lower Vardar valley and extended along the Aegean coast to Thrace. This conflict between geography and nationality is one of the fundamental factors in the modern Eastern European problem.

CHAPTER TWO

EARLY HISTORY

THE IMPORTANCE OF HISTORY IN EASTERN EUROPE

A feature of Eastern Europe which strikes the most casual observer is the large number of nations in proportion to the size of the territory. The whole area is about two-thirds the size of Western Europe. In Western Europe five nations occupy nine-tenths of the area—British, French, Italians, Spaniards and Germans. In Eastern Europe are more than three times as many. All are pressed together in this comparatively small space. None has increased its population or developed its economic and social life sufficiently to become a great nation. Each remained small, and even in its own home each became mixed with its neighbours, having minorities of them in its midst and of its own among those neighbours. The reasons for this state of affairs must be sought in the early history of Eastern Europe.

The following historical survey is divided into four parts, each of which has some bearing on the conditions of modern Eastern Europe. The first deals with the period of colonisation, in which the existing nations occupied the lands they now hold. The second shows how the settled nations were exposed to constant pressure from Germans and Italians in the west and from Tatars and Turks in the east, to the repelling of which they were obliged to devote their whole energies. The third summarises the historical role of the States and Empires created at one time or another by the various nations, to whose glories they still look back at the present time for guidance in their modern policy. The fourth briefly describes the fate of the nations under the rule of the alien Habsburg and Ottoman Empires, before these were affected by modern ideas, and shows how Poland as a Great Power declined and was replaced by the third foreign Empire of Russia. The conditions in which the nations lived under the three Empires determined aspects of their political life which are still valid.

THE MIGRATIONS AND THE COLONISATION PERIOD

Of the peoples that inhabited Eastern Europe at the time of the Roman Empire there remain the Greeks, Albanians and Wallachians. The Greeks occupied in Europe much the same territory as to-day, but also extended farther into Macedonia and Bulgaria. Constantinople was Greek, and there were Greek settlements along the western and northern coasts of the Black Sea, as far as Crimea, while a large part of Asia Minor was inhabited by Greeks. The people of the territories now comprising Albania and Jugoslavia were known as Illyrians, and are considered to have been the ancestors of the modern Albanians. North of the Danube, in Transylvania and in Wallachia, were the Dacians, the forefathers of the Roumanians, whose language has disappeared and of whose way of life little is left but some carvings on Trajan's Column in Rome, in which are represented Dacian headdresses closely resembling those still worn by the peasants of certain villages in Southern Transylvania. Moldavia, Poland, Bohemia and even northern and eastern Hungary never belonged to the Roman Empire, and of their inhabitants nothing remains but a few names of tribes in Roman chronicles.

In the third century the lands beyond the Roman frontier were occupied by the Goths, who came into conflict with the Empire. After over a hundred years of frontier wars the Goths established themselves, with kindred Germanic tribes, in Italy, Gaul and Spain. Their place in Eastern and Central Europe was taken by the Slavs. Of the origin of these little is known except that they came from the plains and marshes of Russia. They first appear in Byzantine chronicles as tributaries of a Mongol tribe called the Avars. The Avars established their rule on the ruins of the Hun Kingdom founded in the fifth century by Attila. Throughout the sixth and seventh centuries the Slavs penetrated west and south. The Poles, Wends, Lusatians and other Slav tribes occupied what are now Poland and Prussia, and advanced to the line of the Elbe. The Czechs took possession of Bohemia. The Slovenes filled the valleys of the Eastern Alps, establishing themselves in the modern Austrian provinces of Carinthia, Styria and Lower Austria. The Croats occupied Illyria. The Serbs and kindred tribes penetrated into Macedonia and even into the Greek Peninsula.

The Slavs were unwarlike people. They spread themselves quietly over the countryside, avoiding strong fortified points, living in the forests and marshes, refusing pitched battles and contenting themselves with repeated small-scale plunder expeditions. In the Baltic and Danubian regions there was no power capable of resisting them. In the Balkans they had to face the Byzantine Empire. But they were fortunate in that the seventh century was one of the most difficult periods in the Empire's history. Threatened in the east by the Sassanid King of Persia, Khusru Parviz, and in the west by the Avars, the emperor had no time to spare for the less dangerous Slav intruders. As soon as the Persian threat was removed, it was replaced by the still more terrible danger of Islam. The Slavs availed themselves of these circumstances to colonise the whole northern part of the Peninsula.

In the second half of the seventh century Wallachia was occupied by a Mongol tribe called the Bulgars. Unable to fight on two fronts, the emperor allowed the Bulgars to cross the Danube and take possession of the fertile plain and uplands between the river and the Balkan Mountains. The Bulgars did not remain content with this limit, but during the following hundred and fifty years penetrated the greater part of the country which now bears their name. In the first years of the ninth century the Bulgar Khan Krum besieged Constantinople. During the ninth and tenth centuries Bulgarian power was one of the chief threats to the Byzantine Empire. The ruling class of Mongol Bulgars adopted the language and customs of the Slav population whom they conquered, and the Bulgarian language of to-day, apart from a number of Turkish words acquired during the Ottoman domination, is purely Slav.

At the end of the eighth century a new Great Power arose in the west in the shape of the Kingdom of Charles the Great, who fought several campaigns on the Elbe, in Bohemia and in Austria against the Slavs, and inflicted a crushing defeat on the Avar Kingdom. The Avars never recovered from this disaster. Their place in Central Europe was taken by a short-lived Slav State, the Moravian Empire, which, under Rastislav (845–70) and Svatopluk (870–94) ruled a large part of the Pannonian Plain. After the death of Svatopluk his Empire was weakened by the quarrels of rival pretenders to the throne, skilfully fostered by the German king.

During the last years of the ninth century a new Mongol tribe, the Magyars, appeared on the scene. Driven from their homes in the steppes of Southern Russia by a kindred tribe, the Pechenegs, they crossed the Carpathians and overran the

Central Plain. By the end of the century the Moravian Empire
had been finally destroyed. In 907 the Magyars routed a
powerful German army on the Marchfeld near Vienna. For
twenty-five years they terrorised Western Europe with their
raids, reaching as far as Benevento, Nîmes and Champagne
and regularly ravaging South Germany and North Italy. This
was one of the darkest periods of the history of Western Europe,
for the Hungarian invasions from the east combined with the
attacks of the Danes from the north and Moslems from the
south to destroy almost all that was left of the civilisation of
the past. The Hungarian menace was removed in 955 by the
victory of Emperor Otto I on the Lechfeld. After this the
Hungarians settled down in the Central Plain. They abandoned
their nomadic habits, ceased to harry their neighbours, and
organised themselves in a State. In the year 1000 their duke,
Vajk, received a royal crown from Pope Sylvester, accepted
Christianity and took the name of Stephen. He was later
canonised, and is the national saint of Hungary.

In the year 1000 the political map of Eastern Europe was
approximately as follows. In the north-west the land between
Elbe and Oder was the object of constant frontier wars between the Saxon Emperors and the Slav tribes. The population
was mostly Slav, but the German element was increasing.
Bohemia was a Slav Dukedom, whose rulers usually recognised
the overlordship of the emperor, but from time to time proclaimed complete independence. East of the Oder and north
of Bohemia was the Kingdom of Poland, which under Boleslav
the Brave (992–1025) extended far eastwards, and reached the
Baltic coast in the north and Slovakia in the south. In the
Baltic Provinces were a number of barbarous Slav and
Lithuanian tribes, at war with each other and with Poland,
Denmark and Sweden. Northern Russia was covered with
trackless forests, inhabited by backward Finnish tribes. In
the south of Russia a semi-civilised State had arisen in the
Principality of Kiev, founded according to tradition by North-
men who had sailed from Sweden up the Baltic rivers, crossed
the watershed and descended the Dniepr to the Black Sea.
The Kiev State had important commercial relations with Constantinople, and in 988 its Grand Duke Vladimir accepted
Christianity.

The Central Plain was occupied by the Kingdom of Hungary.

The original Magyar[1] conquerors soon, like the Bulgars to the south, intermixed with the population whom they conquered, themselves already a mixture of Slav, Avar, Hunnish and aboriginal stock. Unlike the Bulgars, however, the Magyars kept their language, which remains one of the purest in Europe, influenced in spirit by Western languages but unchanged in its word-forms and grammatical structure. Transylvania formed part of Hungary, but retained a large aboriginal population.[2] These were the descendants of the Dacians, who during two hundred years of Roman rule had adopted Latin as their language. The Roumanian language of to-day is mainly Latin in character, though later invasions have added to it many Slav, Hungarian and Turkish words. The population of Transylvania became in the course of the following centuries a mixture of Roumanians, Hungarians and Germans, the latter the descendants of colonists settled there by the Hungarian kings. In its south-eastern corner there established themselves a distinct tribe related to the Magyars, the Szeklers, who have kept to this day certain special characteristics of their own. Moreover, during the Middle Ages a number of similar tribes (Kumans, Pechenegs, etc.) were peaceably settled by the Hungarian kings as 'hospites', and became absorbed in the Hungarian nation. In the northern district of Hungary, in the foothills of the Carpathians, the Slav people of the Slovaks have maintained themselves distinct from the Magyars to this day.

The eastern valleys of the Austrian Alps were at this time still in the hands of the Slovenes, who occupied the north-eastern corner of the Adriatic and the hilly country behind it. Farther south, the former Roman province of Illyria was now the Kingdom of Croatia, which had accepted Christianity in the ninth century. Most of the Dalmatian coast was in Croatian hands, though Italian trading colonies remained

[1] The name 'Magyar' originally belonged to one of the several invading Asiatic tribes which founded the Hungarian State, but was later accepted as the name of the whole Hungarian-speaking nation. In this sense it will be used in this book.

[2] The proportion of Roumanians or Dacians to Hungarians in these earlier centuries is the subject of acrimonious controversy between Hungarian and Roumanian historians, the former claiming that the Roumanians did not enter Transylvania until much later. In the absence of conclusive evidence it seems reasonable to suppose that a substantial Dacian population remained there uninterruptedly, but whether it always outnumbered the Hungarians it is impossible to say.

scattered along it. The Adriatic was the only part of the Mediterranean which was little harried by the Moslem fleets. Here a restricted trade continued between the Byzantine Empire and the young city of Venice, later the rival and enemy of Croatia. Bosnia and Serbia were inhabited by Slav tribes, still heathen, which retained in their forest and mountain fastnesses an independence which their neighbours did not find it worth while to challenge.

At the end of the tenth century the Byzantine Empire had reconquered most of Bulgaria, and in 1018 the Emperor Basil II destroyed the Shishmanid Principality ruled by Tsar Samuel the Bulgarian from his capital at Ohrid in South-Western Macedonia. The Byzantine Empire had not far from Belgrade a frontier with Hungary; north of the Danube Wallachia was the plunder-ground of the nomad tribes of the Russian steppes, Pechenegs, Kumans and others, which crossed the territory of Kiev and poured down to the Danube. The rulers of Wallachia constantly changed, but its population remained Dacians, racially intermixed with their conquerors but retaining a language of predominantly Latin character. Greece, Albania, Macedonia and Thrace remained part of the Byzantine Empire.

It is necessary at this stage to point out the division between the Roman and the Greek Churches. In the ninth century the Greek monks Cyril and Methodius had evangelised the Slavs of Moravia and Bulgaria, and provided for their Church ritual an alphabet suited to their language. If their work had survived, all Eastern Europe from Bohemia and the Carpathians southwards would have come under the ecclesiastical leadership of Constantinople. The irruption of the heathen Magyars destroyed this possibility. The Poles and Czechs were separated by the Hungarians from Constantinople, and, subjected to constant pressure from the German frontier, accepted the Catholic branch of Christianity. The Croats in the same century were converted by missionaries from Rome, and in the last year of the millennium Stephen of Hungary imposed on his people the Western faith. Twelve years earlier Vladimir of Kiev, a prince of irregular sexual morals and the murderer of his own brother, had been converted for political reasons by the emissaries of Constantinople, and thereby won the status of saint. Bulgaria and Wallachia had already been won for Constantinople in the days of Cyril and Methodius, but the Serbs remained heathen, and it was only in the thirteenth century, after long hesitation between the competing Churches, that the Nemanyid Prince of Serbia finally announced his conversion to the Eastern branch. The rivalry between Rome and Constantinople, which had existed since the reign of Constantine, had culminated in open schism in 1054. After this date difference of faith provided a cause of mistrust and even hatred between Western and Eastern Europe which was to play an important part in history. The Eastern or Orthodox Church was one of the main factors which helped to shape the mentality of the Balkan and Russian peoples in a different mould from that of the Western and Central European nations.

In the thirteenth century already Hungarians, Slovenes, Croats, Czechs, Poles and Slovaks were Catholics, while Greeks, Serbs, Bulgarians, Roumanians, Albanians and Russians were Orthodox. With the exception of the Albanians, the religions of these nations were to undergo only small or transitory changes. These changes will be mentioned later, but it may be said that the religious division of the thirteenth century is broadly that of to-day.

GERMAN EXPANSION AND ASIATIC INVASION

Throughout the Middle Ages the Eastern European nations and States were subjected to pressure from the west and east.

Charles the Great began to drive the Slavs back from the Elbe and from Austria, and this work was continued a century after his death by the Saxon emperors. Once the Hungarian menace had diminished the emperors were able to concentrate on the extension of their eastern frontier. This proceeded throughout the tenth and eleventh centuries, and even when the emperor was diverted from it by his quarrel with the Papacy, it was continued by the borderland dukes of the Houses of Welf in Saxony and of Babenberg in Austria.

At first the policy of the Empire was defensive. The frontier wars formed part of the long tradition of resistance to the series of minor raids and major invasions which had plagued Germany for more than five hundred years. But during the eleventh and twelfth centuries a change took place. These centuries were a period of economic development in Western

Europe. There was a considerable growth of population, which combined with the greater internal security to cause men to bring waste land into cultivation, to cut down forests, to drain marshes. In Germany there was a movement towards the east. The borderland magnates encouraged the process. They enlisted the vagrant element, which the rise of population had greatly increased, and settled them on the eastern marches, often on conditions more favourable than those under which serfs lived in the interior of Germany. There began a systematic colonisation of the east by the Germans, which extended at once the German-speaking area in Europe and the private domains of the lords of the marches. While in the Rhineland and on the North Sea coast a commercial German civilisation was developing, based on the democratic institutions of self-governing cities, in the east were created the great feudal and despotic principalities which were ultimately to dominate German history.

The eastward penetration of the Germans, by war and by peaceful means, continued throughout the twelfth and thirteenth centuries. Austria was Germanised except for Carinthia and Styria, which have retained to the present day a considerable Slovene population. German burghers and peasants were invited by the kings of Poland and Bohemia to settle in their countries. Early in the thirteenth century King Andrew II of Hungary invited German Crusaders to Transylvania to help him to resist the Asiatic tribes which crossed the steppes of Russia to harry his frontiers. They were followed by peaceful colonists, the forefathers of the 'Saxon' community which in the following centuries grew up in Southern Transylvania, and has played to the present day an essential part in the cultural and economic life of that province.

In 1228 the Teutonic Order of German Knights were given land in Pomerania and Prussia, and the task of 'evangelising' the heathen Lithuanians and other Baltic tribes. Not content with carrying the Gospel by fire and sword through the Prussian marshes, the knights Germanised the population, built German fortress cities and trading posts, and encroached on the territory of Poland, whose existence they threatened for over two hundred years. So ruthlessly did they do their work as to win the enthusiastic praise of Adolf Hitler in *Mein Kampf*.

Meanwhile farther west the Germanisation of the eastern frontier of the Empire had been progressing uninterruptedly. Particularly zealous in this work was Henry the Lion, Duke of Bavaria and Saxony, the great enemy of the Hohenstaufen Emperor Frederick Barbarossa, who resisted the expansion of Denmark in the Baltic provinces, and gained for Germany much of the territory now known as Saxony—a name then given to Central Germany, west of the Elbe. By the end of the thirteenth century, the Slavs had been driven across the Oder, and German expansion along the Baltic had nearly joined up with the German settlements in East Prussia.

Colonisation on the grand scale came to an end about the middle of the fourteenth century. The German Empire had on its eastern frontier the three organised States of Poland, Bohemia and Hungary. Although the immigration of Germans into those countries continued in the following centuries, the peoples resisted Germanisation, and the countries retained their national character.

Pressure from the east was less permanently dangerous, but hardly less unpleasant. Throughout the eleventh and twelfth centuries South-East Poland, Hungary and Wallachia were raided by different tribes whose original home had been Central Asia, but which now lived a nomadic existence on the Russian steppes. These were a constant nuisance, obliging the threatened countries to devote continuous attention to the frontier, and retarding their internal development. They were overshadowed by the great Tatar invasion of 1241. In the first three decades of the thirteenth century the Tatar hordes, trained into an invincible army by the shepherd's son, Jenghiz Khan, had overrun Northern China, Central Asia, Persia and Russia. In 1241 an army commanded by Batu, a grandson of Jenghiz, invaded Europe. One branch of this army advanced through Poland to Silesia, crushing a German army at the battle of Liegnitz, while the other poured through Hungary and reached the Adriatic coast. Europe was unexpectedly saved from this menace, worse than any since Attila, by the death in distant Central Asia of the Supreme Khan Ogotai, which compelled Batu to withdraw his forces in order to be present at the election of a successor. The Tatars settled in Russia, creating the State of the Golden Horde on the

Lower Volga, and did not repeat the invasion of 1241. But that invasion left marks of devastation in Poland and Hungary from which they did not quickly recover, and for the next two hundred years Tatar incursions on a smaller scale continued to ravage Poland and Wallachia. Even after the Grand Dukes of Moscow had finally defeated the Golden Horde, the Tatars of the Crimea made disastrous plunder raids to the west and south-west.

The Balkan Peninsula was also, though at first on a smaller scale, exposed to pressure from west and east. The tenth and eleventh centuries saw the rise of the Venetian Republic. The first struggle of Venice was with the Croats of Dalmatia, whom she fought in the name of the Byzantine emperor, still recognising the sovereignty of Constantinople over herself. After the conquest of Croatia by Hungary, the relations of Venice and Hungary were for long strained. During the eleventh century Venetian trade began to spread beyond the Adriatic into the Mediterranean. Since the tenth century Moslem sea-power had rapidly declined. The Abbasid Caliphate of Baghdad was a shadow of its former self. It was succeeded in the north by the Seljuk Turks, and in Egypt by the Fatimid dynasty. Of these the former were not interested in the sea, while the latter became unwarlike, and were not averse to trade with the Christians. At the end of the century Sicily was finally conquered from the Moslems by the Normans, who did not seriously threaten the trade of Venice. The commercial and naval power of the Adriatic Republic began to rival that of Byzantine and Arab alike.

On the east the Byzantine Empire was threatened in the eleventh century by the land power of the Seljuk Turks. In 1071 the Byzantine army was defeated at Manzikert by the Seljuk Sultan Alp Arslan, and the Emperor was taken prisoner. This new threat from the east combined with the commercial ambitions of the Italian cities to produce the First Crusade. The appeal of the Pope brought a generous response in Western Europe, then experiencing a wave of religious enthusiasm connected with the quarrel of Pope and Emperor and the Reform of the Church. Knights and men from France, Germany and the other countries of the west set out for Palestine, some going by land through the dominions of the Byzantine Empire and Anatolia, others by sea on Venetian, Pisan and Genoese ships. In 1099 Jerusalem was taken, and Crusader States were set up in Syria on the Western feudal model.

Although relieved by the Crusade from the Seljuk threat, the Byzantine Empire had little reason to be glad of the invasion of the Levant by the west. Now that Moslem sea-power was overthrown, the trade between west and east was carried by Venetian and Genoese ships and need no longer use the land route through the territory ruled from Constantinople. The Eastern Mediterranean became an Italian lake. Chief among the Italian cities was Venice, once a humble vassal of the emperor and now the greatest naval power in Europe. Rivalry between Greek and Italian grew ever more acute. Italian traders obtained invidious privileges, which were the cause of repeated riots of the citizens of Constantinople against the Italian quarter. Finally the Fourth Crusade of 1203 was diverted by the Venetians against the Greek capital. Constantinople was twice besieged and taken, a Latin emperor installed in the imperial palace and Latin principalities founded in Macedonia, Greece and Albania.

The Latin Empire was overthrown in 1261, and the Greek dynasty of the Paleologi restored—with Genoese help—but the great days of Christian Constantinople were over. The Empire in Europe was confined to Thrace and parts of Macedonia and Greece. The Angevins in Durazzo, the Catalans in the Peloponnese, a mass of Western princelings and adventurers reduced the Empire to a pale shadow. The commerce of the Aegean and even of the Black Sea was in the hands of the Genoese or their rivals the Venetians. The remnant of the Empire was weakened by internal quarrels. In 1347 the usurper John Cantacuzene invited on to European soil, to assist his claims, the Turkish tribe of the Ottomans. They never left Europe, and only a hundred years later they were the masters of Constantinople.

The history of Eastern Europe from the settlement of the Hungarians in an organised State (c. 1000) to the fall of Constantinople to the Turks (1453) is marked by almost unceasing wars of defence against pressure from west and east, against the expansion of Germans and Italians and against the invasions of Mongols and Turks. The peoples of Eastern Europe formed a buffer between the west and Asia, allowing the Western nations to develop in comparative security their own civilisation, while the fury of the Asiatic whirlwinds spent itself on their backs. And throughout these centuries their powerful neighbours in the west exploited their weakness to encroach on their territory and ruin their economic life. Impoverished by constant wars, the Eastern European peoples had little opportunity of cultural or economic development.

THE MEDIEVAL STATES OF EASTERN EUROPE

Each of the Eastern European nations had during the Middle Ages a period of independence, and some, even, of greatness.

The First Bulgarian Empire reached its highest point of strength and civilisation in the reign of Tsar Simeon (893–927). It was destroyed by the Byzantine Emperor Basil II at the beginning of the eleventh century. For a hundred and fifty years Bulgaria was ruled again from Constantinople. Then, at the end of the twelfth century, a Second Bulgarian Empire was created under the half-Wallachian (Roumanian) dynasty of Asen. The greatest strength of this Empire coincided with the fall of Byzantium to the Crusaders. The Bulgarians inflicted severe defeats on the Latin emperors. By the middle of the thirteenth century, however, the Second Bulgarian Empire was in decline, being eclipsed by the growing power of Serbia.

The Kingdom of Croatia, after two hundred years of independence, which gave considerable promise of real civilisation, influenced by Venice and Byzantium, was conquered at the beginning of the twelfth century by King Coloman of Hungary. Croatia remained part of Hungary, retaining a certain autonomy and a constitutional law of its own, until 1918.

At the end of the twelfth century Serbia, under Stephen Nemanja, first begins to attract attention. In the third decade of the next century, the eastern form of Christianity became the State religion. During the following hundred and fifty years the Serbian State grew in power and civilisation, being strongly influenced by Byzantine culture, and developing a style of architecture and mural painting with a flavour of its own, to which the monasteries of South Serbia still witness at the present day. It extended its frontiers at the expense of its neighbours, in the first place of the Bulgarians, whose Empire had now split up into several separate principalities. The greatest period of Serbia was the reign of Stephen Dušan (1332–56) who brought under his rule large districts of Macedonia, Albania and Greece. Dušan was a great law-giver, corresponded with the sovereigns of Western Europe, and had a brilliant and civilised court. He attempted to make himself Eastern Emperor by besieging Constantinople, but before he reached the city he suddenly died, it was believed from poison. After his death the Serbian Empire rapidly declined.

The Kingdoms of Bohemia and Hungary developed on the feudal lines then prevalent in Western, Catholic Europe. Bohemia was spared the horrors of the Tatar invasion, and, being geographically more favourably situated than Hungary, was for a time stronger and more prosperous. Otakar II of Bohemia, the most powerful monarch in Central Europe at the time, in 1273 competed for the title of Holy Roman Emperor, against Rudolf of Habsburg, a minor Swiss princeling who had acquired possessions in Austria and then succeeded the House of Babenberg as Duke. The two rivals fought for five years, until Otakar was defeated and killed by Rudolf on the Marchfeld some miles east of Vienna. From this year dates the rise of the House of Habsburg, which later played so great a part in the history of Eastern Europe.

At the beginning of the fourteenth century the two national dynasties of Hungary and Bohemia, the Houses of Árpád and Přemysl, came to an end, and were replaced respectively by the two Western European dynasties of Anjou-Naples and Luxemburg. The two countries were dragged by their rulers into the wars of Italy and France, from which their peoples gained nothing but unnecessary suffering and privation. The second Bohemian ruler of the Luxemburg line, who became Holy Roman Emperor as Charles IV, was an interesting personality. He founded in 1348 the University of Prague, the first in all Central Europe, which was open to the three 'nations' of Czechs, Germans and Poles. Although a German by origin, Charles considered himself a Slav prince, and corresponded as such with Stephen Dušan of Serbia.

Poland in the twelfth century was divided into a number of different principalities, the rulers of which fought each other for overlordship. Nothing was left of the proud Kingdom of Boleslav the Brave. The settlement of the Teutonic Knights in East Prussia and the ravages of the Tatars reduced the

country to a pitiable condition. Not until the beginning of
the fourteenth century was most of Poland reunited under one
prince, who successfully fought the Teutonic Knights and left
a much stronger Kingdom to his successor Casimir III the
Great, who gave it thirty years of peace and internal consolidation. Under Casimir Cracow and other towns developed
real prosperity, and a commercial class began to take a place
in national life. This class consisted, apart from Poles, of
Germans and Jews. King Casimir enabled Jews to settle on
liberal terms in his dominions, and they proved both a source
of revenue to the royal treasury and a valuable element in
the economic life of the country. In 1364 Casimir founded
the University of Cracow, which was to play the chief part
in the cultural life of the Polish people.

In 1382 the Crown of Poland passed to a girl, the Princess
Jadwiga, who four years later was induced by her counsellors
to marry the Grand Duke of Lithuania, Jagiello, who accepted
Christianity and became King of Poland and Lithuania, taking
the Polish name of Wladyslaw. By this marriage Poland was
doubled in area. The Grand Duchy of Lithuania at that time included vast areas of Western Russia. Created by pagan rulers
in the fourteenth century, it reached the Dniepr, included Kiev
and touched the Black Sea. The majority of its inhabitants
were not Lithuanians—these inhabited in the Baltic provinces
approximately the area which formed the Lithuanian State of
1919–40—but Orthodox Russians. For two hundred years
after the accession of Wladyslaw Jagiello, Lithuania possessed
a constantly decreasing degree of autonomy. In 1569 by the
Union of Lublin it was incorporated in Poland. Its ruling
class rapidly adopted Polish speech and manners, but the
masses remained Orthodox in religion and Russian in senti-
ment.

Wladyslaw Jagiello took up with great vigour the fight with
the Teutonic Order. In 1410 the Knights suffered a crushing
defeat at the hands of the Poles in the battle of Grünewald
in East Prussia. War continued intermittently for a further
fifty years. By the Treaty of Torun in 1466 the Knights ceded
to Poland their lands in West Prussia and retained East Prussia
only as vassals of the Polish Crown. For the following two
hundred years Poland had no more trouble from Prussia.
Poland had now become a Great Power. Her economic and

cultural life developed promisingly. The University of Cracow, founded by Casimir, was further endowed and supported by Wladyslaw, from whom it took the name of Jagiellonian University, which it bears to this day.

At the beginning of the fifteenth century occurred a movement of great importance in European history, that of the Hussites. Its founder, the Czech reforming priest Hus, was martyred at Constance, and a combination of Czech nationalist indignation at German penetration of Bohemia, of social discontent and of religious fervour produced the Hussite revolts. Led by brilliant generals, the Hussites for nearly twenty years successfully resisted the attacks of well-equipped 'Crusading' armies recruited by the Pope from all Catholic Europe. Peace was made at last on a basis of compromise, the Emperor Sigismund promising them freedom of conscience. The Hussite wars are the heroic period of Czech history and have had a profound effect on the character of the Czech people. The movement also spread its influence outside Bohemia. The intellectual class of Poland, particularly Cracow University, had many disciples of Hus, while in Hungary his ideas, spread by the lower priesthood among the oppressed serfs, enjoyed much popularity. In both countries Hussite influence prepared the way for the sixteenth-century Reformation.

In the second half of the fifteenth century both Hungary and Bohemia again had national kings of their own. The most illustrious among them was the Hungarian Matthias Corvinus (1459–90), son of a Transylvanian nobleman, John Hunyadi Corvinus.[1] Matthias did much for the internal development of the country, and made his capital, Visegrád, a cultural centre of some importance. Unfortunately his positive achievements were spoiled by his foreign policy. Instead of concentrating on resistance to the Turkish menace now threatening the Danube valley, he wasted his time and resources in wars with Bohemia and Austria. He succeeded in stealing territory from both, but Hungary paid the price of this transitory

[1] Roumanian historians claim Hunyadi as a Roumanian, illegitimate son of Sigismund by a Roumanian peasant girl who took the Emperor's fancy during a hunting expedition in Transylvania. The ethnical origin of Hunyadi may be left to the chauvinist historians of Budapest and Bucarest to fight out between them, but the historical fact is that both Hunyadi and his son considered themselves Hungarians.

aggrandisement soon after his death. His policy inevitably recalls that of his much less distinguished successors of 1938–41 in the face of Adolf Hitler.

The Ottoman Turks, as we have seen, first landed in Europe in 1347. In 1362 they made Adrianople, 140 miles west of Constantinople, their capital. In 1389 at the battle of Kosovo Polje they defeated the Serbian army. Both the Sultan Murad and the Serbian Tsar Lazar lost their lives in the battle, which is the subject of Serbia's greatest epic poem, and which still deeply moves every Serbian peasant to this day. Four years later, Trnovo, the last free capital of Bulgaria, was taken. Although the Ottoman onslaught was then retarded for twenty years by the invasion of Anatolia by the Mongol conqueror Timurlenk, the Western and Central European States did not exploit their opportunity. The Pope was much too interested in the suppression of Hussite heresy, which threatened his personal authority, to call a crusade against the enemies of Christendom, particularly as the prospective victims were only Greek schismatics. The Turks began their advance again. John Hunyadi, the father of Matthias, for some years led mixed Hungarian and Serbian armies against the Turks and repeatedly beat them. In 1444, however, the young king, Wladyslaw III of Poland (since 1440 also King of Hungary), disregarding Hunyadi's advice, invaded Turkish territory, and lost his army and his life on the field of Varna. This was the last expedition from the west to help Constantinople, paid for by the submission of the Eastern Church to Rome.[1] No further help arrived, and in 1453 the Second Rome fell to Muhammad II the Conqueror.

The next seventy years were spent by the Turks in completing the conquest of South-Eastern Europe. The death of Hunyadi removed any danger from the north-west. Serbia and Bosnia were overrun. Venetian possessions in Greece fell, their Greek inhabitants in some places welcoming the Turks as a relief from the oppressive rule of the hated Italians. Two countries offered serious resistance. The Albanian tribesmen, led by George Castriotis, or Skanderbeg, held out for fifteen

---

[1] The Council of Florence in 1439 established the reunion of the two Churches. The measure was extremely unpopular with the Greek masses, and was revoked after the Ottoman conquest, Sultan Muhammad cleverly exploiting Greek hatred of the west by his tolerance towards the Church of Constantinople.

years after the fall of Constantinople. Their fortress capital of Kruja was taken in 1466, Skanderbeg died the following year, and in 1468 the country was effectively subdued. The other country where the Ottomans met with resistance was that which is now called Roumania. The princes of Moldavia and Wallachia gallantly withstood Turkish attacks throughout the second half of the fifteenth century. The most successful was Stephen the Great of Moldavia (1457–1504), who beat the Turks on more than one occasion in open battle. He also fought the Tatars of the Crimea, building against them with the help of Genoese engineers a series of massive fortresses along the Dniestr from Hotin to Akerman, which stand to this day. Moldavia was only conquered by the Turks after Stephen's death.

Having subdued the Balkans and Wallachia, the Turks turned to more ambitious enterprises. They overran Syria, Egypt and North Africa as far as Tunis, and built in the ports of North Africa a fleet which challenged the naval power of Venice and Spain. Suleiman the Magnificent (1521–66) began his reign by the capture of the frontier fortress of Belgrade. In 1526 he invaded Hungary. On the field of Mohács the armies of Hungary and Bohemia were annihilated, and their king, Louis Jagiello, killed. The larger part of Hungary was occupied by the Turks. Three years later Suleiman laid siege to Vienna, but was compelled to retreat without capturing the city. After ten years of frontier fighting between Suleiman and the Habsburg Emperor Ferdinand, the eastern frontier of 'Rump'-Hungary was effectively stabilised. Most of Slovakia and Croatia, and the Hungarian plain west of Lake Balaton, formed the share of the emperor, the successor of Louis Jagiello. Transylvania retained a semi-independent status. The rest of Hungary was left to the Sultan.

AUSTRIA, POLAND, TURKEY AND RUSSIA

The battle of Mohács is an important date in the history of Eastern Europe, for it marks the disappearance of the last independent States of the Danubian Basin, those of the Balkans having disappeared in the course of the preceding century. For the next four hundred years Eastern Europe was ruled by three great Empires, Austria and the Ottoman Empire in the south, and in the north Poland until the end of the eighteenth century, and afterwards Russia. These great States swallowed up the small nations, which do not appear again till modern times.

The death of Louis Jagiello on the battlefield gave Bohemia and the remnant of Hungary to the Habsburg Ferdinand, in accordance with a marriage treaty made by his grandfather with Poland. The crowns of both Kingdoms remained in the possession of the Habsburg dynasty until 1918.

The sixteenth century was the period of Reformation and Counter-Reformation. The ground had been prepared for the new ideas in Austria and Hungary by the Hussite movement, and they spread rapidly in both countries. In the second half of the century came the Catholic reaction. This was at first comparatively mild, relying on persuasion rather than terror. The Jesuits carried out a great work of education, and the high spiritual level of the apostles of the Counter-Reformation brought striking successes. More violent measures were adopted by Ferdinand of Styria, who forcibly converted to Catholicism his Protestant subjects. The prospect of this fanatic's succession to the Bohemian Crown and to the Empire was the cause of the Bohemian revolt which started the Thirty Years' War (1618).

At the battle of the White Mountain (1620) the Bohemian Army was routed, and Czech independence disappeared for three hundred years. The autonomies which Bohemia had retained since Mohács were suppressed. Religious freedom was abolished, and the population mercilessly Catholicised. German nobles and burghers were settled in the country, and the native Czech aristocracy was Germanised. The only positive feature of this dark period was the development of the baroque architecture, essentially bound up with the Counter-Reformation, which made of Prague the most beautiful city of Central Europe. In spite of persecution and enslavement, the Czech people retained its national character, and among the masses of oppressed serfs the religion of Hus did not die out.

Hungary was divided during this period into three pieces. The strip in the north and west which remained under Habsburg rule was exposed to the full pressure of the Catholic reaction under Ferdinand II and his successors. To this was added social oppression by the nobility, intensified after the bloody Peasant War of 1514. Transylvania enjoyed a semi-autonomous status, paying tribute to the Turks but suffering little intervention in its affairs. Here too, social conditions were oppressive, but less so than in the Habsburg portion of Hungary. At the end of the sixteenth century the Roumanian Prince Michael the Brave of Wallachia, also a vassal of the Sultan, invaded Transylvania, and for one year united it with his own realm, an event concerning which Roumanian and Hungarian nationalist historians love to polemise. Early in the seventeenth century Gabriel Bethlen, Prince of Transylvania, skilfully enlarged his dominions at the expense of Habsburg Hungary by well-timed intervention in the Thirty Years' War. Under him and his successors there was at least religious tolerance in Transylvania.

It could be argued that the most fortunate people in Eastern Europe were the subjects of the Ottoman Empire. In many places the Turks were welcomed by the miserable serfs as deliverers. This was notably the case in Hungary. The inhuman repression which followed the Peasant War caused such hatred of the ruling nobility that the peasants failed to perform military service, and the battle of Mohács was lost through numerical inferiority to the Turkish army. In Serbia too the semi-feudal regime had lain heavily on the peasant masses, and the Turks were assisted in their conquest by various peasant rebel chiefs or bandits. The Ottoman regime established after the conquest was not hard for the times. The fury of the conquerors was directed against the aristocracy, which was simply destroyed. The Turkish governors or 'pashas' left the masses of the population to themselves, and taxation was at first not heavy.

The Turks showed considerable tolerance towards the religion of their new subjects. Christians were not usually persecuted. The Patriarch of Constantinople had an officially recognised status as head of the Christian subjects of the Empire. Moslems were socially, politically and militarily privileged, and expressed open contempt for the Christians, but these did not have great hardships to suffer. The majority of the Balkan Christians remained true to their religion, but exceptions were the Albanians and the Bosnians. A majority of the former, and a substantial proportion of the latter, were converted to Islam.

The most irksome institution of the Ottoman Empire was the tribute in children. Christian children were taken from their mothers in infancy, and brought up in special schools in Constantinople as Moslems and as soldiers. These formed the élite of the Ottoman armies, and were called Janissaries. They lived together in special barracks, and were not allowed to marry. They were splendidly disciplined, and proved a match for any soldiers in Europe or Asia. During the seventeenth century, however, their discipline declined, they meddled in politics and raised Sultans to the throne and dethroned them. They obtained the right to marry, and to make their children Janissaries after them. Their increasing unruliness was one of the main causes of the decline of the Empire.

The Peace of Westphalia (1648), which, by dividing Germany into Catholic and Protestant States, weakened the position of Austria in Germany, induced the Habsburgs increasingly to look for compensation towards the Danube valley. Ever since Mohács, there had been intermittent frontier wars between the two Empires, but in the seventeenth century Austria began to take a more aggressive attitude. The Ottoman Empire was already much weaker. Power was in the hands of unscrupulous court cliques, who pursued only their personal aims, and corruption spread down to the lower ranks of administration and army. Threatened by Austrian military successes, the Turks made a last rally. The Albanian Viziers Muhammad and Ahmed Köprülü from 1656 to 1676 cleaned up the Central Government, reconstructed the finances and reformed the armed forces. During this period the Turks completed the occupation of Crete and made extensive conquests in South-Eastern Poland. In 1683 they invaded Christian Hungary and besieged Vienna itself. The city was saved by the Polish king, Sobieski, and this failure marked the beginning of the military collapse of the Turks. By the Treaty of Karlovci (1699) the Turkish part of Hungary was ceded to the Habsburgs. Turkish aggression was never again a danger to Europe.

The sixteenth century was the period of Polish greatness. Poland's military power was impressive, her economic life was developing, and her capital Cracow was a centre of culture, which craftsmen and architects from Italy and Germany competed with Polish artists to beautify, by buildings and sculp-

tures which remain to the present day. Cracow was a centre
of intellectual activity. Its university spread the religious and
philosophical speculations of the Reformation. Yet although
the Reformed religion had a considerable following among the
aristocracy, it did not penetrate to the peasant masses, which
remained faithfully Catholic. The Counter-Reformation, less
bloody in Poland than in the Habsburg dominions, made great
progress. By the middle of the seventeenth century there was
little left of the Reformation in Poland.

The sixteenth century saw the beginning of the long struggle
for predominance in North-Eastern Europe between Poland
and Russia. At first Poland had everything her own way.
The wars between the Transylvanian Prince Stephen Báthory,
who was King of Poland 1576–86, and Ivan IV the Terrible
of Moscow (1533–84) for the possession of Latvia ended to
the advantage of the Poles. Under Sigismund III (1587–1632)
the Polish armies exploited the confusion that fell on Russia
on the extinction of the old dynasty, to invade Russian territory and occupy Moscow. They were expelled in 1613 by a
mass resistance of burghers and peasants, led by the butcher
Minin and Prince Pozharski, but they retained large areas of
Western Russia.

Russia did not become dangerous for more than half a
century after this. The Tsars of the Romanov dynasty devoted
their energy to enslaving to their nobles the peasants who had
saved their country and set them on the throne, while these
same nobles were serving the national enemy. Russia remained backward culturally and militarily, while Poland appeared to be still a great State.

It was during King Sigismund III's reign that the Pope
founded, with the King's support, the Uniate or 'Greek
Catholic' Church. This Church was to recognise the supremacy
of the Pope, but was allowed to conduct its services in Slavonic,
and its priests were allowed to marry. The purpose of the
foundation was to attract the peasants of the eastern borderlands away from the Orthodox Church. It won a number of
converts in Eastern Galicia and in Transylvania, among the
Little Russians and the Roumanians. It fulfilled, however, a
purpose different from that intended by its founders, for it
was in constant conflict with the Roman Catholic Church, and
became in the nineteenth century centres of Ukrainian and

Roumanian nationalism, directed respectively against the Poles and the Hungarians.

During the seventeenth century the south-eastern border was in constant unrest. In this frontier region, where Poland, Moscow, Turkey and the Tatar Khanate of the Crimea met, lived a turbulent population of highly independent-minded peasants and Cossacks. The latter were large bands of horsemen, recruited from peasants who fled from oppressive landlords in Poland and in Russia. The local peasants, whose language was substantially different from Polish or Great Russian, and who were the descendants of the people of the ancient Principality of Kiev, made common cause with the Cossacks, who conducted a 'policy' of their own, now raiding Poland together with the Tatars, now making alliances with Poland, Turkey or Moscow against its rivals. In 1654 a terrible revolt broke out, led by Bohdan Chmielnicki, a victim of the injustice of the Polish landowners. The revolt developed into a 'jacquerie' of the downtrodden peasantry against their lords, in which frightful savagery was committed on both sides. When the Cossacks were at last beaten by the Poles, they appealed for protection to Moscow. The Tsar took up their grievances as an excuse for war with Poland. From this time onwards the Orthodox Little Russian population, the Ukrainian nation of to-day, gravitated towards Moscow, and provided a source of quarrels between Poles and Russians which has its importance even at the present day.

About the same time Poland was menaced by two other new Great Powers. Since the time of Gustavus Adolphus Sweden had embarked on a sensational career of conquest on the southern coast of the Baltic. Swedish troops more than once overran Poland, setting up Swedish puppets on the throne and annexing Polish territory on the Baltic coast. The Swedish menace was removed by Russia, whose armies, reformed by Peter the Great, defeated Charles XII and his ally the Cossack Hetman Mazeppa at the battle of Poltava (1709). By the peace which ended the long Northern War, Sweden ceded her possessions in the Eastern Baltic to Russia. Poland never recovered them.

The other Great Power that threatened Poland was Prussia. The Teutonic Order had been secularised in 1525, and its lands became part of the territory of the House of Brandenburg.

A hundred years later, the 'Great Elector' Frederick William of Brandenburg (1640–88) devoted himself to strengthening his dominions, by centralising the political power in the hands of the Monarchy and by reorganising the army. Successfully tricking in turn the Kings of Sweden and Poland, he obtained recognition of the complete independence of East Prussia from the overlordship of either State (1660). In 1700 Prussia-Brandenburg was recognised by the European Powers as a Kingdom. During the eighteenth century its military strength further increased.

From the beginning of the eighteenth century there was no doubt of the superiority of Russia over Poland. From this time dates also the pressure of Russia towards the Straits. South-Eastern Europe was the field of a three-cornered struggle between Austria, Russia and Turkey. Russia challenged Austria's role of 'defender of Christendom' by posing as the champion of the 'oppressed Orthodox subjects of the Sultan'. The rivalry of Austria and Russia, both in the Balkans and in Poland, might have led to war between the two States, had not Frederick the Great of Prussia succeeded in reconciling them by the Partition of Poland.

Poland was destroyed above all by the indiscipline and lack of patriotism of her nobility. Blind to all but their class interests, and possessing no sense of social responsibility, they tore the country to pieces by their quarrels. The Polish Parliament was monopolised by them. They excluded the burgher class from political life, and ruined the towns by an economic policy dictated solely by the grain-producing landowning interest. They mercilessly exploited the peasantry by heavy taxes, irksome labour duties and oppressive laws. The majority of the members of the Parliament were penniless men of noble origin, forming the retinue of a few great landowners, who ruled vast tracts of the country like independent princes. These magnates often conducted private wars against each other, sometimes appealing to foreign powers to help them. The king was powerless against them, for the Parliament would never allow him sufficient troops, not even in time of national danger. The crowning absurdity was the system of the 'Liberum Veto', which made it possible for one man to prevent the adoption in Parliament of a law desired by all the rest of the House.

In 1772 the first Partition of Poland took place. Russia acquired areas in the north-east inhabited only by Russians, but Austria and Prussia took large chunks of purely Polish territory in the west. During the following twenty years there was a real movement for Reform in Poland, which culminated in the Constitution of 1791, based on the ideas of the French Revolution. Russia and Prussia, which had intrigued in Polish affairs to maintain the old inefficient system that favoured their ambitions, could not tolerate the Reform, and invaded Poland, proclaiming loudly to the public opinion of Europe that they had been compelled to this action in order to 'save Poland from Jacobinism'. The second Partition (1793) gave Russia further areas inhabited mainly by Russians, while Prussia extended her possessions in Poznania. The following year a revolt of desperation against the partitions, led by the patriot revolutionary Kosciuszko and supported by the peasant masses, brought a last invasion from west and east. After some months of quarrelling for the spoils, Austria, Prussia and Russia divided up the remnant of Poland.

At the end of the eighteenth century Russia, Austria and a weakened Ottoman Empire faced each other in Eastern Europe.

CHAPTER THREE

MODERN TIMES

NATIONALITY IN THE BALKANS

The march of Napoleon's armies through Austria, Poland and Russia spread the ideas of the French Revolution, which penetrated to the educated class even among the small subject nations of Eastern Europe. During the nineteenth century Liberalism and Nationalism became the most powerful forces moving these nations.

The first movements for liberation appeared in the Ottoman Empire. In 1804 the peasants of Central Serbia, led by 'Black George' (Kara Djordje), drove the Turks out of their country. It is hardly possible to find any connection between this and the ideas of the Revolution. It was rather a successful peasant revolt, of a type for which there are precedents in the earlier history of the Ottoman Empire. Serbia passed through several changes of fortune in the following years, but in 1829 it was recognised by international treaty as an autonomous principality, under Ottoman suzerainty, and a year later Miloš Obrenović, the rival of Kara Djordje, was invested by the Porte as hereditary Prince.

In 1821 began the Greek War of Independence, to which the ideas of the Revolution certainly made a contribution, by their influence on the Greek educated class. The revolt of the Greeks was also stimulated by the anti-Christian policy of the great reforming Sultan Mahmud II. Mahmud's aim was to reorganise the Turkish army and political machine, to put the troublesome Christians in their place, and to make Turkey again a Great Power. To this end he massacred the Janissaries, who for over a hundred years had been little more than a nuisance to the State, created a new standing army, and hanged the Patriarch of Constantinople at his own palace gate in the Phanar quarter.

This last action hardly made the Sultan popular with western public opinion, which was already wildly enthusiastic for the cause of Hellas pleaded in the poems of Byron. Moreover Russia, eager to use her self-appointed role of 'protectress of the Orthodox' to intervene in Ottoman affairs, also supported the Greek cause. Although the heroic struggle of the Greeks was nearly overcome by the superior Turkish armies, the situation was saved by the Western Powers, whose fleet destroyed at Navarino (1827) the Turkish fleet, and by the Russian army, which advanced as far as Adrianople. The treaty signed in this city in 1829 laid the foundation for Greek independence in 1830.

The following thirty years were filled with the rivalry of Russia and Great Britain in the Straits Question.

As Russia advanced nearer to Constantinople, Britain became increasingly alarmed for the safety of her communications with India. Russian expansion through the Balkans towards the Straits and the Mediterranean; through the Caucasus to Persia and the Gulf; through Central Asia to Afghanistan and the gates of India, all made progress during the century, and all were equally alarming to British statesmen, whose policy, with the exception of a few short intervals, was dominated by fear and distrust of Russia until the eve of the First World War.

In the face of Russian expansion Britain supported the Ottoman Empire, having a common interest with it in the assurance of peace in the Arab world and in the Eastern Mediterranean. This policy involved Britain in extremely complicated and unpleasant situations. British statesmen were obliged to press the Sultan for reforms, which they must have known would remain only on paper; to balance between the rival claims of the Sultan, the rebellious pasha of Egypt, and the insurgent peoples of the Balkans, about all of whom their ignorance was too profound to make possible a sound judgment; and to act at times contrary to British public opinion, outraged by the atrocities committed by the Turks in the repression of the risings. This policy led to the Crimean War, the conflict with Russia at the Congress of Berlin, and repeated crises in Russo-British relations during the last years of the century.

Whether Russia represented a real danger to the British Empire, and whether it was wise for British policy to concentrate on resistance to Russia, sometimes even at the cost of blindness to other dangers much nearer the home country, or to support so rotten an edifice as the nineteenth-century Ottoman Empire, is a question for historians to debate. There are powerful arguments to be used on either side. What is certain is that Anglo-Russian relations for more than fifty years were such as to create, in the minds not only of British statesmen, but of the British public, an antipathy to Russia which was firmly rooted long before the Bolshevik Revolution.

The Russians for their part regarded Britain as a selfish, materialistic Empire, interested only in monopolising the wealth of the world, and viciously determined to deny Russia all access to warm seas and the trade-routes of the Oceans.

Moreover, the small nations of the Balkans, particularly the Serbs and the Bulgarians, convinced themselves that Britain was irrevocably opposed to the liberation of the victims of the Turks, and especially to the freedom of the Slav peoples. Although much has changed since the days of Disraeli, strong traces remain in the Balkans at the present time of this traditional distrust.

Two results of the diplomatic conflicts arising out of the nineteenth-century 'Eastern Question' were the liberation of Roumania and Bulgaria. The former had been since the beginning of the century the battle-ground of Turkey and Russia. Its people had been ruled during the eighteenth century by 'Phanariot'[1] Greek princelings, who bought the governorship from the Ottoman Government and recovered the price by mulcting the unfortunate Roumanians. As the life of a governor was liable to be short, he usually tried to make sure of his profit as quickly as possible, and as the rulers were often changed, the population were reduced by merciless robbery to unspeakable poverty. Social misery combined with the beginnings of nationalism to produce the rebellion of Tudor Vladimirescu (1821), and the Russo-Turkish wars kept the country in a state of unrest and encouraged the hopes of patriots for national freedom.

The rival interests of Britain, Austria and Russia, and the sympathy of Napoleon III for the Roumanian cause, combined, at the Peace Congress which concluded the Crimean War, to favour Roumanian independence. The Treaty of Paris (1856) recognised two independent Principalities of Moldavia and Wallachia, but these almost immediately united under Prince Alexander Cuza. On the latter's overthrow by a palace revolution, Prince Charles of Hohenzollern was chosen as Prince of Roumania in 1866.

[1] The word is taken from Phanar, the name of one of the Greek quarters of Constantinople under the Turks.

Bulgaria's independence came ten years later. The Bulgarian people was forced in the nineteenth century to resist two enemies. The first was the Ottoman regime, which had since the end of the seventeenth century become increasingly inefficient, corrupt and oppressive. The second was the Orthodox hierarchy of Constantinople. The Patriarch and his advisers were Greeks, and attempted to use the Church as a Greek national institution. The liberation of Metropolitan Greece, and the growth of militant Greek nationalism, caused the Greek bishops to attempt the Hellenisation of the non-Greek Balkan Orthodox. In Bulgaria the Church had since the Turkish conquest been the main factor that kept alive the Bulgarian language and Bulgarian patriotism. There was therefore a powerful reaction in the country, which obtained in 1870 the concession of an autonomous Bulgarian Exarchate.

The struggle for Church independence had sharpened Bulgarian national feeling against both Greeks and Turks, and the success of 1870 could not satisfy the people. Led by revolutionaries inspired by the ideas of the age, and helped by the representatives of the 'Slavophile' movement in Russia, the Bulgarians revolted in 1876. A still more serious revolt had already broken out in Bosnia, and its importance was further increased by the declaration of war by Serbia against Turkey.

In 1877 the Russian Government, anxious to fish in troubled waters, and influenced by the genuine enthusiasm of Russian public opinion for the Slav cause, attacked Turkey, enlisting also the not inconsiderable military help of Roumania. The Russian Army reached Thrace and dictated the peace of San Stefano, which created a Bulgaria extending across Macedonia to the Lake of Ohrid. At the Congress of Berlin in the following summer, however, British and Austrian pressure secured a reversal of this Treaty. By the new settlement two separate autonomous States were created, under nominal Ottoman overlordship—Bulgaria, comprising the Danubian and Balkan provinces, and 'Eastern Rumelia', consisting of the Maritsa valley and the Rhodope mountain area.

The settlement was short-lived. In 1885 the two were united, despite Ottoman protests and an attempt by Austria to use the army of Serbia, then under her influence, to prevent it. In 1887 the first Prince of Bulgaria, Alexander of Battenberg, was forced by Russian pressure to abdicate, and his place was taken by Ferdinand of Coburg.

NATIONALITY IN AUSTRIA-HUNGARY

Meanwhile the influences of Liberalism and Nationalism had made themselves felt in Austria. In 1848, a few weeks after the French Revolution, revolution broke out in Vienna. It was accompanied by similar outbreaks in Hungary and Bohemia. The 1848 revolutions were inspired by Liberal ideals, but they were marked by confusion of the national and the social issues. The Hungarian revolution is an excellent example of this. The poet Petöfi and the Socialist Táncsics had social revolutionary aims. They wished to liberate the serfs and give them full political rights, and they envisaged the brotherhood of all subject nations of Austria, peasant serfs like the Hungarians. On the other hand, Kossuth, the best-known figure of the revolution, had strictly nationalist aims. His social ideas were influenced by the Conservative reformer, Széchenyi, who advocated the emancipation of the serfs, but by moderate methods, and at the price of payments which would make the process a long one, and would exclude the poorer serfs from liberation altogether. Moreover Kossuth was inspired by an intolerant nationalism. He wished to free Hungary from the Habsburgs and the German Austrians, but the free Hungary must have her historical frontiers, within which the Magyars would be the dominant race and the other peoples would have an inferior status.

The conception of Kossuth triumphed, and this doomed the revolution to failure. Fearing the intolerance of Kossuth, the other nationalities of historical Hungary supported the Imperial troops against the Magyars. The Croats under Jelačić, and the Transylvanian Roumanians under Avram Iancu, played an important part in the repression of the Hungarian revolution, which was finally crushed by the intervention of Russian troops, sent by the arch-reactionary Tsar Nicholas I to help his fellow-autocrat.

Neither the Croats nor the Roumanians received any mark of gratitude from the court of Vienna. The young Emperor Francis Joseph enforced a reactionary and rigid regime in all parts of the Empire. In 1866, however, Austria was defeated at Königgrätz by Bismarck's Prussia, and it was felt in Vienna that concessions were inevitable if the Empire were to be kept together. In 1867 the 'Compromise' was made by which Austria was converted into a Dual Monarchy, in which foreign policy, military affairs and foreign trade were to be controlled by one Government for the whole Empire, but all other matters were left to the two Governments of Vienna and Budapest. Hungary was given her historical frontiers. The two dominant nations were to be the Germans and the Magyars.

The following fifty years of Austrian history were far from peaceful. The aspirations of the other peoples of the Empire—Czechs, Slovaks, Croats, Slovenes, Serbs, Poles, Italians, Roumanians and Ruthenes—were expressed with increasing force and importance.

The most unruly were the Czechs. After their abortive revolution in 1848, they had at first resigned themselves to the failure of their hopes, and waited quietly for better times. But the new generation was less tolerant. In the eighties and nineties the Czech representatives made louder and more radical demands. An attempt of the Austrian Prime Minister, Taaffe (1879–93), to satisfy Czech wishes failed owing to the intransigence of Czechs and Bohemian Germans alike. The obstinacy of both groups of nationalists increased in the nineties, and Prime Minister Badeni's language law of 1897 was met by parliamentary obstruction, initiated by the Germans and later copied successfully by the Czechs. All devices, including the throwing of ink-pots, were used to render parliamentary business impossible. These were so effective that parliamentary government almost ceased to function, and Austria was ruled by the notorious 'Paragraph XIV'. Yet under the Dual Monarchy the Czechs could hardly complain of 'oppression'. They enjoyed economic prosperity. Bohemia was industrialised, and a Czech bourgeoisie grew up, parallel with a specialised working class, which developed its own Trade Unions and Social Democratic Party. Conditions in the Czech Lands resembled those of progressive industrial Western Europe.

But the Czechs could not remain satisfied with these conditions. The nationally awakened Czech people felt that Bohemia and Moravia were its country, which it alone should rule, and that the Germans of Bohemia and the German court at Vienna were intruders. The bourgeoisie was engaged in a bitter fight for the control of Bohemian industry with the German bourgeoisie. The workers disliked the reactionary political and social framework of the old Empire, and their resentment was easily directed into nationalist channels.

The Bohemian Germans—who only became known after 1918 under the designation 'Sudeten Germans', taken from the name of one of the mountain ranges of Northern Bohemia—were more fanatically chauvinist, and propounded with greater enthusiasm the ridiculous theories of blood and race than any other Germans, the often maligned Prussians included. One of their leaders, the Pan-German Schönerer, had the honour, which he did not live to appreciate, of inspiring the young Vienna house-painter, Adolf Hitler, with the gospel of racial hatred and anti-Semitism. The insufferable arrogance of the Germans united the greater part of the Czech people behind the extreme Czech nationalists. The Czech masses looked towards Russia, the great Slav State, for freedom. The intellectuals read French literature, studied in Paris and tried to interest France in their aspirations. The elderly Professor T. G. Masaryk set his hope on the Anglo-Saxon nations. By the eve of the First World War the Czech nation had become fundamentally disloyal to the Austrian Empire. It was waiting only for the chance to turn and rend it.

The subjects of the Hungarian portion of the Empire were much less fortunate. Hungary had a Parliament, whose history, as many Hungarians proudly point out, goes back to the Golden Bull of 1222, only seven years later than Magna Carta. But the franchise was very limited, and the country was ruled by its traditional aristocracy and 'gentry'. The peasants had been 'emancipated' from the remnants of feudal restrictions, but this did not substantially improve their lot. The land was not theirs. They worked as propertyless paid labourers on the great estates of the landlords. They were badly paid, and their lives were really ordered, even in detail, by their lords. During the nineties and the first decade of the twentieth century many emigrated to America, where there are now more than a million people of Hungarian origin. The last decades of last century were a period of crisis in agriculture all over Europe, since it was then for the first time that overseas grain began seriously to compete in the Western European market. Under pressure of the crisis, many smaller landowners were compelled to sell their land. It was bought partly by the banks and partly by the great families, and the former owners were obliged to find employment elsewhere, mostly in the Civil Service and in the Free Professions. These were the founders of the Hungarian middle class of to-day. Although cut off from the land, they have largely retained the mentality of the traditional aristocracy from which their ancestors sprang, and have thus remained different from the Liberal bourgeoisies of western countries.

Liberal ideas of course influenced Hungarian society, but their bearers were mainly Jewish and German elements, who held from the first a dominant position in industry and commerce, and were also well represented in the Free Professions. The last decades before the First World War brought a considerable measure of industrialisation, almost solely in the Budapest region, but the Magyar element did not play much part in this before 1914.

The main preoccupation of the Hungarian ruling class remained defence against the peasantry. In 1891 and 1894 there were demonstrations by agricultural labourers in various parts of the country. The labourers attempted to organise themselves in a Union, and held in 1897 a Congress in Budapest, which made concrete demands concerning working hours, wages and methods of payment. A year later harvest-workers went on strike in large parts of the country. Non-Magyar workers were brought in to suppress the strikes, which were followed by a law making strikes in agriculture illegal. During the following years the Agrarian Socialist Movement died out, and the discontented agricultural labourers found a way out of their difficulties in emigration to America.

The non-Magyars suffered the same conditions. Apart from the Croats, they had no aristocracy of their own. They were peasant peoples, and had the lot of all peasants under Hungarian rule. The most backward were the Slovaks, Transylvanian Roumanians and Ruthenes.* Among the two former a middle class was slowly rising, composed of small-town lawyers, doctors, priests and school-teachers and a certain number of rich peasants. In Slovakia a prominent part was played by the small Lutheran community, which produced the most

* See pp. 175–9, 201, 300–5, 336.

notable Slovak politician of the period, Milan Hodža. In Transylvania the Roumanian nationalist movement was fostered by the Churches, of which the Orthodox had closer contact with the Kingdom of Roumania, but the Uniate produced a better type of priest and had a more civilising influence. The leader of the nationalist movement, Iuliu Maniu, was a member of the latter Church.

The most liberal Hungarian Nationality Law of 1868 was unfortunately never carried out. Coloman Tisza, Hungarian Premier from 1875 to 1890, attempted to enforce on non-Magyar children the Magyar language and to remove the opportunity of education in their own. It was argued that there must be one State language, compulsory for all. It is true that non-Magyars who learned Hungarian well could study at the university, become officials, and reach, if sufficiently able, the highest ranks in the administration, regardless of their ethnic origin. The 'Magyarisation' policy was less inhuman than the nationalist persecution devised in many States after 1918. But it was a stupid policy and only harmed Hungary. It won the hatred of the masses of non-Magyar nationalities, and strengthened the hands of the various nationalist leaders.

The policy, which was continued by Coloman Tisza's successors right up to the collapse of the Empire, was bitterly and successfully resisted. It completely failed to achieve its object, the more so as the oppressive social policy of the Hungarian landlords drove thousands of Hungarians to emigrate, leaving their places to be filled by more docile Slovaks and Roumanians. The mass emigration of Hungarians allowed the non-Magyars not only to hold their own, but to gain ground, while the 'Magyarisation' policy merely infuriated them, and directed all their discontent against the Hungarian State as such. The Slovaks, especially the Lutheran intellectuals, began to think of a Slav Union with the kindred Czechs, while the Roumanians looked for salvation to their brothers beyond the Carpathians.

THE SOUTHERN SLAV PROBLEM

The rock on which the Empire was wrecked was the Southern Slav Question. During the last thirty years before the First World War the Southern Slav subjects of the Empire were divided as follows. The Slovenes of Carinthia, Carniola and Istria were part of Austria, being mixed in the west with Italians, also subjects of the Empire. The Croats of Dalmatia were under Austria, while the main part of Croatia enjoyed autonomy as a part of the Kingdom of Hungary. It had a substantial minority of Serbs in Lika and Slavonia. In the southern provinces of Hungary (Bačka and Banat),[1] there was a large Serbian, and rather smaller Croatian population. Bosnia—taken by Austria-Hungary in 1878, subject to a theoretical Ottoman 'overlordship', and annexed outright in 1908—had a relative majority of Serbs, a rather smaller number of Moslems, and about 25 % of Croats. The 'Sandjak of Novi Bazar', south-east of Bosnia and also administered by Austria since 1878, was inhabited by Serbs—a portion of whom had been Moslemised—with an Albanian minority. Bosnia and the 'Sandjak' were under the joint administration of Vienna and Budapest. The 'Sandjak' was restored to the Turks in 1908, and conquered by the Serbs in the Balkan wars.

Serbia had hoped in 1875 to acquire Bosnia, and bitterly resented its seizure by Austria. Their resentment was not reflected in Serbian foreign policy as long as the Austrophile Obrenović dynasty retained the throne of Serbia. In 1903, however, Alexander Obrenović was murdered by a conspiracy of officers, and the Karadjordjević Prince Peter became king. Serbian policy turned towards Russia, and the agitation of the Bosnian Serbs against Austria enjoyed the sympathy and support of Belgrade. The Empire replied by an economic war against Serbia, and by arrests and repressive measures in Bosnia.

The threat to the Empire from Serbian irredentism was increased when the Serbs of Austria-Hungary began to collaborate with the Croats. Serbs and Croats have the same language, but are separated by their religion, their alphabet and a thousand years of history. These differences were at first successfully used by successive Governments in Budapest to separate the two kindred peoples.

But the policy of 'Magyarisation' began to be applied in

---

[1] The Bačka is contained between the lower Tisza and the north-to-south course of the Middle Danube. The Banat is bounded by the Tisza in the west, the Danube in the south, the Mures in the north, and the Carpathians in the east. See map on p. 5.

Croatia as well as in the provinces directly ruled from Buda-pest. The Governor interfered with the constitutional liberties of Croatia, and attempted to enforce knowledge of the Hungarian language, which few Croats normally took the trouble to learn. In their discontent with Hungary the Croats began to think of friendship with the Serbs.

The 'Jugoslav idea' was propounded from the sixties onwards by the distinguished Croatian Bishop Štrosmajer, who corresponded on the subject with Gladstone. It was taken up with special enthusiasm by the Dalmatian Croats. Connected by sea with the rest of the Balkan Peninsula; threatened not only by Austro-Hungarian but also by Italian imperialism; needing the support of the Serbs of Lika and Bosnia inhabiting their hinterland; familiarised by their travelling seamen and by their numerous emigrants in America with the ideas of the greater world; the Dalmatians not unnaturally responded more rapidly to the generous idea of 'Jugoslav' unity than the more narrow-minded Croats of Zagreb.

In 1905 a Congress of Serbs and Croats was held at Fiume under the leadership of the Dalmatians Supilo and Trumbić, and approved the Jugoslav ideal. A Serbo-Croatian Coalition was formed, which at first collaborated with Budapest, but when in 1907 a law was passed making Hungarian the official language on the Croatian railways, this collaboration came to an end. For some years the Serbo-Croatian leaders hoped that the accession of Francis Ferdinand would improve their lot, as he had shown a certain sympathy for a 'Trialist solution', which would extend to the South Slav portions of the Empire rights similar to those enjoyed by Hungary under the 1867 'Ausgleich'. As, however, those plans never materialised, and as the international crisis deepened, the radicalism of the Croats and Serbs increased.

There were important elements in Croatia which remained hostile or indifferent to the Jugoslav idea.

The native aristocracy, the Catholic hierarchy, and a large number of intellectuals were against it. They insisted on the immense 'cultural superiority' of the Croats over the benighted Serbs, association with whom would contaminate their purity. The religious barrier was of great importance to the devout. The intellectuals took a profound and complicated

pleasure in declaiming about the mysteries of Croatian Constitutional Law, a subject beyond the grasp of any non-
Croatian mind, and certainly unintelligible to a mere vulgar
Serb. These elements formed an extreme nationalist group,
opposed equally to Hungary and Serbia, and aiming at the
creation of an independent, clerical Croatia. Their leaders
were Starčević and Frank, and they came to be known as
'Frankovci' (Frankists).

Opposed to them was the new Peasant Movement, led by
the two brothers Ante and Stepan Radić, themselves peasants.
These stressed the conflict between the ruling class ('gospoda')
and the peasants, who had worked for centuries for the State
and had been rewarded with exploitation and repression. They
used the language of Socialists, but insisted on the sanctity
of private property in Agriculture. They aimed at Land
Reform and the creation of a Democratic Republic, in which
political power should belong to the peasants. Under a restricted franchise they had no political importance, but their
movement had a big following among the Croatian peasants,
who represented three-quarters of the nation. The Radić
brothers stressed their Slavdom, and called the Serbs brothers,
but did not commit themselves on the question of Jugoslav
unity. They were primarily interested in social reforms and
political democracy, and did not understand the wider problems
of European politics outside Croatia.

POLAND UNDER THE PARTITIONS

Since the Partitions the Polish people, divided between
three States, had not lost its national feeling or its desire for
unity. In the Prussian portion the Poles gained from the
general high level of material civilisation, but were subjected
to political and economic pressure which increased towards
the end of the nineteenth century. The anti-Catholic measures
of Bismarck were applied with special rigour in the Polish
regions. The Polish language was not admitted in the State
administration or State schools. Large public funds were
devoted to the settlement of German colonists on the land
in the Polish provinces. But the Poles successfully resisted
this pressure. They remained true to their religion, which held
its own against the Protestant Germans. They retained their
own language, but learned German perfectly at the same time,

thus being better equipped by the possession of two languages than their German neighbours. They formed their own organisation for the maintenance in Polish hands of landed property, in the face of the State-subsidised colonisation schemes. They developed an urban bourgeoisie of their own. The Polish birth-rate was higher than the German.

Russian rule was hard, owing to the despotic and reactionary nature of the Russian State, but there was less systematic pressure against the Polish language as such than in Prussia. At first the regime was comparatively liberal, Poland enjoying a certain measure of autonomy. After the rising of 1830, however, these special liberties were removed, and unrelieved absolutism set in. As the century advanced, the tendency towards Russification increased. The Russian language was given priority over the Polish in Poland in official business. The rising of 1863 further worsened the lot of the Poles, particularly of the aristocracy and the intellectual class, of whom many were sent to Siberia. Numbers emigrated, mainly to France, where they prepared revolutionary programmes and conspiracies. Polish liberal exiles took part in the various European wars of liberation, especially in Italy.

The Russian regime concentrated its repression against the upper class, but interfered little with the peasantry, which lived a wretched life, suffering more from Polish landlords than from the Russian authorities, which was proved by the small support which it gave to the revolts of 1830 and 1863, inspired by the revolutionary intellectuals of the aristocracy. In general, Russian rule, if seldom sensationally brutal, was unpleasant and unpopular, and won the bitter hatred of the educated class and the indifference of the masses. A certain number of Poles were attracted by the Russian way of life, and became army officers or landowners in Russia proper, losing their sense of Polish nationality. The Russian character is much nearer to the Polish than is the Prussian. But such cases were exceptional. The majority remained uncompromisingly Polish, and never abandoned the hope of a rebirth of Poland.

The Austrian portion of Poland was the happiest. In Galicia the Polish language had equality with the German. There were many Polish schools, and the Polish population was represented both in local administrative bodies and in the

Parliament in Vienna. Polish nobles rose to the highest offices of the State. There was no religious persecution, since Austria-Hungary was a Catholic State.

During the first half of the century the aristocracy dominated political life, but in the second half two new political factors emerged. The first was the Peasant Movement. This had its centre in the western part of Galicia, where there was a considerable number of peasant proprietors, whose level of education and methods of cultivation were comparatively advanced and who had been able to buy land from the landlords. The movement advocated reforms in the interest of the peasantry, but was less radical than the Croatian movement. A political party was founded with the name of Piast, the legendary Polish peasant whom tradition makes the founder of the first dynasty of Polish kings. The second factor was the Polish Social Democratic Party, which grew up as industry began to develop in Galicia. It was not so strong there as in the western part of Russian Poland (Lódz district), but it made some progress. Both the Peasant Movement and the Socialists had contact with their compatriots under Russian rule.

The equivalent of the Piast Party in 'Congress Poland' was the 'Wyzwolenie' group, which was more revolutionary, belonging to the same general movement of thought as the Russian Agrarian Socialists or 'Narodniki', and was at the same time more fervently nationalist. The Socialists of Congress Poland were also more violent and more nationalistic than those of Galicia. Despite their profession of internationalism, they were ardent patriots, to whom the liberation of Poland from Russia was far more important than the achievement of Socialism. One of their leaders, Josef Pilsudski, took refuge in Austrian Poland. Trained in conspiratorial methods by his fight with the Tsarist secret police, he devoted all his energy and intelligence to one aim, the liberation of Russian Poland.

Although Austrian rule was mild, there was one feature of Austrian policy which did not please the Poles. This was the encouragement of the aspirations of the Ruthenes of Eastern Galicia. The people of this region spoke a language distinct from Polish or Russian, which is now known as the Ukrainian language. Throughout their history they had shown a spirit of independence with regard to all their neighbours. The Uniate

Church and the encouragement of Vienna combined to create in their small educated class a national consciousness in the modern sense. The expressions 'Ruthene nation' and 'Ukrainian nation' began to be heard for the first time. The purpose of the Austrian Government was to use them both in internal policy against the Poles, should this become necessary, and in foreign policy against Russia. These tactics were greatly resented by the Poles, who regarded Eastern Galicia as part of the historical territory of Poland. In Russia they were less feared. The Ukrainians of Russia were Orthodox, and in the absence of a religious barrier to emphasise their national individuality, they gave little trouble. They might be dangerous to the St Petersburg Government as discontented peasants, Liberal intellectuals or revolutionaries, but hardly as an Ukrainian nation.

AUSTRO-RUSSIAN RIVALRY IN THE BALKANS

The eighties and nineties were a period of great industrial expansion in Austria. The bourgeoisie of Vienna and Bohemia grew in numbers and wealth. Vienna became the banking centre for all Central and Eastern Europe. Austrian capital took great interest in the development of railways in the Balkans. It was at this time that the lines to Constantinople and Greece, through Bulgaria and Serbia, were built. Economic expansion beyond the frontiers of the Empire, and the desire of the military chiefs to liquidate the tiresome problem of Serbia, combined to recommend a foreign policy of Imperialism. This was supported by Germany, which under Bismarck's leadership had taken steps to reconcile herself with her former rival. Germany too had far-reaching plans of expansion towards the Middle East, later symbolised by German interest in the 'Berlin-Baghdad railway'. Having completed only in 1870 her long and painful recovery from the destruction of the Religious Wars, she was now returning to the medieval policy of expansion towards the east ('Drang nach Osten').

The main obstacle to German and Austrian plans was Russia, whose desire for an outlet to a warm sea made her take an interest in the Straits and the whole Levant, while her traditional interest in the Balkan Orthodox, and particularly in the Slavs among them, provided both an excuse and a motive for expansion. For thirty years after 1870

Germany was able to hold the balance between Austria and Russia. Bismarck laid great stress on the need of Germany for friendship with Russia, and his skilful diplomacy succeeded in preventing an open quarrel between his two Allies. After his dismissal German policy was controlled by the incapable hands of William II. At first, however, circumstances favoured the young emperor. Russia was deeply engaged in the penetration of Manchuria and China, and could not devote much energy to Balkan affairs. William encouraged the Tsar to follow his course, and Austro-Russian relations consequently remained satisfactory. The two Empires collaborated with the other Powers in the Eastern Question, and agreements were reached in the Cretan Question—which provoked the Greco-Turkish War of 1897—and in the Macedonian Question in 1903.

Two years after this, however, Russia was decisively defeated by Japan. Her whole Far Eastern policy was ruined, and she was obliged to return to Europe, to seek compensation in the Balkans. Russia had been since 1891 the ally of France, some of whose leading politicians were only waiting for the opportunity to revenge themselves on Germany for the defeat of 1870. And British policy, disappointed at the failure of repeated approaches to Germany, and alarmed by the growth of the German Navy, had begun to turn towards France. The 'Entente Cordiale' was made in the year of the Russo-Japanese War, and in 1907 it was extended by an Anglo-Russian Agreement, which, though not an Alliance, was an important first step towards the improvement of relations between the two Powers. The stage was set for the First World War.

In 1908 a revolution took place in Constantinople. The army of Salonica, led by the 'Young Turkish' group of revolutionary officers, marched on the capital, and compelled Abdul Hamid to give a Constitution. When in the following year he attempted a counter-revolution he was deposed. The power became concentrated in the hands of the revolutionary organisation 'Committee of Union and Progress'.

The new regime aimed at the modernisation of Turkey, by the introduction of democratic institutions and religious equality, and hoped by these reforms to command the loyalty of all citizens. The personal despotism of Abdul Hamid was to give place to a new Ottoman patriotism. For the first few months there was wild rejoicing, Christians and Moslems embracing each other in the streets of Constantinople. But this noble dream soon melted in the face of unpleasant realities. The Young Turks themselves were not clear about their own intentions. In their minds three distinct ideas were confused. These were Ottoman patriotism, resting on equality and toleration for all national and religious groups, which must repay these blessings by unhesitating loyalty to the Ottoman Empire; Pan-Islamism, which Abdul Hamid had favoured, and which aimed at rallying all Moslem citizens of the Empire, and all Moslem communities beyond its frontiers, in support of Ottoman independence and greatness; and Turkish nationalism, which stressed the interests of the Turkish people, in contrast no less to the Arabs than to the Europeans.

These three ideas were mutually incompatible, and the variation in Young Turkish policy caused by their confusion was one important reason for the failure of the revolution. Another was the unwillingness of the Christian subjects to cooperate with the Government. The revolution had come too late. The evil memories of the old regime were too firmly implanted to be eradicated by any sudden political change, and Balkan nationalism had developed to a point where compromise and collaboration were no longer possible. Finally, even if the Balkan subjects of the Empire had accepted the new situation, they would not have been left alone by the small independent States of the Balkans or by the Great Powers.

Within a few weeks of the Young Turkish Revolution Austria-Hungary announced the annexation of Bosnia, and Ferdinand of Bulgaria declared his complete independence of the Sultan, taking for himself the title of king. Moreover the small Balkan States, alarmed at the possibility of a Turkish revival, drew closer together and formed a Balkan Alliance. In 1911 Italy attacked Turkey, and wrested from her Libya and the Dodecanese Islands. In the following year, encouraged by her weakness, the Balkan Allies, Serbia, Bulgaria, Greece and Montenegro, declared war on Turkey. To the surprise of Europe, they swept all before them. The Turks were driven from Macedonia and Western Thrace, and after a siege of some months Adrianople fell to the Bulgars.

It was in the moment of victory that the tragedy occurred

which has overshadowed Balkan politics to this day. The intrigues of Austria-Hungary, frightened by the successes of the Allies, the inordinate ambition of the German king, Ferdinand of Bulgaria, and the quarrels between Serbs and Bulgarians concerning the partition of Macedonia, of which they had conquered much more than their agreements had provided for, combined to produce the treacherous attack of the Bulgarian Army on the Serbs and Greeks. This perfidy did Bulgaria no good. The Turks seized the opportunity to retake Adrianople, while the Roumanians invaded Bulgaria from the north. By the Treaty of Bucarest Bulgaria ceded Southern Dobrudja to Roumania, while the Serbs took both banks of the Vardar and the Greeks the greater part of the Aegean coastline. Bulgaria retained the port of Dedeagach (Alexandroupolis).

Such was the position in 1914. The Turks had been driven back to Eastern Thrace; an Albanian State had been created in the west of the Peninsula; Serbia and Greece had greatly, and Bulgaria slightly, increased their territory. The centre of disaffection remained the Austro-Hungarian Empire, where the unrest among the subject nations, particularly of the Southern Slavs, was increasing steadily. Then on 28 June 1914, in Sarajevo, the capital of Bosnia, the Archduke Francis Ferdinand and his wife were murdered, and the First World War began.

THE FIRST WORLD WAR AND THE PEACE TREATIES

The alignment of the small Eastern European States in the First World War was that indicated by the result of the Second Balkan War. Bulgaria was wooed by both camps, but decided in favour of the Central Powers, since they could offer much more than the Allies, tied by their obligations to Serbia. Roumania, although bound to the Triple Alliance since 1881, joined the Allies, against the wishes of her German king, for she hoped to gain Transylvania and feared a strengthened Bulgaria. Greece, after a determined attempt to maintain neutrality under her pro-German King Constantine, was forced into the war on the side of the Allies, to whom her natural interests bound her and whose case was pleaded by her greatest modern statesman, Eleutheros Venizelos. Turkey joined the Central Powers, and fought beside her traditional enemy Bulgaria. Ever since the nineties, and especially since the Young Turkish Revolution and the Balkan Wars, German influence had been increasing in Constantinople, furthered by economic penetration and by German military missions sent to instruct the Turkish army. Under the Government of Enver Pasha, the Turkish army fought bravely to the end in a war contrary to the interests of the people.

The subject-nations of Austria-Hungary were compelled to fight for a country which they had come to regard as a prison. The Czechs organised espionage and sabotage in the Czech Lands, and many Czech soldiers deserted to the Russians and formed separate Legions in the Russian army. Transylvanian Roumanians deserted to the Roumanian or Russian armies. On the Serbian front Austro-Hungarian citizens of Serbian origin deserted, and were joined by many Croats. Only on the Italian front were most Austrian subjects loyal, especially the Croats, whose dislike of Italy was traditional.

Serbia and Roumania were overrun. The former had offered a particularly heroic and successful resistance, and its army, after retreating through the mountains of Albania to Corfu, continued the fight on the Salonica front. The latter had a less distinguished record, but it must never be forgotten that, after being driven out of Wallachia, the Roumanian Army, reformed by French officers, put up a magnificent fight in Moldavia in 1917, repelling the Germans despite great inferiority of material at the battle of Mărăşeşti, and winning a tribute for bravery from so fine a judge of war as Marshal Mackensen. The collapse of the Russian front placed Roumania in a difficult position, and, more afraid of revolution within than of the national enemy, her German King Ferdinand made a separate peace with the Central Powers.

The unfortunate Poles were divided between the two camps. The most eminent politician of Congress Poland, Roman Dmowski, declared for full support of the Russian war effort, hoping that British and French influence in St Petersburg would secure at least autonomy under Russian protection for a reunited Poland. A large part of Polish public opinion supported him. His political opponent Pilsudski, in exile in Austria, regarding Russia as the first enemy, formed a Legion of Polish soldiers to fight on the German side. After the German armies had conquered Congress Poland, they set up

a Regency in Warsaw with most inadequate powers, and did
not unite Austrian or Prussian Poland to the Congress Kingdom. The only interest of the Central Powers in Poland was
as a source of cannon-fodder for use on the Western Front.
Disillusioned by this, Pilsudski refused further cooperation,
and was imprisoned at Magdeburg. Meanwhile another Polish
Legion, led by one of his former lieutenants, General Haller,
did fine service with the Allies in France.

The Peace Treaties of 1919, inspired by the principle of self-
determination, preached by President Wilson and accepted
by the other Allied statesmen and by Allied public opinion,
restored Poland, enlarged Roumania, and created three new
States on the Baltic, one in Central Europe (Czechoslovakia)
and one in the Balkans (Jugoslavia). The frontiers of these
States are illustrated by maps, and the political problems
arising from them are discussed in later chapters.

The treaties failed to settle the Aegean Question and the
status of Turkey, which were not decided until 1923, but, as
they are an essential part of the Peace Settlement, must be
summarised here.

The Allied plan amounted to the complete dismemberment
of Turkey. In the north-east an Armenian State was to be
constructed, in accordance with the insistence of President
Wilson. The south-east was to be occupied by French troops,
already installed in Syria. The district of Adalia and the coast
facing Rhodes were to go to Italy. Most of the Aegean coast,
with Smyrna and a large part of the hinterland, were allotted
to the Greeks. Constantinople had been promised to Russia,
but, the Bolshevik Revolution having relieved the Allies of
their obligations, they proposed to make it a 'Free City'. The
unfortunate Sultan saw no alternative but to accept these
terms.

It was in this desperate situation that Mustafa Kemal Pasha,
an officer who had had a part in the 1908 Revolution and had
distinguished himself in the fighting at Gallipoli and in Syria,
raised the standard of revolt. Sent by the Government to
Anatolia 'to restore order', he disobeyed orders and summoned a Congress at Sivas, which met on 23 July 1919,
proclaimed the inviolability of Turkish Anatolia, and appealed
to the Turkish people to defend its home. When it became clear
that the Sultan would not resist the Allies, Kemal called a

National Assembly at Ankara in April 1920, which entrusted him with full powers.

The Greeks, encouraged by Britain, invaded Anatolia, but in August 1921 they were defeated on the Sakarya river by Kemal. The restoration of Constantine in Athens weakened them, both by an intensification of political intrigues within the army, which impaired discipline, and by alienating the Allies, who regarded the king as a friend of their former enemies. Negotiations having failed, fighting continued, and in August 1922 Kemal inflicted a final defeat at Dumlu Pinar and drove the Greeks out of Anatolia. In November Colonels Plastiras and Gonatas made a revolution, executed six prominent royalist politicians and generals and expelled Constantine. These executions accentuated the division of the Greek ruling class into two implacably opposed groups, which has deeply affected Greek political life ever since.

Already in 1921 the French and Italians had abandoned their plans in Anatolia, and the Turkish-Russian frontier had been settled at the expense of Armenia. After some weeks of tension British troops evacuated Constantinople. In July 1923 was signed the Treaty of Lausanne, which abolished the Capitulations and all privileges enjoyed by foreign citizens or religious groups, and left Turkey all Anatolia and Thrace as far as the Maritsa.

This success was due partly to disagreements among the Allies and to Soviet assistance, but its main cause was the patriotism and endurance of the Turkish people, which now at last came into its own. For centuries the Anatolian peasant had borne the burden of the wars of a multi-national Empire of which he knew nothing. World opinion, shocked by the sufferings of the Christians of the Balkans, had shown little interest in the fate of the Turks themselves, who had fared as badly under a corrupt despotism as any other nationality. Kemal's Revolution liberated the last oppressed people of the Ottoman Empire. Since 1923 Kemal Atatürk, his back turned on the internationalism of Constantinople and of Islam, devoted himself to the erection of a Turkish national State which has already taken an honourable place in world affairs.

SOCIAL EVOLUTION: FROM SERFDOM TO LAND REFORM

The depressing effect of constant wars and invasions on the social evolution of Eastern Europe has already been indicated. In 1918 Eastern European society was still predominantly agrarian, and the material and cultural level of the agricultural masses remained low. It could be said that at the end of the First World War the greater part of Eastern Europe had only just emerged from the Feudal Age.

Feudalism was a social order based on precise obligations. The lord held his lands in fief from the Crown, and was obliged in return to serve the king in his wars. The lord in his turn let out parts of his land to vassals, whose services were available to him when he should require them to discharge his military obligations to his sovereign. Beneath the vassal class were the masses of serfs, who cultivated the lord's land, and were assured of his protection and of a number of defined liberties and rights. The essence of Feudalism was the reciprocity of obligations. When these were one-sided, society ceased to be truly feudal.

Feudalism was overthrown in Western Europe by the rise of a commercial class, whose standard was not social obligation but money, and by the concentration of political power in the hands of a centralised Monarchy. Both these phenomena can be observed in the history of Eastern Europe, but on a smaller scale. The Balkan Slav States were destroyed by the Turks before the process had gone far. The Byzantine Empire was never a feudal State in the western sense. It had preserved from Roman times a centralised monarchical system, which never allowed the local magnates to build up very great power, and it had a commercial class which played an important part in the life of the State. During the last two centuries, however, it had been compelled to sacrifice everything to the needs of defence, and had been reduced to the condition of a small impoverished city-state.

In Poland, Bohemia and Hungary, which were feudal States in the true sense of the word, the later Middle Ages saw the beginnings of a commercial life. Feudal ties were loosened. In the Hussite Wars other social classes of the Czech nation besides the nobility played a part. Matthias in Hungary did not rely solely on the nobility for his policy, but was several times in conflict with them. The conception of Society as based on fixed obligations of service between king, noble, vassal and serf was disappearing.

Under Habsburg rule this process was accentuated. The emperor had at his disposal armies from his other dominions, and was not forced to rely on the Hungarian and Bohemian nobility. After the battle of the White Mountain the old Bohemian families were either destroyed or Germanised. The Habsburgs introduced their own favourites, and made a new, German, aristocracy, dependent on them but bound to them by ties stronger than the old obligations of feudalism. Moreover a new German burgher class was a most useful bulwark of Habsburg rule in Bohemia.

In Hungary too the Habsburgs used German troops to maintain their rule, and did not need to pay great respect to the Hungarian nobility. There were repeated conflicts between emperor and nobility, the Hungarian aristocrats sometimes appealing to the Turks for help against Vienna. After the reconquest of Turkish Hungary the pressure of the Monarchy was still stronger, and in the second half of the eighteenth century the Emperor Joseph II resolutely pursued the policy of 'enlightened despotism', building the power of the Monarchy upon a new Imperial bureaucracy.

In Poland the evolution was different. Here the nobility obtained a monopoly of power. In the sixteenth century the kings had built up substantial personal power, and commercial life developed, the monarchy encouraging the bourgeoisie. In the following century, however, the nobility recovered its position. It refused military service even in important national wars, it would not allow the king to form a standing army, it withheld funds even for purposes of national interest, and it secured the exclusion of the bourgeoisie from political life and the maintenance of an economic policy which ruined the towns. It was able to do this because the Polish monarchy was elective, and, although the Jagiello kings were strong enough to secure the succession of their children, when their line came to an end in 1572 the nobility seized the chance to extract fatal concessions from the candidates for the succession. As throughout the seventeenth and eighteenth centuries there were numerous disputed successions, the nobles had frequent opportunities to extort privileges. Already a century before the Partitions Poland had fallen into a state of anarchy. The country was at the mercy of a class deprived of all patriotism or sense of responsibility. Here too the balance of Feudalism was utterly destroyed.

All that remained of feudal society was the subjection of the agricultural masses. Though the ties binding nobility and Crown, and the whole complicated system of vassalage based on military service, had been dissolved, the bond between lord and serf remained, but had ceased to be one of mutual obligation, degenerating into mere one-sided exploitation. The Polish nobility, freed from the restraint of the central Government, wrought their will on their serfs, while the nobility of Hungary and Bohemia, reduced to a secondary role in public affairs, compensated themselves by increasing their pressure on the peasants. These were entirely at the mercy of their lord. If the latter was a just man, they were fortunate. If not, they had no means of defence. Taxes could be raised, irksome and humiliating forms of labour service devised, the traditional rights and freedoms of the village removed, restrictions on the small degree of personal liberty increased. There was little that the serf could do against this. If he appealed to the courts, his case was judged by the nominees of the lord. If he protested, he was dealt with by the lord's armed retainers.

From time to time the serfs of some district would rise, and after a few weeks of desperate resistance would be crushed by the disciplined troops of the nobility. Individuals would fly to the woods or mountains, and form bandit groups that would prey on all classes of the population. Occasionally a major Peasant War would occur. In 1437 Transylvanian small nobles and peasants, Hungarian, Szekler and Roumanian, revolted with success under Budai Nagy Antal. The magnates adopted the usual tactics. They made promises, split the ranks of the rebels by intrigues, then broke their word, attacked the weakened peasants, defeated them and tortured some of their leaders to death.

More important still was the Hungarian revolt of 1514 led by a Szekler noble, George Dózsa. This broke out owing to the cruelty of the nobles towards peasants who wished to go on a Crusade called against the Turks by the Archbishop of Esztergom. The nobles wished to retain the serfs on the land to work for them, and used torture on them or their wives and children, to prevent them from going or compel them to return. The peasant army assembled for the Crusade was turned by Dózsa against the nobles. The programme of Dózsa was based specifically on the principle of human equality. After some weeks of success, during which more than 100,000 peasants joined the revolt, Dózsa's army was beaten by the nobles. He himself was captured and tortured to death with his chief assistants. After this the yoke of serfdom was more firmly planted on the necks of the peasants. Their old rights and feudal liberties were formally abolished, and for three hundred years the theory propounded by the noble legislator Werböczy, that by the revolt the peasants had forfeited all rights, was officially accepted.

In 1573 a fierce revolt broke out in Croatia. It was led by Matija Gubec, a peasant from the hills of Central Croatia. Croatian peasants fought side by side with Slovenes from across the Austrian frontier. They captured a number of castles, and massacred a number of nobles, but were crushed in the end. Gubec was burnt alive in Zagreb, and his followers suffered the usual inhuman acts of repression.

A fourth memorable revolt was that of 1784 in Transylvania, led by the Roumanian peasants Horia, Cloşca and Crişan. Horia was a well-to-do peasant from the Ore Mountains, a region inhabited mainly by Roumanians, the so-called 'Motsi'. He obtained an audience of the Emperor Joseph II on one of the latter's visits to Transylvania, and complained to him of the injustices suffered by the peasants. Some time later Horia himself went to Vienna, and was again received by the emperor, who listened to him with sympathy. On his return he told the peasants that the emperor supported them, and had ordered him to lead them in resistance to the nobles. The rebellion spread all over the central mountain district, and extended into the Mureş valley. It was soon defeated, however, by the nobles. Joseph II disclaimed any sympathy for the rebels, and allowed Horia to be broken on the wheel at Gyulafehérvár (Alba Iulia, Karlsburg or Belgrad). Roumanian historians are inclined to treat this as a nationalist rising. The nobles against whom Horia fought were Hungarians, and it is possible that the national motive played a part. But the movement was essentially a social revolt of the peasant masses against the nobility. After its suppression the rule of the nobility was more rigorously enforced than ever.

The Ottoman Empire was never a feudal State in the sense in which Poland, Hungary and Bohemia had once been. Feudal institutions had existed in medieval Serbia and in the Latin principalities created after 1204 in Greece. In both cases Feudalism had developed in the sense mentioned above, towards a loosening of the ties between the monarch and the nobility, and a tightening of the bondage of the serf. The Ottomans swept this system away. They destroyed the native aristocracy and set up their own military and administrative machinery.

During four hundred years of Turkish rule the Balkans were ruled essentially on military lines. There were Turkish garrisons in strategic points and administrative centres, Turkish governors and prefects, and a Turkish bureaucracy whose main task was the collection of taxes. The Christians were left to their own devices. They did no regular military service, although their children were liable to be taken away and brought up as Janissaries. They had to pay taxes, which were not usually heavy, but sometimes caused great hardship, for the officials were inclined to forget them for years on end and then suddenly, on urgent demand from the central Government, descend on the unhappy peasants and seize all that they had. Life was most uncertain and uncomfortable, but there was, at least during the first two hundred years, probably less systematic exploitation and oppression than in the Habsburg territories.

In Bosnia and Albania a considerable part of the population had accepted Islam. In both countries Moslem, Orthodox and Catholic populations existed side by side, in Albania the Moslems outnumbering the Christians, in Bosnia the Christians the Moslems. The Moslems retained their native language as well as the Christians, and the Turks never attempted to force their own upon them. The Moslem Bosnians and Albanians enjoyed all the privileges of their Turkish fellow-citizens. In both countries a native Moslem aristocracy existed under Ottoman rule, owning the greater part of the land and ruling over the masses of dependent serfs.

In Serbia and Bulgaria the native landowning class almost completely disappeared. Some Turkish pashas obtained large estates, and transmitted them to their children, but these were few. Thus the population of Serbia and Bulgaria consisted mainly of small holders, and such big estates as existed were in the hands of foreigners. The leaders of the people were priests and peasants.

In Greece a similar state of affairs existed, modified, however, by the fact that there was a large and prosperous commercial class. Trade in the Ottoman Empire was largely in the hands of Greeks, and in the chief cities of the Empire, especially Constantinople, there were many wealthy Greek merchants. Moreover the highest places in the hierarchy of the Orthodox Church were held by Greeks. Both the Church and the traders owned some land, and from them arose a limited but important native landowning class.

In Roumania the mass of the people were serfs, living in bondage to an aristocracy of mixed origin. Some of the landowning families were of genuine Wallachian origin, but many had Greek names (e.g. Callimachi or Cantacuzino). The country was ruled by 'Phanariot' Greek princes, wealthy Greeks of Constantinople who bought the principalities at high prices from the Ottoman Government and recouped themselves by merciless extortion.* The merchants of the Danube ports of Roumania were mostly Greeks or Armenians, with a certain number of Jews.

The 'Emancipation' of the Eastern European serfs, the formal destruction of the old system under which they were 'bound to the soil', took place in the nineteenth century. This was done in Austria by the abortive Parliament of 1848. In Hungary it was done by Kossuth's Parliament. The Polish peasants of Congress Poland were emancipated with the other subjects of the Russian Empire. In Roumania the serfs received their freedom during the reign of Cuza. In Greece and Serbia the peasants were free from the moment of national liberation from the Turks.

'Emancipation' meant only that the peasant was free to travel, to seek employment on the estate of another landlord or in the towns. This freedom had small value if his economic condition was unchanged. He had no land, but still depended on the landlord on whose property he worked. Apart from Bohemia and the Łódź area, industry in Eastern Europe de-

* See above, p. 37.

veloped only at the end of the century, and then slowly. The steady growth of population, and the agricultural crisis caused by American competition, even before 1914 depressed the standard of living of the peasantry. Discontent increased, and in progressive intellectual circles in the towns the question of land redistribution was seriously discussed.

In 1907 a peasant rising occurred in Moldavia, where some Jewish tenants had rented land from the estate owners and exploited the peasantry. The revolt spread southwards, and soon lost its anti-Semitic character, becoming a 'jacquerie' against the landowning class. In a few places, particularly in the non-Jewish south-western regions, peasants murdered a few landowners, but generally little violence was done to human life, although a good number of manor houses were burnt down. The repression by the Government, which in its first panic made the usual insincere promises, was, as customary, extremely savage. Some 10,000 peasants were killed fighting or executed afterwards. The revolt succeeded, however, in frightening the ruling class, and talk of Land Reform became commoner both in Roumania and in Austria.

At the outbreak of war Congress Poland and Austria-Hungary were still dominated by great estates. In Galicia the Polish peasants had taken advantage of the agricultural crisis to buy land from the estates, so that this area had already largely lost its pseudo-feudal character. The Hungarian peasants were too depressed to be able to buy, and the estates were sold instead to banks.

In Greece the Venizelos Government began the redistribution of the remaining big estates in the second decade of the century. In Albania the land remained in the hands of the tribal chiefs. In some parts of the Balkan Peninsula the traditional system of the 'Zadruga' survived. This was a sort of family cooperative, in which all worked together under the orders of the head of the family. These 'Zadruge', in which each individual had his or her appointed task, and the proceeds were shared by all, had sometimes as many as a hundred members. This institution has now died out, despite the efforts of some Peasant Party 'ideologues' to revive it.

EVOLUTION OF POLITICAL IDEAS

The cultural life of Eastern Europe in the early Middle Ages was far in advance of that of the West. The Byzantine Empire and its Balkan vassal States were centres of art and civilization. The cultural supremacy of Constantinople might be challenged by Baghdad or Cordoba, but not by any northern capital. In the eleventh century, worn out by centuries of struggle with the barbarians, the Empire entered on its final decline, and the new States that arose in the Balkans, however brilliant their brief periods of triumph, were too furiously engaged in warring with each other to survive long. During the same period the Western States, protected by the Eastern European buffer from Asiatic invasions, developed their own civilisation, based on the remnant of the Roman tradition of Law, preserved by the Catholic Church, and on the growth of a commercial class, which, trading first in the closed Mediterranean, Baltic and North Seas, and then in the open Atlantic, laid the foundations of the modern age.

The Catholic States of Eastern Europe, Poland, Hungary and Bohemia, partook to some extent of the civilisation of the medieval west. The Universities of Prague and Cracow played an honourable part in the intellectual life of Europe. Hungary under Matthias Corvinus could compete with them. The Hussites were the fathers of the whole European Reformation.

The battle of Mohács ended the cultural development of the Danubian peoples, as the fall of Constantinople had ended that of the Balkan peoples. Vienna was not interested in the development of Hungary, a frontier province inhabited by a turbulent alien nobility and ravaged by constant wars. In Bohemia the fanatical energy of Ferdinand II was devoted to the destruction of religious heresy and Czech national liberty. In this atmosphere no cultural life could survive.

Poland remained for a century more a civilised State. In the sixteenth century the Polish nobility and gentry, the backbone of the Constitution, included many educated and enlightened men. In the seventeenth began the decline. The gentry became a rabble of unruly hangers-on of the great nobles, as lacking as their patrons in any sense of responsibility to other classes or understanding of their country's true interests. They cared nothing for education or culture. The university decayed, and the intellectual life of Poland reached a lower level than had been known for three hundred years. Only in the second half of the eighteenth century was an attempt made to revive learning and to make use of the country's wasted resources. Led by a few patriots, the movement resulted in the Constitution of 1791. But it was already too late.

The peoples of the Ottoman Empire were plunged in unrelieved gloom. If material conditions were tolerable, cultural life was non-existent. The masses were completely ignorant. Only the priesthood in Serbia and Bulgaria had some education, and its standards were low. It fulfilled the historic task of keeping alive national consciousness, but it could do no more. The Greek commercial class had contact with the outer world, but the educated merchants were concentrated in a few big cities, and had little influence on the life of the Greek people. The Balkan peasant used primitive methods of cultivation, and had no opportunity of learning better. Moreover Turkish administration, which became increasingly corrupt and inefficient as the Empire declined, had a depressing effect on the morals and mentality of its subjects.

The nineteenth century brought a flood of new ideas to Eastern Europe. The principles of Nationality and Individual Liberty, spread by Napoleon's armies, reached Eastern Europe by two channels.

The first channel was direct contact with France.

Already in Ottoman times there were a number of Greeks who spoke French and had commercial dealings with France. After the liberation of Greece these contacts increased. By the Treaty of Adrianople Roumania was opened to the trade of the Western Powers. France and Britain bought large quantities of Roumanian grain. A commercial bourgeoisie grew up in the Roumanian towns, which besides Jews and Greeks included a number of Roumanians. Both Greeks and Roumanians began to visit France on a greatly increased scale. Possession of the French language became a necessary social accomplishment. Roumanian aristocrats, merchants and country squires sent their children to educate themselves in France.

France was since the Partitions the home of many Polish exiles. Poles had fought in the armies of the Revolution, and

Napoleon had realised part of Polish national hopes by the creation of the short-lived Grand Duchy of Warsaw. After the Vienna Congress, which ignored the rights of the Polish people, and still more after the unsuccessful rising of 1830, Polish intellectuals flocked to France. Moreover in Poland itself the educated class learned French, knowledge of which was considered essential by people of culture throughout the Russian Empire. By learning the French language, by visiting France, and by reading French literature the upper class of Greeks, Poles and Roumanians familiarised themselves with the French conceptions of Liberty and Nationality.

The second channel was through the intermediary of German Liberalism. In the first surge of German resistance to Napoleon, the ideas of Nationality and Liberty had been united, and in the years of struggle against Metternich the German revolutionaries were no less enthusiastic for the freedom of the individual than for the unity of the German nation. Nationalism reached the peoples of Austria-Hungary largely through Germany. Liberalism came through the same channel. A certain number of intellectuals in the Empire had access to French ideas. Knowledge of French, though much less common than knowledge of German, was growing among the new Czech bourgeoisie, and in Hungary such men as the Conservative Széchenyi and the revolutionary poet Petöfi were familiar with French ideas. Among the other nations of Austria-Hungary, however, knowledge of French or of France was at this time very rare. The language learned by Croats, Slovaks or Transylvanian Roumanians aspiring to culture was German, and the new ideas consequently reached them from the German angle.

In Serbia and Bulgaria, Austrian and German trade penetration during the nineteenth century brought knowledge of German and of the Germans. The prestige of the French State, the French language and French ideas were, however, so strong that they attracted both Serbs and Bulgarians. Serbs from the beginning of the century, and Bulgarians after the liberation of their country, began to visit France and to send their children there. By the end of the century French cultural influence and French ideas far surpassed German, and this has remained true in both Serbia and Bulgaria until very recent times.

After the defeat of the German Revolution of 1848 German Nationalism lost much of its original Liberalism. Worship of State and Race, which can be found in the works of Fichte, one of the fathers of the German national revival of the nineteenth century, began to predominate over the principle of Liberty, taken by the Germans from the French Revolution but discarded under the impression of Bismarck's successes.

This change was reflected in the political development of the Austro-Hungarian Monarchy. The Austro-German bourgeoisie of Vienna and Bohemia turned its back on Liberalism, and plunged into an orgy of intolerant romantic nationalism. Liberalism was left more and more to the Jews, who, as a socially inferior group, were naturally more inclined to see the value of individual liberty and equality than the Germans, intoxicated since the victory of 1870 by a sense of the strength of the German people, in which, although Austria had taken no part in the victory, they felt themselves included.

Many Austrian Germans aimed openly at unity with the Reich, seeing in absorption in the new Empire a final submersion of their individuality in a magnificent superhuman machine. Bismarck did not encourage this movement, even though some of its leaders ostentatiously 'converted' themselves from Catholicism to please Prussia. He wished to avoid any conflict with Vienna, whose policy was essentially dynastic and supra-national, and whose alliance was an important part of his diplomatic system.

The association of Liberalism with Jews diminished its prestige. The end of the century saw a wave of anti-Semitism in Austria. Mistrust between Christians and Jews was not new in Central or Eastern Europe, where it had existed in the Middle Ages. But the development of anti-Semitism as a political programme, based partly on economic rivalry between the Jewish and non-Jewish bourgeoisies, and partly on ideological differences, was something new. It is important to note that it made much more rapid progress in Austria than in Germany proper.

Antipathy to Liberalism was further strengthened by the influence of the Roman Catholic Church, which upheld the traditional authoritarian doctrines of Rome and was slightly anti-Semitic. Dr Karl Lueger, the founder of the important Christian Social Party and Mayor of Vienna about the turn

of the century, won great success with a demagogic policy of
Catholicism and anti-Semitism. Thus Pan-Germanism, anti-
Semitism and Catholicism combined to submerge in the
educated class the principles of Liberalism. These same forces
combined forty years later to destroy the Austrian democratic
Republic.

This trend in German Austria inevitably had its effect on
the other parts of the Empire. In Hungary the middle class
was divided between commercial bourgeoisie, bureaucracy and
free professions. The first was mainly Jewish and to some
extent German, the second was chiefly filled with Hungarians,
and the third was disputed between Hungarians and Jews.
The latter were especially strong in journalism, medicine and
the Law. Liberalism was widespread among the Jews. The
Hungarian middle class was more Conservative, looking back
to the traditions of the Hungarian Constitution. It believed
in intellectual freedom within the ruling class, but did not wish
it extended further. In this respect there was little difference
between the Hungarian middle class, of aristocratic origin, and
the great noble families which dominated the country. Both
were Conservative, suspicious of the Jews, influenced by the
Church, and inspired by a powerful, romantic patriotism.

The trends noticed in Vienna existed in Budapest, but they
were less powerful. In Hungary a large part of the population are Calvinists, and the Catholic Church, although occupying a privileged position, did not dominate the country to
the same extent as it dominated Austria. Moreover, although
suspicion of the Jews was traditional, the Hungarians were
more tolerant than the Austrians. The principle of 'Magyarisation' allowed a Jew, as much as any other non-Magyar, to
become a Magyar if he would abandon his former national
allegiance. Many Jews did become assimilated, and came to
regard themselves as Hungarians and to be accepted as such.
This tolerance was made easier by the fact that the Hungarian middle class had not yet engaged in commerce, and
therefore had as yet no economic motive for rivalry with
the Jews.

The other nations of the Empire were influenced by the
same phenomena. The middle class of Croats, Slovaks and
Roumanians, which grew up during this period, became increasingly romantic in its conception of nationalism. Lip-

service was still paid to the ideals of Liberalism, but they came far behind nationalist aims. In Croatia, Slovakia and Slovenia the influence of the Catholic Church was strong, especially in the last, whose national movement followed very closely the lines of the Austrian Christian Social Party.

The evolution of the Czechs, who had attained a higher cultural level, was more complicated. There was little anti-Semitism among them, for their rivals in every sphere of life were the Germans, not the Jews. Although Bohemia and Moravia are usually regarded as Catholic countries, the Catholic Church never had much influence on Czech political opinion. A large part of the new bourgeoisie were Free-Thinkers, and among the people the old Hussite ideas had not died out. The growth of Czech nationalism led to a conscious revival of Hussitism. Romantic nationalism of the German type made progress among the Czechs, as a reaction against the militant nationalism of the Bohemian Germans. In intellectual circles French influence was important, and a strong current of Liberalism continued to play a part in Czech national life. The great apostle of Liberal Democracy, T. G. Masaryk, drew much of his inspiration from British and American Democracy, to which his American wife had introduced him. He bravely criticised the romantic chauvinism of his compatriots. Although he won great unpopularity in political circles, and never had a large following in the Vienna Parliament, his moral influence over the Czech people, and over the intellectuals of the other subject nationalities, was very great.

Towards the end of the century Social Democracy became an important force in Austria-Hungary. Based on German Socialism, the Austrian Social Democratic Party was founded in 1889 by Viktor Adler. It spread to Bohemia, where it acquired followers among both Germans and Czechs. Trade Unions on the German model were formed in the industrial regions of German Austria, Bohemia, Moravia and Galicia. As industrialisation made progress in the Budapest area, in Croatia and in Slovenia, Trade Unions and political organisations of Hungarian, Croatian and Slovene workers also grew up. In the Austrian Parliament of 1906, the first elected by universal franchise, there were many Socialist members, including Germans, Poles and Czechs. In the Budapest Parliament, owing to restricted franchise and slow progress of industrialisation, Socialist representation was small.

It is important to note that Social Democracy came to Eastern Europe from Germany. It succeeded in those regions which were most influenced by Germany, and which were industrialised. In Eastern Europe Social Democratic Movements have always been confined to the industrial workers. They have had little contact with the peasants, partly because they were too much concerned with the problems of Industrial Labour to take much interest in the peasantry, partly because they were prevented by the police from entering the villages to hold meetings or organise propaganda. They did not therefore succeed, as in Italy, in organising an appreciable part of the rural population. In Hungary, Poland and Bohemia they represented a disciplined, progressive and moderate force, capable of playing an important secondary political role. The agrarian masses remained an unstable element, usually conservative, sometimes violently revolutionary, always easily misled and exploited. In the Balkan countries Social Democratic Parties were founded at the end of the century, but played little part in the national life. They were led by intellectuals influenced by French or Russian ideas. They had hardly anything in common with Central European Socialism, and had little human material on which to build.

Shortly before the First World War the Peasant Democratic Movement began to appear in Eastern Europe. The most notable example was the party led by the Radić brothers in Croatia. In Poland there were two groups, Piast in Galicia and Wyzwolenie in Congress Poland. An Agrarian Socialist Movement in Hungary alarmed the ruling class in the nineties, but after some measures of repression it petered out. In Bulgaria a peasant named Stamboliiski built up a group which attracted little attention before the war. In Serbia a number of parties fought each other, proclaiming programmes borrowed from French party politics. As the reality of Serbia was very different from that of France, the parties were obliged to take account of the peasantry, which represented some four-fifths of the nation. After the palace revolution of 1903 the most important group was the Radicals, who for about ten years to some extent represented the aspirations of the peasants. Their spiritual father was Svetozar Marković, whose writings express democratic views influenced by Socialism and by the milieu of a peasant society.

The Peasant Movements varied according to the special circumstances and traditions of the regions in which they arose. Their leaders proclaimed themselves the heirs of the traditions created by the historical heroes and martyrs of the peasant class of their nation. The Hungarian Agrarian Socialists proposed to unveil a statue to Dózsa, whom respectable history text-books represented as a bloodthirsty robber. The Radić brothers stressed their devotion to the memory of Gubec. But besides local traditions, the Peasant Movements were influenced by Russian Agrarian Socialist ideas. During the second half of the nineteenth century there was great enthusiasm among the revolutionary 'intelligentsia' of Russia for the cause of the peasants. The revolutionaries preached a 'Return to the People'. Intellectuals went to the villages and preached revolution to the peasants. These doctrines were not very clear, but their champions believed in a moral superiority of the peasant over the townsman, opposed industrialisation, repudiated western models, and insisted that Russia would find her own solution by a transformation of the State which would base the whole national life on the peasantry. This aim was to be attained by acts of terrorism, and finally by a popular revolution.

The 'Narodniki', as these romantic revolutionaries were called, disagreed violently with the Socialists, who held that only the working class, then just beginning to distinguish itself in Russia, could bring revolution, and that Russia must advance far on the path of industrialisation before she could hope for this. As time passed, the 'Narodniki' lost their romantic *naïveté*, which had provoked nothing but derision among the peasants to whom they preached. They became an organised movement, calling themselves Social Revolutionaries, and probably had the largest following in the country before the Bolshevik Revolution.

The influence of the 'Narodniki' can be traced in the Balkan countries and in Poland. The 'Wyzwolenie' group of Congress Poland had the same ideas, and intended to put them into practice in a liberated Poland. They had good relations with the Russian 'Narodniki', who recognised the right of Poland to freedom. In Roumania the Bessarabian Stere represented

them. This brilliant but unstable man had a great influence
on the Roumanian Peasant Movement and on Roumanian
Socialism.[1] Like Pilsudski, however, he was dominated by
hatred of Russia, which led him to move from extreme Left
to extreme Right and back with amazing facility. To his
influence, and to the erratic character of the Roumanian
intellectual in general, may be attributed the strange antics
of the Roumanian Left. In Bulgaria, where Russian influence
was strong in every field of life, the ideas of the 'Narodniki'
had some influence on the Peasant Movement led by Stamboliiski. In Serbia too they were known to the leaders of
political parties, and even the Radić brothers were affected
by them.

All the Peasant Movements of Eastern Europe aimed at the
transformation of the State in the interests of the peasantry,
and demanded social reforms, economic measures to help the
peasants, and political democracy. Their leaders often expressed themselves in very revolutionary terms, and used the
terminology of class struggle, familiarised by Marxist doctrines, though usually in simpler phrases. They insisted,
however, on the sanctity of private property in agriculture,
and their ideas on the place of industry and of the industrial
working class in society were confused. They consequently
alternated during the following years between revolutionary
violence and extreme Conservatism.

A last current of thought of which mention must be made
is Pan-Slavism. Among the Slav peoples there was a sense
of solidarity, varying in intensity but common to all. The
majority of the small Slav peoples looked to Russia, the only
Slav Great Power, for leadership and protection. This feeling
was strongest in the nineteenth century, and is strongest to-
day among the Orthodox Slav nations, the Serbs and Bulgarians. It is not confined to the intellectuals, but is in fact
strongest among the peasantry. It was before 1914 vigorously
fostered by the priesthood. No Government could ignore it

[1] Stere founded the review *Viaţa Românească* in Bucarest, in which were
expressed in the first decade of the twentieth century the views of the most
brilliant progressive intellectuals of Roumania. The ideas of Peasant Democracy were taking shape at that time in intellectual circles, but a Peasant Party
was founded only at the end of the First World War. Stere survived the war,
but his sudden changes of opinion precluded him from playing a serious part
in the political life of Great Roumania.

without grave risks. Russia was regarded by the masses of both peoples as a God-given Protector.

The same feeling was found in slightly lesser degree among the Czechs. In their long struggle against the Germans the Czech people clung to their sense of Slavdom, and when Russia emerged as a Great Power they were cheered by the consciousness of belonging to a powerful family of nations. In Slovakia the influence of the Catholic Church, which had much more hold on the people than was the case in the Czech Lands, was exerted against that of Russia, but without much success. The Slovaks have remained enthusiastically Pan-Slav.

In Croatia the educated class was profoundly influenced by the Roman Church and attracted by the civilisation of Vienna. Almost absurdly conscious of their 'western culture', Croatian intellectuals have always shown reserve towards Russia. The Croatian peasant masses, however, had a strong Slav consciousness, and have always regarded Russia with sympathetic curiosity. In Slovenia the peasant masses were more profoundly influenced by the Catholic Church than those of Croatia, but the intellectuals, largely as a reaction against the political position of the clergy, were more strongly Slav in feeling.

Pan-Slavism was for the small Slav nations a source of moral support rather than a political programme. They were comforted by the thought of the numerical strength of the Slav nations, and they hoped that Russia would one day free them from German or Turkish tyranny, or, if already liberated, that she would help them against any powerful enemies who might threaten their security. The idea of a great Slav Empire, built at the expense of Hungarian, Latin and Teuton, belonged to the realm of poets' dreams, and was never taken seriously by the peoples or their leaders.

The Russians, for their part, showed reserve towards the Pan-Slavism of the other Slavs. There was real sympathy in the Russian masses and among Russian intellectuals for the other Slavs, and this was at times encouraged by the Tsarist Government, which hoped that the 'Slavophiles' would divert the attention of the Russian people from social questions, and keep the masses from listening to revolutionaries. But if the Tsars found 'Slavophilism' convenient for internal political reasons, they did not base their foreign policy on it. 'Protection of the Orthodox citizens of Turkey' or 'concern for oppressed Slavs' might from time to time be useful excuses for Russian Imperialism, but if circumstances were unfavourable they were forgotten. Pan-Slavism has never played much part in international affairs.

The Polish people, divided between three Empires, was subjected to various forces. French cultural influence was strong in all three territories, especially in Congress Poland. Through French literature, and through the Polish exiles in Paris, the Poles learned the principles of Democracy, including the most advanced political and social theories put forward by French thinkers. From Prussia some learned the methods of an efficient bureaucracy, and a few of the benefits of material civilisation. In their struggle they were led by their Catholic clergy and intellectuals. Most supported politically the German 'Centre' (Catholic) Party, which had its own Trade Unions for the workers. The German Social Democrats also enjoyed some Polish support.

From Russia other Poles learned the methods and mentality of Conspiracy, developed to an art by the Russian revolutionaries in their fight with the Tsarist secret police. They learned from the 'Narodniki' the ideas of terrorism and of peasant revolution. The Social Democrats of Congress Poland acquired some knowledge of Socialism and a great deal of revolutionary ardour. Some Polish intellectuals were attracted by Pan-Slav ideas, and believed in brotherly relations with Russia. Most Poles, however, who had and have a deep sense of Slavdom, excluded Russia in their minds from the Slav brotherhood, preferring to regard themselves as the greatest Slav nation, with a mission of leadership over the others.

In Austria upper-class Poles had experience of limited power in a civilised country, while the peasants learned Democratic ideas and the workers Socialism of the German type, diluted by a certain Austrian mildness. Anti-Semitism existed among Poles of all three territories, but as the main enemy was German or Russian, and the economic rivalry of the Polish and Jewish bourgeoisies was not yet far developed, it did not attain large proportions. All these diverse currents united in one stream of Polish nationalism. The Polish people was firmly united in adversity, and only after independence was achieved did the differences begin to tell.

In the course of this brief historical survey nearly all the problems have been raised which dominate Eastern Europe to-day. It has been shown how a host of separate nations settled on top of each other in Eastern Europe, each of which once had a State of its own built at the expense of its neighbours; how the rise and fall of these short-lived States left many disputed frontier regions, and several inextricably mixed populations; how the States of Eastern Europe served as buffer between the west and the invasions from Asia, allowing other western nations to develop their civilisations in comparative security at the cost of theirs; how Poles, Czechs, Hungarians and Southern Slavs for a thousand years have been forced to defend themselves against the pressure of German expansion; how the Balkan peoples were for four hundred years ruled by the sterile military despotism of the Ottoman Empire; how Turkish methods of government corrupted public morals and denied the subject nations all possibility of education and culture; how in the Baltic and Danubian countries too the promise of the later Middle Ages was succeeded by a long period of decay, in which the cultural life of the upper class was debased, while the masses lived like beasts; how the peoples of Eastern Europe remained agricultural peoples; how different historical experiences made the agricultural society of the Balkans one mainly consisting of small peasant holders, while that of the Danubian and Baltic regions was dominated by big landowners; how in the nineteenth century commerce and industry began to develop in Eastern Europe, and the western ideas of Nationalism, Liberalism and Socialism impinged on these backward peoples.

The problems of to-day arise directly out of this historical evolution. They are the problems of the Peasantry and the Bourgeoisie, of Administration and Education, of Mixed Populations and Small Power Imperialism, of German Expansion and the Great Powers. They form the subject of this book.

Chapter Four

THE PEASANTRY

THE PEASANT COUNTRIES

The countries of Eastern Europe are predominantly agricultural. The population of most of them is composed in majority of peasants. The proportions for the individual States of 1918 are: Roumania 78 %, Bulgaria 80 %, Jugoslavia 75 %, Poland 63 %, Hungary 55 %, Czechoslovakia 34 %.

OFFICIALDOM AND THE PEASANT

The peasant character of these States has always been stressed by their official spokesmen. They declare themselves proud to be 'peasant nations'. Official tourist propaganda is backed up by beautifully illustrated pamphlets showing beautiful peasant girls, dressed in beautiful national costumes. The foreign visitor to an Eastern European country is immediately impressed by the enthusiasm of the well-to-do lawyers and business men of the capital for the peasant masses. The peasants, he is told again and again, are the backbone of the nation. They alone embody the stern, sound traditions and virtues that have carried the nation through the difficult past to the glorious present. On them alone can the nation rely in its direst need. Loving care for their welfare is the one permanent principle of the Government's policy. If the foreign visitor is fortunate enough to make the closer acquaintance of some well-to-do lawyer or business man, he will be invited to his house, and will be shown his host's daughters dressed up in peasant costumes. And very charming they will look too. After a few days' stay in the capital, the foreign visitor will find the Propaganda Ministry most eager to arrange for him to make a Sunday excursion to a not too distant village, where he will see the peasants come out of church in their best clothes. He will be received in a well-selected peasant house with touching hospitality. He will drink several glasses of good local wine. He will admire the rugs and the pottery with which the peasant's house is adorned, and he will have the privilege of watching a number of colourful national dances. The experience is delightful, and is often enough to make the foreign visitor a friend of the country for life, and a staunch supporter, for some years at least, of the good Government under which such happy scenes can take place.

Many delightful books have been published in recent years by self-constituted experts on individual Eastern European countries, and few have failed to stress the paternal relation of the various Governments to the sound, loyal peasantry. The soundness and loyalty of the peasantry is due to its complete contentment with its condition. Some Eastern European countries have made Land Reforms. In these countries the peasants are contented, because the Reforms have finally satisfied their aspirations, and solved all their social problems. In other countries there have been no Reforms, and the land remains in the hands of big landowners. Here also the peasants are contented, because they devotedly love and admire the landowners, who are true fathers of the peasant family. They are glad to be relieved by them of the responsibilities of land ownership. In both reformed and unreformed countries, then, the peasants lead almost idyllic lives, tilling the soil they mystically love, dancing their ancient national dances, clad in their picturesque national costumes and singing the while their soulful national songs.

Such is the picture presented to the foreign visitor by Eastern European officialdom. But if the foreign visitor stays a little longer in the country, if he leaves the capital for the provinces, and drives and walks a little in the countryside, if he travels sometimes in third-class railway carriages and keeps his eyes open, he will find things that he did not expect. He will see mud hovels, adorned by no rugs or pottery, housing families of seven or eight. He will meet peasants returning from their work in tattered rags that do not recall to him the lovely clothes of his first village. He will notice how the young peasant labourers in the train look at the officials who examine their labour permits. Then perhaps on his return to the capital he will meet some town intellectual, who will express to him opinions very different from those of his hospitable lawyer or business man, and will tell him facts not published in the Press or in the Propaganda Ministry pamphlets. Later, they may go together to a village, where he will be introduced to peasants who will put their own views before him. And gradually a picture will form in his mind. The picture will probably be

incomplete and a little distorted, but it will be much nearer
reality than the flights of imagination of the hard-worked
writers employed by the Tourist Department of the Propaganda Ministry.

THE LAND REFORMS

In 1914 the countries of Eastern Europe could be divided
between those based on small peasant proprietors and those
in which large landed estates predominated. The first category
consisted of Serbia, Bulgaria and Greece. To the latter belonged
the territories contained in the Austro-Hungarian Monarchy,
the whole of Poland and the Kingdom of Roumania.

Either during or immediately after the First World War
Land Reforms of one kind or another were planned in all the
areas belonging to the second category. The first country to
act was Roumania. In 1918 the Roumanian Parliament voted
a most radical Land Reform, which was carried out at the end
of the war. It was most effective in the newly annexed province of Bessarabia, where the proximity of the Bolshevik
Revolution made the Government most eager to satisfy the
demands of the peasants. It was also extended to the other
provinces of the country, both old and new, and, although
its application was in some cases delayed or evaded, by 1930
over 4,000,000 hectares of cultivable land had been distributed
to small holders or landless peasant labourers.

In Czechoslovakia a less radical reform distributed among the
Czech and Slovak peasants the estates of the big German and
Hungarian landlords. In Jugoslavia a similar reform divided
up the properties of the Moslem aristocracy in Bosnia, the
Hungarian estates in Bačka and Banat and the possessions
of the Croatian nobility. Both Czechoslovakia and Jugoslavia
thereby became predominantly countries of small peasant
proprietors.

In Hungary a fairly generous Land Reform was planned by
Bethlen's Minister of Agriculture, Nagyatádi Szabó, but when
the latter died suddenly, and the danger of Communism receded with the defeat of the Red Army by Pilsudski in 1921,
the project was abandoned. Between 1921 and 1938 not more
than 271,000 hectares of the big estates were distributed to
the peasants. In Poland ambitious schemes of reform were
discussed in Parliament during the first years, but while the

parties quarrelled over them little was done to put them into practice. After Pilsudski's *coup d'état* in 1926 radical reforms were definitely rejected, and the process of 'moderate' distribution of land was continually slowed up. In the last years before 1939 Land Reform was again treated more seriously by the Minister of Agriculture Poniatowski. Between 1921 and 1937, however, only 2,500,000 hectares had been divided up, a comparatively small amount in a country as large as Poland, and possessing so many vast estates. Hungary and Poland therefore remained countries of big landowners rather than of small holdings. Each has areas, which will be mentioned later, in which peasant holdings are the rule, but on the whole big estates play the chief part in their agriculture.

It is important to note that the two countries in which only minor reforms took place, Hungary and Poland, are those in which the native aristocracy had in the nineteenth century played the leading part in public life and in the national movement. In the countries which made radical reforms either there was no native aristocracy, or it was losing its political importance. In Czechoslovakia the landowning class was almost entirely German or Hungarian. In Jugoslavia part of it was foreign, while part consisted of native elements which had supported the Austro-Hungarian or Turkish regime and had shown no sympathy for the Jugoslav idea. In Roumania the aristocracy of the new provinces was Hungarian or Russian, but in the Old Kingdom it was Roumanian, even if part of it was of Greek origin. This native Roumanian aristocracy had played a prominent part in the national movement before the Liberation and in the political life of the independent State. The Land Reform, however, was voted by the Liberal Party, which represented the rising bourgeoisie, and which by the pro-Entente war policy of its leader Ionel Bratianu had become the great patriotic party of Roumania. One cause of the Liberal Party's support of Land Reform was the desire to destroy the economic basis of power of its political rivals, the Conservative landowners, whose political position was undermined by the voting in the same year of Universal Suffrage. The two measures finally eliminated the Roumanian aristocracy from the political field.

Another point worth stressing is the connection between the Land Reforms and the Bolshevik Revolution. This has already been noted in the case of Roumania. Czechoslovakia and Jugoslavia also had reason to fear Communism, as the sufferings of the war and the excitement of the national revolutions had created in the masses a radical mood, and as sympathy for Russia was traditional in their nations. This fear combined with the principles of bourgeois Liberalism to make the new Governments immediately apply far-reaching measures to satisfy their peasants. In Hungary and Poland, however, the Communist danger took practical form before any specific measures had been decided. In Hungary the Soviet Government of Béla Kun led to civil war and foreign intervention, while Poland, having embarked on an adventure in the Ukraine, was faced with the invasion of the Red Army. When both dangers had been overcome, with foreign aid, the reactionary elements of society acquired prestige, and the opposition to Reform hardened.

The Land Reforms also have a nationalist character which deserves attention. In Transylvania, Slovakia, Bačka and Banat, side by side with Roumanian and Serbian peasants, were landless Hungarian peasant labourers. These, as belonging to the 'enemy nation', received a less than equitable share of the lands of their former Hungarian masters. Moreover, in frontier regions of 'minority' population, actually or potentially hostile to the new States, colonists of the 'State nation' were settled. The most important of these 'colonised' areas were Eastern Poland, Macedonia and Dobrudja, where Poles, Serbs and Roumanians were settled respectively among Ukrainians, White Russians, Albanians and Bulgarians. In these cases the social character of the Reform was partly or wholly superseded by the national. Of this more will be said later.

It should be clearly understood that the motives of the Reforms were political, social and national, not economic. The economic difficulties inherent in the system of small properties were either not foreseen or ignored in the face of political and social necessities. Apart from the considerations noted above, there was a general feeling among educated middle-class people in all the countries under review that as the peasantry had borne the brunt of the war, and had proved itself in the greatest crisis yet known in human history to be in fact the backbone of the nation, it deserved to be given its share of the wealth of the nation. This was thought to override all other arguments. The Land Reforms were not economic measures, and cannot be judged as such.

The difference between countries which had radical Land Reforms and those in which big estates survived is an important one for the following twenty years. Although many of the technical problems of agriculture are the same for both types of society, there are substantial differences between the two in the mode of life of the masses, and these are reflected in the political life of the countries. The two types of society will here be considered separately before an attempt is made to reach certain conclusions on the Eastern European Peasant Problem.

THE PEASANTS IN THE REFORMED STATES SINCE 1918

It had been hoped that the Land Reforms would solve the Peasant Problem, and that the masses, socially satisfied, would form a stable basis of the State. These hopes were not justified. The economic developments of the inter-war period created new problems, and by 1939 the situation of a large part of the Eastern European peasantry was worse than it had been in 1914.

The new peasant owners lacked technical knowledge. As labourers on the big landowners' estates they had had neither opportunity nor inducement to learn modern methods of agriculture. Having become independent owners themselves, they did not know how to develop their land. Agricultural education was not easily available, and had no social prestige. A peasant's son of ambition who could afford a university education preferred to study Law or Medicine and then remain in the town. A number of agricultural experts were trained every year, but they were not enough, and although some of them did splendid work in the villages, others did not take their duties very seriously. The Governments devoted little money or attention to agricultural education.

The peasants also lacked technical equipment. In the Balkans and Poland there are many places where the wooden plough is still used. Many households had no plough at all. More complicated machines—reapers, tractors etc.—were confined to the remaining big estates. The small holders could not afford them, and their use on these tiny properties would have been uneconomic. The medium holders could have used them if they had collaborated with their neighbours and tilled their lands in common, and if they had had credit facilities for making the expensive initial purchase. But the Governments frowned on communal cultivation, and failed to organise a cheap credit system for the peasants. If they wished to use machines, they had to borrow them from the local landowner, often at great cost. In general the new Governments paid little attention to the improvement of agriculture or the assistance of the peasant owners until the World Depression forced these tasks upon them. But during the ten years of comparative prosperity much of the damage was done, for the backward methods and bad management of these years weakened unnecessarily the position of the peasant owners, and made the subsequent burden of the Depression more difficult to bear.

In Eastern Europe it is the custom that the holding is divided on the death of the owner between all his sons. Twenty years of this practice has caused a subdivision of the original holdings of the Land Reforms into a much greater number of tiny plots of land. If a holding consisted of land of different qualities, devoted to different kinds of production, then each son must have a piece of each type. It is arguable that even the original holdings were too small for rational cultivation, but there is no doubt at all of the hopelessly uneconomic nature of the dwarf properties into which they have since been divided. A holding of a few acres may consist of as many as forty small strips, separated from each other by several miles. Large areas of cultivated land were wasted in the form of paths enabling owners to walk from one strip to another. The strips are incapable of efficient production. Even the most casual visitor is impressed by the difference in quality of the crops he sees on a drive through a region such as the Wallachian plain, where small holdings and large estates exist side by side.

The situation of Eastern European agriculture was deeply affected by the competition of overseas cereals in the great European markets. Hungarian wheat, for instance, might compete with American in Vienna, but was undersold in Munich. It was cheaper to transport grain raised on the highly capitalised farms of America by sea from New York or Buenos Aires to Hamburg and Trieste than to bring the products of the less capitalised estates of Hungary, not to

mention the uneconomic holdings of the Balkans, a few
hundred miles. American competition more than balanced
the grain represented by the disappearance of Russian wheat
from the world market after the Revolution. It was felt more
by the big and medium proprietors than by the small holders,
but it influenced directly or indirectly the whole agricultural
population of Eastern Europe.

The World Depression struck Eastern Europe in 1929, and
its worst years were 1932–34. The price of wheat fell by about
one-half in the home markets. Industry suffered too, but the
various cartels were able to some extent to defend industrial
prices. Thus occurred the 'price scissors', the catastrophic
disparity between industrial and agricultural prices. Some
figures are given in full on p. 122.

The Roumanian Trade Cycle Research group calculated an
index of prices of those industrial goods which are bought
by peasants (tools, clothes, town-prepared foodstuffs, etc.) and
compared these with the agricultural price index. The respective
figures, expressed as a percentage of the 1929 level, are in
1932 47·7 for agricultural and 80·9 for this group of industrial
prices; in 1934 44·1 and 82·6. After 1934, owing to Government
help and to expansion of trade with Germany, agricultural
prices began to recover, but they failed to keep pace with
industrial prices, which soared to heights unknown for more
than a decade. The figures for January 1940 in Roumania
are 80 and 159·4.

In Poland the same phenomenon occurred, but the disparity
decreased appreciably during the economic recovery immediately preceding the war. The corresponding figures, expressed as a percentage of the 1928 level, are for 1932 48·9
and 81; for 1934 37 and 70·3; and for 1937 49·2 and 66·1.

Throughout Eastern Europe the purchasing power of the
peasantry failed substantially to recover from the blow dealt
it by this price disparity. The result is a general lowering of
the standard of living, which the war has accentuated. In
particular, being obliged to spend his reduced cash resources
on necessities like clothes, salt, lamp-oil, the peasant cannot
buy tools, still less machines. The hope of escaping from
poverty by increasing his output through more efficient methods is thus removed.

The reduction of purchasing-power caused by the World

Economic Depression has increased other burdens. During the earlier years of comparative prosperity the wealthier peasants had borrowed money, from banks or from individuals, in order to make purchases to improve their lands. The poorer peasants also borrowed money in order to buy food in the critical period of the year, the months before the harvest, when their supplies from the preceding harvest had run out. Borrowing for food was especially common in certain regions, such as Dalmatia, which do not produce cereals, and where the income from other occupations does not suffice for subsistence needs the whole year round. Loans were made at a high rate of interest, particularly those made by individual money-lenders. The rate was often over 20 % and sometimes amounted to 45 %. The fall of agricultural prices enormously increased the burden of these debts, since the peasant now received half as much for his products as earlier, while the sum of his debt remained the same. During the thirties agitation for the annulment of debts was widespread in the Balkan countries. In 1934 Roumania passed a Conversion Law, from which 64 % of the holdings of the country, comprising 58·76 % of the cultivated land, benefited. The total amount of agricultural debts was reduced by 50 %, and the rest was to be paid in the form of annuities of 8 % over a period of twelve years. In Jugoslavia a Conversion Law of the same nature was passed in 1935, which transferred the reduced debt to the State Agrarian Bank. In Bulgaria a number of separate measures were passed during these years, which brought about a similar result. The Conversion Laws relieved the situation, but they still left the peasants with a very considerable burden, and the creditors were unwilling after this experience to make loans. Credit for the peasants remained as difficult as ever.

The same cause increased the burden of taxation. The sums paid in direct taxation by Eastern European peasants seem at first sight very small. But in comparison with the exiguous income of the peasant they represent a very substantial sacrifice. Indirect taxation, mainly in the form of State Monopolies of articles of universal consumption, such as salt, was heavy in the Eastern European States, and weighed most severely on the poorest of the peasants.

These general causes, which operated in all areas of small peasant holdings in Eastern Europe, brought about a striking fall of the standard of living, which had never been high, and at the same time deprived the peasants of the opportunity of improving their condition by more efficient cultivation.

Under pressure of increasing poverty many peasants sold their land. It was acquired in some cases by the landowner formerly expropriated in the Land Reform, in others by a town or village merchant, in others by a rich peasant who had used the period of comparative prosperity to put his property on a firm foundation.

A process of differentiation between rich and poor is taking place among the Eastern European peasantry. Although exact information is too scanty to permit dogmatic statements, it can be safely said that the process is general in the peasant-owner regions. Two classes are forming. The feudal landowner of the old days is replaced by the large medium farmer of above 50 hectares, who may be peasant, merchant or aristocrat by origin. The place of the landless labourer of the period previous to the Reforms is taken by the rural proletariat of dwarf owners.

CATEGORIES OF LAND HOLDINGS

The official statistics of the Eastern European States show three categories of land holdings—big, medium and small. The first may be taken to comprise those above 50 hectares (roughly 125 acres). It includes both great estates—of which there are many in Hungary and Poland, a few in Roumania and hardly any in the other countries—and large farms (say 50–200 hectares)—of which there is a considerable number in all. For the purposes of the present survey these two types of property will be taken as one, and called 'big holdings'. The expression 'great estates' will be used at times to describe properties of several hundred hectares. The differences in absolute size within the 'big holdings' class are striking, but from the economic, social and political points of view they should be regarded as one class. These big holdings can be, and usually are, organised on a rational basis. They produce large quantities of cereals or other agricultural products, and sell to the big internal markets and to foreign countries. They produce the bulk of each country's agricultural exports, and from the point of view of national agriculture are the most important category.

The second category are middle-sized farms between 5 and

50 hectares. These will be referred to henceforth as 'medium holdings'. They produce mainly for their own consumption, and are usually self-supporting in most foodstuffs. Those which are most efficiently exploited may even send their products to the big markets within the country and abroad, but on the whole they limit themselves to the smaller markets near their villages, where they sell for the ready money which they need to pay taxes and to make necessary purchases in the towns. This class of holdings is still fairly numerous in many parts of Eastern Europe, but it is diminishing in the face of the process of differentiation described above.

The third category are properties below 5 hectares. These will be called 'small holdings'. They are usually inadequate for the maintenance of a peasant family. They do not produce sufficient foodstuffs, and the sale in the local market of any surplus which they have of any particular crop does not bring in enough cash to buy those foodstuffs which are not produced. Nor are the animals belonging to the small holder sufficient to make up this deficit. He is obliged for part of the year to seek work elsewhere. This class is being constantly increased by the process of differentiation.

It should be emphasised that the size limits used to define the three categories are inevitably arbitrary. A holding of 5 hectares of exceptionally good land may provide fully for the food needs of a family and bring in adequate cash as well, while one of 50 hectares, if administered with exceptional ability, may reach the economic level of the 'big holdings'. But the three classes undoubtedly exist, and the limits chosen are the most satisfactory possible.

The main strongholds of big estates in Eastern Europe are Eastern Poland (the White Russian provinces and Volhynia) and Central and Eastern Hungary (especially east of the Tisza). These regions have properties of tens of thousands of hectares. The greatest families are the Hungarian Festetics and Esterházy and the Polish Radziwill and Potocki. Although big estates exist in all parts of these two countries, in the other regions they are mixed to a greater extent with medium and small. Hungary west of the Danube is a centre of medium holdings, Western Galicia consists largely of small holdings, while in the central district round Warsaw there were many prosperous medium holdings.

In Roumania the biggest estates are mostly in forest land, but big holdings of cultivable land are also found in parts of Wallachia, Moldavia and Bessarabia. In Dobrudja, whose population is thinly distributed, and where cultivation has only begun on a serious scale since 1918, the average holding is big or medium. In the greater part of the country, however, small holdings predominate. In Jugoslavia small holdings are the rule except for Slavonia and the Voivodina (Bačka and Banat), where the population is less dense and both big and medium holdings are found in considerable numbers. In Bulgaria small holdings are the most numerous but the proportion of medium is high. In Greece small holdings are usual. In Albania large properties are common. The land is organised on a tribal system which does not exist in other countries.

In Czechoslovakia small and medium holdings are the most frequent, but there is a substantial number of large holdings. The peasants of Bohemia-Moravia are the most advanced in our area. Their standard of living normally approximates to that of the farmers of Southern and West Germany. The World Depression hit Czechoslovak agriculture, but the high cultural and economic level of the Czech peasants, and the agricultural protection introduced owing to their political pressure, spared them much of the sufferings of their neighbours. In Slovakia conditions resemble those of other ex-Hungarian provinces that had Land Reforms. The Slovak peasants are small holders with a backward standard of living, buyers rather than sellers of food, whom protection harmed rather than helped.

Roumania, Bulgaria, Hungary, Jugoslavia and Czechoslovakia have published reasonably recent statistics of distribution of land between categories of holdings. The only complete Polish statistics available date from 1921, and show a state of affairs to some extent modified by subsequent Land Reform. These figures are all given on p. 121.

In Poland in 1921 64·7 % of holdings were under 5 hectares and possessed 15·3 % of the land; 34·3 % were between 5 and 50 hectares and possessed 31·8 %; and 1 % were over 50 hectares and possessed 52·9 %. More recent figures show the same proportion of holdings in each category but deliberately conceal the proportion of land possessed by each.

In Hungary 85·2 % of holdings were below 10 joch (about

5 hectares) and possessed 19·1 % of the land; 14·1 % were between 10 and 100 joch and possessed 32·6 %; and 0·7 % were over 100 joch and possessed 48·3 %.

In Czechoslovakia in 1931 71 % of holdings were under 5 hectares and possessed 23 % of the land; 27 % were between 5 and 30 hectares and possessed 51 %; and 2 % were over 30 hectares and possessed 26 %.

In Jugoslavia in 1931 67·8 % of holdings were under 5 hectares and possessed 30·3 % of the cultivable land.

In Roumania in 1930 74·9 % of holdings were under 5 hectares and possessed 35·8 % of the cultivable land; 24·3 % were between 5 and 50 hectares and possessed 45·4 %; and 0·8 % were over 50 hectares and possessed 18·8 %.

In Bulgaria in 1934 62 % of holdings were below 5 hectares and possessed 29 % of the land; 37 % were between 5 and 30 hectares and possessed 65 %; and 1 % were over 30 hectares and possessed 6 %.

Big holdings are important only in Poland and Hungary, medium holdings are more numerous and best provided for in Bulgaria and Poland, but in all six countries small holdings are most numerous and possess much less than their proportionate share of the land.

THE EASTERN EUROPEAN SMALL HOLDER

Eastern European agriculture is extensive. The yield of crops per unit cultivated is small. This explains the failure to compete with overseas agriculture, whose intensive methods greatly reduce costs of production. Small and medium holdings can conduct intensive agriculture if economic circumstances are favourable and standards of education and methods of production are of high quality. This is shown by the case of Denmark, a country of prosperous small farmers. The average production of wheat per hectare for 1933–37 in Denmark was 29·2 quintals, in Bulgaria 11·9, in Hungary 11·8, in Jugoslavia 11, and in Roumania 9·1. The corresponding figures for the four Eastern European countries for maize in the same years were Hungary 18·5, Jugoslavia 16·9, Bulgaria 12·8, and Roumania 9·8. The fact that even Hungary, where agriculture is based on big holdings, has less than half the yield of Denmark shows that agricultural methods are backward in all classes of holding, but it is usually true that in

Eastern Europe the smaller the holding the lower the productivity of the soil. This is due partly to the poverty of the
holders and partly to the fact that the holdings are devoted
mainly to cereals, needed for home consumption, although
cereals are less suitable to small holdings than other types
of crop.

Eastern European small holdings are mainly devoted to
cereals, but they also rear livestock. More prosperous holdings
have oxen or horses for ploughing, cows for milk, pigs for
food and market, and perhaps some poultry. In the mountain
villages of Transylvania and Slovakia the peasants have little
land, and this not very fertile, and they live from their sheep,
sheep-milk cheese or geese. In Croatia livestock farming is
important, and in Central Serbia cereal and pig farming go
side by side. But in the greater part of Eastern Europe, particularly in Roumania and the Balkans, the small holdings
are poorly supplied with livestock.

The researches of groups of students under the supervision
of Professor Gusti of Bucarest in selected typical villages in
the various provinces of Roumania revealed the following
situation. In the plainlands of Wallachia, Bessarabia and
the western frontier region there was one pair of oxen or
horses to between 1·5 and 2 holdings, that is to say between
one-third and one-half of the holdings had no ploughing
animals at all, but were obliged to hire them from their
neighbours. In the mountain districts of Transylvania the
proportion was one pair to 3·5 holdings, and in the mountains of Wallachia and Moldavia (the southern and eastern
slopes of the Carpathians) it was one pair to 6·4 holdings. In
the whole country, in the category of holdings less than 1 hectare 65·2 % have neither oxen nor horses, 51·5 % have no
cow, 60·2 % have no pig and 64·8 % have no sheep. In the
category between 1 and 3 hectares the corresponding figures
are 48·5 %, 36·1 %, 53·8 % and 52·8 %. In the category
between 3 and 5 hectares in the plain regions of the provinces
of Bessarabia, Wallachia and the western frontier only the
percentages of holdings that have no oxen or horses are
respectively 58, 43 and 37. The same percentages for the
same three regions in the category of holdings between 5 and
10 hectares are respectively 30, 21 and 16.

This situation represents a marked decline in the number

of livestock since before 1914. It is due partly to the cultivation of former grazing grounds with cereals, and partly to the
lack of fodder grown in the country. The proportion of cultivable land producing fodder in 1937 was 24·23 % in Denmark, 12·19 % in Czechoslovakia, 10·09 % in Hungary, 6·68 %
in Bulgaria, 5·2 % in Roumania and 4·66 % in Jugoslavia.
The lack of both grazing grounds and fodder is most acute
in the case of Bulgaria, which has 61·4 head of cattle per
10 hectares of pasture or cultivated fodder. Roumania has
17 per 10 hectares, Hungary 12·4 and Jugoslavia 10·3. Czechoslovakia and Hungary are both better supplied with livestock
than the other countries of Eastern Europe. Of the remainder
the most fortunate are probably Poland and Bulgaria, while
the poorest is Roumania. The figures given above for Roumania represent, however, a phenomenon which is common
to some extent to all.

More suitable than cereals for small holdings are vegetables
and industrial plants, whose market value is also considerably
higher. Progress has been made in the cultivation of these
plants in the last years, particularly owing to demand for
them from Germany. Soya beans and sunflower were grown
on a fairly large scale in Northern Bessarabia before the outbreak of the war, and their production has been intensified
since the German occupation. But the quantities produced
are not yet very large. Between 1920 and 1937 the percentages
of cultivable land in Roumania producing vegetables and industrial plants rose respectively from 3·3 to 3·7 and from
2·2 to 3·6. An increase of these crops took place during the
same period, and particularly since the Depression, in Jugoslavia (mainly Croatia) and in Bulgaria. The extension of these
plants over a large area is hampered by the lack of fertilisers.
In the absence of artificial fertilisers, which are beyond the
reach of most small holdings, animal manure is used. But the
shortage of livestock indicated above is a serious obstacle to
an increase of these valuable crops.

The lack of technical equipment has already been mentioned
as a cause of the difficult situation of small holdings. In this
respect Roumania is the poorest of the Eastern European
States. The value of agricultural equipment per hectare in
Roumania is half that in Bulgaria and one-third that in Poland.
The researches of the Gusti group in Roumania showed an

average of one plough to 2·1 holdings in the whole country. In every category of holdings under 10 hectares there was less than one plough per holding. In the category 0–1 hectare there was one plough to 9·6. Holdings of this size are so small that it would be uneconomic for each to have its plough. But for each dwarf owner the cost of hiring a richer neighbour's plough is a heavy burden. For larger holdings permanent possession of a plough is desirable, yet the lowest category in which the average holding has a plough is that between 10 and 25 hectares. A Roumanian agricultural expert[1] in 1939 estimated that the total value of technical equipment of Roumanian agriculture was 14 milliard lei, and that the value needed for efficient agriculture was 30 milliard. If the country had equipment to this value, agricultural output would be raised by 50 %. In this respect Roumania is worse off than her neighbours, but the small holders of Poland, Bulgaria and Jugoslavia have a position only very slightly better.

The small holdings, then, produce cereals and have a small number of animals, but are prevented from keeping many animals by the lack of fodder, and from producing vegetable and industrial crops by the lack of animal manure. Their cereal production is less than it should be owing to lack of technical equipment. The produce of the holdings only partly satisfies the food needs of the family. The surplus that is left of the crops after a part of these needs has been satisfied, must be sold in order to obtain cash with which to buy certain foodstuffs which the holding cannot produce, but must be bought in the towns. This cash income must also suffice to buy a few things besides food, and to pay taxes. But in most cases the foodstuffs produced by the holding are not sufficient to supply the family the whole year round, and the cash income realised by the sale of the surplus is not sufficient to cover necessary expenditure. In the majority of small holdings therefore one or more members of the family is obliged to earn more cash by work outside the family holding. Yet in many cases even this additional income does not cover the minimum necessary consumption.

The main sources of additional income for small holders are labour on the big holdings and seasonal labour in industry.

[1] A. Cherdivarencu, quoted in Madgearu, *op. cit.*

Some regions, where the soil is poor and there are not sufficient occupations outside agriculture, have a large number of peasants seeking temporary work elsewhere. The Bosnian and Dalmatian peasants worked as agricultural labourers on the big and medium holdings of Slavonia, or in the big forest exploitations. Bessarabian land workers were employed in the harvest season in Southern Roumania. The peasants of Northern Transylvania (Maramureş) used, until Transylvania was partitioned by Hitler and Mussolini, to work in the factories of the south and in the Old Kingdom.

The researches of the Gusti group shows the following results for Roumania. They may be considered to represent also the state of affairs in many other parts of Eastern Europe, where such statistics are not available.

Taking all the holdings examined together, including small and medium, selected in the same proportion as the known distribution of land in the country, the average proportion of total family consumption supplied by the produce of the holding was found to be 60–70 %. In the poorer categories of holdings and in the poorer regions, it was much lower. In Transylvania—not one of the poorest provinces of Roumania—in the category of holdings less than 3 hectares, only 17·9 % of family consumption was provided by the holding, and 82·1 % was bought.

In the category below 2 hectares for the whole country 17·3 % of the cash income was derived from the produce of the holding, 59 % from labour outside the holding, and 14·9 % from subsidiary sources. For the category between 2 and 5 hectares the corresponding percentages were 42, 21 and 15·9.

In the category below 3 hectares for the whole country, in 86 % of the holdings expenditure exceeded income. This percentage was 70 for holdings between 3 and 5 hectares and 41 for those between 10 and 20 hectares. It should be remembered that 75 % of all holdings in Roumania are below 5 hectares, and 52 % below 3.

Throughout Eastern Europe the number of families that make their own clothes is decreasing. Even if the women still embroider the special local costumes that are still worn on Sundays and on special occasions, the working clothes are usually bought. Although Eastern European peasants do not have large wardrobes, the necessary minimum of clothes is a heavy charge on their incomes. In the·Transylvanian holdings below 3 hectares examined by the Gusti group, 61·9 % of the family income was spent on clothes. In the same category of holdings in Bessarabia—perhaps the most backward part of Roumania—the average family expenditure consisted of 206 lei (about 4s.) for clothes, 16 lei for the Church. This was all that the average family spent in one year apart from buying food. It is not surprising that with such low purchasing-power the peasants of Eastern Europe are not able adequately to clothe themselves. In most parts of Eastern Europe one will see numbers of peasants in mere rags. In some regions they are the majority. In Bessarabia or Bosnia there are many families in which one pair of shoes has to do for two or three persons.

Housing conditions are usually extremely bad. Most medium holders, and small holders in prosperous districts, have adequate houses, but, often lacking any sense of hygiene, they seldom make the best use of what they have. The majority of small holders live in such wretched and primitive hovels that even the best hygiene experts would have difficulty in making much of them. One bed will often hold six or seven persons, including children. In parts of Bosnia and other poor regions the cow or pig sleeps in the same room as the family. Yet the Eastern European peasant is fond of his house, and all except the hopelessly destitute will take great pains to beautify it, by carving the doorpost, decorating the interior with home-made rugs, or other means.

A factor of some importance in depressing the standard of living of the peasants even lower than it would naturally be is to be found in certain social conventions. Peasant houses often have a 'guest-room', for the entertainment of friends on special occasions, or for any guest who may turn up. The bed is not used except on these occasions, and the family have to confine themselves to one room and a small kitchen, or one room alone. If a girl in the village gets a pair of silk stockings, the other girls must have some too to maintain the family prestige. Fathers will make great sacrifices, and spend too little on food, in order to save money to buy them. In the rich Jugoslav province of Slavonia it is the custom that peasant brides wear old Austrian gold ducats on their wedding costumes. It is the ambition of every girl to have more ducats than her fellows. The honour of the family depends on the expenditure of a large proportion of the earnings of the household on the purchase of these ducats. No girl can hope to find a husband, however admirable she may be in every other respect, unless she has a sufficient number. The purchasing-power immobilised in this useless gold is very considerable. The region is one of the richest, and its peasants have one of the highest income levels, in all Eastern Europe. But this practice prevents social progress which would be otherwise possible.[1]

The food of the peasant population of Eastern Europe is most unsatisfactory. The small holders hardly ever touch meat. It is reserved for special religious festivals, and for the entertainment of guests. A poor man will eagerly slaughter his only pig for a complete stranger. Wheaten bread is eaten in the richer regions. It is fairly widely consumed in Central Serbia, Slavonia, Transylvania, Northern Bulgaria, Slovenia, Southern Poland and most of Czechoslovakia. In the greater part of Poland rye bread takes the place of wheaten even in medium peasant households, and the small holders seldom eat wheat. In most of Roumania, Jugoslavia and Bulgaria the staple diet is maize. The small holders hardly ever get anything else, and even the medium peasants are more accustomed to maize than to wheat. They probably often prefer it. In Bosnia, Macedonia, Dalmatia and Central Croatia maize bread is widely consumed. In Roumania the food of the masses is 'mamaliga', a maize polenta, which is made more tasty by the addition of cheese or onions when these are obtainable. In Bulgaria the diet of maize is supplemented by the same additions, and by large quantities of paprika. The Eastern European countries have a wealth of excellent national dishes of grilled meat and meat-and-vegetable stew, which delight the enterprising foreign visitor, but the latter does not usually realise that these dishes, although 'national' in the sense that they are specific to particular countries or regions, do not reach a very large part of the 'nation'. The peasant masses seldom taste them. Bad bread, cheese, onion and paprika are all that comes their way for most of the year.

[1] This phenomenon is described by a Croatian country woman doctor, Nada Sremec, in her book *Nismo mi krive* ('We are not to blame'), Zagreb, 1939.

Medical research in the Eastern European countries has shown that although the quantity of food consumed by the peasants is sufficient to supply the minimum number of calories, its variety and quality are extremely unsatisfactory. In other words, they get enough to keep alive, but not enough to keep in good health. Here again the difference between categories of small holders must be borne in mind. The very poorest often do not even get the quantitive minimum, whereas holdings of 4 or 5 hectares of good soil in a prosperous region may yield, in kind and in income, sufficient quality as well as sufficient quantity. A special unsatisfactory feature of the diet is its irrēgularity. On the whole the peasants have sufficient good food during the autumn and winter months, when they are inactive. In the spring and summer, however, when they are doing heavy work from dawn to dark, their supplies of food from the previous harvest are coming to an end, and they are undernourished. These months of overwork and inadequate food weaken their bodies, and make them susceptible to disease.

The following figures, published by a Roumanian expert,[1] are of interest. The average yearly consumption per family of three important articles of food in certain Roumanian provinces was as follows (in kg.):

	Meat	Milk	Sugar
In Bessarabia	35·0	102·8	2·4
„ Western Wallachia (Oltenia)	39·5	93·1	2·0
„ Eastern Wallachia	40·7	129·0	3·7
„ Transylvania	41·6	185·0	3·7
„ Moldavia	43·5	162·1	4·1
„ Banat	65·1	187·7	6·2

The Banat is a rich region where medium holdings are numerous, and where even small holders enjoy a fairly high standard of living. The others are regions where small holdings predominate. It should be noted that these figures represent the average consumption for all categories of holdings, including medium. Similar statistics for the small holdings only would show much lower figures.

It is obvious that the conditions described above have an injurious effect upon the health of the peasantry of Eastern Europe. Much of the heaviest work is done in these countries

[1] Dr D. C. Georgescu, *L'alimentation de la population rurále en Roumanie*, quoted in Madgearu, *op. cit.*

by women. The women work in the fields beside the men right up to the last stages of pregnancy. It is still by no means unknown in Roumania, Bulgaria or Jugoslavia for children to be born in the fields. Overwork and insufficient food for young mothers have a fatal effect on the powers of resistance of very small children. Infant mortality in Eastern European countries is from three to four times higher than in Holland. It is highest of all in Roumania, and of the Roumanian provinces the worst is Bessarabia. Tuberculosis is the scourge of the peasant masses. It is high in all the countries under review, particularly in such miserably poor regions as Montenegro. In the Roumanian plains of Wallachia and Moldavia a disease called pellagra is not uncommon. It is due to bad nourishment, and seems to be connected with the unvaried consumption of badly prepared maize flour. It is occasionally found in other European countries such as Italy and Spain, but much the highest rate of occurrence in Europe is that of Roumania.

There is no doubt that in all the countries under review far too little attention has been paid to public health. Medical students who have completed their university courses prefer to set themselves up in the towns, and treat the medical profession only as a means of financial gain and social advancement. The life of a country doctor, or even of a town specialist spending most of his time in the country, does not appeal to most. Yet despite lack of recruits and governmental indifference, an enormous amount has been done in the last twenty years. A small number of public health workers by selfless and unsparing efforts have done little less than miracles. Special mention should be made of the great Jugoslav Dr Andrija Štampar, recognised as one of the greatest experts in public health in the world, who in a few years obtained brilliant results in parts of his country. The pioneers of this work have to face attacks from all sides, accusations of 'Bolshevism' from part of their own profession, and indifference from the peasant masses, whose lack of education does not enable them to understand the importance of hygiene or to make the best even of the scanty resources of food that are at their disposal. All that has been done hitherto is only a beginning. And it cannot progress far unless radical economic and educational reforms are made.

An account of the living conditions of Eastern European small peasants is bound to leave a gloomy impression. The condition is that described above, which is fairly general for the class of holdings below 5 or even below 10 hectares. There are of course regional variations. In the Banat and Slavonia, despite the special local problems created by useless expenditure on conventional luxuries, conditions are mainly good. In the mountain villages of Transylvania there are many prosperous peasants who make a good living from sheep-farming. In the foothills of the Carpathians fruit farmers organised in selling cooperatives enjoy satisfactory incomes. The economies of small holdings in Central Serbia are well balanced between cereals and livestock. Other happy examples could be multiplied.

At the other extreme there is abject misery. Two examples will suffice. There are mountain villages in Dalmatia, in the barren 'karst' desert described in Chapter Two, where people have to walk 20 kilometres to fetch water. A member of the family will set off with a jug in the burning summer heat. When he gets to the spring he will find dozens of others, gathered from other villages whose supplies have dried up. He will have to wait his turn for hours to fill his jug with the diminished trickle of poor water. Then he must walk back 20 kilometres. The precious water will be drunk at once by the family, and almost immediately someone else must set out again on the same journey.

In the western mountains of Transylvania the soil yields little. The peasants' houses are hovels perched on barren hillsides. The produce of the holdings is negligible. Some go to work in the forests, others in the gold-mines of this region. Others have little water-mills of their own, which they work for hours on end, washing slowly through the heaps of clay which they bring up laboriously in barrows, hoping to find a few grains of the precious gold. Others make wooden instruments, little tools and buckets which they load on their carts and carry away to a market. These nomad sellers from the mountains, called 'Motsi', can be met at any hour of the day or night on the roads. Their wanderings took them, in the days before frontiers became steel walls, as far as Constantinople. They still travel down to the Danube at Galaţ. The reward of these distant, painful pilgrimages is a few hundred lei, with which to buy maize to keep their families from starvation. There is a Roumanian rhyme in this district:

Munții noștri aur poartă.
Noi cerșim din poart' în poartă.

'Our mountains bear gold, we go begging from door to door.'

OVERPOPULATION

The fundamental problem of the Eastern European peasantry in all smallholder regions is overpopulation.

At first sight this statement may be surprising. The density of population of the Eastern European States is very much lower than that of the States of the west. But the difference between Eastern and Western Europe is that the former is agrarian, the latter industrialised. A highly industrialised area can support an almost unlimited concentration of population, but the number of people that can be employed in agriculture is much smaller. The degree of overpopulation can therefore only be measured by taking the density of population per unit of cultivable land. Denmark, a largely industrial state with highly developed agriculture, based on intensively cultivated small and medium holdings, has 36·6 people per square kilometre of cultivable land. The corresponding figures for the Danubian and Balkan regions are Hungary 80·6, Roumania 116·3, Bulgaria 119, Jugoslavia 157·4. The contrast is striking.

In some districts of Eastern Europe the pressure of overpopulation is especially severe. In Poland Galicia is heavily overpopulated, particularly the western, Polish-inhabited portion. Most regions of Bulgaria are densely populated. In Jugoslavia the central part of Croatia, north of Zagreb (Zagorje) is heavily populated, and in some districts of Bosnia and Dalmatia there are as many as 300 people to a square mile of cultivable land. In Roumania the most heavily overpopulated regions are Transylvania (145 per square kilometre of cultivable land), Wallachian Mountains (166), Moldavian Mountains (188) and Bukovina (192). The most fortunate regions are Dobrudja (52) and Southern Bessarabia (59). The price of land in Bukovina is four times greater than that in Dobrudja, and the rate of rent is two and a half times greater.

The contrast between density of agricultural population in Eastern and Western Europe becomes more striking when we remember that in the former agriculture is extensive, and in the latter highly intensive. The yield of wheat per hectare in Denmark is, as has been stated above, 29·2 quintals to 9·1 in Roumania, 11 in Jugoslavia, 11·8 in Hungary and 11·9 in Bulgaria. In fact, in Jugoslavia on a given unit of land four times as many people produce three times less wheat than in Denmark.

The overpopulation of the Eastern European countries is, of course, only relative, since if they adopted intensive methods of cultivation and industrialised themselves, they could support much more than their present populations. This is, however, an academic observation. Industrialisation is a long and difficult process. And it has already been shown what causes prevent the rational development of Eastern European agriculture. And meanwhile the populations rapidly increase. The rates of increase of Poland, Jugoslavia, Roumania and Bulgaria are much higher than those of Western European countries. Moreover the predominance in the populations of these countries of young-age-groups ensures the continuance of the increase for a long time ahead. Dr Manuila, head of the Roumanian Statistical Institute, has shown, on the basis of the Roumanian census of 1930, with calculations bringing the figures up to 1937, that the age-group 0–19 represented 46·4 % of the whole population of the country, and 48·2 % of the peasant population.

The pressure of overpopulation in the Eastern European agrarian countries of Poland, Roumania, Jugoslavia and Bulgaria is more severe than in Italy, and very much more severe than in Germany. If the principle of the two Dictators were accepted, that countries suffering from overpopulation have the right to annex their neighbours' territory, then it is the Eastern European countries that should rule Germany and Italy.

Attempts have been made to calculate the percentage of the available man-power of the agrarian nations of Eastern Europe that is at present wasted. A Roumanian estimate puts this percentage at 56·34 in Roumania. The researches of the Gusti group estimated it as 62 % for holdings under 3 hectares—(which, be it remembered, constitute more than half the total number of holdings in Roumania)—and 40 % for those between 3 and 5 hectares. Polish economists calculate that in Poland at least one-third of the available agricultural man-power is wasted. Probably in the four countries under review rather more than a third is superfluous. This could be put more strikingly by saying that, taking together only these four countries, more than 17,000,000 peasants are unemployed. In fact, few of these are quite unemployed. Rather the great majority of all small holders in Eastern Europe are permanently underemployed. The problem of overpopulation and underemployment is as pressing for the States of Eastern Europe as was the problem of industrial unemployment for the States of the west during the worst years of the Depression.

Before attempting to consider the possible lines of treatment for this problem, we must consider briefly the condition of the peasantry in the regions still dominated by big holdings.

THE PEASANT AND THE LANDOWNER IN THE UNRE-FORMED STATES

The strongholds of big holdings in Eastern Europe are Hungary and Eastern Poland. The part of Hungary between the Tisza and the former Roumanian border is, and the Polish provinces of Vilna, Polesia and Volhynia were until 1939, mainly controlled by a few great properties. In Central Hungary, South-Eastern Galicia and Prussian Poland big estates predominate, but to a lesser degree. In Hungary in 1937 Prince Paul Esterházy and Prince George Festetics possessed hereditary entailed properties of 80,000 and 30,000 hectares respectively.[1] The properties of the Radziwill and Potocki families in Poland were of similar proportions. These vast estates support various kinds of economic activity. Both cereals and livestock are produced. The Polish estates included valuable forests, and in both countries large tracts are devoted to hunting. The estates require temporary labourers for the harvest and other busy seasons, and a large number of permanent estate servants to perform the varied tasks necessary throughout the year for the upkeep of the property.

The problems of the population dependent on the large estates were substantially the same in Hungary and Poland. More is known of the Hungarian estates, owing to the work of

[1] See Kovács, *Kivándorlás* and *A néma forradalom*, and Málnási, *A magyar nemzet öszinte története*.

a group of writers who have devoted themselves for ten years to the study of the condition of the rural population. These men, some of whom are themselves country-born, have 'explored' hundreds of villages, and have described what they saw with their own eyes. In Poland valuable economic research has been done, but books of the quality of the Hungarian studies are lacking. The following survey of Hungary is largely applicable to Poland.

The overwhelming majority of the rural population of Hungary are dwarf holders, hired labourers and estate servants. The first have small plots of land round their houses, the second and third have nothing. One of the group of writers mentioned, I. Kovács, estimated the total number of men, women and children belonging to these three categories—the rural proletariat of Hungary—as 3,020,532. Another writer, M. Mátolcsy, estimated the number of agricultural labourers with their families as 1,250,349 and of estate servants as 599,622. The number of dwarf holders would therefore seem to be about 1,200,000.

The dwarf holders have too little land to support their families, although its quality is good. They are therefore obliged to seek work outside their own holdings or to lease land from a landowner. The situation of these tenants is usually little better than that of the landless labourers or servants. During the second half of last century workers on the estates leased land from landlords to build themselves houses. After some years they began to consider these houses and plots as their own, and the Government passed a law enabling them to acquire full rights of ownership. This, however, did not please the landlords. Although the tenants were useful as labourers, they did not wish them to become the legal owners of their plots. If this should happen, the colony of peasant houses would be recognised as a village, and be subject to the State laws as such. The absolute authority of the landowner over them, valid as long as they lived on his property, would cease. For this reason many evicted their tenants. When the latter protested, troops were sent against them. The landowners hired labourers who razed the villages to the ground. The loss to the landowners was not serious, since docile labourers could always be found easily in Hungary. The evictions began in the eighties but they did not cease with the First World War. In 1926 the village of Doc was destroyed by Count Pallavicini. Other minor cases have occurred still more recently.[1] The small tenants of to-day take care not to make claims inconvenient to the landlords. The rent they pay is a heavy burden on their resources, and their income from the sale of their produce is small.

The landless labourers obtain work in the harvest season for a month or two. During the rest of the year they have to find occupation somewhere, in the towns or in odd jobs on the estates. For months they are unemployed. Kovács estimates the average annual cash income of the estates servant-labourer-dwarf holder class at 300 pengö (*ca.* £15); this tallies with the calculation of the Ministry of Agriculture for 1937, which gives for agricultural labourers an average of 200 days' employment per year at 1·5 pengö (1*s.* 6*d.*) per day. Often, however, labourers receive no more than 40–80 filler (4½*d.*–9*d.*) daily wage. It has been calculated that the average wages of men, women and child labourers decreased between 1913 and 1935 by 2·7, 2·35 and 2·72 times respectively.[2] These wages are supplemented in the harvest season by payment in grain, which lasts the family for a part of the year only.

Estate servants are employed the whole year. Their payment is almost wholly in kind. They have to sell a part of this in order to obtain money for the minimum of necessary purchases. Although serfdom was abolished in 1848, the condition of these estate servants is little freer than was that of the serfs. They have the theoretical right to leave the landlord's employ for other work, but this is so circumscribed by restrictions and labour contract regulations as to be virtually worthless. Their lives are ruled by their masters' pleasure. In some cases the landlord and his estate managers may be excellent people, and treat their employees well. In many cases this is not so.

The World Economic Depression affected Hungarian agriculture, but the political power of the landowners was used to shift the burden of the Depression on to the other classes. The Government paid a bonus for wheat exported, which made up most of the difference between the fallen world market price and that to which the landowners had been accustomed. The internal price fell meanwhile by about half, as in neighbouring countries. The estate servants, who received their payment

[1] Kovács, *A néma forradalom.*   [2] Málnási, *op. cit.*

in wheat and had to sell part of this for cash, now obtained far less money with which to buy industrial goods whose price remained fairly stable. The effect of the 'price scissors' was borne mainly by the poorer classes.

It is claimed by apologists of the present system of land distribution in Hungary, that Hungarian agriculture is more efficient than that of countries which have had Land Reforms, since it is organised on a more intensive basis. It is true that some of the large estates are well managed, for instance the Esterházy and the (Jewish) Manfred Weiss properties. But the average yield of wheat per hectare in Hungary is slightly less than that of Bulgaria, and only slightly more than that of Jugoslavia. The difference in the yield of maize is appreciably higher (18·5 quintals as opposed to 16·9 in Jugoslavia and 12·8 in Bulgaria). The management of Hungarian estates is not so efficient as it should be. Many landowners are absentees, leaving the administration in the hands of paid managers, who do not always distinguish themselves by devotion to their duties. Machines are of course more frequently used than would be possible on small peasant holdings, but their use is not as widespread as might be expected. One reason is that human labour is cheaper. The output would no doubt be increased by greater use of machines, but the margin between costs and receipts would be smaller.

The living conditions of the Hungarian rural proletariat are similar to those of the small-holder class of neighbouring countries. Families are packed into small, unhygienic rooms. Some have their own tiny houses, others are crowded together in barracks provided by the estate management for their servants. The discomfort is about the same in each case. Owners of houses have more personal liberty, while estate servants of a benevolent landowner may be sometimes better cared for. The food of the masses is wheaten bread, a little pork fat and small quantities of onion and paprika. It is perhaps slightly better than that of the Balkan peasants, but is most unsatisfactory. Infant mortality is lower than in Roumania, but far higher than in the west. The rate of tuberculosis is the highest in Europe.

One consequence of extreme poverty observed by the 'village explorers' mentioned above, is the prevalence of obscure religious sects. Men and women seek joys that earth will not afford them in the ecstasies of 'Holy Rolling' or similar rites. The researches of these observers suggest a connection between these practices and physical degeneration due to poor nourishment and harsh material conditions. The regions where they are most widespread are some of the poorest in the country.

The population trend in Hungary is quite different to that of the other Eastern European countries. The rate of natural increase is 7·1 in Hungary, as contrasted with 12·5 in Roumania and 13·1 in Jugoslavia. The 'One Child System' is widespread in the Hungarian countryside. It appears to have been imitated from the German peasants of the south-western regions, but its cause is different. The German peasants of Hungary enjoy a high standard of life, and restrict their families in order to be able to give their children luxuries. The same phenomenon can be observed among the rich German and Roumanian peasants of the Banat and the Croats of Slavonia. It is essentially the same as the trend in the prosperous urban societies of the west. In Hungary, however, the one child system is not confined to the rich peasants, but is found also among the miserably poor. The researches of the 'village explorers' show that restriction of the families is often due to poverty. The peasants openly say that they do not want to bring children into the world if they are to live as they themselves have lived. There is no doubt that this trend is spreading, and that it has greatly increased in the last twenty years. Hungarian economists express grave alarm as to the future of the whole nation if present developments continue.

Discussion of the Peasant Problem in Hungary centres round the question of Land Reform. Since the Counter-Revolution of 1920 the various Governments of Hungary have refused to carry out any considerable Land Reform. Since Nazi influence grew in Hungary measures have been passed directed against Jewish landowners. Jewish estates have been expropriated, with some compensation, and their lands distributed. But the recipients of the Jewish land have not usually been landless workers or dwarf holders. Often it has been given to medium or big holders, gendarmes, officials who have proved themselves loyal to the Government, etc. Moreover, Jewish landed property was but a small proportion of the total acreage of land possessed by big estates.

Defenders of the present system point to the misfortunes of the countries which executed Land Reforms, and argue that the experiment was a failure. They admit the need of some reform, but insist that it should be 'moderate', and be made to cover a long period of years, in order to avoid dislocation of production. They oppose any reform which would radically affect the distribution of property. Their arguments are disingenuous. It has been shown that even wheat production, which is the type best suited to large estates, is not noticeably better in Hungary than in neighbouring countries, since the landowners prefer to use cheap human labour to secure a moderate output, rather than buy expensive machines and use really intensive methods. But in any case there is no reason why the agriculture of Hungary should be based on cereals. The country is equally well suited for livestock, vegetable, fruit- and dairy-farming, and for the cultivation of oil plants and industrial crops. These can be particularly well produced on medium and small holdings, as the example of Denmark shows. If the large estates were divided up, peasant owners could, with a little initial help from the Government, make good use of their land. Moreover, Hungary is more favourably situated than her neighbours in two important respects. Her soil is very much more fertile, and she has not a severe over-population problem. At present there is widespread under-employment in Hungary, but this is due, not, as in Poland, Roumania and the Balkans, to pressure of the population on the land, but to the maintenance by the landowners of a large reserve of labour, which depresses wages and enables the land-owners to get an abundant supply of workers whenever they need them. If the land were distributed among them, a very large number of peasant families could obtain a much better living than is now possible, and the agricultural production would soon pass the present level.

Poland, unlike Hungary, suffers from severe overpopulation. But the most overpopulated districts are those where there are fewest great estates, notably Western Galicia. In the eastern regions conditions comparable to those of Hungary exist. Here too there is a reserve of labour and a large number of estate servants with a low standard of living, utterly dependent on the good pleasure of their masters. The distribution of the great estates would not solve all the social problems of the Polish peasantry, nor eliminate overpopulation, but it would relieve the pressure to a considerable extent, and, if accompanied by public works aimed at the reclamation of waste land and marshes, would provide a good living for thousands of families, and bring about a substantial increase of the country's agricultural output.

The question of Land Reform cannot be judged by purely economic standards. The situation of the agricultural proletariat under a system of great estates may not be much more wretched than under a system of small holdings. But the moral factor represented by the vast contrast of wealth between landowner and peasants is of supreme importance. In the countries of small holdings there is some sense of fellowship in misfortune between all. The difference of wealth between a big and a small peasant holder may have the same social significance as that between the landless peasant and the great landowner, but it does not strike the peasant that way. The small and big peasant feel themselves equals in the community of the village. The relationship of landowner to peasant labourer remains, whatever the legal theory, that of master to serf. There are good and bad masters. But the institution of serfdom is a dangerous anachronism in the twentieth century. It creates a condition of smouldering class hatred, in the face of which apparent social stability can be maintained only by the fragile bayonet.

It has already been shown above that Land Reform alone is not sufficient to solve the Peasant Problem. Redistribution of the land is desirable in itself, but it would not suffice to ensure a reasonable livelihood to the peasant masses of Poland, or even of the more favourably placed Hungary. Both countries would face after Land Reform the problems that faced the reformed countries between 1918 and the present day. These problems can be summed up in two tasks: the improvement of agriculture and the transfer of a portion of the rural population from agriculture to other occupations. These will now be briefly examined in turn.

MEASURES TO IMPROVE AGRICULTURE

Measures for the improvement of agriculture in Eastern Europe can be divided into seven categories: technical education, supply of credit, regrouping of the existing strip holdings into more rational units, cultivation of different crops, development of local and international transport, public works, organisation of efficient cooperatives.

Insufficient attention was paid after 1918 to agricultural education. As long as the countries of Eastern Europe remain agricultural countries, a high place should be given in the educational system of the State to training in modern agricultural science. The universities of the Eastern European States teemed with law students. Although study of law is an im-, portant branch of learning in any modern State, it can safely be said that if there had been fewer law graduates and more agricultural experts in Eastern Europe the countries would have gained. What is needed is a comprehensive system of training colleges for the education of professional agricultural experts, technical colleges for peasants who wish to improve their knowledge of agriculture, and a minimum of compulsory agricultural training for all peasants' sons. The training colleges would specialise in the preparation of 'agronomes' who would return after training to the villages, to give the benefit of their expert knowledge and advice to the peasants. Each would have a district assigned to him by the Ministry of Agriculture. The technical colleges would be established in a large number of country towns. Promising peasant children from the surrounding district would be enabled by State scholarships to study there. Finally a minimum of agricultural instruction would be enforced in the schools, and courses for adults also would be arranged. It must be said that something was done in this direction by the Eastern European States between 1918 and the present day, but these attempts were certainly inadequate. Yet without good training in modern agricultural methods an improvement of Eastern European agriculture is impossible. The number and quality of training and technical colleges should be enormously increased. If there is a lack of teachers for the training colleges, then during the first years experts could be employed from the Western European countries and from America.

Agricultural machines and tools should be supplied to the peasants by the State. This could be done either by giving them to the Communes, which would lease them to the peasants at cheap rates, or by selling them to the peasants direct, at cheap prices paid in instalments. The State would in any case make the machines available to the peasants at less than cost price, and the difference would be borne by the Government. Such steps as were taken in this direction after 1918 were quite insufficient. In general the States should organise a system of credit for peasants wishing to make investments to improve their holdings, at a low rate of interest. Money-lending by individuals at rates higher than the official rate should be made illegal in the villages. The Eastern European States during the last twenty years did little more than grope towards this direction.

There has been much talk in recent years in Eastern Europe of 'commassation', by which is meant the regrouping of dwarf holdings into efficient economic units. The land wasted in the form of paths would be brought back into cultivation, and an enormous amount of time spent on walking from one strip to another would be saved. This process has been put into effect in certain regions of Eastern Europe, particularly in Poland and Bulgaria. In the latter country it was only done in villages where a majority of the peasants voted for it. The principle is obviously sound, but it is not easy to realise. In the great plains, where all land is of the same quality, it is comparatively simple. But in hilly or mountainous regions, where there is little good land, and each holding includes strips of varying quality, it is almost impossible to carry out without grave injustice to a number of holders.

There is no doubt that far too great a proportion of the cultivable land of Eastern Europe is devoted to cereals. It is unlikely that Eastern European wheat will be able to compete on a large scale with overseas wheat for a long time. An enormous improvement in the output per unit of land is necessary, and this cannot be obtained in a few years. It may be possible to make trade agreements with the United States, the Argentine and the British Dominions by which certain areas will be recognised as the markets of Eastern European cereals. But it will not be possible to exclude overseas grain altogether from the European market. It seems therefore highly desirable that less cereals and more of other crops should be produced. Vegetables, fruit, dairy produce and industrial plants are, it has been seen already, especially well suited to small holdings. Their prices are better than those of cereals. They would provide a better and more varied diet

for the peasants than maize flour. The market for meat, vegetables, eggs, milk and butter is capable of very great expansion
not only in Eastern but also in Western Europe. These products are less affected by overseas competition. The spreading
of these types of cultivation, the advantages of which are proved
by their success in such regions of Eastern Europe as have ex-
perimented with them—notably Czechoslovakia and some
parts of Poland and Bulgaria—depends on the better organisation by the States of education, technical equipment and credit
for the peasants.

The absence of good communications is one of the main
reasons for the backwardness of agriculture in Eastern Europe.
One of the most striking examples of this is the fruit region
of Bessarabia (Tighina or Bendery). Here splendid fruit and
wine were produced, but rotted in the villages because there
was no means of taking them to the market. Other examples
of the effect of bad communications on the peasants are
Dalmatia, Hercegovina and the Rhodope Mountains of Bulgaria. Three types of transport are needed to increase prosperity
and raise the standard of living in Eastern Europe—communications between villages, between the big internal markets
and between States. The peasants of remote villages should
be able to transport their produce to the local market, in a
larger village some miles away. For this they need roads and
carts. In many regions in Eastern Europe there are no roads
at all, and in still more numerous regions they are abominably
primitive. Carts are reasonably abundant, but more could be
used, and their quality improved. The produce of fertile
regions, and the more prosperous small and medium holdings,
is sent not only to the nearest market, but to the large towns,
the big markets of the countries. For this are needed good
roads, motor-buses and railways. The Governments should
provide large quantities of motor-buses and build first-class
roads. The buses would have to be imported from abroad, but
after some years it might become possible to produce parts
of them within the Eastern European countries. The development of transport on these lines would enable the produce of
remote villages to be brought quickly, efficiently and cheaply
to the town populations. The enormous effect of roads on the
standard of life of the peasants is easily seen in the villages
along the few first-class roads that have already been built

in Eastern Europe. In particular, the peasants, beginning to produce for the towns with which the roads link them, are induced to devote their land to the cultivation of vegetables and fruit, and to concentrate on poultry and dairy-farming. Even the very small holdings gain.

Communications between States benefit in the first place those who produce for the export market. These are at present the big and medium holdings. But as the cultivation of specialised crops proceeds, and Eastern European agriculture becomes generally more intensive, the number of holdings affected by foreign trade will rapidly increase. And even the small holders are already affected indirectly by the state of their country's export trade. Better communications between the countries of Eastern Europe have been impeded hitherto by the difficulty of the terrain, by the fears of the General Staffs of improving their communications with potential enemies, and by the absence in present conditions of a sufficient volume of trade to give obvious justification for the expenses of construction. The first point is of most permanent importance. The resources of the Eastern European States are too slender to enable them to build major roads and railways without some financial help from outside. The elimination of the strategical objection depends on the establishment after the war of a better system of international security than was done after 1918. The third objection is only valid in present conditions. When the agriculture of Eastern Europe is made more efficient, the volume of trade will be there. But the intensification of agriculture is itself dependent on the construction of roads and railways. The vicious circle must be broken.

Some obviously desirable lines of communication deserve mention. Bridges over the Danube are needed between Jugoslavia and Roumania, and between Roumania and Bulgaria. The most suitable places would seem to be at Turnu Severin and Ruse. A major railway is needed from Belgrade to Turnu Severin, which would cross the Danube there, and shorten the journey from Belgrade to Bucarest by ten hours. In Jugoslavia roads or railways are required to connect Belgrade with Montenegro and Central Dalmatia with Bosnia (Knin-Banja Luka). The existing lines from Dubrovnik to Sarajevo, and from Sarajevo through Slavonski Brod to Zagreb and through

Užice to Belgrade should be widened. In Roumania better roads, and possibly more railways should be built through the Carpathian passes, to link up across the Danube with new Bulgarian lines of communication over the Balkan and Rhodope mountains down to the Greek Aegean coast, thus connecting the Baltic with the Mediterranean. Places indicated are the Jiu valley, the Struma valley and the passes in the Rhodope south of Plovdiv. There are already railways through the Red Tower and Predeal passes of the Carpathians, and work has been begun on the Jiu pass. In Bulgaria since the German occupation of the Balkans and dismemberment of Jugoslavia work has been begun on lines from Sofia through the Struma valley towards Salonica and across the eastern Macedonian mountains to Skoplje. The roads constructed for strategic purposes by the Germans will remain after the war as the one useful by-product of Hitler's rule of terror. Construction should be continued, in order to create an adequate network of communications between the four seas.

Public works could greatly improve the prosperity of the peasants, and render possible agriculture in places which at present are mere deserts. Particularly important are irrigation and drainage. The first is required especially in the waterless tracts of Montenegro and Dalmatia. In the same regions drainage is required to deal with the floods that wreck the cultivation of the few fertile 'polja'. Drainage on a vast scale is needed in the marshes of the Danube delta and Polesia. If part of the huge area covered by reeds and waterfowl were dried, living could be found for hundreds of thousands from the overpopulated regions. The success of Land Reform in Eastern Poland is largely dependent on the drainage of the Pripet marshes, which measure would also make possible the construction of a canal system linking the Baltic to the Black Sea through the Vistula, the Dniepr and their tributaries.

COOPERATIVES AND KOLHOZY

Cooperatives were little developed in Eastern Europe. Apart from Czechoslovakia, whose economic and social institutions resembled generally those of the west, cooperation was backward, and was regarded with little favour by the Governments. Those cooperatives which existed were usually either marketing associations for the benefit of the richer peasants or party political organs.

The most efficient cooperatives in Eastern Europe were those of Bulgaria. A well-planned system of 'popular banks' in small towns and large villages, run by the cooperatives, afforded opportunities of cheap credit to a considerable number of peasants. The savings of the Bulgarian peasants even sufficed to carry out important works of construction. Power stations, for instance, were owned by cooperatives.[1] In Poland, Roumania and Serbia there were districts where cooperatives benefited more than the minority of big and medium holders. In the foothills of southern Transylvania and northern Wallachia, for instance, whole villages gained from wine- and fruit-marketing cooperatives. Such successes were often due to the initiative of some enterprising individual and to the proximity of an urban market.

The cooperatives run by political parties should not be underrated. The Slovene Clericals and the Ukrainian Nationalists organised cooperatives which undoubtedly improved the lot of the peasants. In the former case Catholic priests played a prominent part. The cultural level of the peasants is higher in Slovenia than in most of Eastern Europe; and the overpopulation problem is less acute. In Eastern Galicia cooperatives arose from the necessities of the political struggle. The Ukrainian Nationalists had to keep the land in Ukrainian hands, and therefore considered the prosperity of the peasants important. Moreover the Nationalist leaders required the goodwill and active support of the peasants in their bitter struggle with the Poles. The cooperatives run by Uniate priests and the U.N.D.O. party were most efficient, and helped to make Ukrainian Nationalism a mass movement in Eastern Galicia. They even secured to the Galician Ukrainian peasantry a higher standard of living than was possessed by the Polish peasants, who, once Polish independence was achieved, could be safely ignored by the intellectual Polish Nationalists of the towns. A third political cooperative organisation of importance was 'Gospodarska Sloga', run by the Croatian Peasant Party. This was connected with the struggle between Croat and Serb, but was managed for a time by men who genuinely cared more for the welfare of the people than for

[1] Warriner, *The economics of peasant farming*, 1919.

anything else. It paid special attention to the rural proletariat
and to the miserable villages of the 'karst' country of Dalmatia. It organised the peasants for the market, supplied them
with grain for seed, and sent crops to regions threatened with
famine.

Although these three cooperative movements fulfilled a
valuable task, it should be stressed that many other vaunted
cooperative organisations were nothing but propaganda machines for Government, and that others again benefited only
the big holders.

Cooperative production smelt too much of 'Bolshevism'
to receive sympathy from Eastern European Governments.
It is probable that in cereal-producing regions cooperative
cultivation, by making the use of agricultural machines eco-
nomical, would benefit the majority of the peasant population,
even if individual rich holders might suffer loss. It would also
help to solve the hopelessly complicated problem of the small
strip. If the whole cultivable area belonged to the peasant
community as a whole, and the product were shared between
them, the injustice to individuals involved in commassation,
which would give to some none but bad land, could be avoided.

There is a great deal of confused thinking on this subject.
It is always pointed out that the peasants of Eastern Europe
are passionate individualists, and cannot bear to cooperate.
This state of affairs is considered in official circles as most
satisfactory. All means of propaganda are used to prevent the
growth of a spirit of solidarity among the peasants. The well-
known Roumanian landowner and agricultural expert Garoflid
openly argues that, as the peasants are quite incapable of
cooperating, being 'fortunately immune to Communist ideas',
they will never make a success of their holdings, and therefore
the State ought to base its agricultural policy solely on 'efficient
productive units', the large estates and big holders, and let
the 75 % of small holders fend for themselves. In fact, the
peasants should be encouraged to use backward methods of
cultivation, in order to provide a good excuse for the abolition
of the Land Reform.

The advocates of cooperative cultivation are always met
with piercing wails about the 'horrors of the Kolhoz system',
and are denounced as 'Bolsheviks'. They are informed that
the sound, individualistic peasantry of Eastern Europe could

never listen to such ideas. The one nightmare, in fact, which mars the idyllic life the peasantry leads, is the thought that one day the Red Devils might seize their land, and make them work together.

There are several answers to this. The first is that the 'horrors of the Kolhoz system' have been exaggerated. The Russian and Ukrainian peasants who, we were told, 'groaned beneath the tyranny of the Kolhoz', who 'had no stake in the land, and therefore could have no patriotism for the Bolshevik regime', not only fight bravely in the Russian army, but in the occupied provinces, where the German invaders ask nothing better than to be regarded as their 'deliverers from Kolhoz tyranny', form themselves into guerrilla bands to fight in the woods, at risk of horrible reprisals and in conditions of indescribable hardship. The ignorant observer has the impression that life on these Kolhozy must have been something worth fighting for.

The second point is that, if the standard of life of the Russian Kolhoznik is not very high, it does not necessarily follow that the introduction of cooperative cultivation would lower the standard of living of the Eastern European peasantry. The education and skill of the peasantry in the countries to the west and south-west of Russia are in most places superior to those possessed by the Russian peasant at the time when the Kolhoz system was first introduced. Moreover the present standard of living of the masses of the Eastern European peasantry is so low that it could hardly deteriorate.

Further, the system of cooperative cultivation is not indissolubly bound up with political terror. It is perfectly possible to imagine the encouragement by Governments of voluntary associations of peasants. If the experiments proved successful with Government help, they would be voluntarily imitated by the other peasants.

Finally, the individualism of the Eastern European peasant has been misrepresented. It is true that the peasant is devoted to his land, but it is not true that he is irrevocably opposed to collaboration with others. The writer has talked to peasants in the Balkans, fairly prosperous medium holders (10 to 15 hectares), who said: 'We have good land, our own property, but we gain nothing from it. We cannot work it as we should wish, and we have to pay so much for town-made goods and taxes that we have nothing left for ourselves. If we worked the land in common, we should earn more and live better.' Although these views are not necessarily typical, they are fairly widespread. They are more likely to be popular among the wretched dwarf holders than among the medium peasants. As for the passive mass of depressed and ignorant peasants who have not thought this out for themselves because they have never been encouraged to think at all, and who still believe what official people tell them, they could easily be educated by the example of others and by Government propaganda, if the Government would recommend cooperative cultivation, instead of preventing it by a campaign of meaningless invective and police terror.

Unfortunately the notion of cooperative cultivation is bound up in too many people's minds with visions of O.G.P.U. ogres and of poor Nicholas II in the cellar at Ekaterinburg. They are incapable of considering it rationally. This is a pity. It is impossible to say *a priori* whether cooperative cultivation would be a success in the Eastern European countries, but the experiment might be tried on a small scale and with milder methods of persuasion than were adopted in the Soviet Union.

Soviet experience could provide valuable lessons. One is that collectivisation of livestock is a mistake. This led to wholesale slaughter of cattle which paralysed Soviet agriculture for years. A compromise must be found, by which peasant families are allowed to have a limited number of beasts and poultry of their own and a plot of land as a garden producing for their own consumption. Secondly, the harvest should be divided between the members of the cooperative, and the excess sold by the cooperative collectively. If the State insists on taking the crop, this will create in the minds of the peasants an attitude towards the State similar to that formerly felt towards the landlords.

The Soviet Union, as Miss Warriner has shown, achieved greater results in bringing new land under cultivation than in raising the productivity of land previously cultivated. There is little undeveloped land available in Eastern Europe, and for this reason Miss Warriner does not consider that cooperative cultivation could do much for Eastern European agriculture.[1] It should, however, be insisted that the difference in cultural

[1] *Economics of Peasant Farming.*

level between Eastern Europe in 1942 and Imperial Russia in 1917 makes generalisation dangerous, and that the disadvantages of the strip system as hitherto practised in the former are so patent as to require heroic remedies.

INDUSTRIALISATION AND EMIGRATION

The measures summarised above, which would require much time and heavy investments, might be expected to effect a considerable rise in the standard of living, but they would not solve overpopulation.

The Eastern European Governments have begun to recognise the urgent nature of the population problem, but they have been unable or unwilling to do much about it. Their peasant policy has been largely based on that of Germany, aimed at creating a rural middle class. The 'Erbhofgesetz' of 1934 represents the policy of Reichsminister Walter Darré, one of the most eminent Nazi intellectuals. Its purpose is to create hereditary indivisible peasant properties of between 7 and 123 hectares. Their owners will form the solid core of the peasant class, and the agrarian policy of the Reich will be based on them. The rest of the rural population will be absorbed in industry, or will receive holdings carved out of countries conquered by the German sword. In this policy only the mystical trappings are original. It is similar to that of the Tsarist Minister Stolypin, who tried to create a class of prosperous peasant owners, the 'kulaki', who caused trouble to his Bolshevik heirs.

Some Eastern European Governments, convinced that slavish imitation of the German model will solve all their problems, loudly applauded this policy and attempted to introduce it. This is notably true of Roumania under the Dictatorships of Carol II and Antonescu. Unfortunately the conditions of Germany and of Eastern Europe are very different. First, unlike Eastern Europe, Germany has an industrial machine which can absorb vast numbers of workers. Secondly, in Eastern Europe the proportion of peasants possessing less than 7 hectares—the lower limit under the German scheme—is between 75 and 90 %, and even a most careful redistribution of land could not, except perhaps in Hungary, provide for more than a minority on a basis of minimum holdings of 7 hectares. What is to become of the majority?

The official experts shake their heads; shut their eyes, murmur about industrialisation and act as if the majority did not exist.

But the problem must be faced. There are too many people on the land. Even a marked intensivisation of agriculture will not provide for much more than half the present rural population. The only visible outlets are industrialisation and emigration.

Czechoslovakia was a predominantly industrial country and both Hungary and Poland had considerable industries. In the other States industrialisation made progress after 1918, but often on an unsound basis. Artificial industries were created by high tariffs at the cost of the consumer. This is justifiable if the industries are indispensable to the safety of the State. Examples are the 'Astra' armaments works in Roumania and those of Kragujevac in Jugoslavia. The cost was heavy, but could not be avoided in the international circumstances of the last ten years. Many industries in Eastern Europe, however, were not essential, and their cost did not correspond to their utility. Factories were set up to produce luxury goods, for which, owing to low purchasing-power, demand was inevitably small. Sometimes the decision whether to start an industry was quite unrelated to the internal needs of the country. A western capital group might set up a factory to make some article in which it was interested, but was quite indifferent to the desire of the Government to produce a commodity of another kind, considered necessary to the national welfare. If the capital group could bribe the local Minister of Commerce, the industry would be founded, and the Minister would ease his conscience with the reflection that at least the new enterprise would 'give some employment'.

Industrialisation is vitally important to Eastern Europe, but it should serve two aims, the production of articles needed by the population and the employment of as large a number as possible of workers. Special attention should be paid to industries connected with agriculture and foodstuffs. Industrialisation of fruits, animal and dairy produce is most important. Manufacture of jam, butter, cheese, bacon, tinned meat and similar articles would have every prospect of success, both in the home market and in international trade. Native textile industries should produce mainly cheap clothes for the peasants, while expensive cloth for the wealthy class could be imported, as hitherto, from the west. Further possibilities are offered by the development of an agricultural machine industry and by the need for large quantities of vehicles envisaged above. Some time will pass before Eastern Europe can make motor engines or complicated machinery, but simple machines, chassis of motor-buses and the like could be produced within a few years.

Everything must depend on the raising of the purchasing-power of the agrarian masses. This can be done by the measures mentioned in the preceding section, aimed at the encouragement of intensive crops. The growth of industry will also cause an expansion of the town market for foodstuffs, which will further increase the prosperity of the countryside. Once the process is seriously started, it will continue by its own momentum.

The best basis for the industrialisation of Eastern Europe is provided by the agricultural products, raw materials and timber resources in which it is potentially so rich. The industrialisation which did take place after 1918 did not appreciably raise the standard of living of the masses because it was misdirected. Insufficient attention was paid to the industrialisation of agricultural products. Branches of industry requiring specialised skill did not draw on the peasant masses, but on the remnant of the traditional artisan class. The competition of the poverty-stricken peasants for unskilled jobs in industry was such that wages were kept low, and the new workers who increased the population of the towns had not sufficient purchasing-power to increase the demand for the produce of the villages.

It all comes back to the fundamental problem of peasant poverty. Industrialisation is one of the principal cures for agricultural overpopulation, but it will not make progress unless it is planned in accordance with the needs of the country rather than those of foreign capital, unless it makes use of the resources of the country and unless it can supply an increased internal market. Everything must begin from Government action to raise the purchasing-power of the peasants.

Industrialisation on some such lines as these should by the end of a generation bring about great changes to the advantage of the Eastern European peoples. The process will not be swift, even in the most favourable circumstances. But in the end there can be little doubt that the Eastern European nations must be industrialised. It may be regrettable but it is inevitable. It may be that life would be better if steam and motor power were completely destroyed. But it is no use dreaming. Romantic nonsense about the stern virtues of the soil-loving peasants, and sentimental rhapsodies about his beautiful costumes and open-air life, only serve to confuse the issue. There is no need for industrialisation in Eastern Europe to lead to the vast unhealthy urban agglomerations that exist in the west. The future may bring new, more satisfactory, forms. But in the modern world no State can remain predominantly agrarian without suffering exploitation by industrialised States. There is no special virtue in tilling the soil. The peasant is not morally superior to other classes of the population just because he is more often cheated and oppressed. There is no reason why he should lose his patriotism or his value to the State because he ceases to be a peasant. If, instead of declaiming about the peasant, the ruling classes of Eastern Europe would give him food and work, and teach him to adapt himself to a new world, they would do him and their countries a good service.

The second outlet for overpopulation is emigration. At the end of the last century and the beginning of the present, large numbers of peasants left Eastern Europe for the United States, Canada and South America. After the First World War the overseas countries imposed severe restrictions on immigration. These coincided with the intensification of the overpopulation problem, now infinitely more serious than it was in the days of free immigration.

It was part of the old theory of Economic Liberalism that Labour would move to places where employment and wages are better, and that by this means regional differences in prosperity would be evened out. Free Immigration is the corollary to Free Trade. The two disappeared together. It is obvious that even in the most ideal conditions movement of Labour could not be as free as movement of goods, owing to difficulties of language and culture which have nothing to do with economic theory. But if huge, culturally backward populations are cooped up in Eastern Europe in steadily increasing misery, while large tracts of the earth's surface are inhabited by small numbers of people enjoying a strikingly high standard of living, grave political, and even military, problems will be created. The peoples of Eastern Europe have far better right to call themselves 'proletarian nations' than the Germans or Italians. At the present moment, divided between themselves they hardly constitute a threat. But if nothing is done by the Western Powers and the overseas Governments to help them solve their problems, within a generation from the end of this war some discontented Great Power will be found to organise them as a weapon of aggression.

Between the wars there was a considerable immigration into France, consisting mainly of Italians, but also of Poles and Jugoslavs. The attractive force of the French language and culture is such that a large proportion of these immigrants was assimilated within quite a short time. France, a country richly endowed by nature, is underpopulated compared with Germany, still more so when compared with Eastern Europe. Probably immigration from Eastern Europe into France will continue after the war, to the mutual advantage of France, which has need of new strength, and of the immigrants, who need a means of living, at present hardly obtainable in their own countries. But clearly France is not a major field for immigration. In so far as emigration can help to relieve the social problems of Eastern Europe, the countries that first leap to the mind are the British Dominions, South America and the United States. The question must be regarded as of international importance, and be most seriously examined. And just as internal reconstruction in Eastern Europe is impossible as long as western capital takes an intransigent attitude, so even a partial solution of the overpopulation problem is impossible as long as Organised Labour in the overseas countries implacably opposes immigration, which would temporarily lower the wages of unskilled Labour, but would within a few years be a source of increased strength and prosperity.

The measures outlined in the preceding pages are in no way original. Technical education, credit, cultivation of new crops, improvement of transport, public works, planned industrialisation, emigration—these things have been urged for years in Eastern Europe by specialists and even by politicians. But only less than half-hearted attempts have been made to deal with them. There has been enough talk. Action can no longer be deferred. The urgency of these problems will be still greater after the war. The misery and poverty will be greater. Nor will the losses due to famine, disease, war and German exploitation relieve the pressure of overpopulation. In the last war Serbia lost a million out of four million citizens. Although this loss had a fatal effect on the public life of the country, the loss in numbers was more than made good within a few years.

Even if all the measures suggested were put into practice, with pure disinterested goodwill on the part of the Eastern European Governments and altruistic support by the Great Powers, in the best possible of material conditions, they would not solve the Peasant Problem completely, and for the first few years they would hardly have any visible effect. The masses must have patience, it may be argued. True. But the masses will only have patience if they have confidence in their rulers, if they feel that these rulers are *theirs*. And the rulers will only have a chance of success if the political system allows of a minimum of stability, and if the international security of their country is sufficiently well guaranteed to let them get on with the job. These questions must now be examined.

APPENDIX A. LAND DISTRIBUTION STATISTICS

Category of holdings	Percentage of total number of holdings	Percentage of land
CZECHOSLOVAKIA 1931		
0–2 hectares	44·0	7·0
2–5 ,,	27·0	16·0
5–10 ,,	16·0	20·0
10–30 ,,	11·0	31·0
30–100 ,,	1·5	10·0
Over 100 ,,	·5	16·0
POLAND 1921		
0–2 hectares	34·0	15·3
2–5 ,,	30·7	
5–20 ,,	32·0	31·8
20–50 ,,	2·3	
50–100 ,,	·4	9·9
Over 100 ,,	·6	43·0
HUNGARY 1935		
0–1 hold	38·5	1·4
1–5 ,,	34·1	8·6
5–10 ,,	12·6	9·1
10–50 ,,	13·1	26·1
50–100 ,,	1·0	6·5
100–500 ,,	·5	12·3
500–100 ,,	·1	6·0
Over 1000 ,,	·1	30·0
ROUMANIA 1930		
0–1 hectares	18·6	2·1
1–3 ,,	33·5	14·4
3–5 ,,	22·8	19·3
5–10 ,,	17·1	24·2
10–20 ,,	5·5	13·3
20–50 ,,	1·7	7·9
50–100 ,,	·4	4·2
100–500 ,,	·3	7·2
Over 500 ,,	·1	7·4
BULGARIA 1934		
0–2 hectares	23·0	5·0
2–5 ,,	39·0	24·0
5–10 ,,	25·0	32·0
10–30 ,,	12·0	33·0
Over 30 ,,	1·0	6·0

The Polish figures will have been modified to an unknown extent by the redistributions of the last twenty years.

The figures for the other countries will have been modified to some extent by the evolution of the last ten years, which has certainly increased the proportion of holdings below 5 hectares.

The Hungarian 'hold' is rather larger than an acre. There are about two to a hectare.

The sources are official statistics. The Bulgarian figures are taken from Mollov, *Die sozialökonomische Struktur der bulgarischen Landwirtschaft*. The Hungarian figures come from Kovács, *Kivándorlás*. The others are from official handbooks.

APPENDIX B. 'PRICE SCISSORS'

POLAND (1928 = 100)

Year	Index agricultural prices	Index prices industrial goods used by peasants
1930	67·6	98·5
1931	59·5	90·4
1932	48·9	81·0
1933	42·6	72·6
1934	37·0	70·3
1935	35·8	66·3
1936	38·7	64·6
1937	49·2	66·1

ROUMANIA (1929 = 100)

Year	Index agricultural prices	Index prices industrial goods used by peasants
1930	68·2	98·0
1931	50·8	86·6
1932	47·7	80·9
1933	44·9	81·1
1934	44·1	82·6
1935	48·4	90·2
1936	54·0	95·4
1937	64·6	101·8
1938	67·1	99·2
1939	72·7	112·5
Jan. 1940	80·8	159·4

The Polish figures are quoted in Buell, *Poland, key to Europe*, 1939; the Roumanian in Madgearu, *Evolutia economei romanesti*, Bucarest 1940.

CHAPTER FIVE

THE POLITICAL SYSTEM

THE RULING CLASSES

In 1918 the States of Eastern Europe had reached different stages of social evolution. In some the aristocracy of earlier centuries still retained considerable power. In others a modern bourgeoisie was already established. Others again possessed neither aristocracy nor bourgeoisie, and their ruling class was in process of formation. A few words on these differences are necessary as an introduction to a discussion of the political systems of the Eastern European countries.

It has already been pointed out that in Hungary during the second half of the nineteenth century a large part of the land-owning aristocracy was ruined by the agricultural crisis, sold its lands and found employment in the civil service and free professions. Thus was formed a Hungarian middle class, which occupied the social position of a bourgeoisie, but retained the mentality of an aristocracy. The commercial bourgeoisie remained at first mainly Jewish. After 1918, however, the second generation of the Hungarian middle class began to enter trade and industry on a considerable scale, challenging the position of the Jews. The political ruling class of Hungary between the World Wars was a combination of the remaining great families and the aristocratic middle class.

In Poland a similar process had taken place earlier. Already in the eighteenth century the 'szlachta' or country gentry, the basis of Poland's strength in her great days, had been impoverished. Its members first became penniless hangers-on of the magnates. Under the Partitions they drifted, like their Hungarian counterparts, into the civil service and free professions. In the Prussian territory they also entered trade and industry, and during the period of 'denationalising' pressure from Berlin there first appeared the beginnings of a Polish commercial class. In the Russian and Austrian territories the Poles left trade to the large Jewish population, which played a prominent part in the rise of a modern industry at the end of the century. Thus the ruling class of Poland, as of Hungary, comprised a landowning aristocracy and a mainly non-commercial middle class of aristocratic origin. In both countries after 1918 the middle class grew more powerful, and paid more attention to economic affairs, while the influence of the land-owners declined. But the rising middle class kept the mentality of the aristocracy, and still remains different in character from the bourgeoisies of either Western or South-Eastern Europe.

In Roumania the aristocracy had lost ground since the beginning of the century. The Land Reform dealt it a mortal blow. Its place was taken by the new Roumanian middle class, which consisted partly of people of similar origin to the Polish and Hungarian gentries, partly of elements risen from the lower classes. It contained a majority of civil servants and intellectuals, but commerce was also represented in it. Although trade and industry were little developed, and were mainly in the hands of Jews, Roumanians were already before 1918 beginning to take some interest in them. The Roumanian middle class therefore had a more bourgeois character than those of Hungary and Poland. This character was reinforced by the Union of Transylvania and Banat with Roumania. These provinces had virtually no Roumanian aristocracy, and their highest social stratum consisted of the rural and small-town bourgeoisie formed from the peasantry.

A similar situation existed also in Croatia. Here too the aristocracy lost its material power with the Land Reform, and the middle class, formed partly of commercial elements from the Dalmatian coast and partly of recruits from the peasant class, took on a definitely bourgeois character. The Croatian aristocracy ceased to play an active part in public affairs, and all that it left to the middle class was a vague yearning for the lost social glories of the old Empire.

In the Czech Lands the ruling class was a strong bour-geoisie, in which the commercial, intellectual and bureaucratic elements were well balanced. It was recruited from the peasantry during the following years, and also from the in-dustrial working class, already well developed by 1918.

The ruling class of Greece was a strong and wealthy com-mercial and intellectual bourgeoisie, also reinforced during the nineteenth and twentieth centuries from the peasantry.

In Serbia, Bulgaria and Slovakia there was no native aristo-cracy and no old commercial class. The Serbs and Bulgarians were essentially peasant peoples. When they attained inde-pendence, a ruling class was quickly formed of army officers, small-town shopkeepers, artisans and rich peasants. In 1918 the process was not yet far advanced. The Slovaks had a similar rural bourgeoisie, still less developed. The lack of political experience was made up during the following years with the help of the Czechs, who made great efforts to train a Slovak middle class.

In Albania there existed a tribal society based on loyalty to the chief of the clan. There were few literate people, and commercial civilisation had hardly set foot even on the coastal strip facing Italy, still less spread into the mountains. The Albanians were peasants, soldiers and artisans. Their ruling class was an aristocracy which had once played a large part in the affairs of the Ottoman Empire, and had thereby come into contact with the greater world, but had not felt to any notable extent the influence of the new society of nineteenth- and twentieth-century Europe.

The task of the ruling classes of the Eastern European countries after 1918 was to attract to themselves new elements, in order to strengthen themselves against possible revolutionary forces. They needed greatly to increase the number of people interested in the preservation of the existing regime, but had to guard against being swamped by the influx of new recruits.

In Hungary and Poland middle class and aristocracy had to be combined into a new ruling class. A compromise must be found between the interests of each, and the traditional spirit of the aristocracy be passed on to the middle class. Moreover the ruling class, although more numerous and more experienced than those of the Balkan countries, needed to be recruited from below. In both countries there was during the inter-war period a regular, if not very large, stream of recruits from the wealthier strata of the villages. This stream was both absolutely and proportionately greater in Poland than in Hungary.

In the other countries the problem was the creation or enlargement of a bourgeoisie. In Czechoslovakia and Greece, where a substantial bourgeoisie already existed, the task was easier, and less hurried and drastic methods were required, than in Roumania, Yugoslavia and Bulgaria, where this class was only beginning to appear.

The new bourgeoisie was formed from the villages. Sons of rich peasants obtained higher education in the small towns, and came back to the village as teachers or priests. The children of schoolmasters, Orthodox priests, Calvinist and Lutheran pastors could begin with an advantage over the other peasants' children. If they showed ability, they reached the university, the most important step towards social advancement. The main goal of Eastern European university students of humble origin was the Public Administration. It was assumed that every student who passed his examinations had the right to a job in the State apparatus. The job might be of little importance, but it conferred great prestige on the son of a peasant or village priest. Other graduates of the universities, of greater ability and ambition, entered the free professions, set themselves up as lawyers, doctors or engineers and became absorbed in the town population.

The commercial class was formed partly from the same source. During the last years especially the number of young men who have entered trade and industry after higher education has increased. Other sources were the village and small-town shopkeepers and the artisans, whom the State supported in order that they should replace Jews, Armenians, Greeks or other foreign elements which enjoyed a dominant position in commercial life.

By this process, which had begun in the nineteenth century, and developed very rapidly after 1918, was formed in Yugoslavia, Roumania and Bulgaria a bureaucratic, intellectual and commercial bourgeoisie which has constituted the ruling class of those countries during the last twenty years. The same process operated more slowly to strengthen the existing bourgeoisies of Czechoslovakia and Greece and the traditional ruling classes of Hungary and Poland. The political history of the Eastern European countries from 1918 to 1941 is the history of these classes.

THE BOURGEOISIE

It was already obvious in 1918 that industrial States are stronger than agrarian, and in a world of national States it was understandable that each nation should wish to have an industry of its own.

There were a number of reasons for industrialisation in the Eastern European countries. A new industrial system would give the State a greater degree of international prestige, security and independence. It would offer the ruling class a means of enriching itself. It would provide employment for a considerable number of young men of the ruling class, in various business offices, commercial enterprises and managerial posts. It would produce within the State's frontiers a number of commodities purchased by the ruling class, formerly imported from the west. Lastly it would give employment to a part of the labour overflow from the countryside. The last consideration, which has been discussed in the preceding chapter, did not play a big part in the calculation, but all the factors enumerated above contributed to convince the Eastern European Governments of the desirability of increased industrialisation.

As we have seen, the commercial bourgeoisie did not constitute the predominant political factor in all the Eastern European States after 1918. But in all these States the main economic aims of the commercial bourgeoisie were served by the ruling classes and the Governments.

In Poland during the first years after the First World War the middle class was the strongest element, and as a part of it was already engaged in trade and industry, and the reconstruction of the devastated country required a large measure of industrialisation, an economic policy suited to the interests of the commercial bourgeoisie was adopted. When after 1926 the great landowners obtained more influence, they accepted this policy.

In Hungary the strongest element from 1920 onwards was the big landowners, and the commercial class was mainly non-Magyar—Jewish or German. Yet here too the economic policy that was followed was entirely acceptable to the commercial class. The landowners were already in 1918 extremely dependent on the banks, with which the most eminent representative of the landowning class, Prime Minister Count Bethlen, had close relations. Moreover it was hoped by interesting foreign capital in the development of Hungarian industry to win sympathy for Hungarian political aims. Industrial protection was adopted from early in Bethlen's Premiership, and the landowners, whose interest in the export of grain might have been expected to cause them to oppose it, were placated by protection and subsidies for their own products.

In Czechoslovakia industry was firmly established already,

and continued to grow during the following twenty years. The existence beside a prosperous and experienced bourgeoisie of a trained and disciplined working class and a reasonably well-educated and organised peasantry made possible a more balanced State economic policy than was pursued in the other Eastern European countries.

In Roumania, Yugoslavia and Bulgaria the agricultural interest was represented after the Land Reforms by a backward and unorganised peasantry, while political power was concentrated in the hands of a newly created ruling class which was beginning to take an interest in industry and trade, and was encouraged therein by western interests. Consequently the economic policy of these three States was dictated by the interests of the bourgeoisie, which had little need to consider the desires of the other classes.

Thus although the situation of each country differed in some respects from that of its neighbours, it can be said that in all the interests of the commercial class took first place in State economic policy, compromising where necessary with those of the landed oligarchy. This does not mean that State economic policy was directed constantly and consciously against the interests of the small peasants and industrial workers. At times the interests of all coincided. The bourgeoisie, influenced during the first years of Liberal ideology, believed that by its generous Land Reforms, or by the support which it gave to Land Reforms where these had not been carried out, it was defending the interests of the peasantry. Moreover it could point out the great interest of both peasants and workers in the creation of an industry which would supply them with employment and commodities. Yet in fact, if the interests of bourgeoisie, peasantry and working class were not always opposed, they were always different. Industrialisation certainly benefits the peasantry in the long run, but this long-term utility is obscured, for the first years at least, by the burden which it puts upon the poorest classes of the population. During the pre-Depression years the peasantry was neglected by the Eastern European Governments, which devoted themselves to such economic activity as directly interested the ruling class.

The most striking example is to be found in the export taxes levied by the Liberal Party in Roumania on agricultural products between 1919 and 1928.[1] It is calculated that these cost Roumanian agriculture 120,000 million lei. They prevented an accumulation of wealth by the Roumanian peasantry which would have lessened the impact of the Depression. But during these years the peasants seemed to enjoy prosperity. Agricultural prices were little lower than industrial, and the export taxes, though resented, were supported.

When the Depression brought the peasantry throughout Eastern Europe to the verge of ruin, the Governments were obliged to take steps to help them. Conversion laws were passed, and institutions, such as the Grain Monopoly in Czechoslovakia and the Privileged Export Company in Yugoslavia, were formed to secure better agricultural prices. But during and after the Depression, as before it, the interests of the commercial and industrial bourgeoisie took precedence over those of the peasantry and working class. This is clearly seen in the statistics of the agricultural-industrial 'Price scissors'. This disparity was not caused by the Governments, but they did little to mitigate its effects.

Foreign capital played a large part in the economic development of the Eastern European countries after 1918. Its importance was relatively smallest in Czechoslovakia, where native capital predominated. In Roumania the commercial class, represented in the all-powerful Liberal Party of the Bratianus, attempted a policy of economic nationalism, creating obstacles to the investment of foreign capital and hoping that Roumania could industrialise herself by her own resources. This policy caused great hardship, as its burden was shifted on to the poorest class. When in 1928 the Liberal regime was succeeded by that of Maniu, the National Peasant Leader, the barriers were removed, and foreign capital poured into the country. In the other Eastern European countries foreign capital was welcomed from the beginning. In 1932 it was shown at the Stresa Conference which discussed Danubian problems, that the greatest value of investments of foreign capital in this region during the fourteen years following the First World War was in Hungary and the least in Bulgaria. It is a fact, which may or may not be connected

---

[1] The Liberal Party was not in power for the whole of this period, but the two Averescu Governments (1919–22 and 1926–27) were under the influence of its leaders, and pursued a similar economic policy.

with this, that Bulgaria has the most equalitarian social structure in Eastern Europe, and Hungary the least.

The influx of foreign capital undoubtedly assisted the process of industrialisation. From the point of view of the Eastern European States, however, foreign capital has its disadvantages. It is a source of constant annoyance to the nationalist commercial bourgeoisie of the States, for it feels that it does not own its own country's resources, and this hurts its pride. This is particularly the case in the countries where the native commercial class finds itself in conflict with a Jewish commercial class—Hungary, Roumania and Poland. Resentment against the Jews leads to resentment against all 'interfering' foreign interests. Secondly, the foreign capitalists are able to influence the character of the industrialisation, and to prevent the execution of a careful plan. The foreign capitalist will invest in what industries interest him, not in those whose creation the interest of the State requires. Of course these are often the same, but they are not necessarily so. Thirdly, the interest payments are a heavy burden on the resources of the States. In order to maintain good political relations with the creditor countries, the Governments find it necessary to pay regularly, but this means that they cannot spend their revenue on large-scale public works for the benefit of the masses, even if they should wish to do so.

The supply of foreign capital came to an end with the Depression. Payment of interest was suspended in Hungary and other countries. During and after the Depression the Eastern European Governments began not only to interfere in industry, but to found enterprises of their own. Such action was dictated by the general need to assist depressed industry, and by the particular desire to eliminate Jews and other foreign elements. In Hungary and Poland industrial and commercial enterprises were filled with young men of the national middle class, many of whom had no special training, and who performed the functions of a State industrial bureaucracy rather than of independent business men. The Governments increased their control over cartels, and took over completely a number of industries, particularly those connected with war production. The most ambitious venture in State enterprise in Eastern Europe was the Polish Central Industrial Region, where a considerable beginning was made with the creation of vital war industries in an area where it was hoped that they would be out of reach of potential enemies. In Yugoslavia the Government played under Milan Stojadinović an active part in the improvement or creation of metallurgical and chemical enterprises. In Roumania the place of State enterprise was taken by the activity of King Carol II and his close friends, who by various means concentrated in their hands a large part of the total industry of the country.

Whether organised by native private enterprise, by foreign capital or by the State, the new industries laid a heavy burden on the masses. Heavy tariffs protected articles whose price was from 50 to 300 % above that formerly paid for importing them from Western Europe. Many such 'artificial' industries could certainly not be defended on grounds of strategic necessity. They benefited only a small number of persons directly interested in them, and their cost was borne by the poorer section of the town population, and to a lesser extent by the peasantry.

The taxation system was calculated to make the poorer classes pay for the economic programme of the ruling class. Here again Czechoslovakia, whose political and social life approximated to that of a democratic western country, must be excepted. In the other countries of Eastern Europe the main burden was supported by the people. Indirect taxes were especially unjust, being imposed on articles of popular consumption. In the last years before the outbreak of this war, the proportion of indirect to total tax receipts was over 60 % in Yugoslavia and Bulgaria, and over 75 % in Roumania.

An important form of indirect taxation are the various State Monopolies introduced in all the Eastern European countries. The articles subject to these Monopolies were those of most universal consumption, such as salt, tobacco, matches. The Monopolies were extremely important sources of revenue for the State, but this revenue was obtained at the cost of grave social injustice. A striking example is the Yugoslav Tobacco Monopoly, which sold tobacco to the public at a price more than twenty times higher than that which it paid to the producers. The tobacco-growers of Macedonia and Hercegovina, peasant small holders of some of the poorest regions of the country, were compelled to sell their whole crop to the Monopoly at prices arbitrarily fixed by it at a miserably low level. If they withheld a part for their own use, they were liable to fines or imprisonment. The Tobacco Monopoly was therefore not only a most unjust indirect tax, affecting the whole nation, and thus particularly the poorest, but it was also a severe tax on production. It would be easy to quote other examples of unjust taxation from the State Monopolies of Poland, Roumania and Bulgaria.

The proceeds of these taxes were spent on objects of interest to the ruling class. They did not come back to the masses who had paid them in the form of social services, improved communications in rural areas, public works, greater security or better administration. Payment of heavy taxes is bearable if the people feels that the money is being spent in its interest. But in the Eastern European countries a large part of it simply went into the pockets of Ministers and high officials, and the remainder was used for the benefit of a small minority. And the people knew this.

The failure of the economic policy of the Eastern European States to deal with their problems was largely due, as has been seen, to the lack of a thorough plan of industrialisation, to the lack of coordination of industrialisation with the natural products of the countries, and to the preoccupation of industrialists with the export market. It might appear obvious that new industries, artificially created in backward countries, could not compete in the great export markets with the industries of Western Europe and America. The hope of healthy industrialisation lies in the development of the internal market. Only by raising the purchasing-power of the masses, and in particular of the peasantry, could the Eastern European Governments hope to lay the foundation of a healthy industrial system. But this they were unable or unwilling to see, or if they saw it they did nothing about it.

Thus although it would be possible to argue that the long-term interests of the Eastern European ruling classes are identical with those of their peoples, this argument would have little more than academic importance. The fact remains that during twenty years their economic policies, representing what they conceived to be their interests, were in conflict with the interests of their peoples. This cannot be disproved by pointing to the numerous successful enterprises of national importance, for instance the creation of the Polish port of

Gdynia, or by enumerating the superficially impressive palliatives to agrarian distress forced on the Governments by the Depression.

There were three main conflicts of interest: between bourgeoisie and landowners; between bourgeoisie and industrial working class; and between bourgeoisie and peasantry. The most important was the last. The quarrels of the landowners and industrialists were solved by compromise in Hungary and Poland. The quarrels of employers and workers were solved by physical force, to the advantage of employers. But the working class, outside Czechoslovakia—to which, as already noted, this description hardly applies—does not represent a very large part of the population. The fundamental conflict in Eastern Europe is that between the ruling bureaucratic-commercial class and the peasantry.

This issue is usually confused by misplaced emphasis on the superficially intimate connection between the peasantry and the new ruling classes. It is pointed out that in Roumania, Yugoslavia and Bulgaria the majority of the ruling class consists of sons of peasants. This is true but unimportant. Few books have been written on Eastern Europe which do not point out that the Minister or business man of the Balkan States was in most cases born in a village, and could easily go back to his village to-morrow and live as a peasant. There are two answers to this. First, the peasant's son who has risen in society does not go back to the village, except to see his parents or a friend. He lives and works in the town, and his family grows up there. He may keep his house in the village, or build himself a new and better one there, but he will go back there only for short spells on holidays, exactly as an English Beer Lord may spend his holidays in Inverness-shire. He no longer belongs there. Still less do his children. Secondly, the 'sons of peasants' who become Ministers or business men are almost always sons of big holders, schoolmasters or priests, of the 'rural bourgeoisie'. Few are sons of one of the small-holder families which form 70 % of the agrarian population of Eastern Europe. And in 1944 it is still less likely that a member of this agrarian proletariat will rise to a high place than it was in 1918. Village-born politicians may visit the villages at election time, and shake hands with the whole population. But the days of patriarchal beneficence are past. This hand-shaking may once have meant something. To-day it is an empty demagogic gesture. The politicians, the business men and the big bosses of the bureaucracy have no more in common with the village proletariat than has a western industrialist with his workers. They speak the same language, and live in the same geographical area, but their interests, aims and outlook are wide apart.

The western tourist can see this for himself by taking a motor trip of a few miles from any Eastern European capital. He may enjoy an excellent lunch with a friend in a comfortable Bucarest flat, furnished with all the amenities of modern civilisation, and then spend the afternoon in the countryside. Along the asphalt road to Sinaia at the week-end the luxurious cars make an unbroken line. But if he turns off after ten miles on to a side road, the tourist will soon find himself in as primitive a village, with as many dirty, ill-housed, ill-clad, cheerless wretches as he likes. The ruling classes of Eastern Europe do not contain so many millionaires as those of the west. But the contrasts of wealth are more striking, for the bottom level is lower, and on it sit more than half the people.

THE WORKING CLASS

Since the end of the nineteenth century an industrial working class has sprung up in certain areas of Eastern Europe. The oldest and most developed are those of Bohemia-Moravia, the Budapest district and Western Poland (Silesia and Łódź). The railway workers of all the Eastern European countries have by now a tradition of more than one generation. The Roumanian petrol industry has a considerable number of skilled workers, who already form a social class distinct from both bourgeoisie and peasantry. The same is true of parts of Croatia and Slovenia, where Zagreb, Ljubljana, Celje, Maribor form industrial centres of some importance. Since 1918 the growth of industry in all the Eastern European countries, particularly in the cities of the Balkans—Athens, Salonica, Sofia, Belgrade, Bucarest, Plovdiv—has led to a great increase in the number of industrial workers. This new Balkan working class has, however, not yet passed its first generation, and is not always clearly differentiated from the peasantry from which it originated.

The problems of the industrial workers in Bohemia-Moravia,

Silesia, Budapest and Lódž are the same as those of their fellows in Western Europe. In Eastern Poland, Roumania and the Balkan Peninsula, on the other hand, special problems exist, for which parallels could be found in the semi-industrialised countries outside Europe, but which hardly exist in the west. They are due to the close connection between the factory and the village.

Overpopulation in the villages sends the peasants into the towns in search of work. This constant influx of unskilled workers creates a permanent reserve of labour, which the employers can use to keep wages low. When times are good, and wages rise, the influx is correspondingly greater, and the old level of wages is soon restored.

A large part of the influx consists of seasonal labourers, who spend only a few months in the factory and return to their villages with their earnings. These men have their house, and produce part of the food needs of their families, on their holding. They only need sufficient wages to cover their small cash requirements—town-made foodstuffs, clothing and taxes. They are therefore content with a much smaller wage than is needed by a worker who lives with his family in the town. The employers naturally use these cheap workers for as many purposes as possible. Their presence is a factor permanently depressing wages. It affects all but the skilled industrial workers.

The unemployment statistics of the Eastern European States during the last twenty years have not been very striking, even in the Depression years. The reason why they have been comparatively low is that when there is less employment in industry, most of the unskilled workers go home to their villages, and sit there and rot. The State forgets about them, and they do not appear in the official statistics.

A better standard of living for the urban unskilled worker in Eastern Europe depends on the success of measures to deal with the agricultural overpopulation problem. It is unlikely, as was seen in the preceding chapter, that even with the best will in the world very big results could be obtained in this direction for a number of years. But until progress is made towards curing, or at least relieving, the misery of the village, the urban unskilled worker can have little hope.

It is possible to relieve the situation for a short time by

restricting the liberty of the peasants to migrate to the towns. Such measures are only justifiable, however, if accompanied by real attempts to deal with the Peasant Problem. They are dangerous, for they usually lead to laziness on the part of the authorities. It is easy for a Government to use the police to prevent the peasants from leaving their villages, refuse them employment unless they are furnished with a labour permit, and arrest them as 'Bolsheviks' if they object. The classical description of this system is to be found in Silone's magnificent novel about Fascist Italy, *Fontamara*. Most of the Eastern European States offer analogies.

The only solution is that Governments should devote themselves principally to the solution of the Peasant Problem, reduce to some extent the influx into the towns, and establish a minimum wage for urban unskilled workers. But it is much easier to point to the desirability of this 'solution' than to carry it out.

The skilled worker is not immediately threatened by the pressure from the village. He will only be threatened when a large number of unskilled workers learn skilled trades. And in view of the low standard of living and lack of technical education this is not likely to be the case for some years.

The Eastern European Governments conformed with the recommendations of the International Labour Organisation concerning hours and conditions of work, insurance and social services, but many of the measures adopted remained on paper, and in all the countries under review the benefits of such measures were confined to the skilled workers. The condition of the workers was far better in Czechoslovakia than in any of the other Eastern European States. In Hungary it was fairly good for certain skilled trades. The situation of the Hungarian working class was improved by the fact that the pressure of the villages on industrial employment was much smaller than in neighbouring countries to the north, south and east. This was due partly to the absence of an acute overpopulation problem, partly to the fact that the landowners were interested in keeping the surplus agricultural population on the land. They profited from the existence of an agricultural labour reserve, and were not disposed to let the industrialists take this from them. In Poland there was a fairly numerous skilled working class in the old industrial centres, which enjoyed a reasonable standard of living. The Depression caused substantial unemployment in Poland, Czechoslovakia and Hungary, but the development of State enterprise, particularly of the armaments industry, in the last years before the war greatly relieved, even if it did not completely cure, unemployment.

During the twenty years between the two wars, then, the skilled workers of Eastern Europe—who were almost entirely confined to the three most northerly States, and constituted less than half the total number of industrial workers—had a tolerable existence, maintained to a large extent at the expense of the unskilled workers and peasants. Consequently, the skilled workers were not on the whole a revolutionary element in Eastern European politics. The threat to the established order came far more from the peasant masses and the first-generation workers of peasant origin.

Trade Unions prospered only in the three northerly countries, and in the skilled trades. In the metallurgical and textile industries there were strong Trade Unions. Particularly important were the Printers' Unions. In all three countries the Trade Unions were closely connected with the Social Democratic Parties, which had been founded on the model of the German and Austrian parties. In Roumania and the Balkans there were few skilled workers, and German influence was of small importance. In these countries the Trade Unions were less connected with parties. Social Democratic Parties hardly existed. Left intellectuals were influenced by French and Russian rather than German ideas. Communist influence was much stronger than Social Democratic. The only part of the Balkan Peninsula where Social Democratic Trade Unions of the Central European type existed was Slovenia, where Austrian models had been imitated already before the First World War.

Mention should also be made of Catholic and Nationalist Trade Unions. The former were most important in Poznania and Polish Silesia, where they dated from the time of the national struggle under Imperial German rule, in which the Catholic Church had led all classes of the Polish nation. They were also of some importance in Czechoslovakia and Slovenia. The most important nationalist Trade Unions were those connected with the Croatian Peasant Party.

In the three northerly countries the Trade Unions were

able to resist pressure from outside' the working class. The Czechoslovak Trade Unions played an active and constructive part in political life until the destruction of the democratic Republic. In Poland they survived the attacks of Fascist elements until the end. In Hungary the skilled workers were sufficiently strong and important to maintain their Unions until the outbreak of war with Russia. They were helped in this by the difference of interests between the landowners and the industrialists.

In Roumania and the Balkans the Trade Unions were never strong. The absence of a large body of skilled workers, and the low cultural and economic level of the peasant recruits to industry made the task of organisation almost impossible. Moreover, the Governments were terrified of Trade Unions and 'nests of Communism', and used every excuse to repress their activities, organising strike-breakers, constantly backing up employers and putting down strikes by armed force. Two examples of the latter are the 'massacre' of the Jiu valley, carried out by the 'progressive' Government of Iuliu Maniu in 1929, and the railway strike of Bucarest (Grivitsa workshops) in 1934, suppressed by Vaida Voevod and Calinescu at heavy cost of life, after complete violation of promises which had been made in order to secure the evacuation of the shops by the workers. The history of Jugoslavia and Bulgaria during the last twenty years contains more numerous and bloodier examples. In Roumania independent Trade Unions were officially abolished in 1938, and replaced by 'guilds' under the Fascist system erected by King Carol II. In Bulgaria they had no real power after 1923, but existed nominally until the *coup d'état* of 1934, when they were superseded by officially organised Labour institutions. In Jugoslavia they continued to exist in theory until the invasion of the country, although they had long ceased to have any importance, and had been threatened by the official, uniformed 'Trade Unions' created on the Italian model by Stojadinović and Cvetković.

THE EDUCATIONAL SYSTEM

The importance of the educational system in the formation of the new ruling classes of Eastern Europe has already been briefly indicated. The Eastern European States prided themselves particularly on the progress made in Education during the twenty years between the wars. Enormous numbers of schools were built in regions where they had been quite unknown. Universal compulsory elementary education was introduced, and a genuine attempt was made to enable poor children of talent to obtain higher education.

The equality of opportunity was greater in the Balkan States, Roumania and Czechoslovakia than in Poland or Hungary, where the remnants of a feudal society provided an obstacle, and in all the countries under review there is a difference between the pre-Depression and post-Depression periods. During the first years, at least in the 'reformed' States, the possibilities of higher education were far larger than after 1932. The combination of the general economic trends, noted in the previous chapter, with the special effects of the Depression widened the gap between the rich and poor peasants, and the masses sank back into the swamp of hopelessness from which they had emerged for a few years after 1918.

It would be unfair to underestimate the achievements of the Eastern European States in Education. During the twenty years illiteracy was enormously reduced. If it has not been eliminated, if there are still regions in Bosnia and Bessarabia, to take only two examples, where more than 80 % of the population cannot read or write, this cannot be blamed entirely on those in charge of educational policy. The peasants themselves were not always cooperative. Often children needed at home for work in the fields were not allowed by their parents to go to school. A further, almost insuperable, difficulty was the absence of communications, particularly important for the mountain villages of the Balkan Peninsula and the Carpathians. Special problems existed in parts of Central Hungary, where the peasants live, not in compact villages but in individual houses, separated by several hundred yards from their nearest neighbours. The situation of the school is bound to be unfavourable for some outlying families, whose children have to walk a number of miles. The truth is that Education, like Public Health, is dependent on economic improvement and reform, and the deficiencies of the latter in the Eastern European States constantly hampered their extremely praiseworthy efforts in the former.

Sufficient progress was made to stimulate a most striking

appetite for knowledge. The word 'intellectual' has perhaps greater prestige in Eastern Europe than anywhere else in the world. Merchants, soldiers, public officials, love to call themselves by this name. Books are in constant demand, and adults take great trouble to continue their own education long after leaving school or college. The Eastern European universities have produced many distinguished scholars, and Governments have spent large sums on the provision of modern scientific and medical equipment, generously assisted by the Rockefeller and other American foundations. The highest level of Education and Culture was undoubtedly to be found in Czechoslovakia, which could bear comparison with Western Europe. The ancient University of Cracow, and the more modern ones of Budapest and Warsaw attained the highest level. In view of the slender resources at their disposal it must be admitted that the Balkan universities and colleges made great progress. Such men as Professor Slobodan Jovanović of Belgrade would have lent distinction to any university in Europe or the New World.

Yet when all credit is paid to the activities of Ministers of Education, and of a vast anonymous army of selfless and untiring men and women teachers, it must unfortunately be stated that there were grave deficiencies in the content and quality of the education provided. One reason for this was the lack of qualified teaching staff available. Even in Czechoslovakia this defect made itself felt. Slovakia, and still more Ruthenia, had a very small number of educated men, and few of these were willing to devote their lives to educating their less fortunate compatriots. It was necessary to bring in Czechs to direct the schools, and this led to considerable ill-feeling. In Poland, western Galicia and the Prussian territories could provide a substantial number of cultured and capable people, but these were in practice frequently overlooked in favour of less suitable persons from the Russian territory, who had won the gratitude of the Government by political or military services. In Hungary the teaching staff was somewhat more adequate, but this was partly because popular education was relatively less developed than in the neighbouring countries. In the Balkan countries and Roumania the lack of staff was acute. Teachers were insufficiently trained, and education suffered accordingly.

The predominant ideology in Eastern as in Western European educated circles in 1918 was that of Liberalism. The two fundamental principles of this creed were the independence of national States and the liberty of the individual in society.

The conflict between romantic nationalism and individualist equalitarianism, already apparent in Western European intellectual life in the nineteenth century, and especially in the contrast between French and German interpretations of Liberalism, received still greater emphasis after 1918. The difficulties involved in this conflict were too much for the inexperienced teachers of the Eastern European States. They continued to pay lip-service to the ideas of the French Revolution, but they understood little of their implications. In practice they fell back on the safe and easily intelligible doctrines of romantic nationalism.

Emphasis was laid on History, and particularly on the heroic medieval periods in which each Eastern European nation had for a brief span of years dominated its neighbours. Serbian children were taught to look back to the glories of Dušan, Bulgarians to the Empire of Simeon, Roumanians to the wars of Stephen the Great and Michael the Brave. Poles were reminded that their armies had once sat in Moscow, Hungarians that their forefathers had raided as far as Naples or Nîmes. The youth of each nation was taught to regard its neighbours as inferior to itself in culture, moral values and courage.

Analytical historical study hardly existed. Such distinguished historians as the great Roumanian Professor Iorga confined themselves to erudite chronology, written in a highly romantic and bombastic spirit. Critical study of the development of social institutions and ideas was only beginning, and if it received some encouragement in Prague, Budapest and Belgrade, in most Eastern European centres it was frowned upon by the elder generation of professors. If this was true of the universities, it is hardly surprising that in the schools the poorly trained teachers were hardly able to give their pupils more than a grounding in the 'three R's' and a conviction that chauvinism is the highest civic virtue.

The part played by university students in the lives of the Eastern European States forms a sad chapter in the history of the last twenty years. The great majority of Eastern European students are sons and daughters of poor families, enabled by the State to continue their studies. They should constitute the élite of these young nations. It is regrettably true that they did not do so. Only a comparatively small proportion were inspired by a love of learning or a desire to train their intellects for the service of their countries. Their idea of such service was rather that they had an automatic right to a place in the State administration after spending a given number of years at the university. A university diploma was considered a claim on the State for the rest of life. Moreover a great part of their time was spent in political activities, not always of a very creditable kind, which detracted from their work. A number of excellent young men and women completed their training every year, but they seldom formed a very high percentage.

There are of course very great differences between different universities. The best universities were those of Czechoslovakia. The Hungarian universities have a fairly good record, and their faults may be said to be those of all European universities, including those of Great Britain. If too much of the time of the students of Belgrade University was spent on political meetings, it must be emphasised that they rendered an immense service to their own country and to the peoples of the Balkans by their devotion to the principles of political freedom and social justice. During the Jugoslav Dictatorship the only place where free discussion was possible was within the walls of the University of Belgrade, whose autonomy was respected by all Governments: and the intellectual integrity and personal courage of many students and professors were a source of inspiration to their people.

The lowest level in Eastern Europe was that of the Polish and Roumanian universities. These words must not be understood to mean that there were not noble, disinterested and industrious men and women among the professors and students of these two countries. The names of such people would fill many volumes. But in both countries the impatient and discontented idealism of the younger generation and of the intellectual class were exploited by Governments and politicians for the basest purposes.

In Poland bands of anti-Semitic and Fascist students were

used by the National Democratic Party to embarrass the Government, and by the Government against Socialists, Democrats and National Minorities.

In Roumania the students were a simple instrument of the police. Numbers of students were hired for small sums to create disorders at Opposition meetings, in order to provide the Government with a desired excuse for the introduction of martial law and the suppression of inconvenient political organisations. In 1925 the Liberal politician Tatarescu paid students, and provided them with free railway transport to the frontier town of Oradea Mare (Nagyvárad), where the police authorities equipped them with stones to smash the windows of Jewish shops. Some hours of breaking, beating and looting gave the Government what it needed. In the University of Jassy in Moldavia the Iron Guard group grew up in the twenties among students who spent their time almost exclusively in anti-Semitic demonstrations, pogroms, strike-breaking and outrages against 'Communist' intellectuals and workers. The 'hero' Codreanu, one of these students, murdered the Police Prefect of the town, was acquitted and gained a reputation for patriotic courage on the strength of it. When the professors were rash enough to remind the students that they had come to the university to work, the students 'went on strike', and refused to take their examinations. Many of the professors encouraged them.

It is obvious that the responsibility for this horrible state of affairs lies not with the students themselves, but with the Governments and ruling classes, who committed an unforgivable crime against their own peoples by their deliberate perversion of the morals of the growing generation.

The false educational system of Eastern Europe, which at the best encouraged chauvinism and at the worst helped to destroy all conceptions of morality, is one of the fundamental causes of the misfortunes of these peoples. Unhealthy romanticism, national arrogance, intellectual and moral dishonesty were not confined to the schools and universities, but extended to the Press, publications of all sorts, the theatre, official propaganda in the widest sense. The ruling class formed in this atmosphere was hardly likely to make a success of its rule. It had no sense of responsibility towards other classes, no understanding of the principle of individual liberty, no knowledge of the fundamental problems of its country and still less of the character and condition of neighbouring countries. The young generation was brought up to hate and despise other nations, to fear its own people and to see in any proposal for collaboration with other States a poisonous intrigue of 'Reds', Jews and Freemasons. It was deceived by any kind of demagogic anti-Semitic or anti-Democratic agitation, and fell an easy prey to Nazi propaganda. In view of the type of education that the Eastern Europeans received, the surprising thing is, not that Hitler and his minions found sympathisers among them, but that so many did not succumb to his blandishments.

There can be no hope of progress for the peoples of Eastern Europe without a radical reform of Education. Unfortunately, 'solutions' of this problem are not easy to find. Education in Western Europe and America is not so free from faults that we . can quickly prescribe remedies for the misfortunes of Eastern Europe.

It is clear that more provision must be made for the training of school-teachers. A much more extensive and efficient system of teachers' training colleges is required. In this respect it is certain that Western Europe can help, for it has undoubtedly reached a more advanced stage. If the Eastern European States cannot at first find a sufficient number of professors for the training colleges, these could be provided from the west, on the understanding that they would be replaced as soon as possible by their own nationals.

The need for a more ambitious system of technical, medical and agricultural Education has already been indicated. There is room for enormous numbers of village doctors, engineers and agricultural experts in all the Eastern European countries, especially in Roumania, Eastern Poland and the Balkan Peninsula. During the last twenty years the comparatively small development of these branches of study was the more striking in view of the overcrowding of the Law Faculties, whose students in many cases received no more than a training in chauvinism as a preparation for a bureaucratic post. Technical and medical training are of more importance to the backward countries of Eastern Europe than knowledge of the complicated concepts of French Constitutional Law. The over-development of Law study was largely responsible for the grave problem of 'intellectual unemployment', which became most acute in Eastern Europe during the Depression, and provided a generous supply of 'Führers' for the various Fascist movements of Eastern Europe. As long, however, as the social problems of the villages are unsolved, there will be no possibility in a rationally ordered Eastern European State of 'overproduction' of doctors, agricultural experts or engineers.

Far greater attention should be paid to the study of neighbouring nations. During the last twenty years rich Eastern Europeans would send their children to study in France, Germany or even England, but no one ever took the trouble to study the language, social conditions or history of neighbouring peoples. Consequently there were, for instance, hundreds of Roumanians who knew something about France, quite a large number who even intimately understood France, but hardly any who knew anything about Poland, Bulgaria or Jugoslavia. Jugoslavia and Roumania were allies for twenty years, but the attitude of the educated classes of the two peoples to each other was marked by complete ignorance, indifference and contempt. This lack of cultural relations between the Eastern European States was one of the fundamental reasons for their failure to collaborate against common external enemies. It is of great importance that in the new Europe means should be provided for regular exchanges of students, teachers and simple citizens and peasants between the countries of Eastern Europe.

The main object of a new system of Education in Eastern Europe must be the removal of the pernicious spirit of romantic nationalism from the schools, Press and Literature. This is no easy task, and one that does not concern Eastern Europe alone. It should be clearly understood that this is not a plea for the discouragement of ordinary ideas of patriotism. The truth is that the best way to stimulate patriotism is to prevent chauvinism. The chauvinist 'Nationalists' of Eastern Europe were mostly not patriots at all, but acted as dupes and agents of Nazism in betraying their countries to Germany and Italy. The next generation of Eastern Europeans must be taught to combine love of their own country with respect for the liberties of other nations. A new outlook must be built up which will avoid the extremes of romantic nationalism on the one hand and colourless and loquacious cosmopolitanism—of the type not uncommon in certain organisations of Liberal tendencies in post-1918 Britain—on the other.

THE ADMINISTRATION

The Administration of the Eastern European States varied according to their past history. The best was to be found in the regions formerly belonging to Austria—Bohemia and Moravia. Hungary and the provinces formerly belonging to her had a rather more backward system. The worst administration was that of the former Russian and Turkish regions.

In the new States of 1918 regions of Eastern and Western standards were combined together, and this gave rise to special problems, of which more will be said later. In Jugoslavia, Roumania and Poland it may be said with little exaggeration that the Eastern methods prevailed over the Western. In Bulgaria the Eastern system has never been challenged. In Czechoslovakia the Austrian tradition of honest and fairly efficient administration was continued, and in Hungary conditions were, as before the First World War, somewhere between Western and Eastern.

The old Russian bureaucracy was the offspring of Mongol and Byzantine traditions, while that of the Balkans owes its origin to a combination of Byzantine and Turkish conceptions. Both were essentially arbitrary and dictatorial, but their severity was always mitigated by inefficiency and corruption. The Balkan official regards himself as immeasurably superior to the peasants among whom he lives and from whose ranks he has sprung. To be an official is the fondest dream of every able young son of a peasant. The Balkan official does not like to work. He considers himself so fine a fellow that the State and the public should be proud to support him for life, and should not ask him to make efforts that will tax his intellect or character. A visitor to a Balkan Ministry or Police Headquarters in the middle of the morning will find the rooms filled with good-natured fellows comfortably enjoying a cup of Turkish coffee and a chat with their friends. The papers lie on their desks. Outside stand, sit and squat patient queues of peasants awaiting their various permits and receipts.

Foreigners and citizens with 'protekcija'[1] obtain swift and polite attention, but the people can afford to wait. They have waited many hundreds of years already for justice, and a few more hours will not make much difference. Time counts little in the Balkans.

Balkan bureaucracy involves obscure and complicated formalities and documents, the result of an accumulation of laws and taxes superimposed on each other since the beginning of time, which provide a constant source of revenue to the bureaucrat and of annoyance to the citizen. Everything which can be is centralised in the capital. The local official dreads above all responsibility. Everything must be referred to a higher quarter. Days pass before an answer is received, and the citizen may be summoned to the capital, at his own expense in time and money, to settle some trifling formality.

It would be absurd to suggest that contempt for the public, pompous laziness, love of formality and fear of responsibility were the monopoly of Balkan bureaucracy. They are, however, perhaps more marked in the Balkans, Poland and Roumania than in the West. What is more especially Eastern is the corruption of officialdom. Few books on Eastern Europe by tourist 'experts' fail to express indignation at the railway official who let them off with half-price and put the half in his pocket, or at the innkeeper or merchant who changed their money at an illegal rate. Petty corruption is widespread in the lower ranks of every branch of the bureaucracy in Eastern Europe. Its cause is very simple. The official is so badly paid that he cannot support his family without extra sources of revenue. These he finds in minor transgressions of the law and in the granting of minor illegal privileges to those willing to pay for them. As the laws are often cumbrous, stupid, inefficient and oppressive, there is seldom any lack of people ready to bribe an official to ignore or contravene them.

Although this corruption had a bad effect on both officials and citizens, and caused unnecessary hardship to those who were too poor to buy exemptions or precedence, its importance should not be exaggerated. Most petty officials in Eastern Europe are not vicious men. They are kind-hearted souls who

[1] This is the Serbian form of a word used, with different terminations, in all the languages and countries of Eastern Europe, to denote 'special protection', 'connections', 'graft' or 'pull'. It is indispensable for the making of a career.

put their duty to their families before all else, and whom economic pressure compels to take a 'realistic' view of their duty to the nation.

Far more serious was corruption in high places. If petty venality can be cured by raising the salaries of Government servants to a reasonable level, it is much harder to prescribe a cure for the more insidious upper-class corruption. This too is not an exclusively Eastern European phenomenon, but it takes on in Eastern Europe forms comparatively rare in the west.

In Eastern Europe the greatest fortunes are made not in industry or banking but in politics. The Ministries of the Interior and of Foreign Affairs of most of the countries under review possessed large 'discretionary funds', of which the Ministers often embezzled part or all. Ministers of Finance enriched themselves by selling high protective tariffs to industrialists. Ministers of Trade (and even crowned heads of States) received generous allotments of shares from foreign companies anxious for concessions. High officials in Ministries fared little worse than their Ministers. Particularly lucrative was the job of Inspector of the Ministry of Labour. Many inspectors found factory owners extremely grateful for the omission in their reports of certain minor irregularities and deficiencies in the working conditions of their men.

Public officials showed respect to members of the ruling class, particularly to those who made it worth their while, but to the masses they were pitiless. This is true of Hungary and Poland quite as much as of Roumania and the Balkan Peninsula. Taxes were collected with ruthless brutality. This was particularly bad in the last few years, when the Governments needed every penny for their military expenditure, and, as usual, put the main burden on the masses. If a peasant owed arrears of taxes, the gendarmes would come to his house when he was working in the fields—or when he and all adult males in his household were serving in the army. If the women could not pay, the gendarmes seized the few belongings of the household. If the wife and children objected, they were beaten. Outrages of this sort were often committed for the sake of a few pennies.

The most striking example of this sort that came to the knowledge of the author is from Kishinyov (Chişineu), capital of the then Roumanian province of Bessarabia, in the spring of 1940. The gendarmes of this province received orders to collect arrears of taxes from the peasants of the neighbourhood. For two weeks they toured the villages, seizing what they could find, blankets, rugs, tools, any spare clothes. The spoils were sold on their return in the public market of Kishinyov, and realised the impressive sum of 800 lei (about 16s.). Quite apart from the injustice of the procedure and the brutality employed to carry it out, it should be stressed that the State cashed about as much as the salary of one of the gendarmes for the period of collection. To achieve this, many peasant households were deprived of everything but the clothes on the backs of the women, at a time when the men were mobilised on the frontier, liable at any moment to be called upon to fight for their country.

Although cases of this kind may be regarded as rather exceptional, injustice, ruthlessness and brutality were widespread all over Eastern Europe except Czechoslovakia, and even there they were not unknown. These abuses will only be eradicated by an entirely new spirit in Education, but something could be more quickly achieved by the promulgation and enforcement of laws forbidding, with heavy penalties, the confiscation for non-payment of taxes of indispensable household accessories and instruments and the use of physical violence by the gendarmes and police except for cases of violent crime. Such laws or regulations existed in the Eastern European States during part or all of the inter-war period, but no one took any trouble to enforce them, and they were consequently almost universally ignored.

The sufferings of the people were increased by the fact that there was no redress against administrative abuses. The legal experts of the Eastern European States could show the foreign inquirer a most beautiful system of courts and appeals, which appeared on paper at least as advanced as that of France, Britain or the United States. But all this remained on paper. A peasant who complained of an act of injustice was denounced as a 'Communist', sent before a military court, beaten from time to time, and sentenced either to prison or to forced labour under military discipline. If the village mayor collected more than the legal communal tax, and pocketed the difference, only 'Communists' would think of protesting.

A peasant who did not like to have his daughters raped or his property stolen by a gendarme must be a 'Bolshevik'. And in the courts the word of a politically sound, patriotic gendarme was always taken against that of a subversive peasant.

DIFFERENCES OF CULTURAL LEVEL

Special problems were created in provinces which had been ruled by 'Western' methods and owing to the territorial settlement of 1918 came under 'Eastern' administration, or vice versa. Czechoslovakia, Jugoslavia, Roumania and Poland were States of mixed 'Western' and 'Eastern' provinces. The Austrian provinces of Bohemia and Moravia acquired Slovakia and Ruthenia, whose past administration might be described as 'backward Central European'. In this case the more advanced dominated the more backward. Serbia acquired the Austrian provinces of Slovenia and Dalmatia, the Hungarian provinces of Croatia and Voivodina, the Austro-Turkish[1] province of Bosnia and the Turkish province of Macedonia. Roumania acquired the Austrian province of Bukovina, the Hungarian provinces of Transylvania and Banat, and the Russian province of Bessarabia. In both these cases a primitive 'Oriental' State acquired large areas accustomed to more advanced standards of administration than it could provide, and at the same time other areas considerably more backward than it was itself. Poland was composed of a thoroughly Western, a semi-Western and a completely Eastern area. The three sections struggled against each other during the succeeding twenty years, without decisive results, although it might be said on balance that Oriental standards prevailed.

A few words are necessary at this point to illustrate the three types of problem created. These are Western superimposed on Eastern; Eastern superimposed on Western; Eastern superimposed on still more backward Eastern.

The only example of the first type is provided by Czechoslovakia. During twenty years Czech officials and teachers did much to raise the economic and cultural level of Slovakia and Ruthenia. But they met with little gratitude. The leaders of the Slovak people in 1918 were the priesthood. The Lutheran Church represented the intellectual élite of the Slovaks, and

---

[1] Bosnia had been ruled by Austria for forty years (1878–1918), but this period had been too short to obliterate Turkish habits and traditions.

both welcomed the Union of Slovakia with the Czech Lands and cooperated with the Czechs in the task of building up a progressive Slovakia. The Catholic priesthood, however, resented the cultural predominance of the Czechs. Slovak Catholic priests were mostly men of little education, brought up to regard all ideas more recent than the Middle Ages as inventions of the devil. The Czechs, with their emphasis on social services and modern education, were to them a 'godless' folk.

The great influence of the Catholic priests over the Slovak masses was used to inflame violent nationalism, directed equally against Czechs and Hungarians. Obstruction by the Slovaks to reforms convinced the Czechs for their part that the Slovaks were a stupid and reactionary people. The young generation of Slovak intellectuals, brought up in the schools and universities founded by the Czechs, turned against their benefactors with fierce hatred. The antagonism created by the difference in cultural and political traditions of Czechs and Slovaks was a constant source of trouble to the young Republic, and helped to bring about its downfall. In Ruthenia similar factors operated, but the very low level of national consciousness among the Ruthenes, their small numbers, and the hostility of the various Ruthene factions among themselves made the Ruthene Question much less important than the Slovak.

Examples of the second and third types can conveniently be taken from Jugoslavia and Roumania. The difficulties of Poland in connection with this problem of different cultural levels will be briefly mentioned elsewhere.

The ruling class of the Old Kingdoms of Serbia and Roumania (known respectively as 'Srbijanci' and 'Regateni') considered that they had 'liberated' the new provinces, and therefore had a right to the gratitude and respectful deference of their inhabitants.[1] The assumption of this superior moral attitude caused intense resentment among Slovenes, Croats, Transylvanians and Bukovinians, whose reaction was to declaim interminably about the superiority of their own culture,

[1] 'Srbijanac' is a Serb from the pre-1918 Kingdom, as opposed to a Serb from the new provinces across the Sava. These were known as 'Prećani' ('preko' = 'across'). 'Regatean' is a Roumanian of the 'Regat' or Old Kingdom. These three words will be used below

and to denounce the newcomers as 'Byzantine barbarians', or 'Orientals'. This naturally exasperated the 'liberators', and increased their determination to maintain political and economic power in their own hands.

Having in fact suffered heavy casualties and having brought devastation on their homes in a war which they had entered principally in order to win these provinces, the 'liberators' expected that the 'liberated' would pay a large share of the expenses of reconstruction, and gave practical shape to their desire by various economic measures directed against the new provinces to the profit of the old. Moreover, they too often regarded the new provinces as colonies, to be provided with new 'nationally trustworthy' public officials, a convenient field for the employment of the sons of the rapidly forming ruling class. Srbijanci and Regateni officials flooded the new provinces, bringing with them the customs and morals of their Balkan ancestors, diluted with some smattering of French Constitutional Theory acquired from half-digested lectures by graduates of the Sorbonne.

The reactions of the different provinces to this policy varied. The most successful resistance was offered by the Slovenes. They were protected by their language, which is sufficiently different from Serbo-Croatian to make it impossible for large numbers of Srbijanci officials to colonise their country. Moreover they showed themselves eager from the beginning to cooperate with the Serbs in the construction of their common State. Although there were troubles from time to time, it may be said that the Slovenes found a satisfactory place in the life of Jugoslavia. Many Slovenes obtained posts in the administration in other provinces besides their own, and in the Belgrade Ministries, while retaining much of the substance of Home Rule in their own lands.

The Roumanians of Bukovina hardly constituted a serious problem. They continued, with much justification, to complain bitterly of the contrast between the methods of government employed by Bucarest and those to which they had been accustomed under Austria. But their loyalty to the Roumanian State was secured by the fact that they were faced in their own province by the hostility of a Ukrainian Minority of numbers almost equal to their own, against which the help of Bucarest was essential. The least agreeable peculiarities of the Roumanian bureaucracy in Bukovina were concentrated against Ukrainians and Jews, and the Bukovinian Roumanians enjoyed tolerable conditions. In Transylvania the problem was more serious.

Although strongly in favour of unity with the Regat, to which they were tied by fear of the large Hungarian minority in their midst and of the Hungarian State beyond their frontier, the Transylvanian Roumanians deeply resented the penetration of Regateni into their province. The battle for economic and administrative control was fought fiercely between Bucarest and Transylvania for more than a decade. In the end the Transylvanians probably more than held their own, for what they lost in Transylvania they gained in the form of important political, economic and administrative posts occupied by Transylvanians in the Regat.

The most dangerous problem of this kind in Eastern Europe was the Croatian Question, of which more will have to be said later. The Croats had not only regional patriotism and consciousness of superior culture, but a definite sense of separate nationhood. The antagonism of the Croats first against the Srbijanci, and then against all Serbs, only increased with the passage of time. The more the Croatian intellectuals prattled about their 'Thousand years of Culture', the more angry the Serbs became, and the more Serbian officials and gendarmes Belgrade sent to 'keep order' in Croatia, the more implacable became the hatred of the Croats.

Particularly wretched was the fate of the third category, backward areas annexed by 'eastern' States, such as Bessarabia, Macedonia, Polesia and Volhynia. The peoples of these areas lacked the political and cultural standards of the advanced regions, and had neither material nor moral weapons with which to defend themselves. They became the victims of merciless economic exploitation and police brutality. Examples of the 'Raubwirtschaft' to which they were subjected have already been given in the Jugoslav Tobacco Monopoly (which affected above all the peasants of Macedonia), and the tax-collectors of Kishinyov. The 'liberating' officials could beat, rob and rape as they pleased, using the well-worn slogans of 'Bolshevik' and 'enemy of the State' to justify their outrages. This was all the easier because all the areas in question were particularly insecure frontier districts. The result of exploitation and persecution was, however, to turn even the potentially loyal part of the population into real Communists and Separatists.

The importance of these conflicts can hardly be exaggerated. In most of these regions the sources of conflict are very old, but they were greatly intensified by the administrative abuses described above. A good and tactful administration would have softened, and might even with time have eliminated them. The methods practised had disastrous results, which affected not only the provinces in which they were applied, but the whole political life of the States. The example of corruption, greed and violence offered by the 'liberating' bureaucracies had an unfavourable effect on the morals of the victims. When they have had the opportunity the Croats, despite their much-vaunted 'Culture', have shown that they can rival and surpass the Serbs in all the unpleasant characteristics which they attribute to them. After twenty years of Great Roumania the Transylvanians could compete in dishonesty with the Regateni. Moreover the methods of 'Raubwirtschaft' employed in the backward provinces had a degrading influence on the public life and morals of every part of the States which cannot be overestimated. The Srbijanac or the Regatean suffered greater abuses from his own rulers because they had tried them out with such success on his Macedonian and Bessarabian cousins. Oppression, robbery, discontent and disunity were greater throughout Eastern Europe in 1939 than they had been in 1918.

THE POLITICAL SYSTEM

Peasant poverty, bad education, bad administration and an ignorant and irresponsible ruling class destroyed all hope of real Democracy in Eastern Europe between the wars. The prevalent political ideas in 1918 were those of the French Revolution—Freedom, Equality and Brotherhood for all. Their bearers were, however, the educated and semi-educated class, the quickly forming bourgeoisie, whose material interests were opposed, in the short run at least, to those of the peasants and workers, whom they kept in their place by police terror and mulcted by taxation.

In Hungary the Red Revolution and White Counter-Revolution swept away all hope of Democracy. In Czechoslovakia the balance of social forces and the strength of the

Liberal tradition allowed the achievement of some measure of true Democracy. In the other countries of Eastern Europe a pseudo-Democratic system maintained itself for varying periods of years, succumbing in the end to Dictatorship well before the outbreak of war.

The pseudo-Democratic surface of Polish, Roumanian and Balkan politics bore little relation to reality. Exceedingly Liberal Constitutions existed side by side with exceedingly dishonest and unscrupulous police machines, which exercised various forms of most effective political pressure on the unprivileged classes. Elections were seldom more than a farce. Voters were bought or intimidated, votes were forged, ballot-boxes were lost or stolen. A few elections of the inter-war period are worth remembering, either because the electors were given some chance to express their views, or because despite police pressure a Government failed to obtain a large majority. But the great majority of elections were of no interest whatever, for everyone knew the result beforehand. Elections were always accompanied by the most extravagant promises. Freedom, Justice and Prosperity would be established once and for all by each party. With each election the number of voters who listened to these promises decreased. Words like 'Democracy' mean little to an Eastern European peasant at the best of times. After some years of unfortunate experience even the most simple-minded convinced themselves that all this was talk and nothing but talk. All parties and all politicians, they believed, were alike. All were dishonest, and all wanted to get something out of them without giving them more than they could help in return. The quarrels of the parties were just quarrels among the 'gentlemen'. They did not concern the people. An election was rather fun, because it was an opportunity, recurring every few years, to earn a little money and some free šlivovica, vodka or tsuica by selling one's vote to the highest bidder. Outside Czechoslovakia, where the people had political education, and a few special areas like Croatia and Eastern Galicia, where national and political problems existed which interested every individual, party politics was viewed by the masses with increasing apathy.

As the World Depression deepened, social discontent grew. The peasants and workers sank deeper into the squalor of poverty and despair. Even the rich peasants were alienated by the increased abuses of the administration and the police. Disillusioned by the old parties, the people looked for new men. Extremist movements of Left and Right gained ground. The illegal Communists and persecuted Nazi organisations expanded their ranks. Observing the rising tide of misery and hatred, the ruling classes became more and more frightened of their own peoples. Every protest was a sign of 'Bolshevism', and was met with brutal repression as such. One by one the last traces of 'Democracy' disappeared, and pseudo-Parliamentarism gave way to police Dictatorships or Fascist regimes.

It would be a mistake to pretend that there was no difference between pseudo-Parliamentarism and open Dictatorship. Under the former there were at least a few safety valves. The peasants of any given village might hope to obtain small material advantages through the local deputy when the latter's party was in power. Criticism of the Government—often misdirected—was allowed to appear in the Press. If the masses even in the most 'Parliamentary' period had little opportunity to express their views, and little hope of receiving justice, at least intellectuals of the ruling class enjoyed some freedom.

With the establishment of Dictatorships these last trivial blessings were removed. Freedom, prosperity and power were confined to members of the ruling gang. Fine proclamations were issued about National Unity, Moral Regeneration, Non-Party Objectivity and Strong Hands, and foreign journalists could always be found to write sycophantic articles of praise in the World Press. But all this fine talk was insincere. The Dictatorships of Eastern Europe did some good things no doubt. No Government sets out deliberately to ruin its country. Great political, social and economic problems were forced on their attention by the march of events, which they hoped to postpone by various palliative measures. But to deal seriously and radically with the tasks imposed by the national interest was beyond their power. Composed of stupid, timorous, dishonest and pettily cunning men, confronted with internal and international situations that were too difficult for bigger men than they, they could only hesitate, temporise and take the line of least resistance. These 'strong Governments' were no more than greedy, corrupt and brutal class regimes, which did not feed but fed upon their peoples, and whose only strength lay in the bayonets of their gendarmes.

CHAPTER SIX

POLITICAL EXPERIENCE, 1918–39

THE WORKING of the political system described above can best be seen by a brief account of the internal political development of the Eastern European States between the two wars. This account will attempt to present only the most significant problems and events, sparing the reader as much as possible of the chronology of Cabinet crises and electoral manœuvres. It will make no reference, except where this is quite inevitable, to problems connected with the existence of National Minorities, or to international questions. These will be dealt with at greater length in subsequent chapters.

The history of the Eastern European countries in these years falls approximately into three periods. The first is the period of the foundation of the new States and of the revolutionary tide which swept through all Europe after the Russian Revolution and the Versailles Treaty. The second period is one of comparative stability, following on the suppression of revolutionary movements and the reorganisation of the finances and economic life of the European States. The third period is characterised by the World Economic Depression and the rise of German National Socialism.

The transition from pseudo-Democracy to Dictatorship, which can be observed in all but one of the Eastern European States, does not coincide exactly with these main periods, for the Polish and Jugoslav Dictatorships were established during the period of 'prosperity'. But the division into these three periods does represent important changes in the type and intensity of the problems facing Governments and peoples. The following account will pay more attention to the first and third of these periods than to the second. The first is important, for it decided the lines on which the different States were to evolve for two decades. The third is still more important, for it marks the origin of the present situation.

1. POLAND

The German collapse found Poland with two Governments. Pilsudski had been released from prison when the Armistice was signed, and was entrusted with full powers by the Polish

INTERNATIONAL BOUNDARIES
(1918–1939)

Regency Council set up in 1916 by the Central Powers.* He formed a provisional Government in which the moderate Left predominated. At the same time the Allies had recognised the Polish National Committee in Paris, dominated by the Conservative Russophile Dmowski. This awkward situation was brought to an end by the mediation of the great Polish pianist Paderewski, who induced the Allies and the National Committee to recognise Pilsudski as head of the Government of Poland and himself and Dmowski as the Polish delegates at the Peace Conference. The legions of Haller returned from France to Poland, and recognised Pilsudski's authority. In January 1919 the first Sejm (Polish Parliament) was elected on a basis of universal suffrage.

The strongest single party in the Sejm were the National Democrats, Dmowski's followers, known in Poland as the 'Endeks'. They were the party of the Polish middle class, intensely nationalistic, socially Conservative and anti-Semitic. They were strongly Catholic, and throughout the twenty years of Polish independence they enjoyed more support from the Catholic Church than any other group. Their main strength lay in the western, formerly Prussian, regions. In this area before 1918 the Polish national movement had been led by the Catholic Church, and there had been few supporters of the Peasant or Socialist movements. After 1918 Prussian Poland voted fairly solidly for the Endeks.

The Endeks distrusted Pilsudski for a number of reasons. They considered him too revolutionary. They were shocked by his collaboration with Germany and Austria, which, until the Bolshevik Revolution, they regarded as more dangerous and implacable enemies than Russia. Above all, the personal rivalry between Pilsudski and Dmowski was a source of constant bitterness. Although as the years passed the political and ideological differences between the followers of Pilsudski and Dmowski dwindled almost to nothing, the hostility between the two groups remained as strong as ever.

The Polish Socialist Movement, like that of all other countries of Eastern Europe, split in two. Already before the Russian Revolution a part of the Socialists of Congress Poland had belonged to the 'Social Democracy of the Kingdom of Poland and Lithuania', a branch of the Russian Social Demo-

* See above, p. 54.

cratic Federation. This group of Polish Socialists was led by Rosa Luxemburg, and put the social revolution before the national independence of Poland. The majority of Polish Socialists were organised in the Polish Socialist Party (P.P.S.), which, as we have seen,* was above all a patriotic revolutionary party, dominated by the personality of Pilsudski. After the achievement of national independence the P.P.S. was forced to reconsider its attitude. Pilsudski openly abjured Socialism, and a number of former Socialists followed him. The bulk of the party was not, however, prepared simply to turn itself into a bourgeois nationalist organisation. It returned to its original Socialist programme, and remained in Opposition. Part of its following, attracted by Lenin's recognition of the principle of national self-determination, which contrasted with the unbending doctrinaire attitude formerly adopted by Rosa Luxemburg, joined the original adherents of the S.D.K.P.L. to form the Polish Communist Party.

The war with Russia in 1919–21 was a disappointment to the Polish Communists, for the Polish peasants and workers were unmoved by their revolutionary appeals, and took part in the fight against the Soviet forces with enthusiasm. The old hatred of Russia proved stronger than the social discontent caused by the economic confusion that followed the World War. The Polish Communist Party was made illegal after Pilsudski's victory and the ban was never lifted during the twenty years of Polish independence. The leaders lay low, or emigrated to Russia, and their followers ostensibly joined the P.P.S. It was consequently difficult to estimate the strength of Communism in Poland.

The Polish Peasant Movement was divided between the Piast and 'Wyzwolenie' ('Liberation') Parties. The leader of the former, Witos, had a great following in Galicia. He was a man of moderate views, prepared to compromise with anyone, and did not insist on quick changes, not even in the matter of Land Reform. The 'Wyzwolenie' Party inherited from the Russian Peasant Movement much more radical views, and pressed for revolutionary measures. For the first few years the two parties were on bad terms with each other.

The Polish Parliament reflected the deep divisions in the

* See above, pp. 48 and 69.

country. All Poles were united in their determination to guard Polish independence and to make life intolerable for those of their citizens whose loyalties were outside the Polish State. But on everything else they were divided. Personal issues played a dominant part in party squabbles, and difficulties were enormously increased by the fundamental difference in outlook between men of Austrian, Russian and Prussian upbringing.

The tasks facing the Parliament were terrifying. The war had devastated Poland, particularly the central and southern areas. The retreating Russians removed large quantities of industrial equipment and railway rolling stock, which were never recovered. Great numbers of Poles were deported into the interior of Russia, and only found their way back in a slow trickle after many months. The markets of Polish industry and agriculture were disorganised by the new frontiers in Western and Central Europe, and by the disappearance of Russia from World Trade. The Polish currency, connected with the German mark, suffered a catastrophic depreciation. The question of Land Reform had to be settled. The country needed a Constitution. Meanwhile unemployment was increasing, the harvest was bad, and the wretched peasants refused to pay badly needed taxes.

The Constitution was finally voted in 1921. It was based rather on the French than on the American model, and gave the chief powers to the legislature, while strictly limiting the authority of the President. Pilsudski strongly disapproved of this, declaring that he would never stand for the Presidency in order to become a mere cipher, and retired from public life to his country house, which soon became a centre for intrigues against Parliament. Land Reform was delayed by increasing squabbles. Although opposition to the principle of Reform was confined to a small group of Conservative landowners, the politicians could not agree concerning procedure and compensation. Witos was content with quite unambitious schemes. At last a law was passed, which provided for the gradual transfer of property from big landowners to peasants. A given quantity of land was to be divided each year, and the process was not to be completed for more than a decade. The financial crisis became increasingly acute, as the country entered upon a wild inflation. This was ended by the measures of the Endek

Finance Minister, Grabski, who stabilised a new currency, the zloty, at a very high parity.

Despite the unpleasant atmosphere of jealousy and re-crimination, the Polish Parliament had enacted a series of important measures of reconstruction. But the country was still in a parlous condition, and discontent was widespread. The burden of the deflationary policy inaugurated by Grabski fell most heavily on the poor. In 1925 Germany denounced her trade treaty with Poland, and caused a serious crisis in the Polish coal industry, the most important of the country. Meanwhile the old conspirator, Pilsudski, was plotting with his friends. Witos, now Prime Minister, had annoyed many people by his unprincipled manœuvring from one side to another, and was apparently quite unable to meet the needs of the moment. Pilsudski decided to act. In May 1926 he marched on Warsaw, met with little resistance, overthrew Witos and replaced the President of the Republic by a friend of his own, the scientist Mościcki. The period of Parliamentarism was over.

Pilsudski had made his *coup d'état* with the help of the army, of his friends the survivors of his war-time 'Legionaries', and of the Left. He was opposed by the Endeks and the Peasant Party. The Polish workers, suffering from the economic crisis and from bourgeois financial policy, put their hopes in the former Socialist leader. Even the Communists supported Pilsudski. Moscow's policy was at that moment to combine with the Social Democrats, and so the illegal Polish Party followed the P.P.S. Thus the change was carried out by a combination of the most democratic elements with the enemies of Democracy in the army and with the extreme Left.

Once installed, Pilsudski disappointed his Socialist well-wishers. The economic situation was improved, owing to the British coal strike, which gave the Polish coal industry new markets, and by a devaluation of the zloty carried out in the same year. But the political situation was not to the liking of the Left. Although the decision of the workers' leaders to give no support to the Government in the defence of Warsaw against the *coup d'état* had decided the issue in Pilsudski's favour, he showed little gratitude.

As soon as he was firmly in the saddle, he made overtures to the industrialists and the big landowners. The latter had hitherto played no part in the political life of the State. Pilsudski enlisted their support, and caused the process of land redistribution to be slowed up. From 1926 onwards names such as Radziwill and Potocki appear ever more frequently in the political life of the country. Although the big landowners never became the main force in Poland, they exercised an important influence in the direction of social Conservatism and political repression.

For the next nine years Pilsudski ruled Poland, part of the time openly and part of the time from behind the scenes. He was sometimes Prime Minister, always War Minister, and always in control of the army, of which he remained Inspector-General until his death. His nominees were placed in all the strategic positions of the Polish State, in the army, industry, the banks, the press. Critics of the regime said with some justification that Poland had been turned into a colony to provide lucrative jobs for former members of the Pilsudski Legions. Special bitterness was felt by those who had served in Haller's Legions in France. These men had fought no less bravely for Polish freedom, and had not allowed themselves to be exploited by the enemies of their country. But they had no share in the spoils monopolised by the Pilsudski group.

However much one may criticise the policy of the old Marshal, it is impossible to question his disinterested patriotism and his personal integrity. This cannot unfortunately be said of his companions. There were good men among them, but many were of extremely low quality. They formed a close 'Interessengemeinschaft' which ruled and robbed the country for thirteen years, and did much to bring about its ultimate downfall. By their hold on the army and the police, and by their exploitation of Pilsudski's enormous prestige with all classes of the Polish people, they maintained themselves in power to the end.

At first Pilsudski was tolerant towards the Sejm. He made it clear that policy was to be decided in the last resort by himself, but he allowed discussion and criticism of his measures. At the same time he encouraged the formation of a 'Non-Party Block' in Parliament and in the country. This 'Block' was in practice the Pilsudski Party. It was not based on any particular ideology or class. It won some support in all regions and all social strata. Its chief asset was the name of the

Marshal, and it was held together by the members of the gang. It won a relative majority in the elections of 1928, and as the Opposition was itself too disunited to threaten it, it ruled the country without trouble.

During 1929 and 1930 discontent in the country grew more violent. In Parliament the Opposition, led by the Endeks, went so far as to impeach the Finance Minister for having withheld from the public certain items of expenditure. In 1930 big demonstrations were held in Cracow. Pilsudski was alarmed, and decided on drastic measures. At the elections of 1930 the voters were terrorised by the police, and a number of the most eminent Opposition leaders were arrested, imprisoned at Brześć-Litowsk and maltreated. Witos escaped arrest and took refuge in Czechoslovakia, where he was obliged to remain until the eve of the present war. By these means the Government obtained a strong majority in Parliament.

From 1930 onwards the Polish Dictatorship was much more severe, but opposition was not entirely silenced. Speeches were made in Parliament against the regime, and independent newspapers, such as the Socialist *Robotnik* and the Endek *Poznanski Kurir*, expressed a limited criticism. The Government decided to change the Constitution, and thereby reduce the opportunities of interference by the Opposition. It is characteristic of the Pilsudski regime that this was done, not by mere force, but by correct Parliamentary procedure. After the proposals had been resisted by the Opposition, an opportunity occurred when the Opposition Deputies were accidentally absent from the House, and the new Constitution was hurriedly voted by a trick. It gave far greater powers to the President and the Government, and placed on a legal basis the limitation of the action of the legislature. The new Constitution came into force in April 1935.

During these years the administrative system was also revised, in a more centralist sense. The provincial Governors (Wojewodzi) and Prefects of Departments were nominated by the Ministry of the Interior, and controlled the bureaucratic machine. Mayors of towns were to be elected by the public, but the Prefects had a right to veto persons considered undesirable.

A few weeks after the coming into force of the new Constitution, on 12 May, Marshal Pilsudski died, and was mourned by almost the whole nation as her greatest modern son. The verdict of History will be given in course of time. Meanwhile all that can be said is that Pilsudski devoted his life to his country and never failed to put before his own comfort what he considered to be his country's interest. Whether his judgment of the country's interest was sound, and to what extent he can be blamed for the political stagnation and moral corruption which spread over Poland during the last years of his life and after his death, are questions much too complicated to answer in this hurried sketch.

The death of the Marshal deprived the Dictatorship of its Dictator. Power remained in the hands of the gang, which proceeded more rapidly to accumulate wealth and honours, free from the restraints imposed by the stern supervision of Pilsudski. The country was ruled by what was known as the 'Government of the Colonels'. The Colonels were former comrades-in-arms of Pilsudski, big bosses of the Legionaries. The most important were Slawek, the reactionary leader of the 'Non-Party Block'; Beck, the successor of the Francophile August Zaleski as Foreign Minister; and Koc, who represented the trend within the gang that favoured a 'totalitarian' system.

One of the first actions of the gang after the Marshal's death was to pass a law restricting the franchise. This was justified as a measure calculated to eliminate professional politicians from Parliament, and to make the next Sejm less partisan and more patriotic. The law, which was of course intended merely to preserve the monopoly of power in the hands of one particular set of professional politicians, was received with indignation by the Opposition, which ordered a boycott of the elections. These were held in the autumn of 1935, and only 46·5 % of the electorate took part in them, as opposed to 75 % in 1930. The Opposition rightly pointed out that the new Sejm was entirely unrepresentative. Acrimonious disputes raged outside the Sejm between Government and Opposition.

On the Opposition side the most violent abuse came from the Endeks. Picturesque language was used by both sides. Government spokesmen declared that their only aim was to give Poland a new 'élite'. The Endeks had little difficulty in exposing the moral and intellectual quality of the self-constituted élite, and meanwhile poured forth fervent professions of democratic faith, while encouraging students and other toughs to beat up Jews and Socialists. The truth was that the fundamental question in Polish politics was not 'Freedom or Authority?', 'Democracy or Leadership?' or 'Strong Government or Popular Rule?' but 'Which gang shall rule the rest?' Unfortunately for the Endeks the Colonels and their friends managed to keep their grip on the substance of power to the end.

Poland was badly hit by the Depression. Polish exports and imports fell between 1929 and 1934 by 300 % and 400 % respectively (measured by value in zloty). The Government adopted a policy of rigid deflation, weighing most heavily, as usual, on the poorer peasants and on the industrial workers. Unemployment rose between 1931 and 1934 from 220,000 to 414,000.[1] The State budget was reduced by 30 %. Discontent grew among the industrial working class, which had increased considerably in numbers and importance since 1918. The number of workers organised in Trade Unions in 1935 approached a million. Of these the greater part were connected with the Social Democratic Party, although in Silesia and Poznania the Catholic Trade Unions were fairly strong. The economic crisis created among the workers an increasingly radical frame of mind. In 1936 there was a series of strikes in Cracow, Lódź and Upper Silesia. The leaders of the P.P.S. remained cautious and moderate, but the rank and file of the party grew more willing to listen to extreme doctrines. Although the absence of an open Communist Party made it difficult to judge, people of long experience, Poles and foreigners, estimated that illegal Communism was gaining ground even among purely Polish workers.

A radical mood was also to be observed among the peasants. In 1930, after the Brześć arrests, the Piast and Wyzwolenie groups had united to form a single Popular Party ('Stromnictwo Ludowe'). During the following decade the economic situation of the Polish peasantry steadily deteriorated. It was especially severe in Galicia, where overpopulation was more

---

[1] Buell, *Poland, key to Europe*. I am indebted to this book for a number of the details contained in this survey. The unemployment figures quoted refer, of course, only to industry. The agricultural unemployment caused by the Depression and by the more general causes summarised in Chapter Five above, never found its way into official statistics.

acute than in any other large region in Europe. Moreover, the Galician peasant had a much higher cultural level, and used more rational agricultural methods, than the greater part of the Eastern European peasantry, so that further intensification could promise much less than in more backward regions. The root of the trouble was sheer pressure of the population on the land.

The political Dictatorship, the impossibility of bringing complaints to the ears of the authorities, the apparent indifference of the Government to the fate of the peasants, the slowness of the Land Reform, and the brutality of the administration, were all causes of discontent. The result was that Galicia, the main strength of the Peasant Movement, and formerly a centre of Conservatism, became the most radical part of the whole country.

Government spokesmen talked of 'Communism'. In fact it is doubtful whether there was ever much sympathy for Communist ideas among the Polish peasantry, but there is no doubt that there was a growth of revolutionary feeling. The younger members of the Popular Party pressed for a union of all uncompromisingly democratic forces in the country, and this corresponded with the policy of the Popular Front advocated from 1935 to 1939 by Moscow. In Poland this policy took the practical form of a closer collaboration between the Popular and Social Democratic Parties. Such influence as the illegal Communist Movement possessed in village and factory was thrown into the agitation for peasant-worker collaboration, and although the old leaders of both parties maintained an attitude of suspicious reserve, the degree of collaboration achieved was considerable.

In general it may be argued that the peasants were a more revolutionary force than the workers. The Youth Organisation of the Popular Party ('Wici') urged most radical reforms, especially the division of the big estates, the extension of the cooperatives, and the control of political affairs by the peasantry. At the same time the Soviet system of Kolhozy was expressly repudiated. The 'Wici' group insisted that the Polish peasant had always been the mainstay of Polish independence and greatness, and should therefore have a decisive voice in the country's policy. They drew a convincing comparison between the selfish policy of the 'szlachta', which had brought Poland to her ruin in the seventeenth and eighteenth centuries, and that of the Colonels' regime, which was ruining public morals within Poland, and lowering Polish prestige abroad.[1]

During the same period a similar process of radicalisation could be observed in the ranks of the Endeks, but in this case the trend was not to the Left but to the Right. The young generation of educated and semi-educated middle-class families suffered heavily from the Depression. They finished their studies to find that there was no place for them in the free professions or commercial life. They noticed the predominance in both of the Jewish element. To the traditional emotional dislike of the Jews was now added an economic motive. The industrialisation of the preceding decade had already accentuated the rivalry between the Polish and Jewish bourgeoisies, but the Economic Depression and the widespread unemployment of young 'intellectuals' greatly increased it. The younger generation, and especially that part which supported the Endeks, became a prey to anti-Semitic agitation, and passed from anti-Semitism to hatred of Democracy as such and admiration of Fascism. In 1934 a group of young Fascists, discontented with Dmowski's Conservative mentality and methods, broke off from the Endeks. In 1937 this group united with other Fascist groups to form the National Radical ('Nara') Party, which proclaimed a full Nazi programme, and organised acts of hooliganism.

The Government veered from one side to the other. In the autumn of 1935, after the 'successful' elections, Slawek declared that as the aim of a 'non-party' Sejm had been achieved, there was no further need for the Non-Party Block, and accordingly pronounced that organisation dissolved. In October the President called upon Mr Kościalkowski to form a Government. This Government showed a tendency towards reform and greater freedom. Attempts were made to relieve unemployment and to provide public works.[2] An ambitious programme of State enterprise in industry was launched, the main point of which was the creation of the Central Industrial Region mentioned in the preceding chapter. The wave of

---

[1] These views are expounded, for example, in a pamphlet *Walka o nowa Polske* by Milkowski, a member of the 'Wici' group, Warsaw, 1937.

[2] For details see Buell, *op. cit.*

strikes in the next year, however, caused the Government to resign, and it was succeeded by that of General Skladkowski, a friend of Marshal Smigly-Rydż, Pilsudski's successor as Inspector-General of the army.

The new Government relieved the economic situation by defaulting on Poland's foreign debts and introducing exchange control. In the political field it inclined towards a more totalitarian course. At the beginning of 1937 was formed the Camp of National Unity ('Ozon'), a new Government Party led by Colonel Koc, consciously modelled on the totalitarian parties of Fascist countries. A Youth Group was formed called the Union of Young Poland, which aimed at outbidding the 'Naras' in anti-Semitic demagogy.

In August 1937 the Polish peasants organised a strike. They refused to bring their products to the towns, in a desperate attempt to obtain the attention of the Government to their needs. In some of the big towns the workers declared strikes of solidarity. The Government sent the police into the villages and suppressed the strike by force. There were a number of armed conflicts, and the dead were certainly more than the forty-two admitted by the Government. The strike made a deep impression at home and abroad. It showed that the masses in town and country were hostile to the Government, and it was even believed in more than one neighbouring capital that Poland was on the verge of civil war.

The Government decided on a more Liberal policy. Nazi phrases were less frequently used in official speeches. Colonel Koc resigned the leadership of 'Ozon'. The Minister of Agriculture, Poniatowski, began seriously to tackle the problem of Land Reform. The Government devoted attention to propaganda in the villages, attempting to organise governmental peasant Youth Groups, to compete with 'Wici'. In this it was unsuccessful, but there was general recognition of Poniatowski's good intentions. In 1938 intrigues by Slawek within the Government camp caused some alarm, and the President decided to adopt a pronounced Liberal attitude. Impressed by the strength of public opinion, he promised electoral reform and declared the desire of the Government to comply with 'the people's will'.

The elections were held before the execution of the promised electoral reform, and consequently gave the Government a better majority than it could otherwise have expected; 65 % of the voters took part. But the complacence of the Government received a hard blow in December, when municipal elections were held in fifty-two cities. These elections were comparatively free from pressure, and gave the Opposition 639 seats and the Government 383. The elections were a victory for the Socialists rather than for the Endeks, who gained only in the west. The 'Naras' were powerless outside Warsaw.

Knowledge of the strength of democratic feeling in the country undoubtedly influenced the Government to adopt a stubborn attitude towards Nazi claims in 1939. But the deepening of the international crisis did not bring about any political change. It might have been expected that in the greatest danger that ever faced the Polish nation the Government would have wished to strengthen itself by incorporating some representatives of public opinion. The contrary was the case. Witos was at last allowed to return to Poland, but this was the limit of concessions. Well knowing that the Polish people was too patriotic to make serious trouble at such a time, the gang continued to enjoy the good things of life, exploiting the patience of its victims. The international crisis was a perfect excuse for doing nothing. Confident of their hold on army and police, 'cleverly' playing off against each other the different sections of the Opposition, the bosses of the regime prayed that the crisis would last as long as possible, and meanwhile made small preparations either on the home front or on the frontiers.

This happy game was brought abruptly to an end by Adolf Hitler. Militarily and morally unprepared, the Polish people, which had deserved better rulers, offered the German invader a heroic resistance, which it never gave up. A part of the Polish army passed through Roumania and Hungary to France, England and Egypt, and fought most bravely beside its Allies. Still more Polish soldiers, taken prisoner by the Russian invaders, were released from captivity to form further regiments in the army of the United Nations. Besides these some politicians and officials who were lucky enough to get into a car with petrol, escaped into exile. But the bulk of the Polish nation remained behind, and has carried on for longer than any of the suffering nations of Europe, and perhaps with greater courage than any, the unequal struggle with the Nazi murder bands. Now Poland has been liberated, but years of labour will be needed to rebuild her. Friends of the Polish people can at least be sure that it will spare no efforts in its struggle to create conditions of greater liberty and social justice than it knew in the past.

2. CZECHOSLOVAKIA

The legal existence of the Czechoslovak State began on 14 October 1918, when the Czechoslovak National Council in Paris was recognised as Provisional Government by the Allies. Two weeks later the Czechoslovak National Committee in Prague proclaimed the independence of the Historic Lands of Bohemia and Moravia. On the following day (29 October) a meeting of Slovak political leaders at the small town of Turčiansky Svätý Martin declared that there is one single Czechoslovak nation, and that the land of the Slovaks shall form part of a common Czechoslovak State.

Soon after this a National Assembly was set up in Prague, consisting of men chosen by the executive committees of the principal political parties. As Prime Minister was chosen Karel Kramář, the veteran leader of the former Young Czech Party, who had been condemned to death in 1915 by the Austrian Government, but subsequently reprieved. Dr Kramář was the most distinguished of Czech professional politicians, and had become a national hero. From Paris came Dr Beneš, who became Foreign Minister in the Government, and held that post in all subsequent Governments for seventeen years. Later returned the Czechoslovak Legionaries from Russia, after a successful retreat through Siberia, Japan and the United States, led by the greatest living Czech, Professor T. G. Masaryk, who was enthusiastically acclaimed as the President of the Republic.

The Kramář Government was faced with two main problems, financial reorganisation and Land Reform. The first was capably handled by the Finance Minister, Alois Rašin. The old depreciated Austrian Crowns were rapidly called in, and a new Czechoslovak Crown was established. Rašin did not confine himself to deflation, but supplemented his measures of 'economy' by a capital levy, thus distributing the burden more equally among the social classes. It is clear in retrospect that he did his country good service, but this did not save him from unpopularity. In 1923 he was assassinated by a young Communist.

The Land Question, for which the Agrarian Party pressed with special vigour, was tackled by a Reform Law which decreed the division of the large estates, and set up a Land Office to redistribute the land. The Reform was not realised immediately, and it was never so radical in fact as it appeared on paper, but it made an important contribution to social peace and national unity.

In June 1919 municipal elections were held in the Republic. Kramář's party suffered a reverse, and the strongest party were the Social Democrats. Kramář therefore resigned, and Tusar, the Social Democrat leader, formed a Government. Early in 1920 the first parliamentary elections were held, which confirmed the supremacy of the Socialists. Soon after this, however, came the split in the Social Democratic Party, the majority seceding to form the Czechoslovak Communist Party, led by Šmeral, a moderate Socialist who in Habsburg days had opposed the nationalist trend in the Czech Social Democratic Party, and now grouped round him that part of the working class which, national independence achieved, showed impatience with the moderate leadership of the official party.[1] Tusar was obliged to resign, and the Socialist Party was still further weakened two months later by an abortive general strike, launched in connection with a dispute between Social Democrats and Communists for the possession of the Prague building which formed the headquarters of the party and of the working-class movement.

Tusar was succeeded by a 'Cabinet of Officials'. From September 1920 to October 1922 two non-party Governments ruled the country, with the qualified support of most groups in Parliament, the first being led by Dr Jan Černy, the second by Dr Eduard Beneš, Foreign Minister en permanence. In 1922 the Agrarian leader Švehla formed a Government.

The Czechoslovak Parliament bristled with small parties, made possible by the system of Proportional Representation. But a comparatively small number had any real importance.

The National Democrat Party, led by Dr Kramář, was the

[1] See Borkenau, The Communist International.

successor to the Young Czech Party of Habsburg days, and in some ways the equivalent of the Endeks in Poland. It was strongly nationalist, implacably hostile to the Germans and other National Minorities, and equally opposed to Socialism. It represented the wealthy established bourgeoisie. Unlike the Endeks, it was anti-Clerical, for the Catholic Church was regarded as pro-Austrian and therefore hostile to the Republic. The National Democrats lost ground to other parties during the following decade.

The National Socialist Party had been founded at the end of the nineteenth century in opposition to the Young Czechs and Social Democrats. It stood between these two. It was firmly attached to democratic institutions, and violently nationalistic. It differed from the older National Democrats in advocating social reforms. It was in no sense a Nazi Party, having chosen its name long before Hitler made himself known to the world. It had a following in all classes of the population, particularly in the middle class, and it always had a substantial number of seats in Parliament. It included a number of distinguished Czech intellectuals, among them Foreign Minister Beneš.

The Social Democrats had a strong hold on the Czech working class, and after a few years acquired a following also in Slovakia. The German and Hungarian Social Democratic Parties of Czechoslovakia, however, remained independent, and only began to collaborate in the later years. The split of 1920 gave a majority to the Communists, and this was confirmed by the elections of 1925, which returned a much smaller number of Social Democratic members. The Communists retained their political rights throughout the history of the Republic. Their following was not confined to the industrial workers, for they won considerable support among the poor and backward peasants of Slovakia and Ruthenia. The Czechoslovak Communist Party included also Germans and Hungarians. In the elections of 1929 the Social Democrats recovered some ground at the expense of the Communists, who again slightly increased their following in 1935.

The Czech Agrarian Party had existed even before the First World War, although it was less important than the others. In the Republic it soon won a large number of votes. It broadened its national basis by uniting with the Slovak

Agrarians to form the Czechoslovak Republican Party. Although this remained its official title until the end of the Republic, it continued to be known as the Agrarian Party. Its main support was the Czech peasantry and provincial bourgeoisie. The Czech peasants consisted largely of medium holders or big farmers. They had efficient cooperatives and marketing organisations, modern agricultural equipment and a high standard of education. They were able through the Agrarian Party to exercise a considerable political influence.

The Agrarian Party was always in power in Czechoslovakia. Under its able leader, Antonín Švehla, it took part in coalition after coalition, often succeeding by its varied political manœuvres in deciding Cabinet crises to its own advantage. It was the dominant party in the history of independent Czechoslovakia. Its political success attracted to it various elements that had little in common with the peasant class. The National Minorities found that it was to their advantage to vote for it rather than for the specific Minority Parties, since, being as constantly in office as the Minority Parties were out, it was in a position to offer personal material advantages to all its supporters. Thus the Agrarian Party lost before long its character of a specifically peasant party, and became an 'Interessengemeinschaft' of people eager for political and economic spoils.

It would be a mistake to imagine that there is any real resemblance between the Agrarians in Czechoslovakia and the 'Legionary' gang in Poland. The Czechoslovak group did not monopolise power: they only secured a permanent hold on a part of its advantages. Moreover, they were devoted to the traditional conception of Parliamentary Democracy and political liberty, and most of their leaders were probably superior from the moral point of view to the Polish bosses. But it is important to note that they ceased to be a class party of the peasantry. They continued to defend the interests of the comfortable farmers of the Czech Lands, but they paid little attention to the needs of the small holders of the eastern provinces. And as time went on the urban bourgeoisie acquired increasing influence in the party. The National Democrats, at first the party of the industrial and commercial class, lost many of their supporters to the Agrarians. During the last years of the Republic the Agrarian Party had become the main party of capital. Such highly capitalist enterprises as the Živnostenská Banka, the largest Credit institution of the country, played a big part in it.[1]

Conditions in Slovakia were very different from those in the Czech Lands, and the contrast between them is one of the main factors in the history of the Republic. The meeting of Turčiansky Svätý Martin had received the approval of all important Slovak leaders, but it must be stressed that these politically conscious Slovaks were only a minority. The Slovak people was both economically and politically primitive. The social conditions of pre-war Hungary had created discontent, but there was little conscious Slovak nationalism, still less a feeling of common Czechoslovak nationhood. In 1918 most, but not all, Slovaks were probably glad to be rid of the Hungarians, but they regarded the new Republic with little more than bewildered expectancy.

The Czechoslovak idea had been mainly represented in Slovakia by the Lutherans. It received support among a section of the Slovak émigrés in the United States. Among the Czechs it was urged by Masaryk, himself a Slovak from Moravia, who discussed it during his stay in the United States, on the way back from Siberia, in 1918. On 30 June 1918 was signed the famous Pittsburg Agreement, in which Masaryk on behalf of the Czechs promised the Slovak émigrés, on behalf of the Slovak people, a Slovak Diet, autonomous administration and law courts, and the use of the Slovak language as official language in public affairs and schools in Slovakia.

As soon as the Republic was established, and the last Hungarian invasion of Slovakia had been repelled, the trouble began. There was a striking lack of qualified men available for administrative work in Slovakia, and it was inevitable that many places should be occupied by Czechs. The new Czech officials differed in mentality from the Slovaks, and their Liberal, free-thinking outlook caused offence to the devout Catholic population. Moreover the Government in Prague did not seem at all eager to introduce the promised political autonomy. On the contrary, a policy of Centralisa-

[1] The Živnostenská Banka started as a savings bank for small bourgeois and rich peasants, but by the thirties of this century it had become a major capitalist concern.

tion was pursued, and official speeches referred constantly to a single 'Czechoslovak nation'.

In these circumstances the Slovak nationalists split into two parties. The National Party led by Šrobar and Hodža favoured a strongly Czechoslovak policy, although demanding a rather greater measure of decentralisation than as yet existed. The National Party soon afterwards merged with the Agrarian (Czechoslovak Republican) Party, and Hodža ultimately became leader of the whole party in the Republic.

The intransigent autonomists formed themselves into the Slovak People's Party, under the leadership of Father Andrew Hlinka. This turbulent priest surpassed the most chauvinist Czechs in his hatred of Hungary, but reserved some of his most virulent diatribes, often stimulated by copious draughts of šlivovica, for the godless Czechs and their impious Republic. The People's Party was based on the Catholic priesthood and rural bourgeoisie, and had a considerable hold on the peasantry. It was anti-Democratic, anti-Semitic and anti-Socialist. Its general outlook and programme can be compared with the Clerical Fascist Movements of Austria, Spain and Portugal.

In the 1920 elections half the Slovak vote went to the Left, and the other half was fairly equally divided between the National Party and the People's Party. The split in the Labour Movement and the union of the National Party with the Czechoslovak Agrarians notably changed the situation, and at the 1925 elections Hlinka had nearly half the Slovak votes, while the other half was divided between the Agrarians and the Left, of which the Communists had three-quarters. In the 1929 and 1935 elections the People's Party retained about the same number of votes, but a lower percentage. The Agrarians and the Left together had more than half, and of these the Left was the stronger, especially in 1935. Of the two Left parties the Communists were the stronger, but the margin between them and the Social Democrats was reduced in comparison with 1925.

Hlinka, then, never had a clear majority of the Slovaks behind him. But this, as Mr C. A. Macartney rightly points out,[1] does not necessarily mean that the majority of the Slovaks were in favour of a centralist Czechoslovak Republic. The elections were not fought on the issue of Autonomy versus

[1] *Hungary and her successors*, Oxford, 1937.

Centralism, and material advantages were to be gained by voting for the Czechoslovak parties, especially for the always-in-office Agrarians. In fact, apart from the small and cultured Lutheran minority, most Slovaks who voted for the democratic Czechoslovak parties were probably opportunists. Those who felt most strongly were usually Autonomists or Communists.

The main grievance of the political class in Slovakia was the failure to implement the promise of Autonomy. Resentment was felt at the presence of Czech officials. That these were necessary at the beginning, no serious person could doubt. But the Slovaks maintained that many minor posts could perfectly well have been filled by Slovaks, and that the whole Czechoslovak bureaucratic apparatus was too large and cumbrous and expensive, and existed mainly to provide jobs for unwanted Czechs. There was probably some justification for these complaints, but it should be pointed out that the number of Slovaks in public administration steadily increased, that a new generation of Slovak intellectuals was trained in a way that would have been quite impossible under Hungary, and that a large part of this new generation genuinely accepted the 'Czechoslovak idea'. Even so, many remained irreconcilable, and their material grounds for complaint were reinforced by the influence of the Catholic priests, offended by the anti-Clericalism of the Czechs. The *modus vivendi* between Prague and the Vatican did not entirely reassure Slovak Catholics, who were frightened by the prospect that their children might learn in the schools the odious principles of Democracy and Critical Thought. The People's Party embodied these fears and suspicions, and continued to agitate for Autonomy and against collaboration with the Czechs.

In 1928 appeared an article by Professor Tuka, one of the leaders of the Party, asserting that the Proclamation of Turčiansky Svätý Martin had contained a secret clause stating that the Union was only valid for ten years. Tuka argued that, as the promised Autonomy had not been granted, there was now a *vacuum juris*, and the Slovak people had the right to secede. A storm of protest broke out against Tuka, who was arrested and tried for high treason. The trial revealed that he was in touch with Hungary and plotting the disruption of the Republic. He was condemned to the surprisingly severe penalty of fourteen years' imprisonment.

After this spokesmen of the People's Party used more cautious language, but they did not cease to be hostile to the Republic. At the same time they made it clear that they had no desire to return to Hungary. When in 1933 a renegade Slovak priest, Jehlička, accompanied Count Bethlen on a propaganda tour in England, a letter was signed by all Slovak Senators and Deputies of the Prague Parliament other than Communists, disowning Jehlička as a traitor to Slovakia. Yet in the same year, at a big political meeting at Nitra, Hlinka made a demagogic speech, loudly cheered, declaring 'There are no Czechoslovaks. We wish only to be Slovaks.'

Political, administrative and ideological factors affected mainly the Slovak bourgeoisie, but the economic troubles of the country touched the lives of the whole Slovak people. The Slovak iron and textile industries, created under the Hungarian regime, were cut off from their market in Budapest. Iron ore from Slovakia was used to some extent by the heavy industry of the Czech Lands, but the cost of transport was a heavy burden, somewhat relieved as better railway connections were established from east to west. The ironworks, on the other hand, were condemned to stagnation, for they could not compete with the metallurgical industry of Bohemia. They fell into the hands of Czech banks, and were eventually closed down.

These losses mainly affected the industrial workers, but the peasants also suffered severely from the dislocation created by the new frontiers. The inhabitants of the unproductive mountain regions of Slovakia used before 1918 to find work as agricultural labourers in the Hungarian plain. Now, although Czechoslovakia had helped herself to a liberal chunk of the plain, most of this employment was cut off. A large proportion of the peasantry of Slovakia made their living, not from cultivation but from the forests, which supplied the former Hungary with much of her timber. During the first years of the Republic this trade continued, if on a reduced scale. In 1930, however, the Czechoslovak-Hungarian Trade Treaty was denounced and, in accordance with the wish of the Agrarian Party, a policy of strict agricultural protection was adopted. Such a policy raises farming prices, but, as has been seen in Chapter Four, it does not benefit the majority of the agricultural population.

In Slovakia small holdings predominated, whereas in the Czech Lands prosperous medium farms were numerous and even the small holdings were so rationally exploited as to assure a fairly high standard of living. A rise of agricultural prices benefited the Czech peasants, who were interested in the big agricultural markets of the country. The backward Slovak small holders, however, like those of Poland, Roumania and the Balkans, did not produce for the market, but had to buy part of their food. Those engaged in forestry, and the agricultural landless labourers—whom the Czechoslovak Land Reform had by no means fully provided for—had to buy everything. At the same time the denunciation of the Treaty deprived the Slovak forests of their market. The consequence was widespread misery in the lower, and more numerous, strata of the peasant population.

The difference in the standard of living of the Czech and Slovak peasantry grew every year owing to the much higher birthrate of the Slovaks and the absence of employment. Thus the problems of overpopulation and underemployment were little less acute in Slovakia than in the other Eastern European countries. The political stability and freedom of the Republic, and the high standard of living of its Czech majority, hardly concealed the fact that its eastern half was on the same level as Poland, Roumania and the Balkans. The social discontent of the Slovak peasantry and working class caused revolutionary feeling, which was canalised partly by the Communists and partly by Hlinka's demagogic Catholic Nationalism.

The most backward province of Czechoslovakia was its eastern extremity, 'Sub-Carpathian Ruthenia'. The inhabitants were primitive Slav mountaineers, who spoke a number of dialects akin to Ukrainian, Russian, Polish and Slovak. They were divided in religion between the Orthodox and Uniate Churches. The commercial and educated class consisted almost exclusively of Jews and Hungarians before 1918. A few Ruthenes acquired some education, and these were easily attracted to Hungarian culture, and thus willingly accepted Magyarisation. The Uniate clergy was pro-Magyar. During the last years before the First World War nationalism had begun to find its way into the remote Ruthene villages.

Three currents contended with each other, proclaiming respectively Great Russia, Great Ukrainian and local Ruthene nationalism. The majority of the population remained passive, and showed no special desire to separate from Hungary, even responding to Jászi's belated offers to the Hungarian nationalities in November 1918.

The ambition of independence from Hungary was almost wholly confined to emigrants in the United States. These discussed with Masaryk in 1918 the possibility of the incorporation of Ruthenia in the Czechoslovak Republic. In October 1918 the Philadelphia Agreement was signed by Masaryk and by the American Ruthene Žatković, promising autonomy for the Ruthenes as Czechoslovak citizens, and a western boundary to the province which would take in certain regions of Slovakia inhabited principally by Ruthenes.

The confusion caused in Hungary by the Kun regime and the uncompromising attitude of the Poles towards the movement for Ukrainian independence in Eastern Galicia inclined the few 'intellectuals' of Ruthenia towards the Czechoslovak solution, which was urged by Žatković, who came to Europe for the purpose. To these persuasive arguments was added the occupation of Ruthenia's main town, Užhorod, by Czech troops. On 8 May 1919 a Central National Council, presided over by the Uniate priest Vološin, proclaimed the unity of the province with Czechoslovakia.[1]

The Ruthene autonomists were disappointed by events. The promised autonomy was never granted, and in fact no serious attempt was made to realise it. In 1920 Žatković was made Governor of the province, with a Czech Vice-Governor, but, discouraged by the hesitant attitude of Prague, he resigned in the following year. The process of centralisation was pushed ahead. Czech officials flocked into the country, and even Czech colonists benefited from the Land Reform in place of Ruthene peasants. In 1927 the Administrative Law placed Ruthenia on the same footing as Bohemia, Moravia, and Slovakia. All that remained of the projected autonomy was the title of Governor held by the head of the Administration.

---

[1] For this section on Ruthenia, a province which I have never personally visited, I am indebted, apart from conversations with Czech, Roumanian and Hungarian friends, mainly to Macartney, *op. cit.*, to which the reader is referred for further details.

In fact the country was so backward, and its people so lacking in political feeling, that it is highly questionable whether autonomy would have been possible. To put a country in the hands of a few semi-educated, ambitious demagogues is not always the best way to ensure its prosperity. The Czechs can therefore to some extent be pardoned for breaking their word. There is no doubt that the province derived substantial benefits from Czech rule. The administration was honest and conscientious, communications were improved, and better schools were made available than could have been dreamed of before the war of 1914.

Unfortunately, the economic situation was bad, and remained bad. Hungary, the natural market of Ruthenian timber, which used to be floated down the rivers into the plain, was cut off, particularly after 1930. The pressure of the population on the wretched land grew every year. The Ruthene peasants did not find employment in other parts of the Republic, for the Slovaks, suffering from similar if less acute problems, were sufficiently superior in skill to exclude them from the labour market. The strip of plainland in the south of the province was in the hands of Czechs, Jews and Hungarians, and the Slovaks refused to give Ruthenia the eastern districts of Slovakia inhabited by Ruthenes, as they had promised in 1918.

The development of schools during the twenty years of the Republic greatly increased the numbers of the 'intelligentsia' of Ruthenia. Of the three nationalist currents that we have noticed, the 'Ruthene' almost disappeared among the educated class. The peasants may still have called themselves 'Ruthenes' or 'Rusins', but this was no more a sign of Ruthene nationalism than when an Englishman calls himself a Yorkshireman. The Great Russian trend continued to exist, but lost ground, being regarded by the younger generation as out of date, since it was connected with a Russia which had been destroyed once and for all. The Ukrainian current was the strongest, and was fostered by the Uniate priesthood, which abandoned its former Magyar sympathies in favour of the views of the Uniate exiles from Polish Galicia, whom the Czechoslovak authorities allowed to settle in the Republic.

The strongest political parties in Ruthenia were Czecho slovak parties. Here, however, the same must be said as in the case of Slovakia, that this may have been largely due to opportunist considerations, and does not prove that the majority was against autonomy or even positively wished for the survival of the Czechoslovak State. The most powerful of the parties was the Communist, which is easily explained by poverty and pro-Russian feeling. The second was the Agrarian Party, which even slightly surpassed the Communists in the 1929 elections, but fell behind once more in 1935.

There were two specifically Ruthene parties, the Agrarian Opposition and the Fenzig Party. The former was Democratic, and supported autonomy and social measures to benefit the peasantry. The latter had Fascist sympathies, urged anti-Semitic measures and had close relations with Poland. Both obtained substantial numbers of votes at the elections, but neither competed seriously with the two Czechoslovak parties.

By 1922 the influence of the Socialist Movement in Czechoslovakia had appreciably declined, and government was henceforth carried on by party coalitions, in which the increasingly Conservative Agrarians predominated. The next seven years were overshadowed by the figure of Švehla, the clever political tactician, who secured to himself the chief role by skilful bargains, promises and threats. From 1922 to 1925 he ruled with the Socialists, from 1926 to 1929 against them. During these years the currency, which after Rašin's reforms had again begun to totter mildly, was stabilised, Agriculture was supported, cooperatives were encouraged, and social insurance laws were passed.

In 1925 a rupture was caused in the relations of Prague and the Vatican by the departure of the Papal Nuncio from the capital in protest against the nation-wide celebrations of the death of Hus, in which Government and President took part. The Nuncio's action provoked an outburst of anti-Clericalism in the Czech Lands, the Catholic religion being identified in the minds of many with the hated German-Austrians. The Czechoslovak representative at the Vatican was recalled, the breach further increasing the friction between Czechs and Slovaks.

The elections of 1925 returned a small number of Social Democrats, the majority of the working-class votes having been given to the Communists, with whom no party was able or willing to cooperate. Švehla again became Prime Minister, but retired owing to illness, leaving the Government to Černy and a non-party team. The Socialists withdrew from the Cabinet owing to their opposition to tariffs, which weighed most heavily on working-class consumers.

During 1926 Švehla returned to form another Government, from which the Socialists were altogether excluded, but in which for the first time Germans participated, in the person of the German Agrarian and Christian Social leaders. In the following year even Hlinka's Party entered the Government, and in 1928 the quarrel with the Vatican was made up by a *modus vivendi* which gave the Czechoslovak Government the powers which it desired in relation to the Catholic Church. The *modus vivendi* did much to improve Czech-Slovak relations, but the Tuka case in 1929 caused a further deterioration.

The 1929 elections brought an increase of the Socialist vote, and from 1929 to 1932 an Agrarian-Socialist coalition again held power. This time the German Social Democrats, who had hitherto remained aside, joined the coalition. During these years the World Depression hit Czechoslovakia. Particularly severe was the unemployment in the industrial districts. Although the money spent on Social Services was not appreciably reduced, the Government's financial policy was one of deflation, and caused widespread discontent. The situation was somewhat relieved by devaluation of the Crown in 1934. In the same year were created the Grain Monopoly and the State Export Institute, intended to safeguard internal cereal prices and to help industrial exports.

The most striking feature of the 1935 elections was the rise of a new German Party, the Sudetendeutsche Partei, formed from the 'Sudetendeutsche Heimatfront', founded in the preceding year under the leadership of a young gymnastic instructor, Konrad Henlein. This party professed loyalty to the Republic and respect for democratic principles, but it disseminated Nazi views among the German community in Czechoslovakia. In 1935 it had the second largest number of seats of all parliamentary groups, being surpassed only by the Agrarians. The continuance of the economic crisis, which affected most severely the centres of German industry in Bohemia, and the successes of Reich foreign policy, caused the Sd.P. to adopt an increasingly aggressive tone. For the last four years of the Republic, Czechoslovak politics were dominated by the question of the German minority, itself influenced mainly by international events. These matters, and the events which led to the collapse of Czechoslovakia, will be considered in a later chapter.

Czechoslovakia differs from all the other States of Eastern Europe in that she was able to preserve democratic institutions until the end. This remarkable achievement requires some examination. The balance between bourgeoisie, working class and peasantry saved Czechoslovakia from the onesidedness and social strains which proved fatal to the Balkan States. But Austria, whose social structure closely resembled that of Czechoslovakia, after a short period of Socialist rule which forms a parallel to Czechoslovak experience, soon relapsed into Reaction and Dictatorship.

The difference between Austrian and Czechoslovak politics can be partly explained by the greater prosperity of Czechoslovakia, which did not suffer so severely as Austria either in the immediate post-war period or during the World Depression. Another important factor is the absence of Catholic political influence. In the Czech Lands the Catholic political party, led by Monsignor Šramek, accepted Democracy, while the Hlinka party was always too weak to exercise perceptible influence as long as Slovakia was subordinated to the Czech Lands. In Austria, on the other hand, the Catholic influence of the Christian Social Party, under Mgr Seipel, dominated the country and imposed a reactionary policy, developing under Dollfuss and Stahremberg into a bloody class Dictatorship. The Czechs are formally considered a Catholic people, but they have been always influenced by the ideas of Hus, which imply political as well as religious liberty. Moreover, although economic conflicts between Czech bourgeois and workers were no less than those between Austrians, the Czech ruling class never resorted to violent repression.

This is in great part due to the Liberal and humanitarian tradition of the Czech people, represented by all its greatest thinkers. It was personified in the modern Czechoslovak Republic by the President-Liberator, Thomas Masaryk. This truly great man was for half a century a prophet of his people. More than once he made himself unpopular by standing up against militant ignorance, prejudice and chauvinism, but in the end his people realised that he was right, and repaid him with a veneration and love which few statesmen have received. During his last years he constantly used his influence in favour of Democracy, and the feeble attempts to propagate Fascism among the Czechs, made by General Gajda, were crushed without force by the authority of the President's name. As a professor in Prague before 1914 Masaryk had been the political and moral educator of generations of young men not only from the Czech Lands but from all the Slav countries of Europe. His death in 1937 spared him the sight of his country's ruin. He was mourned by his own nation and by friends of human freedom in the whole world.

Czechoslovakia had many faults. Leaving aside altogether the vexed question of National Minorities, there is no doubt that the condition of Slovakia and Ruthenia left much to be desired, even if progress had been made. But this was the only State east of Switzerland and south of the Baltic which for twenty years preserved political liberties and progressive social institutions. Its fall was not only a strategical but a moral loss to all Europe.

3. HUNGARY

Two weeks before Austria-Hungary formally laid down arms, on 16 October 1918, the Hungarian Prime Minister, Wekerle, declared the dissolution of the Union between Austria and Hungary. After a further two weeks Wekerle, too much associated with the unpopular war and the Habsburg regime, was succeeded by the democratic Count Michael Károlyi, who became Prime Minister on 2 November. On the 13th Charles of Habsburg surrendered the reins of government, though without abdicating, and the country became a Republic.

Count Károlyi was an aristocrat of advanced democratic views. He had always opposed the war, and he had made himself widely known as a friend of the Entente and an enthusiast for the ideas of President Wilson. He was not a Socialist, but he wished to introduce full civil liberties, social reforms and Liberal political institutions. On 24 October he had organised a National Council composed of Radicals (his own group) and Social Democrats. Although this Council had no constitutional standing, it soon came to count for more in public opinion than the existing Parliament, elected on the restricted franchise and representing the aristocracy, gentry and upper bourgeoisie. The Budapest garrison declared itself for Károlyi and the Council, and it was this which forced the king to invite Károlyi to form a Government.

Károlyi began his political activity by handing over 50,000 acres of land, his private estate, to the peasants, and he devoted himself to the preparation of a radical Land Reform. A law was passed in December giving the vote to all men over 21 and women over 24, and the convocation of a Constituent Assembly was promised. Károlyi's chief task was the liquidation of the war, and, full of confidence in the declarations of Wilson, he addressed himself to the Allied Command, convinced that a democratic Hungary would receive a kindly hearing. At the same time his friend Professor Jászi, well known as an opponent of the pre-1914 Magyarisation policy and a friend of the non-Magyar nationalities of Hungary, was appointed Minister of Nationalities.

Unfortunately for Károlyi it proved too late to find a compromise between Magyars and non-Magyars within a Hungarian State. Convinced that no Hungarian could be trusted, and attracted by the prospects held out by their kinsmen in Serbia, Bohemia and Roumania, the Croats, Slovaks and Roumanians turned a deaf ear to Jászi's appeals. Only the backward Ruthenes considered them, and they soon yielded to the combination of persuasion and force from Prague. The Allied Great Powers were no more sympathetic. They fully supported the claims of the new States, and their representative in Central Europe, the French General Franchet d'Espérey, adopted a haughty tone towards Károlyi. The cause of Hungarian Democracy left him quite cold.

Meanwhile feeling in Hungary was growing more radical. The war had not caused so much suffering in Hungary as in Austria, since the country's wheat plains had guaranteed her against starvation. Yet the Allied blockade had imposed severe restrictions, and was not lifted with the Armistice. There was general poverty. Prisoners of war were returning from Russia with tales of the great Revolution, which kindled the popular imagination. On 20 March 1919 came an Allied ultimatum demanding the retreat of the Hungarian forces to the frontier prescribed with Czechoslovakia. Patriotic and revolutionary feelings combined. The Left extremists led by

Béla Kun, who soon afterwards became the Communist Party of Hungary, gained strength. Károlyi, bitterly disappointed at the treatment received from the Allies, and convinced that the Hungarian people desired a revolutionary Government such as he was unable to give them, resigned in favour of the Left, and soon afterwards quietly left the country.

The new Government was dominated by Kun, a Hungarian Jew who had been a prisoner of war and, after being released by the Bolsheviks, had taken part in the Russian Revolution. In March 1919 the new Government, in which Kun was Foreign Minister, proclaimed the Hungarian Soviet Republic. All industrial enterprises employing more than 25 persons were Socialised. Church property was confiscated. Priests were allowed to continue in their duties only if they used the pulpit to preach support for the Government. Members of the religious orders were compelled to work in hospitals or other humanitarian enterprises, but were not subjected to severe persecution. Education was reorganised in such a way as to give precedence to scientific study and to the teaching of Socialist principles. All this was done in a hurry, by people who had no experience of political power, but with little bloodshed or violence.

The Land Question was tackled by the Socialisation of some two and a half million acres, but it was not decided whether these should be redistributed as private holdings to the landless peasants or retained as big State farms. Existing small and medium holders were allowed to keep their property, and the leader of the Small Farmers' Party, Stephen Szabó, gave qualified support to the regime. The delay in deciding the fate of the confiscated landed properties undoubtedly caused great disappointment among the peasants, who had expected good things of the Revolution. Their discontent was increased by the heavy requisitions which the Government was forced to impose in order to feed the starving capital, and by the compulsory labour on the Socialised estates, decreed in order to maintain production.

The political organisation of the Hungarian Republic was based on the Soviet system of Soldiers', Workers' and Peasants' Councils. The whole judicial power of the State was put into the hands of these Councils, and special revolutionary tribunals were set up to try political cases.

The Constitution was voted by delegates of the Councils in June.

The Hungarian Soviet's fundamental inner weakness was the absence of trained men. The same difficulty existed in Russia, but the combination of Lenin's genius, the resistance of the countless masses of Russia, and the impregnable vastness of the country secured victory over the foreign enemies, and gave the Soviet regime twenty years in which to train a new generation. Hungary was a small country surrounded by enemies, and the Great Powers were determined not to give its 'Bolsheviks' a chance.

In the early summer of 1919 the Roumanian Army advanced on Budapest, after Kun had rejected the terms of the Allies presented by General Smuts. In this crisis a supreme effort was made by the Hungarian workers, who flocked to join the newly formed Red Army. Led by Walter Böhm, and staffed largely by officers of the Imperial and Royal Army, determined to defend the frontiers, whatever the regime, the Hungarian forces overran most of Slovakia.

This triumph was short-lived. Kun, unable to make up his mind between compliance with the Allied requests and open defiance, unwilling to commit himself wholly to the Russian Soviets—who had, in any case, other things to think about than support of Hungarian Communism—at last accepted, in June, the Allied demand to evacuate Slovakia. Immediately all the internal conflicts, suppressed during the brief period of patriotic exaltation, broke out again. The ex-Imperial officers, utterly disillusioned, went over to the Whites, who, having formed a group in exile in Vienna, now installed themselves in Szeged with Roumanian help. Disputes between Kun and the Trade Unions grew more dangerous, and strikes broke out. In the countryside the peasants made armed risings. At last the regime resorted to terror, and a certain Szamuély toured the provinces and ordered a number of executions. An attempt at a Communist *coup d'état* in Vienna, which, if successful, might have helped the Hungarian situation, was a miserable failure.[1]

The Roumanian Army, not content with occupying the line approved by the Allies, advanced into Hungary proper, determined to suppress the 'godless, Bolshevik regime'. On

[1] See Borkenau, *op. cit.*

1 August Kun resigned and fled the country. The Socialist Peidl, dissociating himself from his former allies, formed a Government, which was overthrown after a few days by one Stephen Friedrich, supported by the Habsburg Archduke Joseph. On 14 November the Roumanians retired from Budapest, collecting on the return journey as much loot as they could lay hands on, and a few days later the Szeged group, led by Admiral Nicholas Horthy, entered the capital.

The months following the flight of Kun were filled with a White Terror which far surpassed anything that had been done by Szamuély at his worst. Those suspected of Communist sympathies were rounded up by terrorist gangs, and beaten, tortured and murdered. A number of 'patriotic' organisations performed the butcher's work with enthusiasm. The most important of these were the 'Awakening Magyars', to which belonged such later eminent figures as Julius Gömbös and Tibor Eckhardt. Jews were specially singled out for persecution, but pure Hungarian workers and peasant labourers also suffered. Many of the leaders of the Counter-Revolution disapproved of these atrocities, but they were either powerless or afraid to prevent them.

In November, Friedrich's Government was replaced by one led by the Clerical Huszár, supported by the troops of Horthy. At the end of January elections were held for a National Assembly. These were based in theory on universal suffrage, but their value was diminished by the fact that the White Terror still continued. The Socialists completely boycotted the elections, and Communists were excluded by law. The largest number of seats was won by the Small Landowners' Party of Szabó, which had 71 deputies, while various Right Wing Nationalist groups made up together 80. The Government was a coalition of these two main elements.

It was decided to call Hungary a Kingdom rather than a Republic, but there was some doubt as to who should be king. Meanwhile Admiral Nicholas Horthy was elected 'Regent' of the Kingdom. The strong opposition of all the neighbouring countries convinced the Government that a restoration of the Habsburg Dynasty would be too dangerous. In April 1921 King Charles returned to Hungary, but was advised by the Regent and the Prime Minister, Count Teleki, the successor to Huszár, to leave. Shortly afterwards Teleki resigned, and was replaced by Count Bethlen. In October a second attempt of Charles to reclaim his Kingdom was defeated. This time the ex-king landed from an aeroplane, and was joined by supporters in Western Hungary (Transdanubia). A few armed clashes took place before he was induced once more to retire. He was sent to Madeira, and there died in the following year. Since 1921 Hungary has remained a Kingdom without a king. For the following ten years Bethlen ruled supreme, and the Habsburg Legitimists were forced into fruitless opposition.

Bethlen was a Calvinist Transylvanian nobleman, a descendant of the famous seventeenth-century Prince of Transylvania. He was the strongest personality in the Szeged group, and Horthy was his nominee rather than he the admiral's. A man of personal integrity, Bethlen did not always surround himself with the best of men. Fanatically determined to restore his country's greatness, and an untiring propagandist of Treaty Revision, he did not pay equal attention to the healing of internal weaknesses and injustices.

Bethlen restored stability and legality to Hungary. His policy was definitely Conservative. He relied on the Nationalist groups, and in February 1922 he united them with the Small Landowners' Party to form a Government block known as the 'Christian and Bourgeois Party of Small Landowners and Agrarians' under his own leadership. The Small Landowners' Party which fused into this new creation had already lost what elements of radicalism it had once possessed, and docilely accepted the social and political *status quo*. Its leader Stephen Nagyatádi-Szabó still cherished the idea of a Land Reform, but his projected law was whittled down almost to nothing, and after his untimely death in 1923 nothing more was heard of it. A negligible quantity of land was transferred from big estates to the peasants, and the old pseudo-feudal system remained essentially unchanged.

Parliamentary institutions remained, for official opinion regarded them as the embodiment of the ancient Hungarian political tradition. But Parliamentary formalities and procedure covered with a thin veneer the substance of Dictatorship. Bethlen himself openly opposed Democracy as a political system. Within the Hungarian ruling class survived a kind of Whiggish Liberalism, which permitted a measure of intellectual freedom. Philosophical and political ideas could be discussed, as long as the fundamental regime was not called in question. Persecution of Jews came to an end. The Press and literature had a fairly free field. The country was ruled by the gentry class, some of whom were landowners, while others were civil servants, army officers or intellectuals. These elements controlled the political power, and were supported by business, which was mostly Jewish but was given the opportunities it required as long as it left politics to the old gang.

The composition of the Parliament reflected this state of affairs. The Government Party was not a real political party, but a collection of individuals of proved loyalty and usefulness to the regime. The Deputies were selected on personal grounds by the leaders of the regime. The Government always had a majority in the elections. Opposition was confined within Parliament to three small groups. A new Independent Small Landowners' Party was formed after the fusion of Szabó's party with Bethlen's block. This new party was led by Gaston Gául, and had for some years a considerable following. It represented the medium peasants of the western plain, but had little in common with the masses of the agricultural proletariat. A second group was the Liberal Party of Rassay, a most distinguished writer and public speaker. It was supported by the democratic section of the intelligentsia. It always had a seat or two in Parliament, and made up to some extent for its small numbers by the quality of its representatives. The third oppositional group were the Social Democrats, who after the end of the White Terror reappeared on the political scene.

Parliament was elected according to a franchise law passed by Bethlen in 1922. This replaced the universal suffrage theoretically observed in the Huszár elections of 1920 by a more complicated system. The electorate was reduced by about 25 %, and intricate restrictions, based on the period of residence and the education of the voter, were imposed. The ballot was secret in the towns, but open in the countryside. By this means the agrarian masses were completely disfranchised. No oppositional parties were allowed into the villages. The gendarmes ruthlessly expelled persons suspected of political agitation. The regime allowed the Social Democrats to preach to the industrial workers, on the understanding that they left the peasants alone. The landowning interest, which, when it did not dominate the Government, at least always had a strong influence on it, had little objection if the workers wanted to abuse the capitalists, were even prepared to see them wring concessions from them. But let them not touch their serfs, or there would be trouble. Consequently, the Social Democrats remained a thoroughly respectable party, and survived, as in Poland, to the end.[1] The Trade Unions were dominated by them, and enjoyed a strong position. During the World Depression there was, of course, discontent among the workers, and the rank and file were always more radical than the Social Democratic leaders. But in Hungary the industrial working class was probably a less dissatisfied and revolutionary element than the peasantry.

The regime described above was little changed throughout the following twenty years, and most of its features exist to this day. Consequently, the political history of Hungary after 1920 makes uninteresting reading. Important political events are few, and the chief personalities are colourless. In the last few years new factors have appeared, but the Bethlen period (1921–31) was one of peaceful stagnation.

The economic situation of Hungary had been unfavourably affected by the Peace Settlement. The Budapest industrial region was cut off from former sources of raw materials on the circumference of the old Hungary. Some industry had been lost in Slovakia, Croatia and Transylvania, and the bulk of Hungarian industry, left inside the Trianon frontiers, had been deprived of much of its market. General dislocation was increased by the civil war, and the first years were marked by a violent inflation.

The financial situation was restored by a League of Nations loan and reconstruction scheme, beginning from 1923. A new currency, the pengö, was introduced in 1925, and, as the internal security and prosperity of the country increased, foreign capital poured in. During the following years some £50,000,000 long-term and £20,000,000 short-term capital was invested, the former being loaned to local authorities, or spent on industry, urban real estate and agricultural mortgages. Industrialisation was pushed ahead on new lines, to suit the new

[1] Despite attacks from the Right, the Government allowed them to exist even after the entry of Hungary into the war in 1941.

situation. From 1924 a system of industrial protection was in force. The banks, connected with foreign banking systems, supplied copious credits to industry. For the next four years there was a rapid growth of industry, particularly of textiles and chemicals.

The first heavy blow to the Hungarian economy was dealt by the denunciation of the Czechoslovak Trade Treaty. This mainly affected agriculture, but the reduction of the pur-chasing-power of the peasant owners and land workers, to whom the big landowners were, thanks to the subsidy system, able to pass on most of the burden of the crisis, reduced the demand for industrial goods. The general fall of agricultural prices in the world followed on the special difficulties created by the lapse of the Treaty. In July 1931 came the banking crisis in Central Europe, precipitated by the collapse of the Wiener Kredit-Anstalt. Hungarian banks were connected through Vienna with the western credit system, and the collapse struck a severe blow to the Hungarian currency. The con-sequent currency difficulties, and the scarcity of foreign ex-change, made almost unobtainable the raw materials needed by Hungarian industry.

During the crisis Count Bethlen gracefully retired from the Premiership, and the ungrateful task was assumed by Count Julius Károlyi, who was succeeded in the following year by his War Minister, General Gömbös. Gömbös was of German origin, and caused some amusement by his unsuccessful attempts to prove a Hungarian noble pedigree. His most outstanding quality was his ambition. Formerly a leading member of the terrorist 'Awakening Magyar' society, he had renounced his old views, and was prepared to come to terms with Jewish bankers and industrialists if that would advance his career. He had almost unlimited energy, and genuine patriotism, but these forces lacked direction. He had great admiration for Mussolini, and was drawn by natural sympathy towards Germany. Vaguely convinced that the future lay with 'totalitarianism', he filled his speeches and official publica-tions with Fascist bombast unintelligible to all but the keenest brains.

Government pressure was not appreciably stronger during his four years of rule than under Bethlen, but the outer façade of Liberalism, carefully polished by his predecessor, began to grow shabby, and cracks and holes became more frequent. International events favoured a Fascist orientation. At the end of the Gömbös period, as at the beginning, the greater part of the Budapest intelligentsia laughed at the pompous phrases of the Hungarian aspirant to Führerdom, and the Hungarian masses remained apathetic. But Gömbös played a part of some importance, not so much because he turned in foreign policy towards the future 'Axis Powers'—for that, granted the nature of the Hungarian regime and the attitude of public opinion to the Peace Treaties, was inevitable—as because he was the first Hungarian Prime Minister actively to favour the propagation of a Fascist ideology among the younger generation.

Anti-Semitism was no new thing in Hungary. What was new was the entry of Hungarians into industry and trade, providing an economic basis for dislike of Jews. The first generation of Hungarian middle class, of gentry origin, had, as we have seen, mainly confined itself to the civil service and free professions. The second generation showed interest in commercial and industrial life. This process began before 1914, but it grew important only after the First World War. It was especially marked after the Depression. Jewish bankers were blamed for the crisis, and the wish was expressed that trade and industry should be put in Hungarian hands. The State took a more active part in the organisation of industry, and used every opportunity to squeeze out Jews and replace them with Hungarians.

From 1933–34 onwards the economic situation began to improve. Increased agricultural subsidies raised the purchasing power at least of the considerable class of independent farmers. The reduction of imports, imposed by the strained currency position, stimulated home industry. Above all, Germany provided an alternative market to that of the unwilling Successor States, and one in which foreign exchange was not needed. At the same time the increased industrialisation brought about a change in the structure of Hungarian foreign trade. In comparison with the period 1926–30, the proportion of exports occupied by foodstuffs and wine diminished, while the share of manufactured goods rose. In the case of imports the share of manufactured goods decreased and that of raw materials increased. This trend was bound to create difficulties, for Germany, now Hungary's best customer, and an important contributory cause of her economic recovery, was interested in the maintenance of Hungarian agriculture at the expense of industry. If Hungary wished to increase her trade with Germany, she must slow up her industrialisation; if she wished to industrialise, she must risk the loss of German commercial favour. This dilemma remained in the next years a fundamental issue in Hungaro-German relations and in Hungarian internal economic affairs.

In 1936 Gömbös died during a visit to Germany, and was succeeded in the Premiership by Darányi, a somewhat colourless individual of pro-German sympathies. He was replaced by Imrédy, the Governor of the National Bank. A brilliant economist, Dr Imrédy was considered an opponent of the German orientation, but once installed in the Premiership he far surpassed his predecessors in the courtship of Hitler. At this time Berlin was developing propaganda among the peasantry of Eastern Europe, and Imrédy, following the German lead, began to talk of Land Reform. This could not please the ruling class, already alarmed at the excessive sympathy of the Prime Minister for the Third Reich. It was discovered that Imrédy had a Jewish grandmother, and, when his frantic and undignified efforts to disprove this assertion had failed, he was compelled, having made himself ridiculous, to resign. His place was taken by Count Paul Teleki, the Premier of 1920–21.

Towards the end of Gömbös' rule Nazi groups began to appear in Hungary. In 1935 and 1937 there were more than ten such groups, all too weak and too passionately jealous of each other to have chances of success. In August 1938, however, the two principal groups, led by a member of the great landowning family of Festetics and by a half-crazy fanatical major named Szálasi, fused to form the Arrow-Cross Party (Nyilas-keresztes párt), whose agitation soon began to assume alarming proportions. The Arrow-Cross preached a combination of anti-Semitism and Land Reform, couched in demagogic and mystical phrases. It had some success among students, unemployed workmen and a part of the rural proletariat. The Government already in 1938 had put Szálasi into prison, but this served only to increase his prestige.

The antics of the Arrow-Cross were not met by any reaction

from the Left. The Government, which frowned on Szálasi's movement, positively forbade anything which smacked of militant Democracy. The Independent Small Landowners' Party, now led by Tibor Eckhardt, once an 'Awakening Magyar' and admirer of Hitler, had fallen on evil days, and had only a small number of supporters either in Parliament or in the country. It shunned political cooperation with the Social Democrats, who for their part dared not show interest in the peasantry.

A phenomenon of some interest was the appearance of a group of young writers who called themselves the 'March Front'—in reference to March 1848, the Hungarian Revolution—and devoted themselves to a serious study of the problems of the Hungarian village, and advocated social reforms. These people were convinced Democrats, and showed the agitation of the Arrow-Cross for Land Reform to be mere dishonest political manœuvre. They never formed a political party, but their writings had an effect on public opinion, by showing the lamentable condition of the people.

In May 1939 Parliamentary elections were held, under a new electoral law, which, despite a certain amount of 'gerrymandering' of constituencies, allowed a wider franchise and gave the secret ballot, at least nominally, to the villages. The usual Governmental majority was obtained, but 43 Hungarian Nazi Deputies appeared in Parliament, 28 of these being followers of Szálasi. The number of Social Democrats was smaller than in the preceding House.

Teleki had the terrible task of steering Hungary through the first two years of the Second World War. Although Central Europe was now completely dominated by Germany, and although Hungary had received two pieces of territory from her neighbours as a German present,[1] Teleki fought stubbornly to retain some measure of independence for his country. His efforts compare favourably with those of Roumania in the same period. When resistance was no longer possible, and his own Regent and General Staff betrayed him, Teleki took the classical way out. Like the class to which he belonged, he was an anachronistic survival from the past. Yet however little one may approve his reactionary outlook, however clearly one may see the fatal defects of the regime he repre-

[1] From Slovakia in 1938, from Roumania in 1940.

sented, it is impossible to withhold sympathy from an honourable man.

It is a strange fact that Hungary, where Reaction and Terror were introduced earlier, and where the people had fewer rights and liberties, retained longer than any other Eastern European State remnants of Liberalism. Even after the outbreak of war with Russia newspapers such as the Liberal *Magyar Nemzet* published articles criticising the New Order; the Liberal leader Rassay and the Social Democrats attacked the Government in Parliament; and members of the former 'March Front' openly discussed the formation of a Popular Front. One of these intellectuals even wrote an article declaring that Hungary in 1941 needed political liberty and national independence, and that these could be obtained only by a revolution of peasants and workers. Until the end of 1943 there was probably less German interference in internal affairs in Hungary than in any other Axis country, Bulgaria, Italy and Spain included. The Arrow-Cross split up again into several squabbling groups, and the Germans ceased to take much interest in them, preferring to work with the traditional ruling class, which ensured internal order and the execution of obligations.

All this was of little importance to the war effort of the United Nations, but it shows that the rulers of Hungary, who reduced to the bare minimum their contribution to the Axis, were not 'Quislings' in the same sense as Antonescu, Pavelić or even Boris.

At the same time it should be emphasised that these rulers belong to the past. Pre-Capitalist Conservatism is an attractive phenomenon, but it has no place in the modern world. A social structure with remnants of Feudalism and an official ideology made up of medieval Clericalism and Romanticism had brought the Hungarian people to a point where it was faced with national extinction. Unless the whole rotten system were swept away, the peasants received the land, and the country were ruled by, and in the interests of, the peasants and workers, the chances of Hungary's survival were poor.

It was the apathy of the oppressed peasantry which lost Hungary the battle of Mohács, and to-day she is surrounded by peoples as vigorous, as gifted and as confident of their own future as the Turks. If the needed revolution takes place in time, this gifted nation, which has given great writers, poets and scientists to the world, may occupy an honourable place in human society.

4. ROUMANIA

Of all the Eastern European States Roumania was the most fortunate at the Peace Settlement. Although defeated in 1918, she acquired from her late Ally, Russia, the partly Roumanian province of Bessarabia, and, having signed a separate peace with Germany, declared war a second time just before the Armistice and presented herself at the Peace Conference as an Allied State. This attitude might have caused indignation to so fierce a statesman as M. Georges Clemenceau, had not he and his colleagues been so frightened of the spectre of Russian Communism that they were willing to welcome any small State prepared to act the part of 'bulwark against the Bolshevik poison'.[1] Roumania's success at the Peace is almost solely due to the panic about Bolshevism, and for the following twenty years Roumanian statesmen cleverly exploited the Bolshevik bogey to extract material benefits from Western Powers.

For more than twenty years Roumanian politicians and propagandists declaimed about their mission as a Christian outpost in the East. When war was declared on Russia in 1941 Bucarest Radio commentators went into ecstasies about the spread of Latin culture across the barbarous steppes. Yet the Roumanian troops did not lag behind their Nordic allies in robbery, torture or massacre of the compatriots of Tolstoy and Dostoevsky, or destruction of the cultural monuments of the Ukraine, Crimea or Caucasus. The sense of Latin crusading superiority proved an expensive luxury, dearly paid by the countless corpses of bewildered Roumanian peasants left rotting in the ruins of Odessa, Sevastopol and Stalingrad.

On 1 December 1918 a meeting representative of the Transylvanian Roumanians at Alba Iulia (Gyulafehérvár) proclaimed the Union of Transylvania with Roumania and of all Roumanians in one State. The meeting had been prepared by

[1] The mixing of metaphors is not mine. It has a venerable history.

the National Council of Transylvanian Roumanians, formed in October and inspired by the Nationalist leader, Iuliu Maniu. Shortly afterwards the Roumanian army entered Transylvania.

In Bucarest the pro-German Government of Marghiloman, set up after the Treaty of Bucarest of 1918, had been succeeded in November by the pro-Allied Liberals under Bratianu, who came to Paris to demand fulfilment of the secret treaty of 1916. This masterpiece of Allied diplomacy had promised Roumania a large part of the Hungarian plain, extending almost to Szeged and Debrecen. The fact that Roumania had signed a separate peace was advanced as a reason for not implementing the agreement, and Roumania had to be content with the whole of Transylvania, most of the Banat and the railway linking Timişoara (Temesvár) with Satu Mare (Szatmár Németi) across a strip of plain inhabited predominantly by Hungarians compactly contiguous to the Hungarian frontier.

This, however, was not enough for the fiery Bratianu, who retired in disgust, and was replaced in Bucarest as Prime Minister by the more accommodating Transylvanian, Maniu's closest friend and colleague, Alexander Vaida-Voevod.[1]

The Vaida Government settled the country's frontiers with the Allies and with Jugoslavia, which acquired a part of the Banat. Vaida wished to come to terms with Soviet Russia about the Bessarabian frontier. This dangerous desire, combined with the fact that he showed a deplorable inclination to collaborate politically with the newly formed and rather radical Peasant Party, induced King Ferdinand to dismiss him. The Premiership was given to the war hero, Marshal Averescu, who proceeded to hold elections.

Elections in Roumania are always won by the Government that makes them, and Averescu's were no exception. A new People's Party sprang out of the ground, with a rousing

---

[1] The Liberal leader's son, the historian George Bratianu, who in 1940–41 successfully competed with Antonescu in subservience to the Germans, has made much of his father's maltreatment in Paris. In February 1940 he published an article in the Nazi periodical *Europäische Revue* arguing that Germany ought, as a revisionist Power, to sympathise with Roumania rather than with Hungary. Not the Magyars, but the Roumanians were the victims of the Trianon Diktat, which had denied them their rightful frontier on the Tisza. It says much for the generosity of the learned professor's feelings for Germany that the events of the following August in no way diminished his enthusiasm for St Adolf, the apostle of Christian Justice.

majority. Its success was due partly to the great popularity of the Marshal with the peasantry of the Old Kingdom (unlike many Roumanian high officers, he had taken interest in the welfare of the simple soldier at the front), partly to the precautionary measures of the gendarmerie. Averescu devoted himself, once firmly established, to the repression of 'Bolshevism'. The most important step taken in this direction had been the Land Reform, voted already during the war. The Reform was most radical in Bessarabia, the province most exposed to 'Communist contagion'. Here the land had been distributed with remarkable haste to the impatient serfs. Evasions were more frequent in the other provinces, but on the whole the Reform was translated from theory into practice, the bulk of the work being done during Averescu's regime.

The Reform did not, however, suffice to put an end to all discontent. The revolutionary unrest that pervaded Europe made itself felt in Roumania too, and the repressive apparatus wielded by the Minister of the Interior, Argetoianu, was kept fully employed. In 1920 a big demonstration of workers in front of the National Theatre in Bucarest was dispersed by firing. By the end of the year the country had been 'pacified' to the satisfaction of the Government.

In 1922, Averescu was succeeded by the Liberals, who had supported him behind the scenes during his period of office, preferring to allow the popular Marshal to take the responsibility for the repression. The Liberals dominated the country until 1928. Although Averescu came to power again in 1926–27, this was with the consent and support of the Liberal leaders and of their non-political patrons in high places. Until his death in 1927 the most prominent figure in Roumanian politics was Ionel Bratianu, himself the son of the veteran Prime Minister of the pre-war period.

Under Bratianu's rule Roumania was governed by the part-Jewish, part-Roumanian commercial, industrial and banking class. Having used the Land Reform to break the power of the old Conservatives, the bourgeoisie considered that it had done enough for the peasantry. Leaving the new peasant owners to get along as best they could without State help, the Liberal Government devoted itself to the industrialisation of the country, making the peasants pay for this by export duties and by general taxation, and trying as far as possible to exclude foreign capital from the process.

The second main principle of the Liberal regime was administrative centralisation. The desire of the Transylvanian Roumanians for a measure of autonomy, which in the first generous moments of Revolution had even been combined with a recognition of the right of non-Roumanians to self-governing institutions, was strenuously resisted. Regateni officials were sent to the new provinces, and the Liberal Party banks worked hard to get control of the incipient Transylvanian industry. The new bureaucracy was compared unfavourably, not only by the National Minorities but by the Roumanian inhabitants, with the Austrian system in Bukovina or the Hungarian in Transylvania. Opposition to the regime increased.

Political opposition came from two sides. The old National Party of Transylvania, led by Maniu and Vaida, had been in opposition since the sudden dismissal of Vaida in 1919. The centralising policy had increased its hostility. It was joined by a number of small groups, centred round the poet Goga, the historian Iorga and the Conservative statesman Tache Ionescu. In 1926 it fused with the other main oppositional element, the Peasant Party of the Regat. This party had been founded at the end of the war by a schoolmaster of peasant family, Ion Mihalache. The enactment of Universal Suffrage in 1918 gave the party a numerous following. Mihalache preached peasant democracy and advocated further measures to supplement the Land Reform. His violent language alarmed King Ferdinand, who was induced by his advisers to regard him as something not much better than a 'Bolshevik'. Mihalache collaborated with a number of other small peasant political groups. The most important of these was led by a Moldavian doctor of medicine, N. Lupu, who later joined forces with Mihalache. The fusion of Maniu's and Mihalache's parties in 1926 created the National Peasant Party, which continued to play an important part in Roumanian political life as long as any remnants of liberty existed.

In 1927 a local economic crisis occurred in Roumania, affecting agricultural prices, which it had always been Liberal policy to keep low in the interests of the urban consumers. In the same year both Ionel Bratianu and King Ferdinand, the irreconcilable opponents of the National Peasant coalition, died. A Regency was appointed for the minority of Ferdinand's young grandson, King Michael. The pressure of the National Peasants increased. A demonstrative 'march on Bucarest' of thousands of peasants was organised. At last, reluctantly, the Regency entrusted Maniu with the Government and with the preparation of elections. These, generally admitted to have been the freest in the whole inter-war history of Roumania, gave the National Peasant Party a majority of over 75 %. It was hoped that a new era would begin.

The hopes entertained of the new Government were nearly all disappointed. Something was done for a part of the peasantry. The export duties were repealed, measures were taken to raise agricultural prices and some encouragement was given to cooperatives and to more rational methods of cultivation. A law was passed in 1929 abolishing the restrictions placed by the makers of the Land Reform on the right of the recipients of land to resell it. It was hoped that free sale of land would help the concentration of holdings and favour the creation of a solid peasant middle class. In fact much more important than the increase of medium farms was the development of the rural proletariat of dwarf holders, described in Chapter Four, which was accentuated by this law. The impoverished small holders sold their land to rich peasants, to the old landowners or to non-rural elements, and sank into ever-deepening misery.

Neither the National Peasant Government nor those which followed it did anything substantial for this rural proletariat— (75 % of the peasantry in 1930 and certainly a higher percentage in 1942). All the measures for the relief of the peasantry adopted in the following twelve years, which at the best were insignificant in comparison with the Governmental eloquence which they inspired, were concerned with the minority of big and medium holdings. Such measures may have had indirect effects on the purchasing-power of the rural proletariat, but these were of very small importance.

Much more important than its legislation for the benefit of the peasants was the National Peasant Government's decision to throw open the country to foreign capital. This was Maniu's main achievement, which won him the undying affection of British, French and American capitalists. The influx of foreign capital undoubtedly eased the economic situation, and thus benefited the Roumanian people as a whole, even if only for a short time and at the expense of creating new problems. It also benefited a number of Maniu's colleagues, who made fortunes with striking speed, their increased incomes being, some unkind people whispered, not unconnected with favours dispensed to western business men. Maniu himself remained coldly incorruptible. No one ever suggested—though he had many enemies—that 'Domnul Presedinte' would think of taking a bribe. This could not, however, be said of all his entourage, which included men whose past services to the national cause, rather than any marked political capacity, had raised to Ministerial rank. The National Peasant Government was no freer of scandals than its predecessors, and these were seized on by its political opponents to discredit its policy. In fact, of course, the accusers were in no way better than the accused. The National Peasant team was not notably inferior to that of other parties. Maniu himself, Mihalache and the economist Madgearu were among the most distinguished of their countrymen.

King Ferdinand's son, Prince Carol, had been obliged during his father's lifetime to renounce his right to the Crown, owing to a morganatic marriage disapproved by Court and Government. Since 1926 he had been living in exile in France. It was known that he was not truly resigned to his fate, and, as discontent grew with the feeble Regency, an increasing number of people, particularly in the ranks of the National Peasant Party, expressed a desire for his return. In June 1930 Carol arrived suddenly by air to reclaim his throne. There is no doubt that the greater part of the politically conscious class of Roumanians were pleased. The young king accepted his father's return, and Maniu also acquiesced. After a formal resignation lasting a few days, he continued his Premiership.

Carol II soon showed that he had no intention of remaining a mere colourless constitutional king. Superficially brilliant and basically ignorant, gifted with enormous energy and unlimited lust for power, a lover of demagogy, melodrama and bombastic speeches, he was determined to be a Great Man, the Saviour and Regenerator of his country. His impressionistic mind was filled with admiration of Mussolini, then still the most picturesque figure on the European political stage, and he set himself to imitate him. In his untiring work, which lasted ten years, he combined a little of the terrorist methods of the Duce with much of the well-tried Balkan procedure of corruption and intrigue. Now Carol is gone, but his deeds live after him. The moral standards of Roumanian political life were never conspicuously high, but there is no doubt that they have fallen considerably since 1930, and that a big share of responsibility for this must be borne by Carol II. For a decade the history of Roumania consisted of this man's flamboyant gestures and cunning manœuvres, set against a drab background of peasant misery and police oppression.

Carol's first aim was to break up the political parties, by winning over to himself the younger and ambitious politicians, pushing out the weak and old, and eliminating those who stuck to their principles by a judicious combination of terror and calumny. He was helped by the attitude of Maniu. Firmly devoted to Democracy, of which the Clerical atmosphere of Blaj[1] and the practice of Hungarian Parliamentarism had implanted in him a somewhat formalistic and legal conception, he was bound to come into conflict with the aspiring autocrat. Unfortunately, he chose as the ground on which to fight Carol the latter's private life. During his exile the king had become attached to a Jewish lady named Magda Wolf or Lupescu. Despite an undertaking to Maniu to sever the connection, the king was no sooner installed in the palace than he brought her from France to Bucarest. This was too much for Maniu, who resigned the Premiership in favour of an insignificant member of his party, a lawyer named Mironescu with business connections.

Bourgeois sexual morality is probably less esteemed in Roumania than anywhere else on the Continent. It was not the right issue on which to base the whole conflict between Democracy and Dictatorship. Moreover the resignation of Maniu, far the strongest personality in his party, left the field clear for royal intrigue. Sedulous flattery of the party bosses won the king first their tolerant sympathy and then their collaboration.

Professor Iorga's immense vanity delivered him into the king's hands. He broke with the National Peasants, and was

---

[1] A small Transylvanian town, centre of the Roumanian Uniate Church, Maniu's home during his earlier political career.

entrusted in 1931 with the Premiership. The elections held under him were regarded even by Roumanian standards as unusually brutal and corrupt. He was assisted as Minister of Interior by Argetoianu, the organiser of the repression of 1919–20.

After a year Iorga was replaced by Vaida, who still nominally belonged to the National Peasant Party, but whom the king's intrigues had irrevocably estranged from Maniu and the democratic elements of the party. In 1934 Vaida openly broke away, and founded a new party, the Roumanian Front, which proclaimed a programme of militant anti-Semitism and denunciation of Democracy. During the following years a number of promising young National Peasants were cajoled or bought, by money or favours, into the king's camp. Maniu found himself gradually abandoned by old friends and by young men of whom he had hoped much. In 1932 he was again Prime Minister for a few weeks, but the Lupescu Question again brought his resignation. The propaganda put about by the king's men, that Maniu was a silly old prig of whom no good would come, had growing success. The rising generation was disillusioned with the National Peasants, and looked elsewhere.

The king did not confine his intrigues to the National Peasants. The other great party, the Liberals, soon became the object of his attentions. The death of Ionel Bratianu, Carol's most implacable enemy, in 1927 had made his task fairly easy. Ionel's brother Constantin was also hostile to the king, but he had not the same iron grip over the party as his masterful brother. His nephew George, a professor of history, with strong political ambitions, was in favour of working with the king, and put himself at the head of an 'activist' group within the party.

The chief obstacle to the king's will among the Liberals was the new party leader, Ion Duca, a man of personal honesty and democratic convictions who distrusted Carol's intentions. In 1933 Duca was entrusted by the king with the Premiership. Shortly afterwards he was murdered by members of the terrorist organisation 'Iron Guard'. His place was taken by the obliging Tatarescu, who ruled the country until December 1937, dutifully carrying out the will of his master the king.

Anti-Semitism was traditional in Roumania, dating from

the early nineteenth century, when Jews began to penetrate the country from east and north. As in Hungary and Poland, it began in the cultural field and spread later into the economic, when the Roumanian educated class started to interest themselves in industry and trade. Roumanian anti-Semitism received literary form in the works of the national poet Eminescu, who was strongly influenced by German romantic nationalism. Its centre was the universities.

In the years after 1918 the University of Jassy, capital of Moldavia, supplied the police with a number of students willing to earn an honest penny as toughs, *agents provocateurs*, strike-breakers or Jew-baiters. These young men acquired their moral and intellectual training in the same school as the German and Italian élites which formed the Sturm-Abteilungen and Fasci di Combattimento, and performed the same heroic feats—with the help of the police—against Jewish materialists, decadent Liberals and Communist scum. They were particularly useful to their employers for the purpose of breaking up political meetings and embarrassing democratic organisations. In 1929 the Prefect of Jassy objected to these disturbances, and attempted to stop them. He was shot dead by a young student, of mixed German-Ukrainian origin, named Corneliu Zelea Codreanu, who was triumphantly acquitted and became the hero of the super-patriots. During the following years Codreanu organised a group of romantic young terrorists. His organisation had at different times different names—'League of the Archangel Michael', 'Iron Guard', 'All for the Fatherland Party'. His main henchman was a Transylvanian priest's son, Motsa, author of a long-winded treatise entitled, not unappropriately, *Wooden Skulls*.[1]

Codreanu's group was benevolently viewed by police chiefs, but it was hardly taken seriously until the return of Carol. From 1930 onwards, however, the Iron Guard was supplied with funds by such politicians as Vaida, Inculets and Tatarescu, on the initiative of the king, who hoped to use its passionate patriotism in the creation of a better Roumania, and its 'heroic' methods for the furtherance of his own designs. Their

---

[1] Motsa's father, an Orthodox 'Protopop', an eminent Roumanian nationalist of Habsburg days, proudly showed me in 1939 a pamphlet written by him twelve years previously, summarising the doctrines of the 'great English scientist, Sir Houston Stewart Chamberlain, Professor at the University of London, brother of the British Foreign Minister'!

finances put on a sound basis, the Guardists could now devote themselves to nation-wide propaganda. The crude nonsense which they talked, and the bloody outrages which they committed, offended decent Roumanian opinion, but no official would do anything against people who so loudly proclaimed their hatred of Jews and Bolsheviks, especially when they were known to enjoy august patronage. Codreanu was acquitted of complicity in the Duca murder, although it was an open secret that he had ordered it. The king may have been shocked by the murder, but he did not stop his subsidies. His intermediaries for the financing of the Guard were MM. Tatarescu and Inculets, the late Prime Minister's right-hand men.

During the thirties the World Economic Depression struck Roumania, and, added to the general economic process described in Chapter Four, created acute misery among the peasantry. The policy of the Liberals had undermined the peasants' prosperity, the National Peasant Governments had done little to improve things, and the second period of Liberal rule was no better. The Roumanian peasants are politically backward, especially in the Old Kingdom. Words like 'Democracy' or 'Dictatorship' meant nothing to them. They had voted for benefits promised them, for personalities they knew, or for cash or tsuica.[1] They understood little of party programmes or political ideologies, but they hoped, now that they had this right of 'choosing their Government', now that everyone seemed to agree that they were the 'sovereign people', that their material lot would improve. When their economic situation grew yearly worse, and the corruption and terror of the bureaucrats who ruled them increased, they lost all faith in parties and politicians.

It was now that the Iron Guard appeared. It promised them an end to the misrule of professional politicians, an end to administrative corruption, an end to the extortions of the Jewish shopkeeper, and more land. The slogan 'Omul şi Pogonul' (one man, one acre) swept the country. Although in fact the possibilities of a new Land Reform were not very large, and would have done little to ease the situation of the peasants, the idea was one which the simplest peasant could

---

[1] The local brandy, made of plums. Votes are bought in Roumania with tsuica, in Jugoslavia with šlivovica and in Poland with vodka.

understand and approve. Moreover the bearers of the slogan
were very unlike the old politicians. They were young men, of
transparent sincerity and of personal courage, and made their
campaigns attractive by picturesque trappings—fiery crosses,
white horses—which appealed to the romantic souls of the
peasants. The Iron Guard, once confined to cranky students
and young girls thrilled by 'the Captain's' beautiful eyes,
became a mass movement.

Discontent in the country became increasingly obvious. In
1933, under Vaida's Government, the railway workers of the
Bucarest workshops had gone on strike, and been suppressed
with bloodshed. Under Tatarescu fights between Iron Guardists
and Democrats in the villages were common. In certain parts
of Transylvania anti-Fascist groups of peasants were organised, in collaboration with Maniu's followers but independently of them. These groups copied some of the Guardist
methods, and drilled in semi-military formations, prepared to
fight for the few liberties they still possessed. Revolutionary
feeling of the Left grew among a part of the younger generation,
which rejected Guardist ideas. But these young Democrats
were as systematically repressed by the authorities as the Iron
Guard was encouraged.

In 1937 elections were due. Although police terror, and the
ability of the king to select Governments as he wished, had
long ago reduced Democracy to a farce, certain formalities
had to be observed. The Government required only 40 % of
the votes, which, according to a law made by the Liberals in
their first period, and never repealed by the democratic
National Peasants, then gave them a majority of the seats in
Parliament. The Liberals had the usual prospect of success,
but they had to count on the opposition of the Iron Guard,
which now had so large a mass following that it decided to
throw over its former patrons. Suddenly came sensational
news. Maniu had made a pact with the Guard. This astonishing
decision, contrary to all the political principles for which the
National Peasant Party had stood, was explained by Maniu's
followers as intended solely to protect both parties from pressure and intimidation. In fact the pact was inexcusable. It
demoralised Maniu's best supporters, the young generation
of militant democrats, and it gave to Codreanu the benefit
of Maniu's personal prestige.

The elections, which were comparatively fair (each party had its own band of toughs, and these approximately neutralised each other), gave the Government 38 % of the votes, the National Peasants 22 % and the Iron Guard 16 %. This represented a defeat for the Government, but not a victory for the National Peasants. Carol, now afraid of the Iron Guard, and unwilling to call on Maniu, invited the elderly Transylvanian poet, Octavian Goga, leader of the Right-Wing anti-Semitic 'National Christian Party', which had polled 9 % of the votes, to form a Government.

Goga proceeded to put his principles into practice. Jews were beaten up all over the country, Jewish enterprises came to a standstill, economic life was dislocated, the British and French Ministers protested, and after a few glorious weeks Goga was dismissed.[1] Carol II then announced that Parliamentary rule had been proved impossible, and that he was compelled in the interests of the people to declare a Dictatorship. A new Constitution was drafted and a plebiscite made on it, which resulted, in the approved Fascist tradition, in an almost unanimous endorsement. The Patriarch was made Prime Minister, and the most important member of the Cabinet was the Minister of the Interior, Armand Călinescu, a promising young leader of the National Peasant Party, who had deserted his chief, Mihalache, at a moment's notice to join the Goga Government, and was retained by the king.

Codreanu was arrested and imprisoned. The following autumn, while the king was returning from a post-Munich visit to the western capitals, Codreanu and thirteen other eminent Guardists were 'shot while trying to escape' in the neighbourhood of Bucarest. In December 1938 Carol decided to give dignity to his regime, and to conform to the latest Fascist models, by creating a monopoly party, the 'Front of National Rebirth'.

Carol had now achieved his aim. Eight years of patient toil had brought their reward. He had broken up the two big parties, isolating the old leaders, Maniu and Constantin Bratianu, and winning over the younger men, impatient for the fruits of power. He had used the Iron Guard to terrorise

---

[1] For a description of the beating of Jewish girl medical students by young Roumanian heroes, see article by G. E. R. Gedye in *New Statesman and Nation*, February 1938.

Roumanian democrats, giving its leaders material help and police protection in their work of perverting the idealism of the younger generation into mere worship of bloodshed and bestiality. Then, when the Guard had captured the imagination of the masses, and was no longer content to be a tool of others, he turned on it and massacred its leaders.

Now the king was supreme. He could rely on the army, the police apparatus was better equipped than ever to repress all expression of popular discontent, and the intellectuals of Bucarest competed with one another to cringe at his feet. He and his friends, the 'Camarilla' grouped round Mme Lupescu, had a firm hold on the economic machine. A large part of Roumanian industry, including important textile, sugar and armament factories, was the king's private property. The National Bank was controlled by nominees of the Camarilla, and malicious gossip had it that it supplied at low rates foreign currency needed to buy raw materials for the royal factories. Carol, dressed in beautiful uniforms designed by himself and manufactured in his own factories, proclaimed a crusade against Corruption. Decree laws were signed abolishing nepotism, and declaring that as from to-morrow class conflicts would cease and Roumanians would be brothers. New men and new methods were needed, said Carol, and filled the highest posts of the Rebirth Front with old politicians (Tatarescu, Vaida, Argetoianu) or renegades from the old parties (Ghelmegeanu, Andrei, and Ralea the king's 'pocket Socialist').

Although of German origin, the king undoubtedly had a strong Roumanian patriotism, but this had in the course of years become inextricably identified with his own ambition. Convinced from the beginning that party politicians were the curse of his country, and that only his personal rule could benefit her, he was now at a loss what to do. Surrounding himself with flatterers and intriguers, and relying on the most flexible, irresolute and incapable of the politicians, he found himself without trustworthy advisers at a time when the tense international situation complicated every problem of home politics. The single powerful personality, Călinescu, who, in a ruthless manner, genuinely attempted to serve his country, was removed by assassination in September 1939.

Carol saw that the country was rotten, that drastic reforms

were needed, but he neither understood what reforms to apply, nor was personally suited to apply them. His speeches stressed his fatherly care for the peasants. An interesting experiment was actually made under his regime, at the suggestion of the well-known sociologist, Professor Gusti. This was the 'Social Service', by which all university and high school students were obliged to spend a year in the village after the conclusion of their courses, engaged in manual work and study of peasant life. It was hoped thereby to create in the younger generation of 'intellectuals' greater knowledge of, and sense of responsibility towards, the peasantry. The idea was a good one, and resulted in the collection of a great deal of valuable material on peasant conditions, comparable to that published by the 'March Front' group in Hungary. The material benefits derived therefrom by the peasants were, however, negligible, and after little more than a year, when it was discovered that many of the chief pillars of the 'Social Service' were secret Iron Guardists and were using the organisation to propagate their creed in the villages, it was suppressed. Other less honest schemes were devised, whose only purpose was advertisement of the regime, such as a 'Sanitary Train' which toured the country and compelled peasants to have baths. The regime solved nothing. It maintained order by its bayonets, collected with extreme brutality taxes urgently needed for rearmament, and produced a plethora of extravagant speeches which provoked silent laughter and hatred.

No one took the regime seriously, not even its apologists. The Roumanian intellectual of the Old Kingdom is an excessively sceptical and critical person. He resented the censorship of the Press, which until 1938 had been able to publish vitriolic polemics. He derived some small consolation from jokes whispered at coffee-house tables. But however much he cursed the regime, he was grateful to it for one thing. It stood between him and the great, dirty, primitive, disinherited masses, whose 'Bolshevik' desire for Social Justice threatened his comforts.

The Roumanian intellectual from Transylvania was a rather different type. He had been brought up in the dull, solid school of Austro-Hungarian Liberalism. He was unfamiliar with the latest ideological and constitutional refinements of Paris, so glibly recited by his Regat colleague, but the necessities of the national struggle had brought him in touch with the peasants, whose political support he needed, and this contact had never been entirely lost after 1918. Consequently, though the majority of the most 'advanced' Regat intellectuals, enthusiastic worshippers at the shrine of French culture, ended by becoming lick-spittle Yes-men or Fascist demagogues, many Transylvanian bourgeois remain firm, unimaginative Democrats to this day.

Their hero has always been Maniu. If he had given them a sign, they would have followed him. But throughout the early thirties, while the remnants of formal Democracy were whittled away before his eyes; throughout the disordered weeks of Goga, when a Democratic revolution might have saved Roumania; throughout the Carol Dictatorship, when the moral and material powers of resistance of the nation were being undermined; and throughout the summer of 1940, when the dismemberment of his own Transylvania was being openly prepared, and the whole people prayed for a leader to call them to arms; 'Domnul Presedinţe' sat tight, issuing at intervals a few typewritten sheets of protest, calmly confident that future history would record that he never did anything a good Christian bourgeois ought not to do.

The masses were silent. In Transylvania the name of Maniu retained enormous prestige among the peasants, particularly the more prosperous and elderly. The younger generation showed impatience. Many of them listened to the Guardists, while some were influenced by Left ideas. There were villages in Transylvania where the peasants discussed with interest events in Spain, China and America. Small peasant democratic organisations were formed, directed solely by real peasants, men whose life was spent in cultivating the earth or shepherding flocks, and who only took to politics because misery and terror forced them. The leaders of such organisations, which carefully excluded the usual type of 'intellectual' demagogue from the towns, sometimes revealed a grasp of political realities lacking in many learned treatises.[1] But they were the minority, and, having been repressed in

[1] For instance, a pamphlet *De ce trebue plugarul român sa nu fie Faşist* (Why the Roumanian ploughman must not be Fascist) states the case for Democracy, and the connection between political liberty and social justice, in terms which could not be bettered by graduates of British universities, and intelligible to the simplest mind.

the days when the Guardists received Government support, were given no more freedom now that the Government had decided to persecute the Guardists.

In the Old Kingdom the peasants were much more backward and apathetic than in Transylvania. They submitted, and when called upon made demonstrations of 'spontaneous' enthusiasm for the regime. But hatred was in their hearts, the hopeless hatred of serfs who have never known freedom, but who from time to time break out into a 'Jacquerie' such as that which devastated Old Roumania in 1907. The working class was never a very strong force in Roumanian politics, even though the development of industry had considerably increased its numbers. Social Democracy never had much influence. Those workers who had political views were mostly Communists. Ever since 1918, however, fear of 'Bolshevism' had induced the authorities to take such strict measures against political and Trade Union activity among the workers that Communism had little chance of spreading. The Roumanian Communist Party consisted of a small group of sectarian intellectuals, of whom the most prominent were Jews or members of the National Minorities. Apart from Bessarabia, whose special conditions will be described later, Communist ideas were not popular outside the industrial wórking class. What did exist, among peasants and workers alike, was strong but undetermined revolutionary feeling. This was exploited by various groups, in 1919 by Averescu, in 1928 by the National Peasants, in the late thirties by the Iron Guard. But the masses were not fundamentally monarchist or republican, democratic or Fascist. They were merely oppressed and dissatisfied. They wanted merely the simple things that no one would give them, more food, more freedom and more justice.

Carol II destroyed or disorganised all opposition inside Roumania. He could be destroyed only from without. This happened when the collapse of France deprived Roumania of her one anchor in a stormy sea. The effect of this disaster on Roumanian intellectuals cannot be overrated. To educated Roumanians, more even than to Poles or Balkanites, France was the chief of the Great Powers and a second fatherland. The South Slavs might still look to Russia, Greece could hope in British sea-power, but for Roumania the fall of France was the end. Implacably opposed to any understanding with

Russia—in which he was only representative of his country's ruling class—Carol II decided to make a last-moment bid for Axis favour. He turned the Rebirth Front into a 'National Party', to be still more totalitarian, and made himself party chief. A few days later Russia took Bessarabia, and the Axis did not stir. In July and August preparations were made for the amputation of Transylvania.

Excitement among the Roumanians of that province reached a feverish pitch. The people wished to fight, however desperate the odds, and expected Maniu, the Grand Old Man of Roumanian Transylvania, to lead them. But Maniu did not move, and at the end of August Carol signed the Vienna Diktat. Popular indignation was intense, and even obtained expression in parts of the country. But once again the Roumanian Democrats were too late. While Maniu hesitated, and no other Democratic leader was available, an Iron Guard demonstration in the streets of Bucarest frightened the king into abdication. His son succeeded him, and before leaving the country Carol entrusted the power to General Ion Antonescu, who some days later formed a Government consisting largely of Iron Guardists, with their leader, Horia Sima, as. Vice-Premier.

The follies and horrors of the Guardist regime are too fresh in the public mind to need much attention here. It is sufficient to recall that they murdered in November 1940 the eminent economist and friend of Maniu, Professor Virgil Madgearu, and the distinguished historian Iorga; that they massacred in cold blood some sixty political prisoners in the fortress of Jilava; that they arrested and tortured a number of British subjects; that their Press went wild with delight that the gang had at last come to power by Hitler's favour,[1] and celebrated as a national victory the loss of a third of the country's territory; that unspeakable atrocities were perpetrated on Jews; and that at last, impatient of the remnants of bourgeois morality of General Antonescu, they organised against him a bloody revolt, which the General bloodily suppressed. The Iron Guard, which began its history as a band of police agents, and had for a time become a mass revolu-

---

[1] Perhaps the highest pitch was reached by the editor of *Porunca Vremii*, the Jew-baiting toady Ilie Radulescu, who described Hitler's 'peace appeal' after the fall of France as 'the greatest manifestation of the human spirit since Christ'.

tionary movement, including beside its crooked or perverted leaders a number of gifted and generous idealists, ended as a murder gang, with no other aim than revenge and destruction. Its surviving leaders were kept in Berlin, ready to be trotted out again if Antonescu showed reluctance to execute his master's orders.

The suppression of the Iron Guard gained Antonescu real support in the country, particularly among the Bucarest bourgeoisie. The same people who had squirmed before Carol II now settled down happily to lick the larger boot of the German conqueror. When in June 1941 Antonescu threw his country into war with Russia, they were delighted. The recovery of Bessarabia meant nothing to them—when it was Roumanian few Bucarest bourgeois ever visited the province. What pleased them was the prospect that the Germans would destroy not only an uncomfortably powerful neighbour, but a dream which had for twenty years held the imagination of part of the masses of Roumania and other countries. The entry of Hitler into Moscow would, they hoped, finally remove the threat to their social privileges. Meanwhile good business was to be done with the German guests who poured into the country. A good time could be had. If the rise of prices weighed heavily on the people, if the peasant's products were requisitioned, if thousands were slaughtered far from their country, that was regrettable, but not very important.

Roumania in 1918 appeared to have shining prospects. She had doubled her territory. She had rich natural resources, able politicians and a numerous people of unspoilt peasants. Her opportunities were better than those of any of her neighbours. But since then she has lost territory, soldiers and honour, and has won the anger of her friends, the scorn of her conquerors and the hatred of her neighbours. She is faced with economic ruin and bloody revolution. This change is not hard to explain.

A large share of responsibility for the tragedy of Roumania falls on two men. The first is Carol II. He broke up the country's democratic organisations, encouraged terrorism, and actively assisted the moral perversion of Roumanian Youth. The evil forces were not created by him, but he gave them their chance. The second is Maniu. His fault is not that he refused to accept the political terms of the king, but that he did so little to further the cause of Democracy. Maniu was right in opposing the influence of Mme Lupescu and in denouncing the corruption that grew up round the throne. He was wrong in basing the issue between the king and himself on a question of private morals, and above all in his inherent inability to take action. His followers were ready to risk their future in the cause of Freedom, but he would not put himself at their head. He received his training in an age and an atmosphere in which moral protest counted for something. He was an anachronism in times when only resolute resistance could save the liberties in which he so firmly believed.

But the main cause of Roumania's collapse was more fundamental. It was the bottomless chasm which separated rulers from ruled. Although the Land Reform liquidated the great estates, the material condition of the peasants was hardly better in Roumania than in Hungary, while their cultural level was considerably lower. All the features noted in the preceding chapter—peasant misery, bureaucratic brutality, false education and a privileged class lacking all sense of social responsibility, whose most brilliant members were ready from one day to the next to betray their principles in exchange for the spoils of office and the royal smile—existed in Roumania in pre-eminent degree. Democracy could not flourish in such an atmosphere. Too busy with their personal interests and ambitions to consider reforms, and blinded by fear of 'Bolshevism', the rulers drifted inevitably towards Fascism and servitude to foreign imperialism. The process of decay has gone further in Roumania than in other parts of Eastern Europe. No progress will be made until the old governing class disappears, and a new one is trained to take its place. The period of transition will be long and bloody, but when it is accomplished the great energies and qualities of the Roumanian people, the second most numerous and perhaps the most naturally talented in all Eastern Europe, will assure to it that honourable position which it has not yet been able to attain.

5. JUGOSLAVIA

The turbulent history of the Jugoslav State can only be understood if some brief account is given of the circumstances in which it was born.

It has been seen* that in 1905 the Fiume Congress inaugurated political collaboration between Serbs and Croats within the Kingdom of Hungary. The new Serbo-Croat Coalition decided at first to cooperate with the Hungarian authorities, but a language dispute brought this cooperation to an end within two years. In 1908 the elections to the Zagreb Diet gave a substantial majority to the supporters of the Coalition. When war broke out, some Dalmatian Croats, of whom the most important were Supilo (the chief organiser of the Fiume Congress), Dr Trumbić, and the famous sculptor Ivan Meštrović, went to neutral Italy, and thence passed to Allied territory, where a 'Jugoslav Committee' was formed, including also several Serbs from Austro-Hungarian territories, the purpose of whose activities was the creation of a single State of all Serbs, Croats and Slovenes.

The Serbian Government was at this time less interested in the creation of 'Jugoslavia' than in the aggrandisement of Serbia. The main national aim was the acquisition of Bosnia, the largest element in whose population consisted of Orthodox Serbs. The proposals for 'Jugoslavia' definitely came from the side of the subjects of Austria-Hungary. They were much more warmly supported by the Serbs 'across the Sava' than by those of the Kingdom of Serbia. After lengthy discussions, however, Pašić, the Serbian Prime Minister, was won, with certain reservations, for the 'Jugoslav' cause. In July 1917 a joint declaration was made in Corfu by Pašić and Trumbić, holding out the prospect of a common State of Serbs, Croats and Slovenes, under the Karadjordjević dynasty, with a democratic system guaranteeing religious freedom and equality, the Constitution to be chosen by a freely elected Constituent Assembly.

The publication of this statement had a considerable effect inside the Monarchy. The members of the Serbo-Croat Coalition in the Zagreb Diet refused the request of the Hungarian Government that they should repudiate it. The 'Jugoslav Club' of members of the Austrian Parliament, consisting of Slovenes and Dalmatian Croats, consented to do so, but few believed in their sincerity. In August 1918 a Slav Congress of the Monarchy was held in Ljubljana, as a result of which was formed a Jugoslav National Council, whose President was

* See above, p. 45.

Father Korošec, the leader of the Slovene Catholics. It was to this Council that on October 28th the Austrian military authorities in Zagreb handed their powers.

Meanwhile differences of opinion between Pašić and Trumbić prevented agreement on the formation of a joint Jugoslav Government. Korošec was sent to Geneva as soon as Austria had formally capitulated, and his arguments, combined with friendly pressure from some Allied quarters, induced Pašić to approve a declaration proclaiming the Union of the two States ruled respectively by the Serbian Government and the Jugoslav National Council. A common Government was to be formed, but the two territories were to have autonomy in all matters other than those of common interest. This statement was never willingly accepted by the Serbian Government or army, and the Council in Zagreb was not quickly informed of it. In Zagreb doubts continued, but finally on 23 November, on the initiative of the leader of the Serbs of the Monarchy, Svetozar Pribičević, the Council decided to proclaim unity with Serbia in a unitary Serbo-Croato-Slovene State, and invited Prince Alexander to assume the Regency. On 1 December the Serbian army entered Zagreb.

Meanwhile on 26 November an Assembly had met at Podgorica, formally deposed King Nicholas and his dynasty, and proclaimed the Union of Montenegro with Serbia. On 16 December a joint session in Belgrade of the Serbian Skupština and the Zagreb Council ratified the Union.

The first Jugoslav Cabinet was formed in January 1919. The Prime Minister was the Serbian statesman Stojan Protić. The Slovene leader Korošec was Vice-Premier, and Dr Trumbić was Minister of Foreign Affairs. A provisional National Assembly was formed of delegates from the Skupština and the National Council, together with representatives of Montenegro and the 'Vojvodina'—as the combined Bačka and Southern Banat were now called. The main work of this Government and Assembly consisted of the signing of the Peace Treaties, immediate measures for the reconstruction of devastated Serbia, and discussion of Land Reform. The latter was intended to enrich the peasants at the expense of the Hungarian and Croatian aristocracies and of the big Moslem landlords of Bosnia. In 1921 elections were held for the Constituent Assembly.

The biggest party in the Assembly was, as was expected, the Serbian Radical Party. This party had dominated the turbulent equalitarian Democracy that was Serbia from 1903 to 1914. It had represented in internal affairs freedom and reform, and in foreign policy friendship with Russia. Its leader Pašić, a fierce patriot and revolutionary from Zaječar near the Bulgarian frontier, was the greatest figure in Serbian politics at the beginning of the century. Already soon after 1903, however, the Radical Party began to change its character. Its leaders dropped their revolutionary phrases and paid less attention either to political liberties or to peasant welfare. Within its ranks the rising bourgeoisie acquired growing influence. This process was greatly increased after 1918. In Jugoslavia the possibilities of money-making were far bigger than in parochial pre-war Serbia. The small shopkeepers and tradesmen of the Belgrade 'Čaršija'[1] grew into big business, and, as political power was the quickest road to business success, they had good reason to strengthen their hold on the Radical Party. The party became increasingly Conservative, and soon definitely placed the interests of the bourgeoisie before those of the peasantry. Its leaders retained their personal contact with the villages. They often showed themselves to the people in small country taverns, drinking šlivovica with the peasants and jovially slapping them on the back. They even continued to feel genuine affection for 'the masses', and were proud that they came of the same stock. But their life and interests were no longer those of the village, and this was reflected in their policy. Nevertheless the Radical Party possessed huge prestige in Serbia. The change in its character was not understood for some years, and even when it had become clear there were still material reasons for supporting it. Like the Agrarian Party in Czechoslovakia, or the Liberal Party in Roumania in the twenties, it was a comparatively benevolent 'Interessengemeinschaft', which, being nearly always in power, was able to assure to its supporters a host of minor advantages. Although it no longer represented their interests, the Serbian peasants did not cease to vote for it, and it remained to the end the strongest party in the old Serbian territory.

[1] This Turkish word, meaning 'market', became used for the business and commercial class of Belgrade. The word acquired a derogatory significance. It is a household word in Jugoslav politics.

The second group in the Assembly was the Democratic Party. The bulk of this party was made up of the Independent Radicals, who had seceded from the Radical Party at the beginning of the century and whose leader was the respectable schoolmaster Ljuba Davidović. These were joined by two smaller Conservative fractions, representing officials and tradesmen, and by Pribičević's 'Prećani' Serbs. Davidović became leader of the new party, which had, like the Radical Party, a mixed bourgeois-peasant following. Its evolution followed that of the Radical Party, but it remained rather more genuinely democratic. In the years of Parliamentary regime it always had a smaller number of supporters than had the Radicals. Its main strength was in Central Serbia.

Another group of some importance was the Agrarian Party, also founded after the war, and intended specifically to represent the peasantry. In the 1921 elections the Agrarians won more than thirty seats. This success was due both to the novelty of the party and to the radical mood of the electors. It was never repeated in subsequent elections. The party kept some following in Bosnia, where many who were unable to vote Communist supported it as the next best thing. Its leader, Jovan Jovanović, enjoyed universal respect as an honourable Serbian patriot, but his party never established itself as *the* party of the peasantry. It, like the Radical and Democratic Parties, was led by intellectuals, tradesmen and townsmen. It remained nothing more than the smallest of three parties for which bourgeois, peasants, intellectuals and workers voted with equal facility and equal lack of conviction.

The third largest party in the 1921 Assembly were the Communists. A Socialist Party had existed in pre-war Serbia, strongly influenced by French and Russian ideas. The absence of an appreciable proletariat and the national antipathy to all things German had prevented the growth of a Social Democratic movement of the Central European type. The Serbian Socialists were led by revolutionary intellectuals and supported by discontented peasants. The Bolshevik Revolution received from them the approval accorded to all things both Russian and revolutionary. When the European Labour Movement split, the majority of the Serbian party went Communist. Enthusiasm for Russia combined with social discontent, caused by economic dislocation in general and the war-time sufferings of Serbia in particular, to win it no less than fifty-four seats in the 1921 elections. It received support also in the newly acquired provinces of Vojvodina and Bosnia. In 1921 the murder of Drašković, the Minister of the Interior, by a young Communist, provided an excuse for the suppression of the party. By a majority vote of the Assembly the Communist members were deprived of their mandates, some were imprisoned, the party and its Press were declared illegal, and for the following twenty years Communist sympathisers were subjected to severe persecution. This fact is as important for the history of Jugoslavia as the transformation of the three democratic parties noted above. It meant that the Left was permanently disfranchised. The official Socialists, representing a small minority of the original Socialist Party, never had much importance, although they included a number of decent and progressive individuals. The Left was driven underground, and a large part of the nation excluded from political life.

In Croatia the 1921 elections brought a surprise. The Croatian Peasant Party, led by Stephen Radić, won the overwhelming majority of the Croatian votes. The restricted Austro-Hungarian franchise had prevented this party from playing a major political part before 1918, but now, on the basis of universal suffrage, it revealed itself as by far the strongest. This gave rise to complications, for in the meeting of the Jugoslav National Council which had in November 1918 announced the Union of Croatia with Serbia the only vote of opposition had been cast by Radić. At that time it had been thought possible to ignore his view, but now he was master of Croatia. This was one of the principal causes of the woes of Jugoslavia.

Stephen Radić was a tribune of the people, devoted to the cause of the peasantry from which he sprang. He was a firm believer in Southern Slav brotherhood, but he imagined this as based on a radical form of peasant Democracy. He was a Republican, and distrusted the Serbian dynasty, army and leading politicians. His distrust was increased when he saw that the Belgrade Government was slow to accept the proffered hand of the Bulgarian peasant leader, Stamboliiski, and ultimately left him to his fate. Radić was a man of fiery temperament, generous impulses and muddled head. He never knew clearly what he wanted, and exasperated the Serbian leaders

by his vague refusal to state his terms. It was a great misfortune for Croatia and for Jugoslavia that his brother Ante
had died before the Union. The two brothers had created the
Peasant Movement. Stepan was the idol of the masses, but
Ante was the political thinker. Had he lived, his wise counsel
might have benefited the Croatian cause. As it was, Stepan
Radić, smarting from a sense of injury, adopted a negative
attitude to the Jugoslav State which did little good either to
himself or to the Croatian people.

He met his match in Pašić. The veteran Serbian statesman
had never been able to conceive of the Jugoslav State as anything but a Greater Serbia. In the Constituent Assembly the
two theses of Centralism and Federalism fought it out. The
Radicals were in favour of uncompromising Centralism, the
Croatian members insisted on a federal solution. The Communists, who might have supported Federalism, were excluded,
and the cause of Centralism was reinforced by Svetozar
Pribičević, who, having begun his career as a supporter of
the fullest Serbo-Croatian collaboration, had become more
Centralist than Pašić himself. Among the members from the
Kingdom of Serbia the followers of Davidović and the Agrarians were more willing to compromise, but preferred on the
whole a centralist solution. The Centralists won. The 'Vidovdan
Constitution', named after St Vitus' Day, the Serbian national
holiday, on which it was voted and on which in 1914 Franz
Ferdinand had been murdered, established a centralised administrative system for the whole State, which was called
'Kingdom of the Serbs, Croats and Slovenes'. Democratic
liberties were assured and proportional representation was
introduced. The king was given large powers of control over
the army, which was to be kept out of politics. The king was
to choose the Prime Minister in accordance with the disposition
of votes in Parliament. As proportional representation favoured
the multiplication of groups, the breadth of his choice was in
practice considerable.

The business of the Constituent Assembly concluded, the
king entrusted the holding of elections to Pašić. The result
was an increased vote for the Radicals and for the Croatian
Peasant Party, a fall in the number of Democrat seats and
heavy loss for the Agrarians. The new Cabinet was formed by
Pašić, who derived some additional support from the Bosnian

Moslems. The Turkish successes in Anatolia had put new heart in the Moslem community, which numbered some 750,000 in Bosnia, and their leaders now demanded the full religious and cultural rights promised by the Constitution. As their demands were moderate, and could not be considered a menace to the security of the State, they were mostly granted. Most Jugoslav Governments in the following twenty years received the support of the Moslem political leaders.

Radić meanwhile continued his opposition, supported by the majority of Croats, who were willing to follow him whatever he did. In 1924 he slipped out of the country and went to Moscow, where the creation of a Peasant International was being considered. Radić, however, was little interested in Soviet plans, and probably intended his visit rather as a means of blackmail on Belgrade than as a serious enterprise. He returned to Jugoslavia, was put in prison, and emerged after some months to join the Government, under the Premiership of Pašić. After a year, however, no progress had been made, for Radić still would not state his conditions and the Serbian politicians were no more disposed to make substantial concessions. In 1926 Radić left the Government. In the following year Svetozar Pribičević, the former apostle of Centralism, who had recently separated from Davidović to form a party of his own, the 'Independent Democratic Party', now reconciled himself with Radić. The two men formed the 'Peasant-Democratic Coalition', which pronounced itself for reform, Democracy and a federal organisation of the State. The leader of the ex-Austro-Hungarian Serbs was once again in alliance with the Croats. From 1927 until the destruction of Jugoslavia, Pribičević's party had the most advanced democratic ideas of all the legal Jugoslav parties. But it had only a small following, consisting largely of intellectuals, including some from the Kingdom of Serbia. It no longer represented the majority of the Serbs of the former Austro-Hungarian territories, many of whom now voted for the parties of the Kingdom.

The crisis came in 1928 when a Montenegrin member stood up in Parliament and shot Radić and two of his followers. The Croatian leader died later in hospital from his wound. The Croatian members left the Parliament, and deadlock was complete. Hatred grew on both sides. On 5 and 6 January

1929 King Alexander received Radić's successor, Dr Maček,
and asked his conditions for acceptance of Jugoslavia and
cooperation with Belgrade. Maček demanded a new Constitution, which would reorganise the State on a basis of seven
federal units—Slovenia, Croatia, Bosnia, Vojvodina, Serbia,
Montenegro and Macedonia—each to have its legislature with
powers over trade and finance other than international, and
over education. Each federal unit would control postal and tele-
graphic services on its territory, and would have its own army,
drawn from men resident in the respective territory, who were
not to be used outside its boundaries without the specific
approval of the local legislature. In his second interview
Maček reduced the number of federal units to five, leaving
Macedonia to Serbia and dividing Bosnia between Croatia and
Serbia. Even in their modified form the demands were clearly
unacceptable, especially those regarding the army. If they
had been put into practice the State would have disappeared.
In these circumstances Alexander saw no alternative but to
take on to his own shoulders the whole responsibility. On
6 January 1929 a royal Dictatorship was introduced.[1]

There is little reason to doubt the patriotic nature of the
king's motives. The squabbles of the politicians during the
preceding ten years had presented a sorry spectacle. Alexander
was by nature intolerant of such behaviour. He never understood the meaning of party politics. He thought in terms of
the Dynasty and the State, and believed the national interest
required the suppression of internal conflicts. He was never
sufficiently interested to find out the nature of these conflicts,
some of which had deeper political, social or ideological roots
than he, with his preference for dramatic military solutions,
could imagine. Brought up at the Court of St Petersburg,
he had no patience with Parliamentary procedure or Democratic methods. His autocratic character had been revealed
in the war, when Colonel Dimitrijević, known by the name
of 'Apis', the most powerful personality in Serbia and the
organiser of Serbian patriotic-revolutionary activities against
the Ottoman and Habsburg Empires during the first ten
years of the century, came into conflict with him, was tried

---

[1] For a full account of King Alexander's version of these negotiations, see
article by Hamilton Fish Armstrong in *Foreign Affairs* of January 1935, based
on an interview given by the King to Mr Armstrong.

by a military court in Salonica for high treason, and executed. This trial, conducted with remarkable haste and in somewhat dubious circumstances, left no mean legacy of hatred behind, for 'Apis' was perhaps the most popular man in the country. Its result, however, was to establish the complete control of Alexander over the army. He never loosened his grip. After the war, Alexander had found it difficult to endure what seemed to him the meanly sordid wranglings of inferior demagogues. He had a horror of 'anarchy' and saw the spectre of 'Bolshevism' lurking in the background. He had probably always considered that Monarchical Dictatorship was the best form of Government, but he could plausibly claim that he had been patient, and that matters had reached so complete an 'impasse' that there was no other way open. He knew that he was assuming a heavy burden, but he was prepared to bear it.

Alexander determined to create by force a new 'Jugoslav patriotism'. He had no more sympathy for Serbian than for Croatian particularism. His first Prime Minister was a soldier, General Pero Zivković. This man had begun his career in 1903, when, a Lieutenant in the Royal Guard, he had opened the palace gates to the conspirators, who, led by 'Apis' Dimitrijević, had murdered King Alexander Obrenović and his hated queen Draga. Fourteen years later he had deserted his former leader, and had been one of the pillars of the prosecution at the Salonica Trial. Since then he had been a devoted henchman of the king. Alexander now attempted, with his new team, to recruit support alike from Serbs and from Croats.

The king was more successful in Serbia than in Croatia. The existence of several Serbian parties enabled him to apply the same tactics of division and manœuvre so skilfully employed by his fellow-monarchs Carol of Roumania and Ferdinand and Boris of Bulgaria. Politicians of all parties were found to serve him, and win thereby both distinction and riches. Of the three main parties the Radical Party supplied the greatest number.

In Croatia these tactics produced no result. The overpowering majority of the people was united round the Croatian Peasant Party, whose leaders remained faithful to the memory of their martyr Radić, and refused to work with a regime which denied them political liberty and federal status. Several individual Croats accepted office under the Dictatorship. These men, however, such as Švrljuga, a Zagreb business man who became Finance Minister, were regarded as traitors by the bulk of the people. They represented no one but themselves, and their adhesion to the regime was not a source of strength.

Thus the Dictatorship, which Alexander had wished to raise above Nationalism, became essentially anti-Croatian. Alexander's principal advisers were Serbian officers or members of the Radical Party, both rigidly 'Great Serb' in outlook. The 'Jugoslav Idea' became confused with 'Great Serbism'. Demands to become 'Jugoslav' were felt by Croats as demands that they should throw over their whole historical heritage and national consciousness, cease to be Croats and become Serbs, citizens of a centralised Serbian State. The old conception of the 'Jugoslav Idea', as brotherhood of South Slav peoples with equal rights, began to be forgotten on both sides.

Serbs of the old generation and of the upper classes, even quite moderate nationalists, were genuinely alarmed by the negative attitude of the Croats to the State, and regarded Croatia almost as an occupied enemy province. It was felt that only Serbs could be trusted, and Serbian officials poured into Croatia. The gendarmerie, which was composed almost exclusively of Serbs, was increased in number, and often behaved not only tactlessly but cruelly. Croatian peasants were terrorised and robbed. Cases of beatings and torture were not infrequent.

The Croats accused the Serbs of exploiting Croatia as a colony. Special indignation was caused by the fact that taxation was higher in Croatia than in Serbia. This was really not so unreasonable as it would seem, for the general level of income, at least during the first decade, was considerably higher in Croatia, and Serbia had suffered so frightfully in the First World War that she could only obtain the means of reconstruction by taxing the new provinces. This the more reasonable Croats would have been willing to accept, had their political demands been taken into consideration and had not the Serbian administration misbehaved in Croatia.

Under the Dictatorship the character of the Croatian Peasant Party underwent an important change. Before the war the bourgeoisie of Croatia had voted for the bourgeois parties in the Zagreb Diet, either for the Serbo-Croatian coalition or for the Frank Party of uncompromising Croatian nationalists. Since the introduction of universal suffrage had assured the predominance of the Peasant Party, the bourgeois parties had been unable to survive independently. Obliged to recognise the supremacy of the Peasant Party for a fact, and convinced of the need of a united front of all Croats against Belgrade, the Croatian bourgeoisie began to enter the Peasant Party. Soon they acquired a predominant influence within it. Originally a social revolutionary movement, the party became a nationalist organisation directed by the urban middle class.

Dr Maček, a small-town lawyer and an intimate collaborator of the Radić brothers, retained contact with the peasants, and had their interests at heart. But many of those who surrounded Maček cared nothing for the peasants' condition. They wished only to cut loose from Belgrade, to set up their own State, and to be top dogs in it. Some of these men had no objection in principle to the methods used by Belgrade. What annoyed them was that they were not themselves able to use these methods for their own advantage. Yet these people had small cause for complaint. They had every opportunity to enrich themselves. It was not only the Belgrade 'Čaršija' that made sensational fortunes, and the 'cultural and moral superiority' of the Croats was hardly confirmed by the proportion of Croats involved in financial and commercial scandals under Jugoslavia. The real sufferers in Croatia were the peasants, on whose backs weighed the burden of the Serbian bureaucracy, and who provided the victims of the police terror. But the loudest shrieks against 'Serbian barbarism' came not from them but from the comfortable Zagreb intellectuals and business men, from that urban ruling class which the Radić brothers had so vehemently attacked in the early days of the Peasant Movement.

The Croatian Peasant Party therefore now consisted of an uneasy marriage of peasant democrats and bourgeois reactionaries. The common struggle kept them together, but there was never much love lost between the Left and Right wings. The Left wing maintained the ideology of Ante Radić, and insisted on political Democracy and social reform: the Right wing prated of 'Croatian millenary culture' and constitutional rights. The Left wing cherished the ideal of a peasant democratic federation of all South Slavs, and therefore hoped for ultimate understanding with the Serbs: the Right wing cared nothing for peasantry, Democracy or Slavdom, but was resolved to break away completely from Serbia and to link up with the Catholic countries of Central and Western Europe.

The Left wing had the support of the greater part of the peasants and of the younger intellectuals, especially those born of peasant stock and educated in the ideas of Radić. The Right wing was strongest in the towns, and especially among the older educated class. Universal suffrage and wider education brought during the twenty years of Jugoslavia a steady flow of recruits for the Croatian upper class. These new bourgeois diluted the old traditional Croatian bourgeoisie with a good deal of new Jugoslav and democratic opinion. Nevertheless the bulk of the Zagreb bourgeoisie probably remained anti-Jugoslav, anti-democratic and socially conservative. These elements acquired growing influence within the Peasant Party, but they were resisted by Maček, who remained to the end devoted both to the old 'Jugoslav Idea' and to Democracy. He was backed by some of the younger intellectual leaders, but did not show sufficient strength in purging the party leadership of reactionary elements.

The extreme Right was represented both within and without the party ranks. The survivors of the Frank Party never even nominally accepted the principles of the Peasant Party. They remained devoted to Clerical Fascist principles such as those that guided Dollfuss in Austria. They enjoyed some support among intellectuals and in the Catholic hierarchy. An extremist group of terrorists, led by the exiled Dr Ante Pavelić, engaged in definite subversive activity. It had an illegal organisation within the country, but its leaders lived in Italy and Hungary. In later years it came under German Nazi influence. Its followers called themselves 'Ustaše'.

It would be a mistake to imagine that only Croatia suffered under King Alexander's Dictatorship. The lot of the Serbs also deteriorated rapidly. The beneficiaries of the Dictatorship were the clique of politicians in power, and their dependents and supporters in the country. As in Zagreb, so in Belgrade fortunes were made in politics and in business. While the rulers enriched themselves, the people was impoverished.

The peasants' condition followed the same process as in other Balkan countries, as described in Chapter Four. The

World Depression made it worse. Some measures were carried out to assist the peasants, notably the foundation in 1929 of the Agrarian Bank and the creation of the Privileged Export Institute intended to protect cereal prices. But these measures benefited principally the big and medium holders of Slavonia and Vojvodina. The peasants of Serbia, Bosnia, Montenegro and Macedonia derived little advantage from them, least of all the small holders. Discontent grew, and was mercilessly suppressed by the gendarmes. The reorganisation of the administrative system, introduced by Alexander, which substituted for thirty-three Departments nine 'Banovine' or Provinces, cutting across historic boundaries, did nothing to improve the quality of the bureaucracy. The authorities were obsessed by the 'Bolshevik danger'. Arrests, beatings, tortures and deaths 'while trying to escape' became familiar phenomena.

One of the main centres of radical feeling was the University of Belgrade. Students had played a glorious part in the winning of Serbian independence, and the autonomy of the university was respected as a sacred tradition even under the Dictatorship. Professors were chosen only for their academic qualifications, and students were able within the university walls freely to express their views. Many of the students were sons of poor peasant families. By great efforts their parents had scraped together the small sums necessary to transport them to the capital and to pay their entrance fees. Having once obtained admission to the university the students kept themselves alive by earning a few pence as tram-drivers, waiters or window-cleaners. Undernourished and weak in health, worn out by the double strain of physical and intellectual labour, they grew up to hate the system which caused their sufferings. Familiarised by their teachers with the old principles of Liberty, Equality and Fraternity, they saw around them nothing but injustice, repression and silence. Protests against abuses brought down on their heads the persecution of the apparatus of the Dictatorship. They were driven to the conclusion that only revolutionary methods and solutions could improve the lot of the Serbian people and make Jugoslavia a decent country.

In the Eastern European countries the leaders of every generation are those who obtain higher education, the main mechanism by which the ruling class is created. In Serbia, which between 1912 and 1918 lost one million out of four and a half million inhabitants, the generation which grew up since the war was more important than in any other country of Europe. The future of Serbia depended and depends on those who passed through the University of Belgrade between 1918 and 1941.

The rulers of Jugoslavia between 1918 and 1941 consisted partly of the pre-1914 generation, honest and democratic citizens who cared genuinely for the interests of the people, but who were too old to understand the needs of the modern age, and partly of the war generation which had emerged crippled from the catastrophe and was concerned only to compensate itself for its sufferings by riches and power gained at any price. The old generation had lost contact with the people. The middle generation cared nothing for the people. The young generation ignored the first and revolted fiercely against the second. These young men believed that the knowledge and opportunity which education had given them should be used, not to cheat, exploit and oppress the class from which they had risen, but to enlighten it, to help their own brothers and sisters by their own efforts to improve their condition. Like the Russian intellectuals of the seventies who set themselves to 'return to the people', the Serbian students devoted themselves to the service of the people. The movement suffered, perhaps, from a certain naïve and exalted romanticism, but it had a serious effect on the life of the Serbian people. Its followers gave many proofs of resolution, courage and sincerity. In a country where learning and knowledge enjoy immense prestige, where the peasant's son who has a university degree is regarded as a prophet in his own village, the movement was bound to have a powerful influence.

The leaders of the young generation, on whom the future of Serbia depended, were revolutionaries. Their own personal experiences and the general political and economic evolution of the country strengthened their revolutionary convictions. Both by deliberate propaganda and by personal example they spread their ideas in the country. Sympathy for revolutionary ideas increased among peasants and townsmen, especially among the younger generation. None of these tendencies were reflected on the surface of political life, in the manœuvres of the official political parties, in which the younger generation had no say. But beneath the waters new forces were being created. Only when the brutal levelling might of the conqueror had destroyed the old State apparatus did these forces make themselves manifest.

King Alexander was not unaware of the abuses that went on under his Dictatorship, of the corruption, brutality and terror. He attempted to change his advisers. Živković was succeeded by civilians, who were changed in turn. But the system remained. The Dictatorship, introduced to end the conflicts of Jugoslav politics, solved nothing. 'Jugoslav patriotism' remained a phrase: Serbian and Croatian chauvinism survived. Social discontent and political rivalries were repressed by force but were not removed. Hatred was only the more powerful for being driven underground. During his last years it is believed that the king was convinced of the need for greater freedom. Some claim that he intended to replace his 1931 Constitution—which had superseded the 'Vidovdan Constitution' and legalised the Dictatorship—by something more democratic. If such were Alexander's intentions, he never achieved them. On 9 October 1934 he was murdered at Marseilles, together with the French Foreign Minister, Barthou, by a Macedonian terrorist. The plot had been prepared by I.M.R.O.* and Pavelić, with the help of the Italian and Hungarian authorities.

With the disastrous international consequences of the Marseilles murder we shall deal later.† Its immediate result within Jugoslavia was to rally the people as never before. The crime was repudiated by the majority of Croats, who had the less reason for pleasure in view of the connection with it of Italy, whose designs on Dalmatia were well known. In Serbia the news caused a rage of offended patriotism. Many who had cursed the king in his lifetime were loud in condemnation of the outrage. The Karadjordjević dynasty was the Serbs' own dynasty. They might quarrel with it, but that was an internal squabble. Intervention from outside was intolerable. The impressive processions which greeted the coffin of the king on its passage through the country were an unmistakable demonstration of national solidarity.

Alexander's will appointed as First Regent his cousin Prince Paul. Paul was little known in Jugoslavia. He had kept out

* See below, p. 244.　　　　　　† See pp. 377–8.

of politics, which interested him little, and had devoted himself to the formation of a fine art collection. Educated in England, he felt more at home in a western capital than in his own country. He neither understood nor liked the Serbs. He was incapable of mixing with peasants, as his cousin had gladly done, both at the front and as peace-time king. Paul shared Alexander's horror of 'Bolshevism', which was augmented by an almost pathological antipathy to the 'vulgar masses'. Thrust against his will into the unpleasant situation of Balkan Dictator, he tried his best, according to his lights, but he was not the man for the job. Disliking all Jugoslavs who were not 'Europeanised', he had no reason to prefer Serbs to Croats. He seemed therefore comparatively well equipped to come to an agreement with the latter. Dr Maček was released from prison, and expressed high hopes of the Prince Regent. Liberal-minded Serbs also hoped that a more tolerant regime would be instituted.

Paul replaced Uzunović as Premier by the Foreign Minister Jevtić, who held elections in 1935, receiving approximately 1,700,000 votes to the 1,000,000 of the Opposition. The electoral law gave him a much bigger majority of seats in the Parliament. After some months, however, the strong 'Great Serb' views of Jevtić caused the Prince Regent, genuinely eager to reach an agreement with the Croats, to replace him by a Radical Party politician, Dr Milan Stojadinović, a banker enjoying connections with the English business world, who had distinguished himself by a pamphlet advocating the restoration of diplomatic relations between Jugoslavia and the Soviet Union.

Stojadinović, once firmly in power, belied the general expectations. So far from courting Moscow, he went out of his way to please the Fascist Powers. In this he carried out the orders of Paul, who, frankly bored by internal politics, showed greater interest in foreign policy, for which he felt his knowledge of Western Europe suited him. The real direction of Jugoslavia's foreign policy lay in Paul's hands from 1934 to 1941.

In internal affairs Stojadinović disappointed those who had expected a more democratic regime. Police pressure was only very slightly relaxed. The activities of the Croatian Peasant Party were tolerated, but the Prime Minister did not seem in a hurry to settle matters with Maček. Government was carried on by a new party, the 'Jugoslav Radical Union', known by the initials of its Serbian words J.R.Z. This was formed of three groups—a section of the Serbian Radical Party, led by Stojadinović; the Moslem party of Bosnia, led by Dr Spaho; and the Slovene 'Clerical' Party led by the veteran Monsignor Anton Korošec.

The Moslems took little part in political life. Traditionally opportunists, the Moslem leaders, who before 1914 had supported the Austrian regime, supported most Governments of Jugoslavia. Their main concern was to secure material advantages for their co-religionaries. In this they were particularly successful during the rule of J.R.Z. Spaho was Minister of Communications, and it became a standing joke that railway jobs were monopolised by befezzed Bosnians. Content with these solid gains, Spaho interfered little in political life. The real power in Jugoslavia lay in the hands of Stojadinović and Korošec, both of whom were in turn dependent on the goodwill of the Prince Regent.

Korošec was one of the most striking and complex personalities of Jugoslav politics. Already in Habsburg days a leader of the Slovenes, he continued under Jugoslavia to defend his people's interests. The Slovenes were not satisfied with the centralist Constitution, even if in practice the difference between the Slovene and Serbo-Croatian languages ensured that the administration of Slovenia was carried on by Slovenes. Insistence on Slovene rights had earned Korošec internment for a time under Alexander. Now, as the second most important leader of J.R.Z., he was in a position to obtain all desired advantages for Slovenia save legal autonomy.

Under the J.R.Z. Governments the Slovenes not only controlled their own homeland, but began to 'colonise' Serbia. The number of Slovenes in the Ministries of Belgrade was considerable, and both Serbs and Croats complained that the Slovenes were unduly privileged. The truth is that the superior education and industriousness of the Slovenes—far more marked than the much-vaunted but rather doubtful 'Cultural superiority of Croats over Serbs'—obtained for them the same sort of position that Scots have long enjoyed south of the Border.

In Slovenia Korošec enjoyed great prestige, both for his

past record and because of his successes in 'placing' his country-men, but not all loved him. He relied on the Catholic priests, the peasantry and that section of the intelligentsia which was influenced by the Church. In the villages the priests wielded great power. The efficient cooperative system had been largely built up, and was mainly controlled, by priests. The standard of education of both priests and peasants was much higher than in Croatia or Serbia, and the priesthood could be considered a fairly progressive element. The peasants were also better off, and suffered less from overpopulation, than their neighbours to the south. Although there was discontent, it was not so widespread as elsewhere, and the majority of peasants still had confidence in the priests and gave their votes to the Clericals.

In the towns the situation was different. The greater part of the Slovene intelligentsia was anti-Clerical. Many supported the Liberal Party, led by Dr Kramer, which had fused during Alexander's rule with the ultra-centralist Jugoslav National Party of Živković and Jevtić. Besides the Liberals there were in Slovenia a substantial number of Social Democrats. These had grown up in Habsburg days under the influence of Viennese Social Democracy, and dominated the Trade Unions in the industrial areas of Slovenia. Communist influence was smaller in Slovenia than in Croatia, let alone Serbia, but it was growing among the younger generation, especially among the students.

Korošec was violently opposed to anything which smelt of the Left. He thundered in his speeches against 'Bolshevism'. Not content with keeping the Slovene Left well in control, he determined to purge Serbia also of 'Reds'. As Minister of the Interior he was particularly alarmed by the radicalism of the Belgrade students, but not even he was able to interfere with the autonomy of the university. He had a strong personal influence on Prince Paul, however, and used it to prevent any increase of political liberty, such as might have given not Bolsheviks but even respectable democrats a chance to express their views.

At the same time Korošec, as a Catholic and a Slovene, was keen to settle the Croatian problem and to obtain legal autonomy for Slovenia. It was his idea to make a Concordat with the Vatican, giving the Catholic Church a number of advantages. It was hoped that this would appeal to the more conservative Croats, and that Maček might be induced to find a basis of agreement which would not necessitate the introduction of a democratic system.

It might be considered reasonable that the Government should seek an understanding with the Vatican. Yet the Concordat provoked a fury of opposition in Serbia. The Orthodox Church saw in it a threat to its own position. It claimed that the Concordat gave the Roman Church privileges denied to other religious communities. Distrust of Catholicism, tied up in their minds with the hereditary enemies Austria, Hungary and Italy, is deeply rooted in the Serbs. Moreover the Orthodox Church, which normally plays little part in politics but comes to the front when the nation is in danger, commands a profound loyalty. An attack on the Church is felt by the Serbs, probably the least religious people in Eastern Europe, as an attack on the whole nation. A storm of indignation was let loose by the Church, and all the oppositional elements in Serbia centred round it. In the middle of the agitation the Patriarch died, and the rumour was spread that he had been poisoned. Meanwhile Maček wisely refused to treat the Concordat as an overture, and the majority of the Croats remained quite indifferent.

Out of the Concordat crisis resulted an important political event. In the autumn of 1937 the Serbian Radical,[1] Democratic and Agrarian Parties made an agreement with the Croatian Peasant Party and with the Independent Democratic Party led by Vilder and Budisavljević, the successors of Pribičević.[2] The new political alliance declared its intention to work in harmony for the establishment of democratic government and the solution of the Croatian Question.

A wave of enthusiasm swept the country. The Serbian people wished to satisfy the wishes of the Croats, and looked on Maček as the principal champion of Democracy, which they so dearly desired to see in Serbia. It was felt that the Serbs had suffered long enough from their rulers' failure to solve the Croatian Question. This had been evoked for eight years as a reason for upholding Dictatorship, and a growing

[1] The section which had remained in opposition to Stojadinović, who had of course taken a large number of former Radical supporters with him.

[2] Pribičević had been interned in painful conditions by King Alexander, but released on the personal intercession of President Masaryk. His health was broken, and he died soon afterwards in Paris.

number of Serbs had convinced themselves that there was no desire in high places to solve it, that it was being deliberately used to plant the yoke more firmly on the shoulders of both peoples. The height of Serbo-Croatian friendship was reached in August 1938, when Dr Maček came to Belgrade to confer with the Serbian leaders, and was met at the railway station by a crowd of some 50,000, of which the majority were Serbian peasants who had walked miles or had spent their few pennies on transport, to come and cheer the Croatian leader. When Maček described the terror of the gendarmes on a Dalmatian island, and asked his audience, 'Can you expect men who have suffered like this to fight for the State that oppresses them?', the Serbs cried, 'No, and we wouldn't either'. This was a sad reflection on the condition of the country, and.yet a cause of hope, in so far as the meeting showed real solidarity of the Serbian and Croatian peoples.

The bitterness of the people's mood, and Serbian enthusiasm for Maček, deeply alarmed Regent and Government. The elections of 11 December gave the Government a majority of only 54 % of the votes to the United Opposition's 44 %. Maček's candidates swept the field in Croatia, but in Serbia the Opposition was less successful. This was largely due to pressure and bribery by the Government. Although the Serbian oppositional parties only won a few seats in Bosnia and Central Serbia and one at Veles in Macedonia, a considerable number of oppositional votes were recorded in many of the constituencies won by the Government. Apart from Slovenia, where Korošec had the situation well in hand, the Government's most striking successes were won in regions inhabited by national minorities—Germans, Albanians and Hungarians. This fact increased public indignation with the Premier, who had bought electoral support from the minorities at the price of material concessions resented in a time of international uncertainty and tension.

Seeing that universal hatred of Stojadinović was an obstacle to internal appeasement in general and agreement with the Croats in particular, Paul replaced him in February 1939 by Dragiša Cvetković, a Radical party boss who had become mayor of Niš and who had followed Stojadinović into J.R.Z. He was known mainly for his organising of the unpopular uniformed Governmental 'Trade Unions' ('Jugoras'), created on the Italian model. A man of limited intelligence, Cvetković was willing to carry out any orders given by the Prince Regent. Having no clearly defined political past, he was an acceptable partner in negotiations with the Croats.

Impressed by the March Czechoslovak crisis, Paul ordered Cvetković to open negotiations in April. Two possible methods were available. One was to form at once a National Government of Concentration, including representatives of all the Serbian parties, and then consider thoroughly the best means to solve the Croatian Question. The other was to open discussions between the J.R.Z. Government and Maček on the basis of the definition of the powers to be attributed to autonomous Croatia and the territorial boundaries that were to be assigned to it. The former method meant to abandon the monopolistic position occupied by J.R.Z.: the latter involved the risk of sharpening Serbo-Croatian nationalist antagonism.

Eager to avoid a democratisation of Serbia, which Korošec had little difficulty in representing to him as a prelude to the introduction of 'Bolshevism', Paul decided on the second method. The temptation to drive a wedge between Maček and his allies was too strong to be resisted. Maček for a time hesitated whether to accept negotiations on a basis which implied betrayal of his friends. But the impatience of his own supporters to obtain the best possible terms; the pressure of the rapidly deteriorating international situation, which made Jugoslav unity more necessary than ever; and the obvious unwillingness of Paul and Korošec to consider the point of view of the Serbian Opposition, induced him to begin discussions. These broke down after some weeks, but were resumed in the later summer, and resulted in the 'Agreement' ('Sporazum') of 26 August.

This created a single Croatian 'Banovina', comprising the former provinces of the Sava and the coast, together with a part of Bosnia and Hercegovina (Travnik and Mostar districts). After some discussion it was decided to include Dubrovnik, but not Syrmia (Srem, i.e. the area west of Belgrade between the Sava and the Danube), since, although it had been part of historical Croatia, the majority of its population were Serbs. The 'Banovina' was given considerable powers, matters of national interest being reserved for the Central Government. As 'Ban' was appointed a man of well-proven Jugoslav feelings, Dr Ivan Šubašić. The Croats entered the Government, Maček becoming Vice-Premier and his collaborator Šutej Minister of Finance. Several members of the Croatian Peasant and Independent Democratic Parties were made Senators. Of the Serbian parties, the Agrarians expressed qualified approval, and one of their leaders, Dr Ćubrilović, became with the consent of his party Minister of Agriculture. Radicals and Democrats remained in opposition.

The European War broke out a week later, and Paul congratulated himself that he had managed things nicely. Unfortunately the situation was little improved. The Democrats and Radicals, bitterly disappointed at being left out of the Government, accused Maček of having 'betrayed Serbian Democracy'. Small though were the grounds for these gentlemen to pose as champions of Democracy, there was nevertheless sufficient superficial justification for the charge to cause trouble. The Serbian people was prepared to admit that the outbreak of war was not the moment to carry out radical changes in the form of Government, but it was still disappointed that this was not done. Enthusiasm for Maček waned. It was known that the frontiers of the Croatian 'Banovina' did not satisfy the full territorial demands of the Croats, and fears were expressed on the Serbian side that further pieces of Bosnia would be surrendered. The demand was raised for a separate 'Serbian Banovina' and for the definition of Serbian territory. The Serbian people felt that it had been cheated of its rights. It had created Jugoslavia, at the cost of a quarter of its population killed in six years of war, and now the Croats were enjoying privileges which a Serbian Prince and Serbian Premier withheld from Serbs. This mood of frustration was fully exploited by the Radical and Democratic leaders, whom the mistaken decision of Paul had freed from the responsibility of signing the 'Sporazum'. These politicians irresponsibly let loose a campaign of agitation against the Croats, and succeeded in restoring some of the old nationalist ill-feeling of ten years earlier.

The Croats for their part were not satisfied. The legal quibblers of the Zagreb coffee-houses still wearisomely argued that Croatia had been freer under Hungary when, although three-quarters of the nation was disfranchised, the sacred constitutional rights of the Croatian Kingdom were officially recognised. The peasants were impatient that radical reforms were not carried out. For decades Peasant Party spokesmen had promised them that, when they came to power, the Zagreb 'gospoda' would be ousted and the peasants would themselves rule their country. Now nothing of the sort had happened. The war situation was not favourable to social reforms, and the party was led by bourgeois. Croatian Fascists inside and outside the party used these discontents and disillusionments to make mischief. Individual Serbs were murdered by terrorists, and Maček took no strong measures against the guilty.

Maček refused to admit that the Croatian Peasant Party was no longer able to hold its Right and Left wings. The democratic element in the party was numerically by far the stronger. If he had relied solely on it, Maček would have had at least 70 % of the Croatian votes. But he and his bourgeois advisers were not content with a majority: they must still have the totalitarian unanimity which they had enjoyed during the national struggle. Maček believed that he could drive both horses at once. So he and his friends went out of their way to humour the Extreme Right, to keep them in the party, and to take the wind out of the sails of the small irreconcilable Pavelić faction. To this end various official Croatian speakers made demagogic anti-Serbian speeches, re-opening all the wounds of the past. These were seized on by the inflamed nationalists in Belgrade, who published newspapers and pamphlets vehemently attacking the Croats. When these were suppressed by the authorities, indignation merely increased, and there was talk of a dictatorship of Croats over Serbs in Belgrade itself. And these Serbian protests were used by the Croatian extremists to whip up hatred of Serbs in Croatia.

All this was profoundly distasteful to Maček, who never abandoned his aim of a democratic, peasant-ruled, progressive federation of all South Slavs. But this dream receded while Maček left freedom to those who were sabotaging his ideas, sabotaging Croatian Democracy and sabotaging the Jugoslav State. And all this might have been prevented if Prince Paul had not been so afraid of 'Bolshevism' and if the politicians of J.R.Z. had not been so fond of power.

Another cause of demoralisation was the German-Soviet Pact. Sympathy for Russia was as widespread in Jugoslavia

as hatred of Germany. The majority of Jugoslavs, especially
the Serbian younger generation, hoped for the victory of the
Allies, but Moscow's *volte-face* obliged a part of them now to
concentrate their attacks on 'Anglo-French Imperialism', to
the malicious delight of the Germans. The result was to unite
Serbian opinion against the Left. Korošec and the Right, who
welcomed any opportunity of action against 'Bolshevism',
found themselves in agreement with the democratic middle
class, bitterly offended by the insults thrown at its spiritual
fatherland France. The university was closed for a time, and
political meetings there were banned. But the catchwords
against the Allies spread to some extent among the peasants
and workers, reinforced by the general desire for peace.

The events of the last six months of Jugoslav independence
will be considered later, but a few general remarks may ter-
minate this survey of Jugoslav internal politics between 1918
and 1939.

The Serbs are, with the possible exception of the Greeks,
the most politically minded, and the most devoted to Liberty,
of all the peoples of Eastern Europe. It would have been
difficult to impose Dictatorship on them but for two factors.
The first was the loss in war of a million out of four and a
half million Serbs. The nation was deprived of the flower of
a whole generation, and only the very old and the young were
left. The second factor was the Croatian Question, which was
made the permanent excuse for maintenance of a Dictatorship
from which in the long run the greatest sufferers were the
Serbs themselves. The Dictatorship of King Alexander never
dealt with the Croatian Question, preferring to wait for a
feeling of Jugoslav patriotism to create itself out of the void.
Finally Prince Paul attempted to solve the question in a manner
which unfortunately made possible a recrudescence of hatred
between Serbs and Croats, whom the Dictatorship and the
international danger had previously brought closer together.

Two more points deserve mention. One is the absence of
political representation of the peasantry. Radić had been a
great peasant leader, but after his death his party became a
bourgeois nationalist organisation. Rather more was done for
the Croatian than for the Serbian peasant, thanks to such
institutions as 'Gospodarska Sloga', but in the political field the
peasants were definitely relegated to the background. In Serbia

there was no real peasant movement at all, either in power or in opposition. The Agrarian Party followed the same process as the other Serbian bourgeois parties. It had its full complement of business men, small-town traders, urban intellectuals and public officials. It was a party of the peasantry only in the sense that it relied on peasant votes, and that its leaders possessed proficiency in a style of tavern oratory which commended itself to some, but increasingly few, peasants.

The second point arises partly out of this political vacuum and partly out of the war losses. It is the estrangement between the younger and older generations. The young men were brought up to value the principle of Liberty, whether embodied in the national epics known to every Serb or in the French Liberal and revolutionary literature which was the chief intellectual sustenance of the more educated. But in their country they saw no liberty, only injustice and silence. They realised that the old Serbian parties had become meaningless, and convinced themselves that much more radical ideas, methods and solutions were required. Many of them were Communists and all were called 'Communist' as a term of abuse. The fact remains that this younger generation, which fought for four years in the mountains against overwhelming odds and defended the honour of its country which the official political and military leaders cast in the slime, wants something new. It will not be satisfied with the old lies and promises, but will insist on honesty and justice. It is filled with revolutionary fire, but it is free from the racial hatred and national intolerance which distorted the idealism of its contemporaries in so many other lands. It believes in a new political and social order, and it believes in solidarity and equality of Serbs, Croats and Slovenes. To it belongs the future.

6. BULGARIA

The history of Bulgaria since 1918 begins, like that of the other defeated country of Eastern Europe, Hungary, with a revolutionary outburst followed by a period of bloody reaction.

Bulgaria had entered the war on the side of Germany, but not even the acquisition of Macedonia from Serbia had inspired the Bulgarian people with much enthusiasm for it. It was felt that Bulgaria's action was a betrayal of Russia, who had liberated her from the Turks. It is true that Bulgarian soldiers fought dutifully, even on the Dobrudja front against Russian troops. Yet it was in Bulgaria that the collapse of the Central Powers began, on the Salonica front in the autumn of 1918. At the end of September King Ferdinand released the peasant leader, Alexander Stamboliiski, whose criticism of Bulgaria's war against Russia had caused him earlier to be arrested, and now appealed to him to use his authority with the peasant soldiers to make them continue the fight.

Stamboliiski refused, and one of his friends, Daskalov, organised a 'Republic' of mutinous soldiers at Radomir. The 'Republican' Army marched on Sofia, but was repelled with German help by General Protogerov. Daskalov and Stamboliiski went into hiding. Popular feeling against Ferdinand grew. He was hated for his German origin, despotic inclinations and political intrigues. On 6 October he abdicated in favour of his son Boris. An Armistice was signed, and a coalition Ministry was formed. In the summer of 1919 this Ministry was joined by Stamboliiski, who had meanwhile come out of hiding and had been amnestied. The elections of August 1919 gave a large following, though not an absolute majority, to his party, and in October Stamboliiski became Prime Minister.

Stamboliiski was himself a peasant, and devoted his life to the cause of the peasants' political rights. The Peasant Movement which he founded did not greatly influence Bulgarian politics before the war, but the general misery and discontent caused by six years of fighting brought it mass support. The Bulgarian peasants, who formed 80 % of the nation, wanted a break with the past, what an intellectual would call a political and social revolution. They hoped that Stamboliiski would give it to them. Stamboliiski firmly believed that the State should be run by the peasants themselves, and that the bourgeoisie should definitely take second place.

Stamboliiski's ideas were not limited to the frontiers of Bulgaria. Always a champion of the solidarity of peasant peoples, he dreamed of a Balkan Federation, and regarded as the first step towards this the creation of a South Slav Union, to stretch from Mount Triglav in the Slovene Alps to the shore of the Black Sea. His general outlook was similar to that of Radić, but more clearly defined and wider in scope. It was his misfortune that the men in power in Belgrade after the war were incapable of grasping such ideas. Pašić and his friends could think only in terms of 'Greater Serbia', of which 'the Bulgarians' were 'hereditary enemies', and King Alexander was too frightened of 'Bolshevism' to see in Stamboliiski more than a dangerous agitator. And so in the moment of his danger Jugoslavia, whose friendship was his dearest wish, did not stir to save him.

Stamboliiski was in power for nearly four years, and during this period he attempted much for the people. He carried out a further Land Reform, destroying the very few remaining large properties. As a consequence of tnis, holdings of more than 30 hectares occupied in 1934 not more than 6 % of the land, while holdings between 5 and 20 hectares formed a little less than half the total number of holdings, and occupied almost exactly half the land. Thus Bulgaria, with its much larger proportion of medium holdings and its utter absence of large estates, has a healthier property structure in agriculture than any other State of Eastern Europe. Despite the country's political misfortunes, this fact has been a source of strength to it in the last twenty years, and, although ever since the Liberation Bulgaria was a fairly equalitarian country, the final readjustments are due to Stamboliiski. He also attempted to reform the legal system, in order to make justice cheaper and more accessible to the people. He made changes in the taxation, in order more fairly to distribute property. He carried out valuable public works, and introduced the Compulsory Labour Service, which took the place of the Military Service forbidden by the Treaty of Neuilly, and aimed at maintaining a spirit of patriotism and national solidarity, while using a year in the life of young Bulgarians for purposes of national value.

The second most important political group in Bulgaria during Stamboliiski's rule were the Communists. The Bulgarian Socialist Party had in 1903 split into the 'Narrow' and 'Broad' factions.[1] The former later joined the Third International and became the Bulgarian Communist Party. In the 1919 Parliament they had 47 seats, and 25 % of the votes, while the Socialists had 28 seats. Relations between

[1] See Borkenau, *op. cit.*

Stamboliiski and the Communists were uneasy. In the
autumn of 1919 the Communists organised a railway strike,
which lasted two months. Stamboliiski used force sparingly,
and came to an agreement with them on the basis of desired
reforms. They retained a substantial following after Stamboliiski's two Parliamentary elections of 1920 and 1923, and
enjoyed greater freedom than in any Eastern European country
at this time except Czechoslovakia.

Stamboliiski's strenuous attempts at a reconciliation with
Jugoslavia won him the bitter hatred of Bulgarian nationalists,
and in particular of the Macedonian *émigrés*. Bulgaria was
full of refugees from Macedonia, many of them men whose
abominable cruelties against the Serbs in that province during
the war had made it unsafe for them to remain. They were
particularly numerous in Sofia. The Internal Macedonian
Revolutionary Organisation (I.M.R.O.) was a power in the
land.[1] To these men and their Bulgarian friends any negotiations with Jugoslavia were treason. In 1921 they murdered
Stamboliiski's War Minister, Alexander Dimitrov, on his return
from a visit to Belgrade. I.M.R.O. established itself in South-
Western Bulgaria, the small piece of Macedonia left to Bulgaria by the Peace Treaties, and organised terrorist expeditions into Jugoslavia, hoping thus to embarrass the Government. But Stamboliiski was set on an understanding with
Belgrade. He arrested a number of prominent Macedonians,
but was unable to clear up the I.M.R.O. nest in the south-
west owing to the sympathy extended to the terrorists in
high quarters in the army. In May 1923 Stamboliiski signed
a Convention at Niš, by which the Jugoslav and Bulgarian
Governments agreed to take concerted action against the
terrorists.

Opposition to Stamboliiski was not confined to the Macedonians. The ambitions of the bourgeois politicians had been
thwarted, and men of genuine Liberal feelings had been
offended. Stamboliiski's personal manner was overbearing
and tactless. He had among his colleagues men of inferior
morals and intelligence. Agrarian politicians made demagogic
speeches attacking the town population in bulk. Sofia was
filled with uncouth peasants, who, made dizzy by unexpected

[1] This organisation, and the Macedonian Question in general, are discussed
in the next chapter.

power, abused it wildly. Members of the party demanded all sorts of material privileges. Corruption and scandals were widespread.

In April 1923 elections were held, which, not without the use of judicious pressure, resulted in an overwhelming victory for Stamboliiski. The premier made some indiscreet remarks about his intention to deprive the king of his prerogatives by changing the Constitution. Relations between premier and king were cool but outwardly correct. Whether Boris was privy to the plot which overthrew Stamboliiski is a question still hotly debated in Bulgaria. The usually accepted view is that he was not, but Agrarian supporters doubt this, and it is interesting that in a debate in the Parliament in the autumn of 1938 ex-Premier Tsankov declared that he was unable to tell where the responsibility for those events lay, for 'although he knew, his lips were sealed'.

However this may be, it is certain that in bourgeoisie, army and I.M.R.O. opposition to Stamboliiski was intense. In May a plot was made. The conspirators were led by Professor Tsankov and collaborated with the army. General Volkov enlisted the support of Ivan Mihailov, the assistant of Todor Alexandrov the I.M.R.O. leader, and on 9 June Colonel Velchev and his men took possession of Sofia without bloodshed or disturbance. Tsankov and his political colleagues presented themselves at the palace, and induced the king, after some hesitation, to recognise them as the Government. Meanwhile Stamboliiski was at his home in the country. He led the peasants for a couple of days in a hopeless resistance. Poorly armed and unorganised, they were quickly overcome by the regular forces sent against them. Stamboliiski was captured on 12 June and brought to the town of Tatar Pazardjik. He was then taken by some Macedonian terrorists, who led him back to his home, where they mutilated and tortured him, made him dig his own grave and finally finished him off. Some thousands of peasants were massacred.

Representatives of the victorious Allies in Sofia were rather glad that this boorish demagogue was out of the way, and closed their eyes to the horrors which accompanied it. They were to regret it eighteen years later. Especially were the Jugoslavs to regret it, for if the 'Bolshevik' Stamboliiski had survived, and his party had been freely able to appeal to the

Bulgarian peasants, Hitler would not have passed unopposed through Bulgaria to destroy Jugoslavia from behind.

During the fateful days the Communists had not stirred. They openly declared that the quarrels of the urban and rural bourgeoisie were of no interest to the Bulgarian workers. In September, after the Tsankov regime was firmly installed, they realised its reactionary character and made a belated rising, in which they were joined by a part of the Agrarians. The rising broke out at Nova Zagora and spread to other parts of the country. It was doomed to failure. The army crushed it, and bands of Macedonian terrorists 'cleaned up' afterwards. The numbers killed in cold blood are variously estimated between 10,000 and 30,000. Many more were beaten, imprisoned and tortured.

Stamboliiski had serious faults, but he sincerely worked for the good of the common people and for friendship with neighbouring countries. After his murder foreign policy fell into the hands of the chauvinists, and the interests of the people were subordinated to those of a small clique. The hope of Democracy in Bulgaria was buried.

The next years were a period of disorder and outrages which gave Bulgaria an unenviable notoriety. Some members of the Tsankov Government were decent citizens, whose wish was not to revenge themselves on their political adversaries, but simply to give the country peace. For instance the Finance Minister, Peter Todorov, refused to allow indiscriminate expulsion of Agrarian sympathisers from his Ministry. Another moderating influence was the Socialist Kazazov. But in fact the Government was not in a position to prevent atrocities. In November elections were held, at which, despite police pressure, a number of Agrarian Deputies were elected. One of these was Petkov, a close collaborator of Stamboliiski, who was in prison during the elections. He was released to take up his seat in Parliament, and murdered in the street by Macedonians.

In 1925 a bomb exploded in Sofia Cathedral at a service which King Boris was to have attended. Fortunately for him, the King[1] was late, but over a hundred persons were killed.

---

[1] The King of Bulgaria is officially known as 'Tsar' or Emperor, this title being derived from the medieval Bulgarian Empire. We shall here continue to use the word 'King'.

The authors of the outrage were two Communists, who appear to have acted without the instructions of the official party leaders. The incident provided an excellent excuse for the repression of suspected Communist and Agrarian sympathisers. Masses of arrests were made, over three hundred death sentences pronounced by the courts, and hundreds more 'unofficially' murdered by the police or the Macedonians. Police headquarters in Sofia was the scene of unspeakable tortures.

For more than ten years all Bulgaria was terrorised by I.M.R.O. Not content with murder expeditions into Jugoslavia, the Macedonians made it their job to 'liquidate' any Bulgarian political leader who advocated friendship with Bulgaria's neighbours or democratic government. Moreover the Macedonians quarrelled fiercely among themselves. In 1924 their leader Todor Alexandrov had been murdered, shortly after he had made a declaration in favour of Moscow, which was then interested in Radić's idea of a Balkan Slav Federation. This declaration could not be welcome to the Bulgarian military chiefs, who always regarded Macedonia as a part of Bulgaria and would not tolerate any tendency of I.M.R.O. towards independent Macedonian aspirations. It was believed by many that the Bulgarian army leaders were a party to Alexandrov's murder. The latter was succeeded as leader of I.M.R.O. by Ivan Mihailov, his young assistant, who had organised some of the more revolting atrocities of 1923, and who maintained excellent relations with the War Minister, General Volkov.[1] Four years later Mihailov's men murdered the remaining veteran of I.M.R.O., General Protogerov, who had also inclined in his last years to the idea of a free Macedonia in a South Slav Federation. This murder did not close the feud in I.M.R.O.'s ranks, for the general's followers put up a long, secret and bloody resistance. For the following years Protogerovists and Mihailovists shot each other almost daily in the streets of Sofia. Evening battles in the cafés were a common occurrence. The police kept out of them, partly from a natural desire to avoid straying bullets, partly because the Mihailovists enjoyed protection in high places.

The Governments were powerless. Tsankov was succeeded in 1925 by the colourless Liapchev, who gave the Macedonians

[1] For particulars of Alexandrov's death see Swire, *Bulgarian Conspiracy*.

a free hand. To take action against these 'brave patriots' was as impossible as in the case of the Roumanian Iron Guard in the early thirties. I.M.R.O. had the protection of the War Minister, Volkov, and Volkov enjoyed the confidence of the king. The activities of the Macedonians both against Bulgarian democrats and against Jugoslavia were subsidised from Italy, which gave moral and diplomatic support to the Bulgarian Government in its intransigent policy towards its neighbours. The collaboration of Italy and Bulgaria was consolidated by the marriage in 1930 of King Boris to Princess Giovanna of Savoy. In 1929 Volkov resigned from the War Ministry and was made Bulgarian Minister in Rome. The policy of Sofia did not change. Meanwhile popular discontent grew. It was not confined to the wretched peasantry and terrorised working class, but extended to the educated middle class, which, although nationalist in outlook and resentful of the Neuilly Treaty, was sick of the unceasing crimes and confusion. In 1930 a major scandal was caused when two officers were tortured to make them confess to imaginary acts of espionage. The case was made public and disgusted all decent people with the regime.[1] Meanwhile the World Economic Crisis deepened and the plight of the peasantry grew rapidly worse.

In 1931 elections were held. A coalition of oppositional bourgeois parties with the moderate Agrarians led by Gichev, won a large majority. Malinov, the Premier of 1918, universally respected as an honest patriot and a democrat, became Prime Minister. It was hoped that great things would happen. But there was little change. I.M.R.O. still ruled unchallenged in Petrich Department in South-Western Bulgaria. The army did nothing against them, and the whole civil administration was in their hands. Malinov resigned, and was succeeded by Mushanov. The Government tolerated and was tolerated by I.M.R.O. Gichev, the Agrarian leader, was prepared to collaborate with Fascist Italy. The uncompromising Agrarian leaders, the unswerving disciples of Stamboliiski, were in exile in Belgrade. Only in 1933, after popular pressure, did the Government permit their return. Back in Sofia, they put forward in a review entitled *Pladne* their demand for radical reforms in the interest of the peasantry, and for a greater measure of democratic liberty.

[1] For details of this case see Swire, *op. cit.*

Discontent in the country grew. The Communist Party had been banned since the cathedral outrage, but in the 1931 elections the Bulgarian Labour Party had won some seats. This party was merely the old Communist Party under a new name with new leaders. In 1932 municipal elections were held in Sofia, and the Labour Party won an absolute majority of all votes. The election was promptly annulled. I.M.R.O. and its patrons were alarmed. In 1933 one of the Labour Party Deputies, Traikov, who had dared to ask for the introduction of the eight-hour day in all industrial enterprises, was murdered by the terrorists.

It became obvious that the new Government was little better than the old, and quite powerless to deal with the Macedonians. A number of intellectuals connected with the review *Zveno*, and including Todorov and Kazazov, both former members of the Tsankov conspiracy of 1923, sharply criticised the Government. They had close relations with the army. A special position of influence over the younger officers was held by Colonel Damian Velchev. He had been the technical organiser of the 1923 *coup d'état*, but he had had no part in the massacre that followed it. He had kept out of politics, but his indignation had steadily grown as he saw the abuses committed by the High Command, and the benevolent attitude adopted towards the I.M.R.O. terrorists, who were reducing the country to a shambles. He believed in the necessity of friendly relations between Jugoslavia and Bulgaria, and convinced himself that this could be attained only by a thorough purge in Bulgaria. A man of powerful personality, he exercised over his brother-officers an attraction similar to that formerly possessed by 'Apis' Dimitrijević in Serbia. He built up a large following in the army, and had devoted friends among the 'Zveno' group.

In 1933, on the insistence of Velchev, King Boris had induced the Government to take steps against I.M.R.O. Arrests were made, and comparative order was restored in the capital. But in the provinces acts of terrorism continued, and no attempt was made to touch the Petrich stronghold. The weakness of the Government was shown by constant squabbles between Gichev's Agrarians and Mushanov, which led to the Cabinet crisis in the spring of 1934. On 19 May a military revolution took place. Velchev's officers took possession of the capital, Mushanov and his Ministers were dismissed, and a Government was formed of soldiers and members of the 'Zveno' group.

The new Government was an unconcealed Dictatorship, but it was not Fascist. It set up no complex bureaucracy of new vested interests, and did not introduce the demagogic trappings inseparable from Fascism. It abolished all political parties. This was small loss, for the bourgeois parties represented next to nothing and devoted themselves to personal squabbles, while the two big parties, the Agrarians and the Communists, had been powerless since 1923. The new rulers were not out for personal advantage. They were that rare phenomenon, a group of patriots determined, not by bombastic speeches but by acts, to clean up the country. This does not mean that all their decisions were wise, or that they thoroughly understood the country's needs. It means only that their purpose was honourable.

Finance Minister Todorov introduced measures reducing peasant debts, and reorganised the credit system of the country, creating a new State Credit Bank. An attempt was made to reform Education, giving greater weight to technical and scientific branches. Doctors were encouraged to work in the villages, where the peasants badly needed medical attention, rather than to pile up in the towns, where there was already a surplus of 'intellectuals'. State Monopolies were created for tobacco, salt and alcohol, which soon became fraught with the abuses described in the preceding chapter. Trade Unions were abolished, and their place was taken by 'non-political unions' based on 'corporative' principles. How these would have worked out if the Government of 19 May had remained in power is difficult to say. This Government was not particularly representative of the bourgeoisie. Its action was prompted by the soldier's distrust of 'politics' rather than by the desire to help employers against their men. The Velchev group were not concerned to deprive the working class of its rights. After the overthrow of Velchev, however, the 'non-political unions' were used quite unscrupulously by subsequent Governments, and the workers were more helpless than ever.

Undoubtedly the greatest achievement of the men of 19 May was the liquidation of I.M.R.O. In a few days the army had driven the terrorists out of Petrich Department and rounded up their leaders. Ivan Mihailov escaped to Turkey. What all previous Governments had feared to attempt, was quickly and easily accomplished. This action won the Government enormous popularity in the country. The gangster band, extolled by professional patriots as the defender of the national ideal, had done far more harm for sixteen years to the Bulgarian people than to the 'enemy' Serbs. As long as it existed, the peaceful citizen and peasant could not go about their daily business in security.

In foreign policy the Government made two changes equally popular with the majority of Bulgarians. It restored diplomatic relations with Russia, and it sought reconciliation with Jugoslavia. The general hatred of I.M.R.O. had caused a powerful reaction of Bulgarian public opinion in favour of friendship with the Serbs. This had been for years the main idea of Damian Velchev, who showed himself therein a pupil of Stamboliiski. The notion of South Slav solidarity spread steadily during the thirties, and was made the chief principle of the new Government's policy. The suppression of I.M.R.O. convinced Belgrade of the sincerity of Bulgarian overtures. In September 1934 King Alexander visited Sofia. Even the king's murder only two weeks later by a Macedonian did not prevent the progress of friendly relations between the two Slav countries.

Velchev himself had not entered the Cabinet. His friend Colonel Kimon Georgiev was Prime Minister. Velchev stayed in the background, but his influence was decisive. It provoked jealousy in powerful quarters. It was no secret that relations between Velchev and the king were strained. Rumours spread in the army and in political circles that Velchev was preparing a republic. In January 1935 a dispute occurred between Velchev and his military colleagues, skilfully exploited by the king. Kimon Georgiev resigned and Velchev withdrew from politics. A Government was formed by General Zlatev, and this was replaced in turn a few months later by one led by Toshev, a man of Macedonian sympathies and a willing instrument of the king. In July Velchev left the country for Belgrade, but in October he returned illegally and was arrested. He was accused of preparing a Republican conspiracy, and on 22 February condemned to death. A month later, in response to requests from within Bulgaria and abroad, the sentence was commuted to imprisonment for life.[1]

The removal of Damian Velchev left King Boris undisputed master of Bulgaria. A quiet and somewhat mysterious man, the king had long played an obscure but important part behind the scenes. Now he openly assumed responsibility for the country's affairs. He retained the dictatorial system created by 19 May, refusing to go back to the previous 'Parliamentary' party politics. The Dictatorship became his own personal despotism. The army was sent back to its barracks, and ordered to forget about politics and concentrate on loyalty to the king. Boris ruled through individuals chosen by himself, supported by the police and administrative apparatus.

There has been much discussion of the king's personality during the last six years in the Balkans. The official version is that he is a modest, upright, patriotic Bulgarian, fond of his people and enormously popular, passionately interested in botany and a skilled railway-engine driver. He has been described by eminent people as 'the greatest friend of Britain' and 'the best Democrat in the Balkans'. The Opposition make him out a monster of cruelty and perfidy. He never, according to this theory, forgot that his father was a German. He determined from the first to be Germany's chief instrument in the Balkans. He it was who arranged the overthrow of Stamboliiski and ensured political and financial support to I.M.R.O. All the crimes and horrors perpetrated by the Bulgarian police should be attributed to him. Which of these theories is true it is not for me to say. The case of Boris of Bulgaria can be safely left to the experts. Here a brief summary of facts will suffice.

In foreign policy Boris pursued the line of reconciliation with Jugoslavia, which led to the Jugoslav-Bulgarian pact of Eternal Friendship in 1937. This pact was immensely popular in both countries. Jugoslavia had always been willing to make friends with Bulgaria, provided that the Macedonian Question was buried. On the Bulgarian side a policy of friendship was imposed by public opinion, whose truest interpreters in this connection were Velchev and the 'Pladne' group of Agrarians. Boris satisfied the popular desire by the pact, but his sincerity

---

[1] Details of the Georgiev regime and of the Velchev trial will be found in Swire, *op. cit.* The author was a personal friend of Velchev.

is open to question. The pact was signed by two Governments that in no way represented their peoples, and it never had much value.[1]

Boris also continued the policy of Velchev in so far as he never allowed I.M.R.O. to recover its former position. Petrić Department remained fully under Government control and Macedonian terrorism was a thing of the past. But among the king's advisers were men of known anti-Jugoslav feelings, who had had intimate connections with the Macedonians. Extreme nationalist organisations such as the 'Ratnitsi' and the 'Otets Paisi' Society were allowed to make propaganda for a Greater Bulgaria with the San Stefano frontiers. Ex-Premier Tsankov worked to build up a party modelled specifically on German National Socialism. At the same time the Velchevists and Agrarians, the proven friends of Jugoslavia, were subjected to close police supervision

In 1938 the king decided to broaden the basis of support for his regime. There was much talk of a 'democratisation' of Bulgaria. In the spring Parliamentary elections were held, the first since 1931. Candidates were not allowed to represent parties, but were supposed to stand on their merits as individuals. The men chosen as Government candidates were 'non-political', that is to say, people ready to act as polite Yes-men for the Government. Every difficulty was put in the way of oppositional candidates wishing to visit their constituencies. Voters were terrorised and bribed in the usual Balkan manner. Nevertheless about one-third of the Deputies returned were in opposition to the Government. Soon after the opening of Parliament the few Communist members were deprived of their seats, and some months later the representatives of the 'Pladne' group were likewise expelled. The remaining oppositional members proved fairly docile, and were in any case in no position to influence policy. Further elections at the beginning of the present war gave the Government the required large majority.

The seven years of the Royal Dictatorship were quiet. The army submitted to the king's will, and the police had the situation well in hand. Government pressure increased after the German occupation, and the growth of discontent, caused

[1] The international implications of the pact are discussed in Chapter Nine below, p. 390.

by the shortage of commodities attendant on war conditions, was answered by more ruthless repression. Minor plots by Communists or Agrarians were announced from time to time, but public order and the safety of the regime were not seriously threatened while Boris lived.

Yet that there was widespread opposition to the regime on both internal and external policy could hardly be doubted. Of all the States of Eastern Europe, Bulgaria has had since 1918 the most stormy history. It was inconceivable that all the strains and stresses of the last twenty years could have been finally removed. During this period Bulgaria has suffered from the same bitter division between rulers and ruled that afflicted her neighbours. This fact is not modified by the comparative absence of striking contrasts in wealth.

It is true that social differences played a less important part in Bulgaria than in Roumania and Jugoslavia. This is explained partly by the more equalitarian structure of peasant society in Bulgaria and partly by the fact that defeat in war and loss of territory deprived the ruling class of the opportunities for enrichment that existed in the victorious small States. This could be seen even from the outward appearance of the capital. Sofia is a sober, clean and unimpressive city. Its centre consists of straight, orderly streets with houses all of much the same height, few of them new. It contrasts with Belgrade and Bucarest, busy, crowded, modern cities, where ten-storey skyscrapers have sprung up chaotically next to low, red-tiled Turkish hovels.

The division between rulers and ruled in Bulgaria was much more political than social or economic. The ruling class of civil servants, army officers, tradesmen and intellectuals jealously maintained by force their supremacy over the people. The peasants and workers, who suffered less from purely economic exploitation than those of the northern neighbour countries, wished to wrest political power from their masters. During the four years of Stamboliiski's Government they had some success, and the bitterness of the passions aroused on both sides is proved by the ferocity with which the attempt was repressed. Torture was regularly used in all the Eastern European States but none has a record of such systematic and uninterrupted brutality as Bulgaria.

Nevertheless it was doubtful whether all this brutality had

stamped out opposition. The name of Stamboliiski was still treasured as that of a saint by most Bulgarian peasants. It had become a symbol of Revolution. Whether the Agrarian Movement was still strong is more questionable. After Stamboliiski's death the Agrarians split into several factions. The most important of these were led by Gichev and by the 'Pladne' group. The latter were more radical and more honest, and probably enjoyed a more numerous following. The fact that there had been no really free elections for nearly twenty years made it difficult to judge.

It should be emphasised that the Agrarians were never a political party in the strict sense of the word. From 1919 to 1923 there was a tremendous wave of peasant revolutionary feeling, whose exponent was Stamboliiski, the beloved popular tribune. But the number of organised members of the Agrarian Party was never clearly defined. Still less certain was the Agrarian programme. The revolutionary party which did possess an efficient organisation, clearly defined doctrine and a considerable number of fanatically brave and devoted supporters, was the Communist. Academic discussions as to whether 'the masses like Communist doctrine' are meaningless. The idea which the Communist leaders preach to the people is the simple one of Revolution. Revolution is also the slogan of the Agrarians. Agrarians and Communists have often collaborated, and at least since 1923 they have not interfered with each other. It is therefore doubtful whether the Bulgarian peasant has a very clear idea in his mind of the difference between Agrarians and Communists, or whether there is any distinct Agrarian 'ideology' which can compete with that of the Communists. The question of Property may be a stumblingblock between the Communist and the richer peasants, but is unlikely to be of much importance for the poorer majority. Revolution, which all understand and many desire, is the declared aim of both parties. It is therefore quite possible, in favourable circumstances, that the Communists might capture the Agrarian, or the Agrarians the Communist, following among the peasants. Among the industrial workers, whose numbers have, as elsewhere in the Balkans, risen in the past twenty years, it is unlikely that the Agrarians could compete with the Communists.

The Communists possess one great advantage over all other

parties in their connection with Russia. All classes in Bulgaria love and admire Russia, the 'liberator' of the country. The successful resistance of the Red Army will enormously have increased the prestige of Russia in Bulgaria, and nowhere more than among the peasants. In so far as the Communists, who have shown themselves skilled in underground work, are able to convince the people that Russia will be the greatest European Power after the war, and that they themselves represent the 'Idea of the Future', they may hope for big successes.

One thing is certain, that the peasants, treasuring the memory of Stamboliiski and looking with hope to Russia, the traditional protector, will play an important part in the Bulgaria of the future.

POLITICAL CURRENTS IN EASTERN EUROPE

Most of the political struggles of the Eastern European States during the last twenty years were fought between different small groups within narrow ruling classes, over the heads of the peoples. These struggles were no more than scrambles for power, for material advantages and for personal prestige between ambitious individuals and interested cliques. The individuals and cliques were not concerned to better the lot of the people, and only considered reforms or measures of relief when ineluctable circumstances imposed these on them. They won power by elections, at which the 'sovereign people' was supposed to decide, but whose results were in fact determined mainly by pressure and bribery, and partly by competition in demagogic promises, which no party had any intention of fulfilling. To the politicians the people was 'the masses', electoral currency, the passive objects of their policy. Such was the basis of the quarrels between Endeks and Pilsudskists in Poland, between Radicals, Democrats and Agrarians in Serbia, and between the bourgeois parties in Roumania and Bulgaria.

As soon as the passive 'masses' expressed impatience at this delicate game, and took a hand themselves, or threatened to do so, the rival cliques in the ruling class united against them. When popular discontent assumed alarming proportions, the remnants of Democracy were liquidated and bare Dictatorships took their place.

These Dictatorships were not Fascist regimes in the proper sense of the word. Carol II in Roumania tried to ape Fascism by his Front of National Rebirth, but never succeeded in raising the minimum of popular enthusiasm necessary for Fascism. Specifically Fascist movements, such as the Polish National Radicals, Hungarian Arrow-Cross Party and Roumanian Iron Guard, failed in their purposes. The first two never attained power, while the third made such a mess of its brief period of government that it discredited itself in all classes of the nation.

The Eastern European Dictatorships relied not even on artificially stimulated popular enthusiasm, but on police pressure. In Roumania, Jugoslavia and Bulgaria they were personal autocracies directed by hereditary monarchs. In Hungary power was controlled by an alliance of the aristocracy with a middle class of aristocratic origin, in Poland by a clique of diverse antecedents bound together by material interests and loyalty to a leader. These regimes had no such basis of support as those of Hitler and Mussolini. They were able to survive because they had a firm grasp on the bureaucratic and military machines, because the peoples were backward and apathetic, and because the bourgeoisie would always support them in case of need. Certainly a part of the bourgeois and intellectual classes suffered from these regimes. Certainly criticism of them was loud and fierce in bourgeois and intellectual circles. But if ever the regime were radically threatened from below, the great majority of bourgeois and intellectuals would rally round it.

Everywhere in Eastern Europe much had been expected of the Peasant Parties, and everywhere these expectations were disappointed. Some of these parties were rendered helpless by terror exercised from above (Bulgaria and Poland). Others collapsed from internal decay (Serbia and Roumania). Others came under the control of the urban bourgeoisie (Czechoslovakia) or of nationalist intellectuals (Croatia). In one country, Hungary, no Peasant Party existed at all.

The organisation of a Peasant Movement is at the best of times a difficult task. The peasants live scattered in villages. They know their neighbours, but they are not usually interested in the outside world. They are intensely suspicious of all who come to them from the towns. Yet in the last fifty years the influence of the outside world on the village has greatly

increased. The desire of peasants for education is most impressive. The affairs of the capital, of foreign countries, even
of distant continents, are now discussed in village taverns. The
passion of Greeks and Serbs for politics is a byword. Among
other Eastern European nations, too, such leaders as Radić,
Stamboliiski and Witos succeeded in interesting the peasants
in public affairs, in convincing them that their social aspirations could be satisfied only by political action. Outwardly
impressive movements were built up. The prospects of an
organised peasantry as a political force seemed bright.

The failure of these hopes can be variously explained. The
peasants were seldom sufficiently educated to be able actually
to lead the parties. Even parties founded by peasants soon
attracted non-peasant elements when they attained success
in the elections. Radić and Mihalache, for instance, allowed
themselves to be influenced, or were succeeded, by non-peasant
politicians. The influx of non-peasant elements created an
ever-widening gap between leaders and peasants.

Moreover, whether peasants or bourgeois, the leaders of the
Peasant Parties had no clearly defined aims. They swayed
from Left to Right, now proclaiming the sanctity of Property
against 'Bolshevism', now demanding a Social Revolution.
Especially uncertain was their attitude to industry and to the
working class. On the one hand the peasants had a traditional
distrust of the towns, whose expensive goods absorbed their
small cash incomes and whose citizens squeezed the last penny
out of them in taxes. On the other hand the peasants had
common interests with the working class against the rulers.
Bourgeois politicians within and without the Peasant Parties
deliberately sought to use the peasants as a prop to a policy
directed against the working class. The Peasant Party leaders
propagated romantic ideas about the special virtues supposed
to be the monopoly possession of the peasant class. These only
confused the political issues, and turned solely to the advantage
of the ruling class.

The Peasant Parties usually represented the interests of
the big and medium holders, those whom the Russians call
'kulaki'. They stood for high agricultural prices and protection, which benefit the wealthy peasants but increase the
misery of a large part of the small-holder class which has to
buy its food. The most successful of the Peasant Parties

during the last twenty years was undoubtedly the Czechoslovak Agrarian Party, which defended the interests of the
Czech medium farmers and did next to nothing for the rural
proletariat of Slovakia. The Peasant Parties in general paid
little attention to the needs of the 60–80 % of small holders,
which, we have seen, are different from and often even con-
tradictory to those of the 'kulaki'.

There is little point in saying that the 'kulaki' are the most
valuable element in the peasant class, who have reached by
harder work than their neighbours their present fortunate
position. Even where this is true it is of little importance.
For in all Eastern Europe except the Czech Lands the rural
proletariat forms more than half the peasant population. There
can be neither social peace nor political stability as long as
the interests of the rural proletariat are ignored. And the
Peasant Parties have seldom done anything but ignore them.
They have confined themselves to pressing for high prices
to benefit the 'kulaki' and for marketing cooperatives to
strengthen these prices. They will not even admit the existence
of a division between rich and poor peasants. Representing
the former, they claim to speak in the name of all. They prate
about a special Peasant Democracy, possessing superior moral
values lacking in industrial society. They ignore two plain
facts. The first is that the peasant lives best, and possesses
to the greatest degree those qualities of independent judgment
and sound patriotism of which they talk so much, precisely
where he is brought into closest contact with industrial society
and where his agriculture is most highly capitalised (e.g.
Denmark or Switzerland). The second is that for the surplus
population of Eastern Europe, which amounts perhaps to
one-half of the small-holder class or one-third of the whole
peasantry, the only hope of a better life lies in employment in
industry, either within their own country or, by emigration,
beyond its borders.

The brutal truth is that the Peasant States can only become
prosperous and healthy when they cease to be Peasant States.
Yet even if industrialisation is pushed ahead with greatly
increased speed and efficiency, and unlimited possibilities of
emigration are provided, the peasant character of the Eastern
European States will not quickly change. For many years
there will exist a numerous class of poor small-holders. The

interests of this class are sufficiently important to justify the existence of special political groups. But the Peasant Parties of the last twenty years did not represent these interests. To that fact as much as to police persecution is due their general failure.

The extent of Communist influence is difficult to assess. Communist organisations existed in all the countries of Eastern Europe. The only legal party in the last decade was the Czecho-slovak, which had an important following among the Czech workers and the Slovak and Ruthene peasants. The Bulgarian party was believed to be well organised underground. The Polish party had a large following before 1939, but was always handicapped by the national antipathy to Russia, presumably strengthened by the events of September 1939. The Jugoslav party had one opportunity—in 1920—of presenting itself to the electorate, when it had a considerable success. It was much persecuted but was probably fairly strong. The Hungarian and Roumanian parties were small, and were most effectively suppressed by the police.

The Communist parties depended less on winning votes in elections than on an organisation of disciplined cadres, which kept the movement in being even under rigorous persecution. The cadres were recruited from the industrial working class and from a part of the intelligentsia. These, the élite of the movement, studied and discussed political problems, decided, on the basis of an examination of conditions in the country and of the wishes of the International, the policy of the local party, and set themselves by secret propaganda to spread ideas among the people, to win sympathisers and create a mass movement.

The people did not need to understand fully the doctrines of Marx and Lenin, and little attempt was made to interpret these doctrines to them. Communist propagandists concen-trated on two simple ideas, which everyone could understand and large numbers approved—Social Justice and Revolution. These two ideas, whose great merit from the point of view of propaganda is that they defy precise definition, and can be interpreted by each individual as he pleases, undoubtedly appealed to a very large number of peasants and workers, and a considerable number of educated middle-class people as well, in Eastern Europe.

Most western observers of Eastern Europe make a grave error when they estimate the attitude of the Eastern European peasants to Communism in terms of the situation which it is calculated that the peasants would occupy if the Soviet system were introduced there. The Eastern European peasants do not think in these terms at all. They know very little about the Soviet system.

Two arguments are usually advanced to show that the Eastern European peasants are 'immune to Communism', namely, that they dread the introduction of the Kolhoz system and that they are deeply religious. Neither is very true.

The wealthy peasants may fear collectivisation of their farms, but even this is far from universal.* The mass of wretched small-holders, however, have little or nothing to lose, and are more aware of this than ever.

The religious barrier is stronger in Catholic than in Orthodox countries. It is probably most important in Poland and Slovenia. In Croatia and Slovakia it is to some extent counteracted by the strength of sympathy for Russia. The Orthodox peoples, and especially the Serbs and Bulgarians, take their religion very lightly. They resent an attack on their Church from without, but for reasons of national pride rather than of religious piety.† Pro-Russian feeling based on Slav solidarity is far stronger than fear of Russian anti-religious policy. Even the priests are often strongly pro-Soviet, although aware that the Orthodox Tsar has given place to the 'godless' Stalin. If the Orthodox bishops frequently denounce Communism, many of the village priests fear it but little, and even sympathise with it. In Roumania there is no Slavophile feeling to counteract the influence of the Church, but that influence itself is not very strong. Some priests, who were fanatical members of the Iron Guard, and were persecuted as such, were respected. On the whole, however, Roumanian priests have a very low moral standard, and the identification of the Church with the State authorities and the wealthy classes has greatly reduced its influence since the heroic days when it was the champion of the nation in the struggle against the Turks.

Even in regions where religious belief is firmly implanted, there is often resentment against the priests. Polish and

* See above, p. 112.   † See above, pp. 29, 71.

Croatian peasants are mostly good Catholics, but the Polish and Croatian Peasant Movements had always an anti-Clerical aspect. Eastern European peasants have natural religious feeling, consisting rather of a vague mystical belief in the supernatural, than of deep intellectual conviction of the dogmas of the Church. Persecution of the fundamental religious feeling would no doubt provoke bitter hostility. But Communist propagandists do not attack religious feeling. They attack only the priests, and this often increases rather than diminishes their standing with the peasants. Moreover, in Russia itself for several years the Government has shown considerable religious tolerance, being concerned not to suppress the religious faith of the individual, but to prevent the growth of a wealthy and powerfully organised Church. In the present war even the organised Church has received recognition.

The attitude of the Eastern European peasants to Communism is determined not by fear of collectivisation or religious persecution, but by the degree of sympathy for Russia and by the extent of the popular desire for Revolution.

Sympathy for Russia has always been strong in the Czech Lands, Serbia and Bulgaria, and fairly strong in Croatia, Slovenia and Slovakia. It is absent in Hungary and Roumania, and is replaced by active antipathy in the Polish-inhabited parts of Poland.

Revolutionary feeling is fairly strong all over Eastern Europe. Desire for violent change, and distrust of everything said by the ruling class, have produced a curious state of affairs. The common people of Eastern Europe do not understand the doctrines of Communism, but they have heard often enough the word 'Communism'. This word has for twenty years been hurled by their rulers against all who have stood up for the simple rights of the people. Ordinary men and women who have asked for reforms, protested against bureaucratic abuses, or resisted the gendarmerie in the execution of some wanton act of brutality, have been denounced as 'Bolsheviks' or 'Communists', beaten, tortured, sentenced to long terms of imprisonment or killed. The principle of the Eastern European Governments has been 'Kill your man first, and prove that he was a Communist afterwards'. This principle has been turned against its users. For by a process similar to that used on Pavlov's dogs, whose mouths were

made to water by the ringing of a bell associated with food-
time, the word 'Communism', whose political significance is
unknown to the Eastern European peasants, has come to be
associated with the fight of brave men and women for freedom,
has become identified with civil liberties. The consequence is
that Russia is regarded by large numbers of peasants, who
are not members of any organised Communist Party, as a
country where 'there are no masters', where the common
people is in control.

Two examples from the personal experience of the writer
may help to explain this mentality. Two Roumanian peasants,
prosperous medium farmers, respected as leaders in their
village, said to me: 'Our priests and officials tell us that over
in Russia the small, humble people are terribly oppressed.
What we cannot understand is why our priests and officials
are so indignant at the sufferings of the small, humble people
over in Russia, when they care so little about their sufferings
here in Roumania.' In a Serbian village we were discussing
the Moscow trials. Shortly before, the Jugoslav War Minister
had resigned in somewhat dubious circumstances. A peasant
said to me: 'Russia must be a grand country. There the big
men get punished when they do wrong, because the people
rule. Here if we don't pay our taxes we get into trouble at
once, but the big men can steal as much as they like without
harm.' All the others present heartily agreed.

Although Communist ideas are not widely understood, very
little is known of conditions in Russia, and the organised Communist Parties are not very strong, the prestige of the word
'Communism' stands high. Connected vaguely with Revolution, Liberty and Russia, it is regarded by many Eastern
European peasants with prudent benevolence. In very general
terms the regional distribution of such sympathy may be
indicated as follows. It is strongest in Serbia and Bulgaria,
where the Slav and the revolutionary factors combine. It is
also strong in Slovakia and Croatia, where both factors exist
in somewhat lesser degree; in the Czech Lands and Slovenia,
where the Slav factor is stronger than the revolutionary, but
the latter has been strengthened by the social misery attendant
on foreign oppression; and in Hungary and Roumania, where
the Slav factor is absent but the revolutionary is extremely
powerful. It is perhaps least in Poland, where revolutionary

feeling has long been strong, but hatred of Russia is deeply rooted. It may be that the achievements of the Soviet Union in the Allied cause have diminished the anti-Russian feelings of Poles living under German oppression in Poland, but in the absence of evidence it is unwise to speculate. Certainly no change is noticeable among the Poles in exile. Probably Communism will attract few Poles as long as it is identified with Russia. Finally mention should be made of certain areas in Eastern Europe where, at least up to 1940, sympathy for Russia and for Communism was for special reasons unusually strong. These are the Polish north-eastern borderlands, from the Vilna province to Polesia; Bessarabia; and Ruthenia. Here national affinity combined with extreme poverty and, in the first two cases, an exceptional degree of political oppression.*

If such was the state of affairs in Eastern Europe before the war, it is unlikely that it has been changed by subsequent events. The desire for Revolution can only have been increased by the greater poverty and the more brutal repression of discontent caused by German conquest or 'peaceful penetration'. It is probably strongest of all in the countries formally allied with the Axis. The fact that Hungary and Roumania are at war with Russia will not have diminished the revolutionary mood of the two peoples, which hate the Germans quite as much as the Russians, and have every reason to dislike their own ruling classes. In Bulgaria sympathy for Russia is notoriously so strong that the Government is afraid to send the army to fight on the Eastern Front. In countries occupied and conquered by the Axis the hatred and energy of the peoples is chiefly directed towards the national fight for freedom. But this does not mean that the desire for Revolution has disappeared, or that the peoples wish to return to the conditions of 1918–41. Of all the Eastern European peoples only the Czechs have something good to look back to, and even they will not be left unaffected by the change of spirit that Hitler has brought to Europe. The other peoples, like the Czechs, are resolved to win back their national freedom, but that is not enough. This freedom must have a new content.

Is Democracy possible in Eastern Europe? This question

* See pp. 328, 337 and 395.

has been often asked and variously answered. Some give an enthusiastic affirmative and believe that as soon as a commission of brilliant lawyers have drawn up a Constitution based on French Law, and a Parliament has been set up with western rules of procedure, all will go smoothly. Elections will be free, and the sovereign people will decide. Others give an equally enthusiastic denial. The peoples of Eastern Europe are 'not ripe for Democracy'. They 'need a strong hand'. 'National unity' has to be 'forged by heroic methods'.

Both these commonly proclaimed views are wrong. It is, of course, perfectly true that the Eastern European peoples are politically backward. Their history is long, but it contains gaps. Constant wars and foreign rule retarded their political and social development. They do not understand the complexities of Parliamentary procedure and Constitutional Law. They dearly need Education in Citizenship. All this is true. It is also true that the problems that most nearly affect their lives are economic and social rather than political. What the people wants is more to eat, more land, more justice and more personal security. What the people needs is better agriculture, better prospects of employment in industry, better bureaucracy and better law-courts. These things it could receive, theoretically speaking, as well from a despotism as from a democratic Government.

But practical experience has shown that despotisms in Eastern Europe do not generally give the people these things. The men who become despots do not generally possess a well-developed sense of responsibility to their peoples. They are often themselves excellent examples of the lack of Education in Citizenship which they so rightly denounce in their peoples. They talk much of national unity, strong hands and heroic methods, but they do nothing but maintain by force a monopoly of power in the hands of a restricted and not too honourable clique. They make no reforms but palliatives. They make no change in the spirit or the system of Education. They devote themselves partly to enriching themselves and their friends, partly to playing clever little games in international diplomacy. While by their magnificent foreign policy they seek to carve themselves a niche in the temple of History, the voice of their peoples goes unheard. Even if they were inclined to listen to it, they could not, for it has no other means of expression than the moving demonstrations of devoted enthusiasm staged by the flunkeys whom they pay to flatter them. And when real danger threatens, they have unpleasant surprises.

Unfortunately, moral, intellectual and cultural deficiencies are not confined to the peoples, but are possessed in still greater measure by the rulers. As the rulers are indifferent to the fate of their peoples; as the condition of Eastern Europe will remain unhealthy so long as the peoples are robbed and oppressed by irresponsible cliques; as the continuance of an unhealthy condition in Eastern Europe is a menace to the rest of the Continent; and as it is undesirable for international reasons that any single Great Power should directly rule all Eastern Europe; it is hard to escape the conclusion that popular representation in Government, and popular influence on policy, should be increased.

How this can be done is for the constitutional lawyer to say. The layman can only name a few conditions essential to success. Local Government officials should be elected by the people. It is especially important that mayors of villages should be men possessing the confidence of the peasants, rather than nobodies nominated by the Minister of the Interior for their 'safe' political opinions or services rendered to a party. Elections to the legislative body of the country must be free, and the ballot must be secret. Bribery and intimidation of electors, and falsification of votes by such well-tried methods as 'losing the urns', must be punished by severe penalties. Restrictions must be placed on the number of political parties, aimed at eliminating the multiplication of groups with no other justification for existence than the ambitions of their leaders. Parties avowedly working for the destruction of political liberties must not be tolerated. The Press must be free to criticise the Government.

The most essential condition of all for the establishment of democratic Government in Eastern Europe is an improvement and intensification of general Education. This means not only the education of youth, but the raising of the tone of the Press, Literature and all forms of expression of public opinion.

The problems of political structure, party government, freedom of the Press, public opinion, and Education are far from solution in Britain, and we cannot expect that Eastern Europe will easily cope with them. But it should be emphasised that these problems are as important to the Eastern Europeans as to us. These peoples may be behind us in some ways, but they can learn from our mistakes. They are not wild savages, to be permanently cowed by lion-tamers, snake-charmers and witch-doctors. They are Europeans, who have shown their worth in more than one historical crisis. No political system which fails to take account of fundamental conditions can bring them peace or prosperity, or itself hope long to survive.

Chapter Seven

MINORITIES AND MIXED POPULATIONS

The Problem of Minorities

We have seen already that a large number of nations were during the last thousand years compressed within the comparatively small space of Eastern Europe. The nations occupied certain areas in the course of the period of invasions between the sixth and thirteenth centuries. Their distribution was modified by the pressure of the Germanic Empire and the Venetian Republic from the west, and of the Ottoman Turks from the east. Further modifications were introduced by the westward advance of Russia, and by the resettlement that accompanied the reconquest of the Middle Danube from the Turks. By the eighteenth century the Eastern European nations occupied approximately the same territory as to-day.

Each of these nations has some history of independence, but this is more continuous, and more strongly impressed on the national consciousness, in some cases than in others. For long periods the whole of Eastern Europe was ruled by three Empires which, although not National States in the modern sense of the word, relied for their organisation mainly on three nations which do not properly belong to the area we have taken as 'Eastern Europe', the Germans, Russians and Turks. Under these Empires certain nations, which had enjoyed a longer uninterrupted period of independence, and had been less thoroughly subjected, retained a privileged position, or at least put up a national opposition too strong ever to be entirely broken. These were the Poles and Hungarians, and to a lesser extent the Greeks. The Czechs and Croats obtained occasional recognition of their historical rights, but this did not always have much practical value. The remaining nations of Eastern Europe were completely submerged for centuries on end.

The 'historical' nations had for centuries ruled territories inhabited largely by people speaking other languages and professing other religions than their own. The educated class of the 'historical' nations considered the frontiers of their States, the restoration of whose independence became their constant aim during the years of foreign rule, to be determined by historical rights. They never conceived of their States as based on the ethnical principle, and do not so conceive of them to this day.

The 'disinherited' or 'non-historical' nations hardly had an educated class at all before the middle of last century. Some of these nations were entirely subjected to one Empire (the Bulgarians under the Ottomans or the Slovaks under the Magyars are examples), while others were divided between two or three Empires (Roumanians, Poles and Serbs).

The rise of modern nationalism slowly affected the nations of Eastern Europe. Some of these attained whole or partial independence in the course of the nineteenth century. Finally, in 1918, the statesmen of Western Europe and the United States proclaimed the ethnical principle as the basis on which the frontiers of Eastern Europe should be drawn, and the Treaties of Versailles, St Germain, Trianon and Neuilly were regarded as embodying that principle.

The 1919 Treaties set up a system of frontiers which approximated more closely to the ethnical divisions than any previous system in the history of Eastern Europe. The new frontiers did not, however, correspond in all cases with these divisions. Large numbers of people were left on the wrong side of the frontiers, and their existence gave rise to a series of international problems commonly summarised under the name of Minority Problems. The 1919 statesmen realised that these problems, which revisions of frontiers could have mitigated but could not have eliminated, would cause trouble in the post-war years, and they obliged the Successor States to accept 'Minority Treaties', intended to guarantee certain minimum conditions to the minorities. The faithful execution of these Treaties was to be ensured by the League of Nations. In fact appeals were made to the League from time to time by the minorities, but the grievances were not removed, and no means was found in practice of enforcing the execution of obligations assumed. The Treaties were resented by the Successor States as limitations of their sovereignty, while the minorities complained that they were quite ineffectual as guarantees of their rights, and even declared that they had never been intended to be seriously used.

Three separate types of Minority Problem should be distinguished.

There are national minorities in border regions. Their situation is due to a conflict of the ethnical principle with historical, strategical or economic considerations. Northern and Western Bohemia are mainly inhabited by Germans, but they were given to Czechoslovakia in 1918 on the grounds that they formed part of the historical Kingdom of Bohemia. Eastern Galicia was taken by Poland, despite its Ukrainian population, because it was a historical Polish province. The Kosovo region of Southern Serbia has a large Albanian population, but is associated in the minds of all Serbs with one of the most glorious episodes of the national history. The northern fringe of the Hungarian plain was taken by Czechoslovakia on the grounds that, although its population is mainly Hungarian, a strip of fertile land was necessary to the economic life of Slovakia. The plainland west of the Transylvanian Western Mountains was assigned to Roumania in order to give that country a railway line of economic and military importance connecting north and south. The Caribrod district on the Bulgarian, and the Subotica and Baranya areas on the Hungarian frontier, were given to Jugoslavia for strategic reasons. In areas of this kind minorities are separated by what seems to them an arbitrary line from the main body of their peoples, with whose countries they are immediately contiguous.

A second type of national minority are those separated by great distances from their own country. The most important minority of this kind are the Jews, who have no country of their own, but are plentifully distributed through certain areas of Eastern Europe. Also important are the German minorities scattered from the Middle Danube to the Eastern Carpathians and the Black Sea. Less numerous or powerful are the Greeks of the Black Sea ports; the Vlachs of Macedonia, the Pindus and the Balkan Range; and the Armenians found in some of the older towns of the former Ottoman dominions.

The third type are the inhabitants of certain regions of exceedingly mixed population. Such regions are the Banat, Dobrudja, Bessarabia, Transylvania and Macedonia. The Banat is inhabited mainly by Roumanians, Serbs, Hungarians and Germans, but there are also smaller settlements of Slovaks, Ruthenes and peasants speaking special Slavonic dialects peculiar to this region. The Dobrudja has a population of Turks, Bulgarians, Roumanians, Greeks and small Tatar tribes and religious sects. The Black Sea coast-line was not inhabited until the end of last century by Roumanians, who have never been a seafaring people. The trade was handled by Greeks and Armenians, and the craftsmen of the towns and the peasants of the sparsely inhabited countryside were Turks and Slavs. A mixture similar to that of the Dobrudja exists in Southern Bessarabia, with the addition of a numerous Russo-Ukrainian element and a German minority of nearly 100,000. Central Bessarabia has a mainly Roumanian population, with Russians and Jews in the towns, while in the north the dominant element is Ukrainian, with substantial minorities of Russians, Roumanians and Jews. Transylvania is the home of Roumanians, Hungarians and Germans, closely interwoven with each other, with small settlements of Ruthenes and Slovaks and a strong urban Jewish element. Macedonia is perhaps the most hopelessly mixed region of all. Here are Serbs, Greeks, Bulgarians, Albanians, Turks and Vlachs, besides a large number of people speaking Slav dialects which are neither Serbian nor Bulgarian, and small settlements of Armenians and Jews.

Each of these mixed regions has some history of its own, and has at some time or other provided a subject for international disputes. Transylvania and Macedonia, however, unlike the other regions of the kind, have a very long and distinct history, and there exists even to-day something like a Transylvanian or Macedonian patriotism.

The three types of national minority described give rise to different types of problem. The frontier minorities can be satisfied by revision of frontiers or by the provision of special facilities and rights. The case of the isolated minorities is more difficult, as the majority nations are faced with the task of assimilating, or of finding a place in their midst for, essentially alien elements. Finally, in the mixed regions the problem is not one of guaranteeing minority rights at all, but of rendering possible the peaceful coexistence of a number of different national groups, each of which regards the region as its home. Transylvania, for instance, cannot be considered as a Roumanian province with a Hungarian minority or as a Hungarian province with a Roumanian minority. It is the home of both Roumanians and Hungarians, both of whom have lived there far longer than any historical records that can be considered as reliable. Until the two nations can live together in peace and friendship it is inconceivable that the country can have any prosperity or security.

The 'solution' or mitigation of the Minorities Question, which did so much to poison the atmosphere of Eastern Europe between 1918 and 1941, is dependent on three types of measure. The conditions of the minorities should be improved by the concession and enforcement of greater political, economic and cultural rights. The numbers of the minorities should be reduced by the readjustment of national boundaries where this can be shown to be desirable. The importance of frontiers should be reduced by weakening the connection between nationality and the apparatus of State.

The sufferings of the minorities during the inter-war period were due fundamentally to two causes, the bad system of Government prevailing in Eastern Europe and the identification of nationality with the State apparatus. It is inconceivable that national minorities can enjoy decent treatment in States organised on a basis of economic exploitation, social oppression, corruption, torture and terrorism. Not only the minorities, but all but a few members of the majority nation suffer from these things, and to talk in such conditions of human rights and protection of minorities is merely a joke in bad taste. Moreover, the identification of nationality—or language—with State apparatus makes permanent friendship and mutual loyalty between the majority and minority nations within a State impossible. As long as these two things are identified, the minorities, however well treated, will desire incorporation in another State, where their kinsmen are the majority, or the creation of a new State in which they shall form the majority, while the majority nations will regard the minorities, however well they behave, as a potential danger to their State. As long as this is the case, mutual confidence and friendship are impossible.

The problem can only be solved if it is possible to combine free use of the language of birth, and recognition of the personal nationality of the citizen, with loyalty to a State which stands above the ethnical principle and includes men of different nations. The only States in the modern world which have attempted this solution are the Soviet Union and Switzerland. Switzerland was formed by the association over a period of centuries of free men of different language. The Swiss example cannot be followed in a few years or even in a few generations. The Soviet Union, however, attempted systematically to deal with the modern principle of nationality—which never faced the founders of the Swiss Republic—on the basis of combining cultural autonomy with State unity. The degree of success achieved has formed a subject for much interested controversy during the last twenty years. It is impossible to give a categorical answer, but the loyalty with which soldiers, peasants and townsmen of non-Russian origin have served the Soviet Union in her hour of peril would suggest that considerable success was attained.

Is it possible to apply a similar solution in Eastern Europe? The psychological and cultural differences between the nations of Eastern Europe and those of the Soviet Union would of course call for different methods, but it might be possible to adopt the same principle. It is probable that different classes would react differently to it. It has often been said that the peasant is the bearer of the national idea. This catchword is repeated on every possible occasion by the middle-class intellectual chauvinists of Eastern Europe.

It is true to this extent, that during the centuries of foreign rule the national language and customs of Eastern Europe were preserved by the peasantry, which remained unaffected by those of the alien ruling class, with which it had little contact. The peasant clings stubbornly to his language and customs, and resists any attempts made to denationalise him. It is not true, however, that the Eastern European peasantry is the bearer of the national idea, if by that expression is meant the nationalist ideology of the nineteenth and twentieth centuries. That ideology is essentially intellectual, and was introduced into Eastern Europe by men who had studied it in the classrooms of Paris or had heard the version of it proclaimed by the German romantic distorters of the Principles of 1789. The Eastern European peasant does not and cannot understand the refinements of constitutional law or the various theories of historical rights and national sovereignty.

It is quite probable that the principle of cultural autonomy and State unity would be acceptable to the Eastern European peasant. His national character would be assured against any denationalisation, and he would serve the State as he has always served, but with greater enthusiasm if the new State was reformed in his interest, was a Welfare State instead of a Robber State.

It is doubtful, however, whether the nationalist intellectual class, and its pupils in army, bureaucracy and commerce—the ruling class of Eastern Europe from 1918 to 1941—could ever accept this principle. These people could not be satisfied by cultural autonomy. They require nothing less than a National State, in which the whole military, bureaucratic and commercial apparatus of State Sovereignty is monopolised by them as rulers of the majority nation within the State. They require this partly because it affords them opportunities of personal enrichment and power which would be denied them under any other system, and partly because their ideological leaders have for fifty years or more been convinced, and have implanted in their own heads the conviction, that no nation can escape physical annihilation that does not possess a Sovereign State of its own, equipped with all the tools of modern 'Integral Nationalism'.

This dogma is shrieked forth with fanatical and wearisome frenzy by the representatives of the educated classes of the Eastern European (and, for that matter, of other) nations. The fact that it is historically untrue, and almost meaningless, in no way diminishes its importance. It is believed by the educated class of oppressed minorities and oppressing majorities alike. The tearful bleatings of the former and the confident brayings of the latter blend most unharmoniously in a deafening cacophonous chorus.

A solution based on cultural autonomy and super-national States can only hope to succeed if the ruling class of 1918 to 1941 is rendered entirely powerless. During twenty or thirty years it should be possible to train a new generation, capable of supplying industry, commerce, the bureaucracy and the free professions with men loyal to the ideas of the new system. This result appears to have been achieved in the Soviet Union by somewhat drastic methods. If the attempt were made in Eastern Europe, it might be possible, in view of the fact that the general level of civilisation there is appreciably higher than that of the Russia of 1917, to achieve the result desired by a less painful process. If, however, political power and the control of education remain in the hands of the ruling classes of 1918–41 there is no prospect that a new system, other than that of Sovereign States, could succeed. In this case the Minorities Problem will continue to give trouble.

It is not enough to remove political power from the old ruling classes and to bring up a new generation of intellectuals to understand that the national idea and State apparatus need not be connected; it is also necessary to create a new State loyalty.

The French-, German- and Italian-speaking citizens of Switzerland do not consider themselves Frenchmen, Germans or Italians. They violently repudiate any suggestion to this effect. They are Swiss and only Swiss. In the Soviet Union the language and cultural rights of the different national groups are recognised, but at the same time the Moscow Government has been at pains to stimulate 'Soviet patriotism'. Official statements speak not of the Russian people or the Ukrainian people or the Uzbek people, but of 'the Soviet people'. It appears—in the nature of things concrete irrefutable proof is unobtainable—that this policy has been successful. The question presents itself, whether a higher loyalty can be created which will be accepted by the nations of Eastern Europe.

A great part of Eastern Europe was once ruled by the Habsburg Monarchy. This State was based on the dynasty and on a super-national aristocracy closely attached to it. The Habsburg dynasty was almost wholly free from nationalist bias, but it was paralysed by its ignorance and fear of the people whom it ruled. It could work only through the aristocracy and was unable to understand the needs or wishes of the rest of the population. The growth in the nineteenth century of nationalist movements among the subject peoples, and of social movements among the subject classes created problems which the Habsburgs were incapable of facing. The collapse of the Empire was delayed by the fact that it suited the interests of the compact and powerful Reich to support it, but the defeat of Germany in war brought inevitably the dissolution of its fragile ally. After 1918 Eastern Europe was organised on the basis of National States. The policy of all these States was dictated by modern romantic nationalism, which made reconciliation and cooperation of majorities and minorities impossible.

If the Minorities Problem is not faced with realism and courage at the end of this war, it will be an important contributory cause for another European War. Apart from frontier changes, which can greatly mitigate but cannot finally solve the problem, three types of solution deserve consideration. One is denationalisation. By drastic police pressure, economic discrimination, and the denial of all cultural rights, 'Integral Nationalists' hope to annihilate national minorities, to turn Ukrainians into Poles, Albanians into Serbs, Slovaks into Hungarians. If such a policy could be pursued for a hundred years it might achieve its aim. Unfortunately, human experience suggests that the European wars to which it invariably gives rise do not leave sufficiently long intervals between them to give it a fair chance. And, although 'Integral Nationalists' would bitterly dispute this, it is probable that most Europeans would prefer to avoid a cyclical series of European wars even at the cost of allowing a few million people to retain the language and customs of their birth.

A second type of solution is the exchange of populations. This has on paper an attractive simplicity, but entails in practice unspeakable sufferings and general cultural impoverishment. The most striking case recorded is the exchange of Greeks from Asia Minor and of Turks from Greece. This gave to the two States a purer ethnical composition, but undoubtedly brought about a most regrettable lowering of civilisation in the Levant, and should be regarded not as a triumph of international statesmanship but as a dismal confession of human failure. It is doubtful whether it is suitable for imitation anywhere in Europe.

The third type of solution is that commonly associated with the word 'Federation'. It implies the combination within one larger unit of a number of former National States. Within this larger federal unit the different nations would enjoy full protection for their national languages, customs and cultures, but decisions on foreign policy, trade with areas outside the Federation, and military affairs, would be taken by the Central Federal Government.

The word 'Federation' enjoys at present a vague popularity. There is even an inclination to regard it as a cure for all troubles. It should be understood that the creation of a Federation is only a structural measure. Everything depends on the content of the structure. It is possible to conceive a Federation run by Catholics in the interest of the Catholic

Church, by industrialists in the interest of industrialists, by kulaki in the interest of kulaki, by workers in the interest of workers, or by the people in the interest of the people. No Federation and no National State, in Eastern Europe or elsewhere, will succeed unless it ensures minimum standards of good Government and an educational system which fosters loyalty to itself.

Further, although the purpose of Federation is to reduce the importance of frontiers, it is a mistake to imagine that these will no longer have any importance at all. Administrative boundaries will be required within the territory of the Federation, and these will have to be drawn as far as possible in accordance with linguistic boundaries. Still more important will be the settlement of the external frontiers of each Federation, and the decision which nations should combine with which to make a Federation.

These problems, connected with the possibility of a Federal solution for Eastern Europe, will be mentioned again later. Enough has been said here of the general lines on which a solution of Minority Problems could be attempted. Those who wish to study the problem in detail should read the works of Mr C. A. Macartney.[1] The present chapter will deal with certain special problems connected with the existence of minorities. These are the German and Jewish minorities in Eastern Europe, and the mixed regions of Transylvania and Macedonia.

The German Minorities

The German minorities within the area under review should be divided at the start into two categories, those inhabiting regions more or less contiguous to the Reich and those separated by considerable distances from it. To the former category belong the Germans of Bohemia, Silesia and Pomerania, to the latter those of Hungary, Jugoslavia, Roumania and the rest of Poland.

The Germans of Western Poland and of Bohemia were the ruling race during the nineteenth century and up to 1918. In Poland their supremacy was rigorously enforced by the

[1] *National States and National Minorities*, 1934; *Hungary and her Successors*, 1937; *Problems of the Danube Basin*, 1942.

power of the German Empire. In Bohemia the situation was more uncertain, for although the Emperor Francis Joseph preferred the Germans to the Czechs, he was not interested in nationalist theories, and did not hesitate to support the Czechs against the Germans when that seemed to suit the interests of his dynasty. In both countries the German supremacy was strongly resisted in the political, economic and cultural fields by the more numerous but less fortunate Slav peoples.

The German communities elsewhere in Eastern Europe are the descendants of settlers imported by various rulers, who enjoyed for longer or shorter periods a number of material privileges, but until the arrival of Adolf Hitler's hordes never enjoyed political power over the nations among whom they lived. The most interesting case are the 'Saxons' of Transylvania, who settled in the south of that province in the thirteenth century, and during the Reformation in Hungary adopted Lutheranism. Their number in 1930 was 237,000. German settlers in the interior of Poland and Hungary have been there for centuries. The large colonies of 'Swabians', who have remained Catholics, now established in the Banat and the Bačka, were settled there in the eighteenth century, after these lands were reconquered from the Turks, when the Habsburgs did not completely restore them to Hungary, but kept part of them under a separate administration as the 'Military Frontier'. A large colony of Germans was settled in Southern Bessarabia in the nineteenth century by the Imperial Russian Government.

The settlement of 1918 converted the Germans of Bohemia, Silesia and Pomerania from masters into second-class citizens, while the Germans of Eastern Europe merely changed masters. The latter found Roumanian and Serbian rule in some ways more painful than Hungarian. The bureaucracy was more brutal and less honest, and life became more complicated. But the leaders of the German minorities soon made agreements with the new Governments, and during the post-war years they had little cause for complaint, and behaved as quiet and loyal citizens. It is even arguable that they were better off than under Hungary, for the Serbs and Roumanians, fearing Hungarian Revisionism more than anything else, regarding the Hungarian minorities in the new provinces as irreconcilable, and remembering that during their struggle against Budapest the Swabians had shown no hostility to them, favoured the German minorities at the expense of the Hungarians. During the preceding fifty years many Swabians had become Magyarised. The new Governments made it their business to re-Germanise peasants who considered themselves Hungarians but bore German names. The Swabians of the Satu Mare district in North-Western Transylvania and others in different parts of the Banat were 'saved for Germandom' with the help of the Roumanian and Jugoslav authorities.

The Germans of Bohemia and Western Poland on the other hand bitterly resented the change. The latter consistently refused to admit that Poland was more than a temporary aberration of the peacemakers, in which attitude they were supported by the various Governments in Berlin. Both the German minority and the Polish authorities adopted a provocative attitude, and even such respectable German statesmen as Stresemann were determined to recover for Germany the 'Corridor', Danzig and Pomerania.

The Czechoslovak Germans hoped to be allowed to join either Germany or the Austrian Republic. The Czechoslovak Government insisted on the sanctity of the historical Bohemian frontiers. On 4 March 1919 big demonstrations were staged by the Germans in a number of Bohemian towns. The Czechoslovak police fired on the demonstrators, and more than fifty Germans were killed. Relations between Czechs and Germans continued to be as bad as they could be for some time. After a few years, however, as it became clear that the prospects of a reversal of the 1919 settlement were not great, a will to understanding began to appear on both sides. In 1925 representatives of the German Agrarians and Clericals entered the Prague Government, and were followed in 1929 by those of the Social Democrats, who had some time before this decided on political collaboration with the Czechoslovak Social Democrats.

The advent of the National Socialists to power in Germany in 1933 had an immediate and profound effect on the German minorities all over Eastern Europe. The only German minority in which resistance to the Nazi ideology might have been expected was that of Czechoslovakia. The three and a half million Czechoslovak Germans included all social classes, and had been exposed to all political and religious influences.

There were German Socialists, Communists, Conservatives, Fascists, Liberals, Agrarians and Clericals. It might have been expected that many of these would reject the Nazi ideology. This was not, however, what happened. A section of the Bohemian German bourgeoisie had always held radical nationalist views. These people had followed the Pan-German Schönerer under Austria-Hungary, and sympathised with the extreme nationalist groups in the Reich after 1918. When Hitler came to power they became Nazis. A large part of the younger generation of Bohemian Germans held somewhat aloof from the political parties in the first post-war period. They joined a number of gymnastic societies, which pursued apparently harmless aims, but actually fostered extreme nationalism, combined with various obscure mystical doctrines and a passion for conspiracy. In 1934 one of the leaders of the 'Turnverband', one of the gymnastic organisations, Konrad Henlein, came forward as the leader of a new Bohemian German political organisation, the 'Sudetendeutsche Heimat-front'. In the following year this was converted into a party, 'Sudetendeutsche Partei' (Sd.P.), which won two-thirds of the German votes in the Parliamentary elections of that year and the second largest number of seats of all parties in the Prague Parliament.[1]

Henlein had the support of the nationalist bourgeoisie and of the younger generation connected with the gymnastic societies, but he would not have had such success without the support of a section of the working class. This he won owing to the despair of the German workers of the depressed industrial areas. The World Depression had hit the old established industries, which were mainly German, more severely than the more modern and more heavily subsidised industries created in recent years by the Czechs in the interior of the country. The German industries had lost markets by the changes of frontier of 1919, and the Prague Government had been less interested in restoring the fortunes of German enterprises, many of which were directed by men known as implacable enemies of the Republic, than in creating a highly skilled

[1] For a full, scientific and objective account of political currents among the Bohemian Germans during this century, and for the whole background of the 'Sudeten crisis', see Elisabeth Wiskemann, *Czechs and Germans*, Oxford University Press, 1938.

Czech industry. Government contracts were given to Czech firms rather than to German, Czech workers were employed in preference to German, and not much was done for the relief of the German unemployed.

These economic hardships were well exploited by Nazi propaganda, and, combined with the constant irritation caused by minor local disputes about schools and about the language of administration, were offered as proof of deliberate and systematic persecution of the Germans by the Czechs, to whom were attributed diabolical plans for the extermination of the whole German population of Czechoslovakia.

In fact the Czechs showed remarkable tolerance towards their Germans, and very little that could be called persecution took place. If the average Czech regarded Germans as unreliable citizens, subsequent events seem thoroughly to have justified this point of view. As for the petty quarrels between local officialdom and the German population, they may have caused general annoyance, but were certainly not sufficient to create a major national and international problem.

The real basis of the question was the fact that the Germans regarded themselves as the race appointed by God to rule in Bohemia. They despised the Czechs, and could never admit them to a status of equality with themselves, still less accept subordination to them. The slender hope of a reconciliation of German and Czech workers on the basis of Socialism and Democracy was destroyed by the sufferings of the Depression period and by the spectacular successes of Hitler. During the last years of the Republic the politics of the Sudeten Germans lost all sense. For instance, in the summer of 1937 German Socialist workers declared a strike in Gablonz against their German employer. The latter appealed to Henlein for strike-breakers, who were promptly provided. It might have been expected that this would wreck the prospect of Sd.P. in the eyes of the German workers. Not at all. Meanwhile General Franco captured Bilbao and Hitler's stock stood higher than ever. The enthusiasm of the Germans of all classes for Sd.P. increased.

The three remaining German parties, the Agrarians, Clericals and Social Democrats, continued to collaborate with Prague, but their following rapidly declined. This decline was not appreciably arrested by the conclusion in February 1937 of an agreement between these 'Activists' and the Government, which promised substantial economic and cultural concessions to the Germans. These were denounced as mere tricks by Sd.P., and the 'Activist' leaders were pilloried as traitors. In April 1938, impressed by the Austrian Anschluss, many Agrarians and Clericals joined the Sd.P. Only the Social Democrats and the German supporters of the Czechoslovak Communist Party remained opposed to Henlein.

In the districts of German majority the terror of Sd.P. reached remarkable lengths. The Prague Government, frightened of the criticism of the British and French pro-Nazis, who let out a deafening screech whenever it was reported that a German had been pushed off the kerb accidentally by a Czech, allowed Henlein to do more or less what he liked with the Social Democrats. A Socialist schoolmistress in a small German town which I visited in the summer of 1938, who tried to prevent her pupils from kicking little Jews in the classroom, was shown by them the lamp-post on which she would be hanged when He should come. Social Democrat Party meetings were attended by Henleinist photographers who announced that everyone whose face appeared on their photographs would be put in a concentration camp or suffer a worse fate.

Henlein himself, who had sworn himself purple about his devotion to Democracy, and had made in 1934 on the respectable members of Chatham House the impression of a mild and charming Liberal, at last came out with demands for complete Nazification of German Bohemia and the adoption by Czechoslovakia of a foreign policy to be dictated by Berlin. In March 1939, while the Gestapo was merrily arresting, beating and murdering Czechs in the city below, the Führer allowed his puppet Henlein the pleasure of giving a party to his friends in the historic Hrad, the citadel of Prague that had been the home of Charles IV and of Thomas Masaryk.[1]

The triumph of Nazi ideas was even swifter and easier among the other German minorities of Eastern Europe. The Polish Germans were never loyal at heart to the new State. Their agitation was less violent after the 1934 German-Polish Treaty, but the situation was not fundamentally changed. The Polish

---

[1] For the international aspect of the 'Sudeten German Question' and German policy in Czechoslovakia, see below, pp. 391–5.

Government never allowed the formation of an official Nazi organisation among their Germans, but Nazi ideas spread rapidly. They affected even the German settlements of Congress Poland and Galicia, which before 1918 had had no reason for enmity with the Poles, and might have become loyal Polish citizens but for Hitler.

In 1937 a joint declaration was made by the Berlin and Warsaw Governments, promising to respect the rights of the minorities of each nation in the other's country to schools and cultural associations. The declaration was quite insincere, and remained inoperative. The diplomatic friendship of the two States did not modify the fundamental hatred of the Polish and German peoples. Provocation and terrorism took place on both sides, although there is no doubt that the Polish minority in Germany was far worse treated than the German minority in Poland. The Polish Germans kept fairly quiet, but maintained relations with their Gestapo chiefs within and without the country. In the short German-Polish war they did their Fifth Column work with exemplary efficiency, and distinguished themselves still more after the conquest of Poland by their zeal as spies, informers, torturers and executioners.

Trianon Hungary had in 1918 a population of some 550,000 'Swabian' Germans. These are mostly settled in Western and South-Western Hungary, in 'Transdanubia' and in the Pécs region. Between 1867 and 1918 a considerable number had become Magyarised. Hungary has with greater insistence and greater success than any other Eastern European State resisted German claims for autonomy. In 1930 the official statistics revealed only 475,000 Germans, a fall of 75,000 in about a decade. This drew from the mild Liberal Professor Bleyer, then leader of the harmless 'Ungarländisch-deutsches Verbildungsverein', which Budapest had allowed to be founded in 1924, a protest, which let loose in the Hungarian Press a frenzied outburst of anti-German feeling.

From 1933 onwards the Reich began to show more interest in the fate of the Germans of Hungary. Emissaries of the Nazi organisations concerned with Germans abroad toured Hungary and agitated. The more active elements among the Hungarian Germans, and especially the younger generation, became Nazis. In December 1938 a new organisation, 'Volksbund der Deutschen in Ungarn', was founded by a Nazi named Basch. The Imrédy Government made concessions to the German minority and tolerated Nazi propaganda among them. Magyarised Germans were encouraged by Basch's men to return to their 'Germandom', and the apparent invincibility of Hitler provided a strong inducement to this effect. In the 1939 elections Basch made a pact with the Government Party, and won two-thirds of the German vote. Since then the arrogance of the 'Volksbund' has steadily increased, but Budapest has not yet gone beyond concessions reconcilable with the independence of the Hungarian State.

The Germans of Jugoslavia during the period 1918–41 fall into four groups. The most numerous were the 'Swabians' of the Bačka and Banat, who numbered 328,000 in 1921. In Croatia were 123,000, mostly settled in the plain of Slavonia. In Slovenia were about 40,000 and in Bosnia some 15,000. Of these the most fortunate were those of Bačka and Banat, who were supported by the Belgrade Government against the Hungarian minority. They founded in 1920 a 'Schwäbisch-deutscher Kulturbund', which enjoyed substantial cultural rights. The Germans of Bosnia, mostly ex-Austrian officials, and those of Croatia were less popular than those of Bačka and Banat, but managed to get on fairly well with their neighbours. In Slovenia the situation was more tense. The Germans had ruled the Slovenes for centuries, and made themselves thoroughly hated. They could hardly expect to receive much affection now that their subjects had become their masters. The attitude of the Slovenes to the Germans was made still less cordial on account of the intolerance, real or alleged, of the Vienna Government towards the much more numerous Slovene minority in Carinthia and Styria. However the unfriendliness of the Slovenes towards the Germans in their midst could certainly not be described as 'persecution', and the numbers involved were too small to constitute a serious problem.

Nazi ideas penetrated among the Jugoslav Germans from 1933 onwards. A German from Osijek in Slavonia, named Altgayer, founded an association independent of the 'Kulturbund' and openly sympathetic to National Socialism. After the Anschluss Altgayer put forward demands for autonomy on lines similar to those of Henlein. After Munich Altgayer was admitted to the 'Kulturbund', which had until then adopted a more cautious attitude, but now accepted the Nazi ideology. The 'Kulturbund' gave valuable electoral help to Milan Stojadinović in December 1938, receiving in return a number of concessions which included the right to buy land in the frontier regions. During the following years the German minority in Jugoslavia prepared itself for the role of Fifth Column, which it duly fulfilled in the spring of 1941. It is now performing the usual prodigies of valour and chivalry in the duties assigned to it by the Armies of Occupation.

The Roumanian Germans also fall into a number of groups. The most important are the 237,000 Saxons of Transylvania and the 223,000 Swabians of the Banat, the former Lutheran, the latter Catholic. There are also 70,000 Germans in Bukovina, while the colony in Bessarabia numbered 80,000 until the summer of 1940, when by agreement between Berlin and Moscow the greater part of these were brought back to Germany after the Soviet annexation of that province.

The cause of 'Germandom' undoubtedly benefited by the creation of Great Roumania, for not only did the Roumanian authorities go out of their way to re-Germanise the Magyarised Swabians, but close contact was established between the highly race-conscious Saxons and the remote Bessarabian Germans, who had been cut off from their kinsmen for more than a century. From 1918 to 1930 the distinctions between Saxons and Swabians made political unity difficult. In 1930 a Saxon named Fabritius started an 'Erneuerungsbewegung' based on the principles of National Socialism, then not yet in power in the Reich. Shortly afterwards he and another Saxon Nazi named Gust founded a Nazi Party of Germans in Roumania, which enjoyed support among Swabians as well as Saxons. In 1934 this party was dissolved by the Bucarest Government, but soon reappeared under another name. The following years saw a good deal of confusion in Roumanian German politics. Fabritius quarrelled with Gust, and both with the more Conservative leaders of the Saxons. But these quarrels were of a personal nature, and in no way impeded the spread of Nazi sympathies among all Roumanian Germans, especially among the young. The older Germans claimed to be opposed to Nazism.

Not long before the outbreak of war I visited a German

village in Transylvania with the Roumanian Prefect of the Department. The German mayor of the village regaled us for hours with excellent wine and passionate professions of hatred for the Nazis. Afterwards the Prefect told me that he had seen a photograph of the mayor's son in the presence of Hitler, and that there was a long dossier of Nazi activities to the mayor's credit. In fact the Roumanian authorities knew pretty well what was going on, and tolerated it.

After September 1940 the last signs of official resentment against the German minority disappeared. Under the Iron Guard regime there was a drive for the 'Roumanisation' of Jewish firms. This consisted, in practice, in replacing Jewish industrialists and shopkeepers by Saxons and Swabians. A few plums were doled out to deserving Roumanians. The same policy was continued by Antonescu after he had liquidated the Iron Guard.

The policy originally proclaimed by Hitler was the unification of all Germans in the Reich. This was at first considered by all serious observers of European politics outside Germany to be mere rhetoric. The distances separating many German communities from Germany seemed too great. The plan has now, however, been almost completely realised. The Germans of Czechoslovakia and Poland have been incorporated, together with those two countries, in Great Germany. The same has been done in Slovenia, and in the Jugoslav Banat the German Army of Occupation gives the dominant role to the local Germans. In Roumania the Germans are a dominant nation within the nation.

The Germans of the Baltic States were withdrawn during the period of German-Soviet collaboration, and some of the Germans of Croatia have been recalled, owing to the uncertainty of life in a country where Jugoslav patriot forces are still active, but it is too early to say whether this represents Hitler's final intention.

The arrogant behaviour of the German minorities in Eastern Europe, and the many abominable crimes which they have committed, make the prospects of their remaining there exceedingly uncertain. It seems inconceivable that Poles, Czechs or Jugoslavs could ever wish again to have German citizens in their countries, and the hatred of the peoples of Hungary and Roumania for their German neighbours is likely to be little less fierce. For several centuries the German minorities lived peacefully among Serbs, Hungarians and Roumanians. They were contented with their lot and tolerant towards their neighbours, and their example contributed to the economic and cultural progress of the more primitive nations. In Transylvania beautiful monuments of medieval German civilisation survive in the old quarters of the Saxon towns of Hermannstadt, Schässburg and Kronstadt.[1]

The Germans played in the past an essential part in shaping the character of Eastern European culture, and it might have been hoped in normal times that they would continue to be a progressive and valuable factor. Adolf Hitler cared for none of these things. He staked all on establishing German domination over all Europe. He forced all Germans beyond the frontiers of the Reich to become tools of his policy of expansion. After his fall it will be impossible for Germans to live side by side with those whom they have betrayed and terrorised. Many will be massacred in revenge, others will be expelled from their homes, others compelled to abjure their German character. No one can yet predict the details, but it is probably safe to say that the historic mission of the Germans in Eastern Europe is at an end.

The problem of the Germans of Bohemia and Western Poland is more difficult. A few words will be said of the latter at a later stage.* As for the former, they present almost insoluble difficulties. About one-third of the inhabitants of Bohemia-Moravia were Germans in 1938. Can Germans and Czechs ever live together again in peace? As long as the Czechoslovak Republic existed, there were people of both nations who believed in the possibility. I once attended a joint meeting of the German and Czech Social Democratic parties in Pilsen. It was not long before Munich. I travelled in a special train with some hundred Germans from a small town in Western Bohemia. We got out at a station on the outskirts of the city and marched to the main square where the meeting took place. As we passed in the early morning the streets were lined on both sides with cheering crowds, in some places ten deep, not party members but simple

---

[1] The Roumanian and Hungarian names of these towns are respectively Sibiu, Şighişoara, Braşov and Nagyszeben, Segesvár, Brassó.

* See below, p. 321.

Czech citizens, who shouted 'Long live our German friends'. And the Germans answered 'Long live the Czechoslovak Republic'. It was a moving experience. Terrorised by Henlein's gangs for months past, these Germans enjoyed for a day the strange experience of being greeted as friends—by Czechs.

But Heydrich's torture chambers and firing squads will not have left much of those emotions. It is hardly credible that the two nations can be friends again. And yet it is difficult to exterminate three and a half million people, and still more difficult for a numerically small nation, whose rate of increase is not very high, to take their place. The separation of the German districts from the rest of Bohemia is no solution, for, apart from the fanatical devotion of the Czech educated class to their historic frontiers, there can be no doubt that Czechoslovakia, or any composite Western Slav or Danubian State which may take its place, must have the strategic frontier of the Bohemian mountains. There are areas, such as Egerland, where German populations could be detached from Bohemia without weakening the strategic position, but such minor revision would only affect a few hundred thousand. Substantially, Bohemia must remain in Czech hands, and something will have to be done with its German inhabitants. The question will give the peacemakers plenty of fun.

THE JEWISH MINORITIES

The Jews are an element even more foreign to Eastern Europe than are the Germans. Their presence constitutes an exceptionally difficult problem. They are of two kinds, the Western or Sephardic and the Eastern or Askenazi.

The former speak Spanish, and are the descendants of the Jews who, after being expelled from Spain by Ferdinand and Isabella at the end of the fifteenth century, took refuge in the Ottoman Empire. The most important colony of Sephardic Jews is in Salonica, but they are to be met with in Istanbul, Sofia, Sarajevo and other Balkan towns, and have even penetrated recently into the Danubian Basin. The Askenazi are descendants of the Jews settled in the fourteenth century by King Casimir III of Poland. The earlier origin of these Jews is obscure. Some were real children of the original Diaspora, others were descended from the Khazars, a Mongol tribe inhabiting the steppes of Southern Russia, which in the ninth century adopted the Jewish religion.

The Jews flourished in Poland during the Middle Ages, and on the collapse of the Polish State became divided between Austria and Russia. Their lot was very much better in the former, and the Russian pogroms of the nineteenth century caused an increasing number to take refuge over the Austrian and Roumanian borders. From the thirties onwards they began to penetrate Moldavia, encouraged by the development of trade following the abolition of Turkish commercial restrictions in the Principalities by the 1829 Treaty of Adrianople. After 1848 they began to pour into Hungary, where the prevalence of Liberal ideas and the indifference of the landowning class to commerce gave them their opportunity.

At the beginning of the present war the Jews of Eastern Europe were distributed approximately as follows. About three million inhabited Poland, this number including refugees from Western Russia, itself part of historical Poland. Roumania housed between half and three-quarters of a million.[1] Hungarian Jews amounted to nearly half a million. In Slovakia and Croatia there were a certain number of Jews, and in Ruthenia the Czechoslovak census of 1930 showed 80,000 out of 700,000. In the Balkans Jews are not numerous, and do not play a part of much importance. They will be ignored in the present survey, which will confine itself almost entirely to the Jews of Poland, Roumania and Hungary.

The main line of division among the Jews of Eastern Europe is between those who desire assimilation and those who cling to their separate Jewish nationality. There are Jews who, while retaining their Jewish religion, consider themselves primarily to be citizens of the country in which they live, and conform in every possible way to the customs of their neighbours. They are Polish, Roumanian or Hungarian citizens of Jewish religion. Some go so far in this direction as to abandon their religion. They wish to forget their Jewish origin altogether, and to sub-

---

[1] The census of 1930 gave 562,000 for the whole of Great Roumania. The director of the census, the American-trained statistician Sabin Manuila, was accused by the Iron Guard and the Goga-Cuza group of fraudulently reducing the number of Jews in order to reassure the people about the 'Jewish peril'. The number may be somewhat larger if all assimilated Jews are included, but is certainly well under a million.

merge themselves in the surrounding nation. They accept Catholicism, Orthodoxy or remain Free Thinkers. The majority of Eastern European Jews, however, show no desire for assimilation. They retain not only their religion, but all the special characteristics of dress and habit which distinguish them from non-Jews. The ghetto district of Cracow or Czernowitz is little less different from the Christian quarter than is an Arab town from the west end of London.

The Eastern European Jews are mostly engaged in commerce and the free professions. The industry of Poland, Roumania and Hungary in 1918 was mostly in the hands of Jews, who also dominated banking. These were the upper class of Jews, a numerically small group of rich and powerful men. More typical of Jewish life are the small shopkeepers found in most towns, large and small, in these countries. Some Jews are industrial workers, but these are more numerous in old industrial centres such as Budapest or Lódz than in the new industries created since 1918. In the free professions medicine, journalism and law have a special attraction for Jews. There are not many in the teaching profession, and they were effectively excluded from the civil service and the army. In a few places, such as Maramureş in Northern Transylvania, a few Jewish peasants are to be found, but these are exceptional. In pre-1918 Roumania, and in Hungary until recent times, Jews rented land from big landowners and let it out again to the peasants.

The causes of the unpopularity of the Jews are various. The native intellectual class resents the greater mental agility of the Jews, who usually prove themselves quicker and more able than their Polish, Roumanian and Hungarian rivals. The mentality of the Jew is entirely alien to the romantic nationalism which spread over Eastern Europe from the second half of last century onwards. The romantic nationalists at once recognised the Jewish intellectual as an enemy, and their literary works have always been richly spiced with polemics against the Jews.

The Eastern European peasants are suspicious of the Jews. In Moldavia, Northern Transylvania, Galicia, Eastern Poland and parts of Hungary the shopkeepers and moneylenders of the small towns and large villages are Jews. The small cash incomes of the peasants are paid to a Jew. All the cash of the village disappears into the Jew's pocket. Cash is so scarce and so important to the peasant that it is easily identified with wealth. The Jew may have a miserable little shop and live wretchedly, but the fact that he absorbs the money resources of the region makes the peasant think that he is the richest man there, that he is preying upon the whole population.

Finally, the native bourgeoisies hate the Jewish bourgeoisie. This most potent cause of race hatred has only grown up in the last generation. The spread of education in the Eastern European countries brought a much greater production of 'intellectuals'. Graduates of universities, colleges and even secondary schools expect as a right a place either in the civil service or in the free professions. The bureaucracy of the Eastern European States has been distended to an almost incredible extent, but it still could not provide places for all. The free professions were filled, in proportions ranging from a quarter to two-thirds, with Jews. The Depression years further intensified intellectual unemployment and gave a stronger stimulus to anti-Semitism. Moreover, since 1918 the younger generation of the Polish, Roumanian and Hungarian bourgeoisies has shown much more interest than before in industrial and commercial life. The domination of the economic life of the nation by an alien element became a subject of increasing resentment. In these circumstances anti-Semitic propaganda, partly rooted in the native brand of romantic nationalism and partly imported from Berlin, was bound to achieve big results.

The resistance to anti-Semitism was strongest in Hungary. A large number of Jews had become completely Magyarised between 1867 and 1918. The Hungarian Government was prepared to give them all rights provided that they became Hungarians before all else. This they were willing to do, and were genuinely accepted by the Hungarians as belonging to their nation. They even intermarried with the aristocracy. After 1918 those who became Czechoslovak, Jugoslav or Roumanian citizens demonstrated their loyalty and gratitude by insisting, contrary to all their material interests, on calling themselves Hungarians. Only when the policy of Budapest became less Liberal, and a new generation of Jews grew up in the Succession States, did they begin to waver in their allegiance.

In Trianon Hungary there was an outburst of anti-Semitism during the Counter-Revolution, due partly to the fact that some of the Communist leaders had been Jews and partly to the influence of militant Catholicism among the counter-revolutionaries. This was, however, only a passing phase, and under the Bethlen regime Jews had as much liberty as other Hungarian citizens, provided that they held respectable political opinions.

Only during Gömbös' Government did anti-Semitism reappear on a big scale. Even under Bethlen the attendance of Jewish students at universities had been limited. Now a clamour began for their exclusion from the free professions and commerce, and the successes of Hitler lent the clamour greater importance. Both Gömbös and his successors resisted anti-Semitic pressure, but as the years passed the number of restrictions increased. All anti-Jewish laws, however, prescribed different treatment for newly arrived, unassimilated Jews and for those who had been long established in Hungary. To this day the Jews have better treatment in Hungary than elsewhere in Eastern Europe.[1]

The Jews of Poland and Roumania fared less happily. They were more bitterly hated, for they were more alien from their neighbours than were the Hungarian Jews, had a greater stranglehold on economic life, and had to do with a more primitive and more brutal class of people. In both countries pogroms occurred at steadily decreasing intervals, in which the university students and the police had their special parts to play. Physical violence alternated with economic measures depriving thousands of the means of livelihood. The situation of the Jews of Poland and Roumania was already desperate in 1939. Since the German occupation of both countries it has become unimaginable.

During the inter-war period Jews individually supported various political parties, but the official Jewish organisations generally supported the Governments in power—Bethlen, Pilsudski, Carol II, etc. Among the Jewish masses two main ideas spread—Communism and Zionism. As the tide of anti-Semitism rose around them, even those who desired assimila-

[1] This was written before the Nazi occupation of Hungary, one of the first results of which was a wholesale persecution of the Jews. According to a statement of the first Hungarian government after the liberation (Premier General Miklos), out of just under 1,000,000 Hungarian Jews, less than 200,000 were left in 1945.

tion found themselves forced towards one or other of these extremes. Zionism was to some extent supported by the Governments, especially by Poland, which showed a lively interest in British immigration policy in Palestine. It attracted a considerable number of Jews.

Communism commended itself rather as a counsel of despair than as a positive faith. The younger generation of Jews in Bessarabia, Bukovina, Moldavia and Eastern Poland could look forward to nothing. They were pushed mercilessly out of trade and industry. Even the licences of small shopkeepers were removed. The older generation simply resigned themselves. A Jewish shopkeeper is essentially a 'capitalist'. He cannot 'go Bolshevik' overnight. The old men could not easily abandon the habits of thought of a lifetime. They had ,not many years to live. They just faced the prospect of sitting and rotting. The young men could not do this. They could not consent to die before they had begun to live. Communism alone offered them hope, and they clutched at it, thereby providing the Governments with further excuses for persecution.

Anti-Semitism is one of the most obnoxious diseases of modern Europe. It is incompatible with civilisation and peace. It is obnoxious for three reasons. In the first place it causes humiliation and suffering to large numbers of innocent people. If some guilty persons suffer with the innocent, they do so not on account of their guilt but on account of their race. Secondly, it demoralises the persecuting nation. In Roumania, for instance, a great part of the younger generation was irreparably corrupted by the school of Jew-baiting in which it was trained by its professors and policemen. If the educated youth of a nation is brought up to despise, hate, insult, beat and torture a section of the population, if it is taught by its leaders to regard the beating of an old man or a girl student of another race as an act of heroism and chivalry, this will have an effect on the moral life and standards of the whole nation. Thirdly, anti-Semitism menaces directly the material interests of the majority nations of the States where it flourishes. It is the classical means of diverting the attention of the most ignorant part of the people from the need for social reforms. As soon as social discontent assumes alarming proportions, the landowners, capitalists, bureaucrats and military chiefs subsidise some adventurer to start an anti-Semitic movement, provide him with bands of toughs and provocative literature, and soon a demagogic 'movement' is in full swing, which puts the blame for all the sufferings of the people on to the Jews. The ruling class is saved. Not only is anti-Semitism unpleasant for the Jews and bad for the morals of their neighbours, but as long as it is strong there can be no hope of thorough political or social reforms.

Much can be done to remove the causes of anti-Semitism if the economic and political reforms sketched in earlier chapters are carried out. If the economic condition of the peasantry is improved, especially if an efficient system of cheap credit is provided, the Jewish usurer, like his 'Aryan' colleague, will lose his power. The improvement of industrial conditions, free development of Trade Unions, and introduction of modern social services will make the industrialist, whether Jewish or not, less formidable. The reform of the administration will put an end to the corrupt practices of the police, and will make 'diversionary' pogroms impossible. Above all, the development of education in a new spirit, opposed to the old romantic nationalism, will train a new generation to regard citizens of Jewish origin as equal to all others.

Everything should be done to distribute the Jewish population more equally between different professions. If the Jews possessed in some parts of Eastern Europe a stranglehold over trade and industry, this was because they were unable to enter other professions. Poles, Roumanians and Hungarians complained of the large numbers of Jewish lawyers and bankers, but they would not hear of allowing Jews to become civil servants or army officers. These occupations should be opened to Jews, who should also be encouraged to become industrial workers or even peasants. That Jews are capable of this is shown by the experience of Palestine, where Jewish agricultural settlements have attained great success. Moreover, there is plenty of room in some of the free professions for Jews and 'Aryans'. It is absurd to exclude Jews from medicine when hundreds of peasants die yearly for lack of adequate medical attention. This profession at least should be able for a generation to absorb all those who enter it, whatever their racial origin.

All these things can help to reduce anti-Semitism and to

mitigate the intensity of the Jewish Question, but it is doubtful
if they can solve it. The fact remains that the majority of
Eastern European Jews are an alien element, bound by no
tie of sympathy or understanding of the peoples among whom
they live. The minority of assimilated Jews may perhaps still
hope to submerge themselves in the neighbour nations,
although even this will be difficult after the experiences of
the last five years. It is true that the Jewish Question seems
well on its way to solution in the Soviet Union, where most
Jews have turned their backs on the past and accepted Soviet
patriotism as their first loyalty. But the Soviet Union, a vast
country of almost unlimited human and material possibilities,
cannot be compared with the small countries of Eastern
Europe.

Hitler's hordes have exploited to the full every latent reserve
of anti-Semitism in every country which they have over-
whelmed. Atrocities have been committed by Germans and
Roumanians far surpassing the worst achievements of the
pogroms of Tsarist Russia. In Hungary the Jews have fared
better, but they have still had much to suffer. In Poland common disaster may have drawn Poles and Jews together, but
it is doubtful whether this can efface the memory of the
outrages committed, and greater outrages planned, by the
Polish Fascists. It is difficult to believe that the Eastern
European Jews can have much confidence in the prospect of
peaceful coexistence with their Roumanian, Polish and Hungarian neighbours. Much will depend on the political, economic
and social regime of Eastern Europe, but always at the back
of the mind of the Jew will be the memory of the terrible
years 1933–44, the most terrible in the history of his race,
and the fear of their repetition. At the same time it is doubtful
whether the young nations of Eastern Europe, whatever their
political, economic and social regime, will for long tolerate
in the most prominent places of their economic and intellectual
life people whom they cannot help regarding as strangers,
or whether the Jews will be able sufficiently quickly to adapt
themselves to new occupations to be able to avert a recurrence
of the danger.

A part at least of the Jews of Eastern Europe will have to
find a home elsewhere. The Eastern European Jews form only
part, though perhaps the most important part, of the World

Jewish Question, one of the most difficult of the questions which will face the statesmen of the next generation. It must be faced with realism and courage if the hateful poison of anti-Semitism is to be removed from the modern world.

A home must be found somewhere for the Jews. It does not necessarily follow that Palestine is the best place, or that the Palestinian Arabs should pay the bill of the whole of Europe. But somewhere a home must be found, and somehow a means must be discovered of saving the Jew from the hateful role of scapegoat of political gangsters, and of harnessing to the cause of human civilisation his reserves of material and spiritual strength. Until this is done there will be no real peace for Jew or Gentile, in Europe or beyond.

TRANSYLVANIA

Transylvania is the most individual province in all Eastern Europe. No one who has experienced the peculiar beauty of its landscape, the charm of its people and the complex fascination of its problems, can ever keep his thoughts for long away from it or be happy until he has revisited it yet again.

Transylvania is bounded on the east and south by the main range of the Carpathians. Its natural limit in the west is the crest of the smaller range of the Ore Mountains,[1] which run from north to south and are crossed only by the rivers Mureş, Criş and Someş.[2] The natural limit in the north is the Carpathians, which at the meeting-place of Transylvania with the Bukovina bend round and run from east to west.

The historical Transylvania is a plateau contained within these mountain walls, but the name is often used to describe all former Hungarian territory taken by Roumania in 1918. This includes three distinct regions other than historical Transylvania. The first is Maramureş (Mármaros), a wild and beautiful region in the extreme north, cut off from historical Transylvania by mountains and connected with the outer world by the upper valley of the Tisza. The second consists of the valleys of the western slopes of the Ore Mountains,

---

[1] This is a translation of the German name (Erzgebirge). The Roumanians call them Western Mountains (Munţii Apuşeni). The former name is used here as more convenient and less confusing.

[2] The Hungarian names are Maros, Körös and Szamos.

together with a strip of plain beyond them which contains the towns of Satu Mare (Szatmár), Oradea Mare (Nagyvárad or Grosswardein) and Arad. This region was given by the Roumanians the name Crişana, after the river Criş which flows out through it to join the Tisza within the borders of Trianon Hungary. The third region is the Banat. This consists mainly of the plain contained between the rivers Tisza, Danube and Mureş, but includes also some of the foothills of the Carpathians. There is some confusion as to its boundary with Transylvania in the north. If this is taken as the river Mureş, the Banat extends beyond the Carpathians, and such towns as Déva, in the Mureş valley, usually considered as part of Transylvania, belong to the Banat.

These distinctions are, however, somewhat pedantic, and for the purposes of this survey Transylvania will be taken to mean the whole area contained by the Carpathians on north, south and east and by the Ore Mountains in the west. Where reference is intended also to Maramureş, Crişana or Banat, they will be specifically mentioned.

The population of Transylvania proper according to Hungarian statistics of 1910 included 1,472,000 Roumanians, 918,000 Hungarians and 234,000 Germans. The Roumanian census of 1930 gives the total population as 2,871,000, of which 1,658,000 were Roumanians, 827,000 Hungarians and 237,000, Germans. The total population of Transylvania, Maramureş, Crişana and Banat was shown by the same census as 5,543,000, of which 3,206,000 Roumanians comprised 58 %, 1,354,000 Hungarians 26·7 %, and 543,000 Germans 9·8 %. There were small minorities of Jews, Ruthenes, Slovaks, Serbs and Armenians.

The main strongholds of the Roumanians are the county of Hunedoara in the south-west, the Ore Mountains and the counties of Maramureş and Năsăud in the north. The most purely Hungarian district is the three south-eastern counties of Háromszék, Csík and Udvarhely inhabited by Szeklers, descendants of a tribe distinct from the original Magyars but now completely Hungarian in speech and feeling. The most important German settlements are in the southern counties of Târnava Mare, Târnava Mică, Făgăraş, Sibiu and Braşov. An isolated German colony of some importance exists near Bistritsa (Beszterce). Elsewhere the proportions of the nationalities approximate to those for Transylvania as a whole. In Crişana the mountainous regions have almost purely Roumanian populations, the northern part of the plain has a strong Hungarian majority, while in the south, towards Arad, the Roumanians are most numerous, followed closely by the Hungarians, with a small number of Germans and Slovaks. The main German settlement in Crişana is in the neighbourhood of Satu Mare (Szatmár). In the Banat the strongest element are the Roumanians, followed by the Germans. The Hungarians number about 100,000.

In the towns of Transylvania, Crişana and Banat the Roumanians are comparatively weak. Arad, Oradea and Satu Mare are predominantly Hungarian and Jewish. Târgu Mureş (Márosvásárhely) is essentially Hungarian, and even Cluj (Kolozsvár) retained under Roumanian rule a slight Hungarian majority. Sibiu (Hermannstadt or Nagyszeben) is half-German, half-Roumanian. In Timişoara (Temesvár) and Braşov (Brassó or Kronstadt) the three nationalities are almost equally represented.

Transylvania was the scene of the Dacian Kingdom conquered in the second century from its ruler Decebalus by the Emperor Trajan. The ruins of its capital Sarmizegetusa still remain. After a period of Roman rule the country relapsed into confusion, and was the scene of the wave of invasions described in an earlier chapter. In the ninth century arrived the Hungarians. Nobody knows what happened to the Dacians, who were then already certainly intermingled with Slavs, as place-names still testify. The Hungarian chauvinist historians assert that they all fled to Wallachia, and did not return for centuries afterwards, while the Roumanian chauvinist historians declare that they always remained a majority of the population. Two things are certain. One is that on the threshold of the modern age Transylvania contained a large number of peasants speaking a mainly Latin language, which it is reasonable to suppose is a corrupted remnant of the language introduced by Trajan's legions. The second is that during the Middle Ages and up to the nineteenth century Transylvania was recognised as being a country of three 'nations', which did not include the Roumanians or Wallachs (Hungarian Oláh, Slav Vlah). The three 'nations' were the Magyars, Saxons and Szeklers (Hungarian Székély).

Each of the 'nations' had its own autonomous organisations, which it retained under the Hungarian Crown, or under the independent Princes of Transylvania during the period when the Turks ruled part of Hungary proper. The Roumanians, however, had no special rights. They were serfs of the Hungarian ruling class. How many there were of them, how many immigrated from beyond the Carpathians, will not be proved even by a thousand years of chauvinist polemics. It is probable that there were always some, but that the proportion grew in their favour after the retreat of the Turks from Central Europe. They are certainly not, as Roumanian schoolchildren are still taught, the racial descendants of Trajan's Legions, but they are an essential element, and to-day the most numerous element, in the population of Transylvania. They have at least as good a right as their opponents to regard themselves as the oldest nation of the country.

During the centuries the Szeklers lost their language and their special national characteristics, and became simply Hungarians. To-day they speak the same language as the people of Trianon Hungary, and regard themselves as Hungarians. Differences of psychology and of social structure between them and the other Hungarians remain, but these do not affect their national consciousness.

The Szeklers are mountaineers, while the great majority of Hungarians outside the Szekler country are plainsmen. The Szekler peasants have mostly owned their land for generations back. Great estates did not predominate in their country as they did in the rest of Transylvania and of Hungary. The small nobility was numerous and even the serfs retained far greater freedom than other Hungarian serfs. Consequently a certain democratic tradition and a spirit of sturdy independence have long prevailed among the Szeklers. They have always been inclined to despise the other Hungarians, and even express their contempt to this day. There have been repeated conflicts between Szeklers and Magyars during the history of Transylvania, the Szeklers even siding at times with the Roumanians against the Magyars. But it is absurd to imagine that these differences could make the Szeklers deny their Hungarian nationality. The Roumanians have during their twenty years' rule attempted to prove that the Szeklers are Magyarised Roumanians. This is not only historically untrue but irrelevant. The worthy Roumanian chauvinist doctors of Cluj University who collected Szekler blood samples and declared that they showed greater racial affinity with Roumanian than with Hungarian blood were wasting their time. The Szeklers feel themselves Hungarians, and for more than a century they have been Hungarians.

To-day Transylvania is still a country of three nations, but the 'nations' have changed. Instead of Saxons, Magyars and Szeklers we have Roumanians, Magyars and Saxons. The policy of Hitler towards all German minorities in Eastern Europe has, we have seen, made the future of the Saxons problematical. The future of Transylvania therefore now depends, more than ever before, on the relations between Hungarians and Roumanians.

The Roumanians of Transylvania were not recognised as a nation in the Middle Ages, and they probably did not even feel themselves as such. Signs of national consciousness begin to appear in Horia's Peasant Revolt in 1784. In the nineteenth century the creation of an independent Roumania east of the Carpathians had an effect on the Transylvanian Roumanians, and the nationalist movement in Transylvania grew rapidly. In 1918 the opportunity of separation from Hungary and union with Roumania, which few Transylvanians would have believed possible a few years before, offered itself and was accepted with enthusiasm.

Under Great Roumania the Hungarians, who had been for over a thousand years the ruling race, became second-class citizens in Transylvania. It was inconceivable that this position could be accepted by the educated class of Hungarians within one generation. It could hardly be said that the Hungarians were 'oppressed' by the Roumanians. They kept most of their schools, although the Roumanian authorities interfered with the teaching in them in a number of irksome ways. They were allowed to publish a large number of newspapers, periodicals and books, and to import literature from Hungary. Their Churches were not persecuted, even if the Roumanian authorities did favour Germans for the highest positions in the Catholic Church, and insisted on building large and often not beautiful Orthodox Churches in towns and villages predominantly Hungarian. There were constant causes of irritation, but these were not very important, and the Roumanians were quite entitled to point out that the Hungarians had far greater cultural liberty than the Roumanians had had under the rule of Budapest, when no Roumanian could hope to rise in the social scale, or to attain higher education, without knowledge of the Magyar language.

More justifiable annoyance was caused by the flood of Roumanian officials, many of Regatean origin, who flooded the province, and by the difficulties put in the way of Hungarians seeking State employment. Particular resentment was felt at the language examinations imposed on Hungarian candidates. Although it was reasonable that knowledge of the Roumanian language should be expected of all State employees, the examination was often deliberately unfair, and came to be regarded simply as an excuse to kick out old, and refuse admission to young, Hungarian officials. This became more acute in later years, for the overproduction of 'intellectuals' in Roumania, and the growth of extreme nationalist movements (Iron Guard, Goga-Cuzists, Vaidists, etc.) made it still more difficult for Hungarians to enter the bureaucracy.

Yet the fundamental cause of trouble lay not in these particular grievances but in the fact that the educated Hungarian could never regard the Roumanian as his equal, or accept the 1919 settlement as lasting. Between the educated Hungarian, brought up in the spirit of the Hungarian ruling class, and the upstart Roumanian no compromise was possible. The Roumanians might have had more success with the depressed class of Hungarians, with the peasants and workers. The Roumanian Land Reform benefited a number of Hungarian peasants. A Hungarian estimate quoted by Mr C. A. Macartney[1] declares that 73 % of the redistributed land was given to Roumanians and 27 % to members of the minorities (this means almost solely Hungarians, as the Germans nearly all had enough land, and the other minorities are of negligible importance). The proportions of the two nationalities in the category of holdings receiving land under the Reform (0–5 hectares) were, according to this estimate, 68 % Roumanians and 32 % minorities. Considering the fierceness of national feeling on both sides, it must be admitted that these figures show a surprisingly generous attitude on the part of the Roumanians. It may even be argued, as Roumanian apologists

[1] *Hungary and her successors.*

do argue, that the Hungarian population of Transylvania gained more than it lost from the Union with Roumania, for the loss to a small number of big landowners was far more than compensated by the gains of a large number of Hungarian peasants.

This must be reckoned a solid achievement to the credit of the Roumanian regime, but it should not be considered to prove that the Hungarian masses of Transylvania were thereby reconciled to that regime. Land Reform, as we have seen, does not suffice to solve the social problems or raise the standard of living of the peasantry. The Hungarian peasants of Transylvania suffered, along with their Roumanian neighbours, from the economic crisis and political terror that characterised Roumanian history from 1918 to 1940. As a national minority, they suffered even more from the political terror than did the Roumanians. Their condition did not change appreciably under the various Party Governments that succeeded each other in Bucarest.

Discontent with corruption, brutality and economic misery was widespread in the whole. State, but among the Transylvanian Hungarians it was inevitable that it should be diverted into nationalist channels. The Hungarian peasants had little reason to love their own ruling class, but they could not be expected to consider oppression by a foreign ruling class as preferable to oppression by people of their own nation. A minority, influenced by the ideas of the extreme Left, remained equally opposed to the Bucarest and Budapest regimes, but the majority allowed themselves to be convinced by the intellectuals and politicians of the old Transylvanian Hungarian ruling class, and regarded Roumanian rule as the cause of all their woes. Active preference for Roumanian rule could not be found anywhere among Transylvanian Hungarians.

In August 1940, wishing to bring all South-Eastern Europe under their control, and finding the existence of frontier disputes and revisionist claims in that region inconvenient, the Axis Dictators themselves decided to 'solve' the Transylvanian Question by Partition. The Vienna 'Award' gave about half of Transylvania, including Cluj (Kolozsvár) and the Szekler counties to Hungary. Hungary received about 900,000 Hungarians and 1,400,000 Roumanians. The north-eastern part of the territory ceded is inhabited by a solid block of Roumanians.

The partition led to great economic difficulties. The railway line connecting Cluj (Kolozsvár) with Târgu Mureş (Máros-vásárhely) was interrupted by the frontier, which thus deprived the Szekler country of adequate communications with north and west. Moreover for years past large numbers of Szeklers had found employment in the Braşov region, and even across the Carpathians in the Old Kingdom of Roumania. Bucarest was full of Szekler servant-girls. These opportunities were now cut off, as the new frontier was treated by each side as a wall of steel to keep out the citizens and goods of the other. The peasants of Maramureş and of the mountainous region of Năsăud had since time immemorial found temporary work in the south of Transylvania. Their homelands are miserably poor and hopelessly overpopulated, and their dependence on the more prosperous regions of the south had increased with the growth of population between 1918 and 1940. These are only some examples of the economic dislocation caused by the Vienna 'Award'.

Moreover this decision satisfied neither party. Far from settling the problem, it only exacerbated feeling on both sides. Relations between Hungary and Roumania have never been so bad as since August 1940. Hungary feels she has been cheated of part of what is hers, while Roumania will never be content until she has recovered all. The partition affords excellent opportunities for propaganda by both belligerent sides in the war, which have, however, been more successfully used by the Axis than by the Allies. Although the development of the Roumano-Hungarian conflict into armed hostilities would embarrass Hitler, it is unlikely that this will happen before the end of the war, while meantime Hitler has an excellent means, by alternate blackmail and bribery, of obtaining from each side a maximum contingent of cannon-fodder for the Russian front.

Hungarian rule over all Transylvania, Roumanian rule over all Transylvania, and partition having all proved unsatisfactory, how can the problem be dealt with? The attitude of the nationalists on each side is irreconcilable. The Roumanians rightly insist that they form the majority of the population, and have a much greater rate of increase, which within a few years will give them twice as many nationals as the Hungarians. To this sound and compelling argument they add a wealth of verbiage about historical missions, Latin races and superior cultures which need not be taken very seriously. The Hungarians point out with equal truth that it is they who have given Transylvania its peculiar character, that for a thousand years the culture of Transylvania has been essentially Hungarian. They are not a mere 'minority' in a Roumanian province. Transylvania is *their* home, and should belong to them. They add with some justification that administrative and cultural conditions have deteriorated since Transylvania has been Roumanian, to which the Roumanians reply also with some justification that the Land Reform carried out by them created in Transylvania healthier social conditions than existed in Trianon Hungary. And so the polemics go on.

The present partition is entirely unsatisfactory, and it is hard to see any other line of demarcation that would be substantially better. It is equally difficult to believe that the restitution of the whole of Transylvania either to Roumania or to Hungary could bring a solution, as long as either country remained organised as a nationalist State. No nationalist Government in Bucarest or Budapest would treat as equal citizens members of another nationality. This has been abundantly proved by the experience of the last seventy years.

There is a school of thought on either side which favours regional autonomy for the province. But the Hungarian autonomists are as insistent that this autonomous Transylvania should form part of Hungary as are the Roumanian autonomists that it should belong to a nationalist Roumanian State. In fact past experience suggests that it is unlikely that any Roumanian or Hungarian Government which received Transylvania on condition that it should be autonomous would execute its promise, or if it did so that it would maintain it for long. Moreover, even if a real measure of autonomy were granted, there would still be grave dangers. The Roumanian population of an autonomous Transylvania forming part of a nationalist Hungarian State, however free and happy it might be, could never forget that across the mountains was a Roumanian nationalist State, in which its kinsmen were not only free and happy, but were the dominant nation. And the same would be true of the Hungarian population if the autonomous Transylvania belonged to nationalist Roumania.

However honourable the intentions of the central Government, there would be a dominant nation and a secondary nation, and the latter would feel it had two countries, its own homeland and 'the other country' beyond the mountains. This state of affairs could not be satisfactory in the long run. It would therefore seem that a more radical solution is required. Two such types of solution present themselves as possible.

The first is an exchange of populations. If it were attempted merely to exchange the Roumanians in the western districts against the Hungarians in the eastern districts, this could only result in a partition of Transylvania, which is a natural unit, the disruption of which can only cause dislocation in the economic, social and cultural fields. There are too many Hungarians in Transylvania for it to be possible to settle them all in the western plain beyond the mountains. Even if they were all concentrated in the west, and the Roumanians in the east, they would extend into the heart of Transylvania proper, and the essential unity of the province would be destroyed. If, however, the expulsion of the Germans accompanied the exchange of populations between Hungary and Roumania, it is possible to conceive an ethnographical redistribution which would leave Transylvania whole. The Saxons of Transylvania and the Swabians of the Banat and of Trianon Hungary would be expelled to Germany, and the place of the latter would be taken by the Transylvanian Hungarians, of the former by Roumanians from the western plain and the Banat, which would be ceded to Hungary. The place of 750,000 Swabians in Hungary proper and in Banat would be taken by an equal number of Transylvanian Hungarians, while the remaining 400,000 or so would find a home in those parts of Crişana and Banat formerly inhabited by Roumanians, side by side with the existing 500,000 odd Hungarians of those regions. Transylvania proper would remain in Roumanian hands, and would have a purely Roumanian population.

This solution is essentially that of an arm-chair expert, and of a nationalist intellectual at that. It takes no account of the suffering involved. It takes no account of the devotion of the peasant to his home and his land as such, things much more important to him than the theories of elegant intellectual speculators in the coffee-houses of Bucarest and Budapest. It is moreover entirely favourable to Roumania. For this reason it is urged by Roumanian nationalists and by their apologists in the Allied camp. It has the outward appearance of an 'impartial' solution, in which the only losers would be the hated Germans. In fact, it means the destruction of a thousand-year-old tradition to please a group of perverse fanatics who have nothing in common with their people, and who, together with their fellows in other countries, have brought Europe nothing but disaster. The Szekler mountaineers must be torn from their home of centuries and be dumped in a plain they neither know nor love, and the Roumanian peasants of Arad and the Banat must be uprooted from the land they have enriched and be cast on the barren slopes of the Szekler country, of whose problems they have neither experience nor understanding—in order to afford some Bucarest professor material for a bombastic lecture on the beauties of 'Integral Nationalism'. Yet it is difficult to see what grounds the United Nations can have to favour the Roumanian nationalists.

There remains the possibility of a federal solution. This would recognise that Transylvania is neither Roumanian nor Hungarian, but has a peculiar character and unity of its own, to which both nations have contributed and can contribute in future. Transylvania would form an autonomous unit within a larger federation which would include not only Roumania and Hungary but several other neighbouring States. Within Transylvania the Roumanian and Hungarian languages would have absolute equality, posts in the civil service would be allotted as far as possible in accordance with the numerical proportions of the two nationalities, and the new generation of civil servants and intellectuals would be brought up to be bilingual.

Whether such a solution is possible depends above all on the general international distribution of power at the end of the present war, and especially on the attitude of the British, Soviet and Polish Governments. An independent Transylvanian State could never maintain itself. It would be too small, its economic resources would not suffice, and it would be permanently at the mercy of whichever of its neighbours happened to be the stronger. A 'Transylvanian solution' of the problem, as opposed to a Roumanian nationalist or Hungarian nationalist solution, depends therefore on the creation of a larger Federation. Here we can only consider briefly what is likely to be the attitude of the Transylvanians themselves.

There is no doubt that there is a big difference between the attitudes of the Hungarians and Roumanians of Budapest and Bucarest on the one hand and of those of Transylvania on the other.

During the centuries of Transylvanian independence there grew up among Transylvanian Hungarians, at least among those of education, a sense of being different from other Hungarians, a kind of special Transylvanian patriotism. This survived under the Dual System, and the union of Transylvania to Roumania strengthened it. The intellectual and political life of the Transylvanian Hungarians for the last twenty years has followed different lines from those of Trianon Hungary. The differences of mentality are no less profound between the Roumanians of Transylvania and of the Old Kingdom. The combination of Turco-Byzantine practice and French theory which characterises the intellectuals of the Old Kingdom is alien to those Transylvanian Roumanians who can remember clearly Habsburg times. The introduction of Balkan standards of administration and justice, and the centralising tendencies of Bucarest, were bitterly resented in Transylvania. Right up till the partition of 1940 Transylvanians used the most violent language in criticism of everything connected with the Regateans. Yet, as Mr Macartney rightly points out,[1] the Transylvanian Roumanians were no less determined to maintain their national domination over the Hungarians than were the Regateans.

The old generation had grown up in the struggle against Budapest. They might have acquired in the old Empire moral standards which made them despise the Regateans, but mistrust of the Hungarians was second nature to them. The new generation not only was brought up to believe in Great Roumania but accepted many of the customs of the Old Kingdom most abominated by their fathers. Enterprising young Transylvanians settled in Bucarest and made them-

---

[1] *Hungary and her Successors.* For a short account of Hungarian currents of opinion in Transylvania after 1918, see Szekfü, *Három nemzedék.*

selves careers. They showed themselves quite capable of standing up to the Regateans on their own ground and with their own methods. Moreover, the growth of extreme nationalism among the younger generation in the whole country, represented especially by the Iron Guard, increased the intolerance of the Roumanians of Transylvania towards their Hungarian neighbours. Thus, although both Roumanians and Hungarians of Transylvania still feel different from, and superior to, their kinsmen of the two small Kingdoms, yet both would probably prefer to be united with their kinsmen, and neither have much affection or even tolerance towards each other.

And yet the two nations have much in common. They are the only non-Slav nations in Eastern Europe, surrounded by Slavs to north and south and threatened by the ever-recurring thrust of the Germans into the Danube Basin. The Hungarians and Roumanians are the two essentially Danubian nations, occupying the space between the Alps and the Black Sea, a space distinct from the Baltic Region or the Balkan Peninsula. These two nations know each other perhaps better than any other pair of nations in Eastern Europe. Hungarian culture has in spite of everything a strange fascination for Roumanians in Transylvania. Even in the younger generation of intellectuals, which did not need to know the Hungarian language in order to make a career in Great Roumania, many have taken the trouble to learn it. It is interesting that the Hungarian poet Petöfi has always been especially admired in Roumania, and the Roumanian poet Eminescu in Hungary.

The circumstances of the last centuries made Hungary the close ally, or even the vassal, of the Germans, whether those of Vienna or of Berlin. This pro-German orientation of Hungarian policy is contrary to the historical traditions and the emotional sympathies of the Hungarian people. It has once already brought Hungary to disaster. This war will prove once and for all its fatal mistakenness. It is associated with a ruling class which for social and political reasons alike is doomed to destruction. It is inevitable that the new Hungary should turn its back on Germany, and look for friends elsewhere. It is not likely to find them, for the first years at least, among the Southern Slavs, Czechs or Slovaks, or even among the Poles, especially as the traditional Polish ruling class, whose personal ties with the Hungarian aristocracy were the main basis of Hungaro-Polish friendship, is likely to be considerably weakened. There remain the Roumanians, whom the defeat of the Germans, whose bewildered and unwilling tools they have been since 1940, is likely to leave in a condition of physical and moral collapse. Will the Roumanians and Hungarians fly at each other's throats, or will they try to make friends, and stand together against common dangers? If they do the former, they are likely to be engulfed by the Slav flood from north and south. And although it is easy to say that by joining the Axis they have 'deserved their fate', it is not for the good of European peace or stability that two nations, which have an essential place in Eastern Europe, should be submerged.

Both Hungarian and Roumanian nationalists have shown themselves incompetent to deal with the Transylvanian Question. At present both nations are dissatisfied. As long as either the Roumanians or the Hungarians had the whole, the contented party was unwilling to make concessions to the discontented. Now that neither has what it wants, perhaps the possibility of agreement is greater. Apart from the anger of the chauvinists of Budapest and Bucarest at the loss of part of the swag, there was a much deeper feeling of bitterness in Transylvania itself. Transylvanian Roumanians felt that the Regateans had let them down, that they had sold to Hitler and Horthy a slice of a Transylvania of which they knew nothing and cared less, in order to avoid the unpleasantness of war, to retain a comfortable life and to achieve petty political ambitions. Transylvanian Hungarians felt that Budapest had betrayed them by accepting from the hands of the Dictators less than the whole. The men of Budapest showed thereby that they scorned the sacred unity of Transylvania and its age-old Hungarian tradition. The depth of this disillusionment could not escape any foreign observer who, during the critical days of 1940, travelled in Transylvania and kept his eyes and ears open.

Nationalism and partition have failed. There remains— friendship. In spite of everything there are on both sides a considerable number of able and intelligent people who wish to solve the problem on this basis. Thoughtful Hungarians realise that their nation is in the minority, and that population trends are such that it is not likely ever to become a majority. If, despite this, Hungary were to seize Transylvania, using some temporary favourable opportunity, she could never feel secure in possession, perpetually threatened by a Roumania growing in population and in economic and military power. But within an autonomous Transylvania, member of a larger Federation, the Hungarians could use their superior education and skill to ensure an influence greater than their numbers would suggest. On the Roumanian side desire for friendship is not lacking. Not all the younger generation accepted the extravagant nationalism of the Iron Guardists and their like. Part of this generation, which received less publicity in the Press of the world, and suffered persecution from the Royal Dictatorship and its successors, believed in reconciliation of the two nations on the basis of real Democracy and Social Justice. These people still exist, and perhaps one day we shall hear more of them.

MACEDONIA

The name Macedonia has had slightly different connotations at different periods of history. To-day it is used to describe the country traversed by the river Vardar. In the north it touches the plain of Kosovo and the upper valley of the Morava. Its western limit is the mountain range running south on the left bank of the Drin to the lakes of Ohrid and Prespa. From Kastoria it runs roughly due east to the Gulf of Salonica. Its eastern boundary is the western end of the Rhodope Mountains and the river Mesta. It does not include the peninsula of Chalcidice. The natural centre of the life of Macedonia is Salonica. The second town in population and importance is Skoplje on the Vardar. Other centres of some significance are Bitolj and Florina in the west, Seres in the extreme east and Veles on the Vardar. Macedonia is bounded by high mountains to the east, west and south, and its interior consists mostly of hilly country, rising in the neighbourhood of Bitolj to over 8000 ft. Its only plainland is in the lower valleys of the Vardar, between Lake Yannitsa and Salonica, and of the Struma, south of Seres. It is essentially an agricultural region, industry being confined to Salonica and Skoplje cities. Cereals are produced on a small scale in suitable places. Two of the main crops are opium-poppies and tobacco. A considerable part of the population makes its living from pasturing sheep in the mountains.

No reliable statistics exist for the ethnical composition of Macedonia. Whereas a comparison of Hungarian and Roumanian census returns makes possible a fairly accurate picture of the truth in Transylvania, this is quite impossible in the case of Macedonia. Macedonian peasants describe themselves as Turks, Greeks, Bulgarians or Serbs according to political circumstances, and no one knows what the truth is, not even the peasants themselves.

It is probably true that to-day the great majority of the population of Greek Macedonia is really Greek. Greek refugees from Asia Minor were colonised in Macedonia after 1923, and an exchange of populations took place between Bulgaria and Greece, which removed many, although not all, Slavs. Of those who remained many were Hellenised, at least in the post-1918 generation.

In the parts of Macedonia belonging between 1918 and 1941 to Jugoslavia and Bulgaria, the majority of the population is Slav. These Slavs speak various dialects, distinct from literary Serbian and Bulgarian. Some consider themselves Bulgarians, others Serbs, others merely 'Slavs' or 'Macedonians'. Besides the Slavs there is a numerous Albanian population, mostly in the west, between Tetovo and Ohrid, but some scattered over the province as a whole. There is a fairly small Turkish minority, consisting mainly of artisans and shopkeepers in the towns. A further element are the Vlachs, who speak a language similar to Roumanian, and are mostly shepherds in the hills. A certain number of Greeks are found outside the area belonging to Greece. Lastly in Salonica itself there is a large community of Sephardic Jews.

Macedonia first attracts attention in the fourth century B.C. as the home of Philip and Alexander. It passed two hundred years later under Roman rule, and was part of the Byzantine Empire until the ninth century, when it was conquered by the Bulgarians. During the following centuries Macedonia was the centre in turn of various Bulgarian, Serbian and Latin principalities until conquered by the Turks.

After four centuries of silent stagnation the Macedonians began to awaken at the end of last century. The movement was at first social and religious. The peasantry wished to free itself from the oppressive, incompetent and corrupt yoke of the Ottoman Empire, and the Christians to rid themselves of the Moslem domination which made them second-class citizens. The conflict within the Orthodox Church between Bulgarians and Greeks, which led to the establishment of the Bulgarian Exarchate in 1870, created furious rivalry in 'cultural' propaganda between the two nations. The Bulgarian and Greek Governments spent lavish sums on the construction of schools in Macedonia, designed to convince the sons of Macedonian peasants that they were respectively Greeks or Bulgarians. Armed bands of Greek and Bulgarian 'komitadjis'[1] fought not only the Turks but each other. Later the Serbs, too, took a hand.

In this struggle of all against all the Ottoman Government relied at first not only on the Ottoman armed forces and the Turkish and Albanian populations, but on the support of all the European Great Powers other than Russia, which was at this time too much engaged in Asia to do much. But feeling became too strong, and the pace of events too fast, for the European statesmen, who were poorly informed of the facts, and took refuge in pious hopes that the Balkan peoples would behave themselves 'in a more civilised manner'.

In 1896 the Macedonian Slav Damian Gruev and a few friends founded the Internal Macedonian Revolutionary Organisation. Its aim was the liberation of Macedonia from the Ottoman regime. It was not at first hostile to any nation inhabiting Macedonia, not even to the Turkish nation. Its leaders had for some time friendly relations with the men of the Young Turkish Movement, then preparing themselves for revolt against the absolutism of Abdul Hamid. In free Macedonia Greeks, Slavs, Albanians and Vlachs were to enjoy equal rights, and for some years members of all these nations collaborated in I.M.R.O.

A few months before the foundation of I.M.R.O., at the end of 1895, had been set up in Sofia a 'Supreme Committee', consisting of refugees from Macedonia who accepted the thesis of Bulgarian nationalists that Macedonians are Bulgarians, and that Macedonia should belong to Bulgaria. One of the

---

[1] This word is used all over the Balkans to denote guerrilla troops. It is a Turkish word, derived from the European word 'committee'.

most prominent 'Supremists' was Protogerov, who became a general in the Bulgarian Army.

Although these two organisations long ago lost their original character, the division of principle noted at their foundation has remained fundamental in Macedonian politics ever since. On the one hand are the Bulgarian nationalists, on the other the Macedonian autonomists. I.M.R.O. for the first twenty years of its existence represented the latter tendency. It gradually became more and more Slav, losing the support first of the Greeks and then of the Albanians and Vlachs. But it continued to insist that the Macedonian Slavs are neither Bulgarians nor Serbs, but a separate branch of the Slav race. The 'Supreme Committee' as such ceased to play an open part, but 'Supremists' penetrated I.M.R.O. to an increasing extent. The conflict of aims was thus transferred within the organisation itself.

During the nineties and the first decade of this century, a series of local revolts took place, of greater or lesser importance, characterised by actions of extraordinary heroism and savagery on both sides, and always followed by brutal repression by the Turks. The Young Turkish Revolution did not improve the situation, and after a brief period of apparent reconciliation between Moslems and Christians the old disorders broke out again. Bands from Serbia and Bulgaria joined in the fray. In 1912 came the Balkan Alliance of Serbia, Greece, Bulgaria and Montenegro, followed by the Balkan Wars. These resulted in the partition of Macedonia between the Allies, and then the loss by Bulgaria of most of her share. The settlement dissatisfied both the Macedonian autonomists, who still predominated in I.M.R.O., and saw the ruin of their hopes of independent Macedonia, and the 'Supremists', who felt themselves robbed of their part of the loot. Hence closer relations between the two groups, and an increase of 'Supremist' influence inside I.M.R.O.

The intervention of Bulgaria in the First World War on the side of the Central Powers led to Bulgarian occupation of Macedonia. The wretched inhabitants, who had been forced during three years of Serbian rule to adopt names ending in -itch, were now compelled by the threat of imprisonment, torture or death to change the endings to -ov. Then came the Allied victory, the return of the Serbs, and more reprisals, followed by mass changing of name endings from -ov back to -itch again.

After 1918 the leader of I.M.R.O. was Todor Alexandrov. As the greater part of Macedonia had fallen to Jugoslavia, that State became I.M.R.O.'s chief enemy, and I.M.R.O. again had common interests with the Sofia nationalists. The latter were willing to hand over to the effective control of I.M.R.O. the small Bulgarian portion of Macedonia (Petrich Department) in return for the help of I.M.R.O. terrorists against Jugoslavia and against democratic elements within Bulgaria. I.M.R.O. helped to overthrow Stamboliiski, and one of its promising young men, Ivan Mihailov, eagerly accepted the job of assisting the Bulgarian political police. Alexandrov himself showed misgivings at this policy. Together with the former 'Supremist', General Protogerov, he insisted on independence of action for the Macedonians. In 1924 representatives of Alexandrov conferred in Vienna with one Vlahov, a Macedonian of Communist sympathies, connected with the Soviet Government, and reached agreement on a basis of Macedonian autonomy within a Balkan Federation, to be founded on principles of Peasant Democracy. A periodical, *Fédération balkanique*, edited by a Bulgarian Communist, was launched in Vienna, and its first number contained a manifesto signed by Alexandrov and Protogerov. The alliance of the I.M.R.O. chief with the Left undoubtedly alarmed the Sofia army chiefs and nationalist politicians, besides annoying their Italian patrons. In August Alexandrov was murdered, some believe on the instructions of Mihailov and his protector War Minister Volkov.*

In October of the same year Vlahov founded a separate Macedonian movement known thenceforth as the Obedinena movement, which preached Federation on Communist lines. This group had the support of Macedonian Communists, and was closely connected with the Bulgarian Communist movement. Protogerov, who had been with Alexandrov when he was murdered, and whom Mihailov's men accused of complicity in the crime, inclined towards the Obedinena group. Although he never accepted a Communist programme, he favoured increasingly a Federalist solution of the Macedonian Question. In 1928 he was murdered by Mihailov's agents.

* See above, p. 247.

The effective leadership of his group was assumed by Pero Shandanov, who collaborated with the Velchev group* and maintained friendly relations with Obedinena. Mihailov obtained control of I.M.R.O., and used it in collaboration with the Sofia Governments until its suppression by Velchev and Georgiev in 1934.

Macedonia is at present again under Bulgarian occupation. This is the fourth change in its ownership since the Turks were driven out. Each change was accompanied by bloody acts of vengeance and severe repression. The accounts published in the British Press since May 1941 suggest that the Bulgarians have behaved less vindictively than they did in 1915, or than did the Serbs in 1913 or 1918. If this is true, it may be hoped that the reaction of the Serbs after the defeat of Germany will also be less bloody than before, and that Serbophile and Bulgarophile Macedonians may eventually be reconciled. But the future of Macedonia is extremely obscure. It is not only impossible to guess what is the state of opinion there at present: it is impossible to say what was the state of opinion under twenty years of Jugoslav rule.

During the first years the province was in permanent disorder. Komitadji bands from Bulgaria raided across the frontier, and found support from members of I.M.R.O. in villages in Jugoslav territory. The Komitadjis massacred those known to be supporters of Jugoslavia, and the Jugoslav authorities replied by arresting, beating or killing suspected or known Bulgarophiles ('Bugarashi'). After some years the terrorism declined. Even those who sympathised with I.M.R.O. became tired of the dreary repetition of outrages and reprisals. As there seemed no prospect of the overthrow of the Jugoslav regime, most people became resigned to it, and a very large number of Macedonians genuinely accepted it. Order was reestablished and people could go about their business without fear of sudden death. Yet many abuses and causes of complaint remained. Serbian 'colonists', war volunteers and other people known to be politically reliable, were settled on land taken from the former Turkish Beys, which was only to a small extent distributed to the local inhabitants. Officials and schoolmasters from Belgrade and Central Serbia made themselves objectionable. People were victimised in a number

* See above, p. 249.

of minor ways for using their native dialect instead of Serbian. The injustice of the Tobacco Monopoly's price policy* was particularly resented. In general, administrative brutality, Serbian chauvinism, political corruption and economic exploitation were more flagrant in Macedonia than in any other part of Jugoslavia. Discontent was therefore acute, and was used by extremist political groups.

Since Mihailov took command, I.M.R.O. definitely advocated incorporation of Macedonia in Bulgaria. Within Jugoslav Macedonia a substantial number of people, especially on the left bank of the Vardar, felt themselves to be Bulgarians. These people helped the Bulgarian cause, at first by violence and in later years by silent subversive work, pretending to accept Belgrade's wishes, making friends with the supporters of Stojadinović—who in his need for support somewhere, and in his desire to please the Axis, made dangerous concessions to anti-Jugoslav Macedonians, even entrusting notorious 'Bugarashi' with positions of importance in the State administration—and generally preparing themselves for their day. During the Jugoslav campaign they did valuable Fifth Column work for the Axis, and they welcomed the subsequent annexation of Macedonia by Bulgaria.

Since occupation Sofia has made it perfectly clear that it regards Macedonia as an integral part of Bulgaria. It appears to be having no patience with Macedonian autonomists, and to have given high posts in the administration mostly to people brought in from Bulgaria, some of these being Macedonian refugees established for twenty years or more in Bulgaria, others being Bulgarians with no connection at all with Macedonia. It is possible, although little has appeared in the Press to confirm it, that this policy has lost or will lose support in Macedonia for the Bulgarian orientation. It must be realised, however, that disillusioned Bulgarophiles are not likely ever to become apostles of Serbian centralism.

The other extremist movement which was strong in Macedonia under Jugoslav rule is the Communist movement. A large part of the votes won by the Serbian Communists in 1921 came from Macedonia. The Communist Federalist programme of Vlahov's Obedinena group undoubtedly enjoyed a

* See above, pp. 244, 247.

large body of support within Macedonia. The programme of the Communists of all Jugoslavia included federal autonomy within Jugoslavia for Macedonia. The most active element in the Communist movement in Macedonia were ex-students of Belgrade University of Macedonian origin. Their ideas certainly spread among the educated class and among the small working class of the towns.

It is difficult to say what the villages thought of them. In general there is strong sympathy among Macedonian peasants for Russia, and the phenomenon described above,* of the identification of the word 'Communism' with civil liberties, exists as much in Macedonia as in other parts of Jugoslavia. At the same time the strength of I.M.R.O. ideas in the villages should not be underestimated. Which of the two movements will be the stronger will depend on the extent to which the annexation has raised the prestige of the 'Bugarashi' or to which the economic difficulties consequent upon war conditions have been attributed to them.

Apart from these extremes there has always been a body of moderate opinion. Many Macedonians accepted Jugoslavia, and hope that it will be restored. Others wish to see a Southern Slav Federation, including Bulgaria as well as the former territories of Jugoslavia, in which Macedonia should have autonomous status. This idea extends far beyond the extreme Left. It would even have support from some followers of I.M.R.O. It may be that it would be supported by the majority of the population. This it is not possible to say with certainty, for there has been no means for at least thirty years of discovering, objectively, what is the opinion of the Macedonians.

The creation of an independent Macedonian State can hardly be considered a serious political proposal. The natural commercial outlet and capital of Macedonia is Salonica, an essentially Greek city, which no Greek patriot could consider abandoning. Moreover, that portion of Macedonia which from 1918 has belonged to Greece is inhabited predominantly by Greeks. The triangle Edessa-Kastoria-Florina, in the north-west corner, is the only area whose population is still mainly Slav. To unite a solidly Greek province with a solidly Slav province, cutting both off from their kinsmen in North and South, is absurd.

* See above, pp. 221, 240.

The Greeks and Slavs are capable of living peacefully side by side, but not as citizens of an artificially created new State.

The real Macedonian Problem is the problem of Jugoslav Macedonia. Here neither Serbian nor Bulgarian rule has benefited the people. The people of Jugoslav Macedonia are in fact neither Serbs nor Bulgarians, and they have had reason to dislike almost equally the dictatorial nationalist centralism of Belgrade and the dictatorial centralist nationalism of Sofia. Probably the only method which offers any promise of a satisfactory solution is that of regional autonomy within a federal Jugoslavia. This would mean that the administration, school system and economic life of Macedonia would be conducted by Macedonians, men born and bred in the province; that the State authorities would officially recognise that the Macedonians are neither Serbs nor Bulgars, but a separate branch of the South Slavs; and that in all matters affecting State policy the Macedonians would accept the authority of the Central Government.

The Macedonian Problem is essentially an internal problem of Jugoslavia. If the relations between Macedonians and Serbs can be cleared in the manner described above, then minor territorial questions, such as Florina or Petrich, can be settled with little difficulty between the Governments of Jugoslavia, Greece and Bulgaria.

The Macedonian Problem cannot be solved independently of the Balkan Problem as a whole. Everything depends on the type of regimes that prevail in the Balkan States after the war. If the old nationalist claims are supreme, then Macedonia will again be a cause of international rivalries. Neither Serbian, Greek nor Bulgarian nationalists will consider Macedonian autonomy as a solution, but will reserve to themselves with passionate enthusiasm the right to fight for the bodies of the Macedonians. If, however, power is in the hands of those who reject the past, and desire a political and social New Deal for the Balkans, then the Balkan peoples, Macedonians included, will be able through their own representatives to solve the problems of their mutual relations.

We have considered in this chapter the problems of National Minorities and Mixed Populations from the point of view of the people concerned. In order to complete the picture we must also examine the other aspect of the question, the attitude adopted during the last twenty years by the nationalist ruling classes of Eastern European States which contain alien minorities, or which have minorities of their own nationality beyond their borders. Small-Power Imperialisms form the subject of the next chapter.

CHAPTER EIGHT

SMALL-POWER IMPERIALISMS

POLISH IMPERIALISM

THE LAST hundred years have been the century of nationalism, and the States created or revived by the 1919 Peace Treaties were regarded as National States. Among these States was Poland. Yet the Polish ruling class and Polish intellectuals had aimed at the restoration of a Poland bounded by the frontiers of 1772. These frontiers would not in any way correspond with ethnical boundaries, and a State contained within them would not be a National State.

Historical Poland was not a National State, but a multi-national Empire which arose in the course of centuries when the dogma of Nationalism, as understood in modern times, did not exist. Poland was destroyed at the end of the eighteenth century, but a movement for its restoration continued to exist in all three portions of the dismembered State. This movement consisted only of people of Polish language and nationality. Among these Poles a nationalism in the modern sense developed, from the time of the French Revolution onwards. Its aim appeared to the outside world to be to liberate the Poles, that is the people of Polish language and nationality, from the yoke of Prussia, Russia and Austria. The Polish national movement enjoyed much sympathy abroad, particularly in France, Britain, Italy and the United States of America. In fact, however, the aim of this movement, as conceived by its political and intellectual leaders, was not merely the liberation of Poles from foreign rule, but the restoration of Historical Poland, a State including millions of people who were not Poles, and who during the course of the nineteenth century had developed for themselves a much stronger national consciousness than they had possessed in the days when Historical Poland existed. The fact that the true political aim of the Polish ruling class was not nationalist at all but imperialist, that it involved the domination of Poles over large numbers of people of origin other than Polish, has never been sufficiently understood in Western Europe, and this failure to understand it has been responsible for errors in the policy of the Western Powers towards Poland.

Poland did not obtain at the Peace Conference the frontiers

of 1772. She obtained considerably less than she would have liked in the west. Although in 1772 East Prussia already formed part of the Kingdom of Prussia, its rulers had from 1464 to 1657 acknowledged the suzerainty of the King of Poland. Polish statesmen in 1919 were extremely anxious concerning Polish access to the Baltic, and would have liked to acquire part at least of East Prussia. Liberal opinion in the western countries, voiced by President Wilson, was, however, opposed to large-scale mutilation of Germany, and not only would not consider giving Poland East Prussia, but would not even leave her the port of Danzig, at the mouth of the Vistula, which was instead made into an international 'free city'. The German-Polish frontier ultimately followed closely the line of the ethnical boundary. Certain areas whose population was predominantly Polish, and whose fate was left to the decision of a plebiscite of the people themselves, remained in Germany.

In the east the demarcation of a frontier was bound in the best of circumstances to be exceedingly difficult. In the Middle Ages the whole area from the Elbe to the Volga was inhabited by Slavs, whose dialects varied from one region to another, but who had no national consciousness whatever. With the passing of centuries two powerful States grew up, Poland and Moscow, the one Catholic the other Orthodox. Literary Polish and Russian languages began to crystallise. But between the regions unmistakably Polish and those unmistakably Russian remained a long and broad belt, inhabited by people still speaking undetermined dialects, whose religion might be Catholic, Uniate or Orthodox.

During the nineteenth century attempts were made to develop two distinct literary languages in this area, White Russian and Ukrainian. The second was the more successful, as the century produced a great Ukrainian poet, Taras Shevchenko, and Ukrainian literature and nationalism were encouraged in one part of Ukrainian territory, Eastern Galicia, by the Austrian authorities. Moreover, the growth of Ukrainian nationalism was helped by the memories of the medieval principality of Kiev, and by the fact that the Cossacks of the Dniepr region had for centuries maintained a life and a society distinct from those of Poland or Moscow, and had enjoyed effective political autonomy. Even so, there remained in the Polish-Russian borderlands numbers of peasants without clearly defined national character, who described themselves as 'people from here' ('tutejszi').

In these circumstances it was unlikely that Polish and Russian nationalists would be able to agree on a frontier, particularly as the situation in 1918 was complicated by the existence of various Ukrainian 'Governments' with armed forces of their own, and by the fact that civil war was raging between Reds and Whites in Russia. The western statesmen believed that the Whites would win the civil war, and considered themselves too much bound to Russia as their Ally to give the new Polish State much territory which could be claimed to be Russian. They therefore proposed a frontier corresponding approximately with the ethnical boundary, the so-called 'Curzon line'. This the Poles refused. They first of all overthrew the Ukrainian 'Government' in Eastern Galicia, and later, in conjunction with one of the Ukrainian leaders, Petliura, invaded the Ukraine, advancing beyond the frontiers even of 1772. The result of this enterprise was the invasion of Poland by the Red Army, which was arrested at the last moment near Warsaw by Weygand and Pilsudski. After this the Russians retreated. The western Powers, seeing that the project of an independent Ukraine had collapsed, and that there was no immediate prospect of the overthrow of the Bolshevik regime, gave their blessing to the Poles, who came to terms with the Soviet Government by the Treaty of Riga. This gave Poland less than the frontiers of 1772, but recognised as part of Poland territories containing between three and eight million Ukrainians and between one and two million White Russians.

Poland is the first and the most loyal of our Allies in the present war. The heroism of Polish resistance to the Germans, both during and after the 1939 campaign, the terrible sufferings incurred from our common enemy, and the fact that, unlike all other conquered countries in Europe, Poland has produced no Quisling to work with the Germans, give the Polish people a special place in the affections of the United Nations, and particularly of the British. The settlement of the boundaries of Poland will be one of the most difficult tasks of the Peace. The utmost consideration must be shown to the wishes of the Polish people.

Poland is, as her history has shown, exceptionally vulnerable to attack from either of her great neighbours. Moreover the Polish people is increasing at a rapid rate. Agricultural over-population is probably more acute in Poland than in any other country of Eastern Europe, and the misery caused to the peasantry is increased by the unjust distribution of wealth, and in particular by the existence of vast landed properties held by a few aristocratic families. Polish statesmen will have to face most difficult internal and international pro-blems.

The measures they adopt will inevitably depend to a large extent on the political outlook and the social origin of those who will be the leaders of the Polish people at the Peace. If the old ruling class is firmly in power, then internal reforms will be neglected, and an attempt will be made both to find partial relief for internal problems and to further personal ambitions and class interests by the acquisition of as large as possible an area of non-Polish territory. If new men decide, then internal reforms will play a bigger part. But in any case certain essential duties will confront any conceivable combination of Polish leaders. They will insist on the liberation of all Poles in Europe from foreign rule; they will seek to assure the strategical position of their country, and especially its access to the sea, by favourable frontiers; they will require the help of their Allies not only for the reconstruction of devastated areas, but for the assurance of a means of livelihood for the depressed agricultural population; and they will wish to realise part of the historical aims desired by part of the Polish people. We shall here consider briefly the problems of Poland's frontiers with Germany, Lithuania and the Soviet Union.

There is no doubt whatever of the vital importance to Poland of safe access to the sea. The fact that the Vistula, the greatest trade artery in Poland, is dominated by Danzig, a German city, constitutes a permanent threat to Poland. The population of the lower, as well as the upper, valley of the Vistula, is predominantly Polish. The trade of Poland with Western Europe must go largely by the Baltic route. This trade, particularly with Great Britain, was steadily increasing up to the outbreak of war. Both Danzig and the newly created port of Gdynia, the greatest testimony during the last twenty years to the energy and the economic efficiency of Poland, prospered exceedingly during this period.

Events have shown, however, that the solution of 1918, the so-called 'Polish Corridor', was a bad one. The inconvenience caused to German citizens and goods crossing Polish territory to East Prussia, about which German propaganda howled with such frenzy for twenty years, was a minor objection. The real weakness of the solution was that it did not in fact do what it was supposed to do, guarantee Polish access to the sea. German armies in East Prussia and Pomerania could easily combine, as they did in 1939, to cut the narrow northern extremity of the 'Corridor'.

The menace of East Prussia to Poland must be finally removed. The least that can be demanded is that East Prussia should be garrisoned by Polish troops, and that if they are removed, it and a substantial area to the west of the Polish-German frontier in Pomerania should be permanently demilitarised. In view, however, of the unfortunate experience of the demilitarisation of the Rhineland after the last war, it is to be expected that the majority of Poles will demand the permanent incorporation of all East Prussia in Poland. It will be pointed out that East Prussia was once part of Historical Poland, but the reason for the demand will not be historical but strategical.

To give East Prussia to Poland would be contrary to the ethnical principle. If, however, the Germans support a Dictator who considers that Germans were created by God to rule, torture and exploit tens of millions of non-Germans, they have small right to complain if a few million of their own people are subjected to foreign rule. The experience of the last century is such that any observer of Eastern European politics, who wishes to see anything like lasting peace, must hesitate to recommend any measure which will place a large number of nationally conscious people under the rule of another nation. Yet the geographical and strategical circumstances in the case of East Prussia are such that it might be considered an exception. And in any case it is probable that the Poles will take the law into their own hands, occupy the region, exterminate a large number of Germans, expel still more, and attempt forcibly to Polonise the remainder.

nor cared about Marxist doctrines, but they understood, and welcomed, the idea of a revolution which would give them the land of the local count or prince, and the opportunity to cut the throats of some of the local officials. Their expectations were to some extent fulfilled when the Red Army occupied the region.

What impression a year and a half of Soviet rule made on the Polish White Russians, there is insufficient sound information to enable us to judge. It is likely that they gained from the change. Their standard of living could hardly have fallen lower, and no political regime could have been stricter than what they had been accustomed to under Poland. Moreover, they no longer suffered from discrimination on grounds of language. Until the German occupation in 1941 the White Russian Socialist Soviet Republic, with its capital at Minsk, was one of the sixteen constituent Republics of the Soviet Union. The centralised Soviet system left little political power to the Minsk authorities, but it is undeniable that the use of the White Russian language was consistently encouraged. A literary language was stabilised by the publication of numerous periodicals and newspapers, besides large editions of translations into White Russian of World Literature. An attempt was even made to create an original White Russian verse and prose literature.

The depressed peasants of the marshy borderlands could not be expected suddenly to turn into poets, but the fact that they were allowed to use their own language in private life and in their relations with the authorities was an improvement in their daily life which they could all appreciate. In view of the bitter memories of Polish rule, the practical value of Soviet reforms, and the general attraction of Russia, the vast Empire that had been the home of their fathers, it is probable that the majority of the population of Polish White Russia would prefer union with their kinsmen in the Soviet Republic of White Russia rather than a return to Polish rule. The creation of an independent White Russian sovereign State does not seem a serious possibility.

The Ukrainian Question is more complicated. In considering the Ukrainian-inhabited regions of Poland, a distinction must at once be made between Eastern Galicia and Volhynia. The inhabitants of the latter are mainly Orthodox. The eighteenth-century partitions gave Volhynia to Russia. The Ukrainians of this province lived in the closest contact with those of the Russian Ukraine proper. The Galician Ukrainians, on the other hand, became Austrian citizens. The Austrian authorities, as we have seen, encouraged the development of a separate Ukrainian nationalism, directed equally against Russians and Poles. This was helped by the fact that the Galicians are Uniates, and that their Church therefore strengthened their consciousness of being different from the Russians. The Ukrainians of Galicia thus undoubtedly developed a strong national consciousness in the modern sense of the word.

The struggle between Poles and Ukrainians in Galicia was bitter even before the First World War. Whereas in the White Russian borderlands of Poland and in Volhynia the Polish element was represented almost exclusively by the landowners, reinforced after the restoration of Poland by the bureaucracy and 'colonists', in Galicia the two nations overlapped. There are districts of mixed Polish and Ukrainian population, where both elements have been long established. Both nations have in Galicia their intellectuals, merchants, peasants and industrial workers, and each of these classes has been in contact and conflict with the corresponding class of the other nation.

Galicia has for centuries been one of the most essentially Polish provinces of Poland. Lwow, the capital of Eastern Galicia, was from 1918 to 1939 a predominantly Polish city. The rise of Ukrainian nationalism has threatened the hold of the Poles on a province to which they have strong sentimental attachments. The struggle has therefore been bitter on both sides.

Something has been said in the second and third chapters of the earlier history of the Ukraine. In the nineteenth century a Ukrainian nationalist movement developed not only in Galicia but in the Russian Ukraine. Shevchenko's poems gave an impulse to the movement. Ukrainian intellectuals tried to show that the medieval Principality of Kiev had been a Ukrainian National State, that the shifting of the centre of gravity of Russia from Kiev to Moscow after the Tatar Conquest was an act of nationalist oppression of Ukrainians by Muscovites, that both Bohdan Chmielnicki and Mazeppa were conscious Ukrainian nationalists, and that everything of cultural value in the history and art of 'Russia' is of Ukrainian origin—hypotheses which no impartial historian can regard very seriously.

During the last decades of the Tsardom the Ukrainian movement acquired some political importance. It is doubtful whether its aims were of interest to any but a small group of intellectuals, but social conditions in Russia were such that these, by exploiting, as did the Russian Social Revolutionaries and Social Democrats, the land-hunger of the peasantry, might in favourable circumstances create a powerful mass movement in the Ukraine. Their opportunity came with the collapse of the Russian Empire in the First World War. A Ukrainian National Council (Rada) was formed by the nationalists in 1917, and, assuming the right to speak for the Ukrainian people, came to terms with the Central Powers, who by the Treaty of Brest-Litovsk compelled the Bolshevik Government to recognise a Ukrainian State comprising not only the Russian Ukraine but the Cholm district in the west and a part of Galicia and Bukovina. The Rada promised to deliver to the Central Powers large quantities of cereals. The Ukrainian peasants, however, resented the presence of German troops, and objected to the requisitions carried out by the Ukrainian nationalists for the benefit of their German friends. Their passive resistance so considerably reduced the amount of grain received that the Germans lost patience with the inefficient Rada, and installed a puppet of their own, the reactionary Hetman Skoropadski, who proposed to restore the big estates, broken up during the preceding months by the action of the peasants themselves, in order the more efficiently to ensure production and delivery of cereals. This policy was naturally highly unpopular. In the autumn of 1918 Skoropadski was overthrown by one of the Rada leaders, Simon Petliura. In November a Western Ukrainian Republic was proclaimed by Ukrainian nationalists in Galicia. The Western Powers could not make up their minds, and confusion reigned in the east. By the summer of 1919 the Poles had conquered all Galicia. In the Russian Ukraine a three-cornered struggle went on between the Bolsheviks, their Russian nationalist enemy General Denikin, and the Ukrainian forces of Petliura. The Ukrainian peasants, tired of the constant changes of ruling cliques, each accompanied by bloodshed and devastation, and eager above all things to obtain the land, showed increasing preference for the Bolsheviks, who ultimately cleared the Ukraine of their opponents. Of the Ukrainian nationalists some went over to Denikin, who was in turn beaten, while Petliura himself fled to Warsaw.

In April 1920 Petliura and Pilsudski made an agreement to create a 'federal' State, to include Poland and the whole Ukraine. The Polish imperialists hoped thus to dominate a huge area greater than the Poland of 1772, while Petliura had no alternative but to rely on Polish military help for the attainment of his designs, no doubt hoping that if such a State came into being the Ukrainians, numbering over 40,000,000 in contrast to some 25,000,000 Poles, would eventually play a dominant part. The price of Pilsudski's help was the categorical renunciation by Petliura of Eastern Galicia, which won him the name of traitor from many of his supporters. The whole scheme came to nothing owing to the successful resistance of the Red Army and the indifference of the Ukrainian peasantry, to whom the Bolsheviks had given the land.

By 1921 the hopes of the Ukrainian nationalists had been completely shattered. The territory inhabited by Ukrainians was divided between four States. Over 30,000,000 remained in the Soviet Union, of which the Ukrainian Soviet Socialist Republic formed one of the constituent republics. Nearly 1,000,000 were citizens of Roumania, being mainly concentrated in Northern Bukovina and the northern and southern extremities of Bessarabia. Poland acquired a number variously estimated by Ukrainian and Polish nationalists between three and ten millions (six is perhaps about the right number). Czechoslovakia by acquiring the former Hungarian province of Ruthenia received some 500,000 subjects of uncertain nationality approximating to Ukrainian.

The fate of the Ukrainians since 1921 has been the subject of so much controversy that it is very difficult to discover even the faintest shadow of the truth. Something has already been said of the political history of Ruthenia, whose importance for the Ukrainian Question as a whole has been grossly exaggerated.* Any estimate of the condition of the Soviet Ukraine must depend on the attitude of its author to the Soviet regime as a whole. Without taking sides in this matter it is perhaps possible to say the following.

* See above, pp. 330–4, also below, pp. 340, 350.

The sufferings of the Ukrainians have been the sufferings of the subjects of the Soviet Union as a whole. The execution of the Soviet·economic programme has imposed heavy sacrifices on the whole population of the Union, including the Ukrainians. The prosperous upper class of the peasantry in the Ukraine, as in other parts of the Soviet Union, resisted the policy of collectivisation of the land. This resistance, and the reprisals executed by Moscow, resulted in the death by starvation of hundreds of thousands, perhaps millions, of peasants, and not only those of the prosperous class. The Ukraine, as the most fertile agricultural region of the Soviet Union, perhaps suffered especially severely from the famine of 1933. Moreover the Soviet regime does not allow free expression of opinion on matters of political principle, and there was as little political freedom, in the western sense of the word, in the Ukraine as elsewhere in Soviet territory. But there is little evidence to show that under the Soviet regime the Ukrainians have been victims of nationalist oppression, directed towards imposing on them Great Russian language and culture. Without claiming expert knowledge of the subject, but after having read a good deal of polemical literature of various origins, I am far from convinced that there is any truth in such accusations. On the contrary, the Soviet regime has given an enormous impulse to the publication of Ukrainian literature, both original and in translation. Whereas under the Tsardom it was difficult to obtain publication in Ukrainian even for the works of great writers like Shevchenko, the new regime deliberately encouraged it. The Ukrainians, like other Eastern European nations, have a great desire and respect for learning. The Soviet regime has made energetic and successful efforts to combat illiteracy, and has provided the Ukrainian nation with an enormous mass of printed material, from great literature to technical treatises and Communist polemics. The use of the Ukrainian language in public affairs and in private life has been encouraged. The administration has been largely in the hands of Ukrainians. Such distinguished Ukrainians as the historian Hrushevski have for a time at least given support to the Soviet regime.

During the last years before the war German interest in the Ukrainian Question and the activities of German agents in the Ukraine caused a certain suspicion in Moscow of the more prominent figures in the Soviet Ukraine. Yet the loyalty of the great majority of Ukrainians appears to have been demonstrated during the German-Soviet war. Not only the population of the industrial towns, which even before the revolution consisted largely of Great Russians, but the peasant masses have offered stubborn resistance to the German invaders.

Discussions of whether the Ukrainians fared better under the Soviet or Polish regime are mostly based on confusion of thought. The truth is that different classes suffered in each case. A rich peasant, a merchant or an intellectual brought up in ideas of romantic nationalism undoubtedly fared better in Poland. Although the Polish censorship was fairly severe, the Ukrainian nationalists of Galicia were usually able to publish their views in Poland. The newspaper *Dilo* in Lwow expressed romantic nationalist views, thinly covered by a veneer of Liberalism. Books were published in Ukrainian in the same city. Ukrainian merchants made money and Ukrainian kulaki maintained a good standard of living. On the other hand, it is arguable that the small holders and landless peasants, who certainly formed together with the small industrial working class the majority of the population in Eastern Galicia, had a more wretched existence than the corresponding class in the Soviet Ukraine. The misery caused by agricultural overpopulation was made more unbearable by the existence of a considerable number of big estates and by the general brutality of the Polish bureaucracy. Poverty and oppression were still worse in Volhynia, where the power of the landowners was greater and the material and cultural level of the Ukrainian peasants was as low as that of the White Russians to their north.

Between 1921 and 1939 the majority of the Galician Ukrainians supported the U.N.D.O. party (Ukrainian National Democratic Union). With this party was connected a system of cooperatives* which did much to improve the lot of a part at least of the peasantry, not excluding the small holders. In Volhynia, owing to the miserable social conditions and the close connection of the population with that on the other side of the frontier, Soviet influence was the strongest. The fact that the Orthodox Church was persecuted in the Soviet Union

* See above, p. 111.

did not deter the majority of Volhynian Ukrainians. After all, the people of the Ukraine were their brothers in religion and in language, and as for persecution of the Orthodox Church, they had plenty of that from the Poles, who, urged on by their Catholic priests, burnt down their churches and ploughed the land on their sites.

In September 1922 the Polish Parliament passed a law recognising the right of the Ukrainian parts of Poland to autonomy. Definitions of the nature of this autonomy, and of the area to which it should apply, formed the subject of endless discussions during the Parliamentary period, and when Pilsudski's Dictatorship was established the project was shelved. Polish nationalists openly proclaimed that the aim of the Polish State was to assimilate all Slav minorities into the Polish nation. Polish 'colonists' were settled in Ukrainian territories. Polish officials and gendarmes poured in. Polish priests demanded the building of Catholic churches in Ukrainian villages, to provide for the spiritual needs of a handful of bureaucrats and policemen, and displayed remarkable zeal and ingenuity in 'converting' the eastern heretics.

The Volhynians suffered most, as they were more primitive and more defenceless. The Galicians put up strong resistance. The U.N.D.O. party protested through legal channels, and strengthened the economic and cultural organisations of the nationalist movement. Some more impatient spirits engaged in terrorism. Members of various extremist organisations, centred in Western Europe, took to burning crops. Such acts infuriated Polish public opinion, and provided the Polish extremists with an excuse for repression. In 1930 'pacifying expeditions' were sent to the Ukrainian provinces. Whole villages were burnt down, numbers of innocent peasants were killed, and abominable tortures and outrages were committed on men, women and children. The official justification for this bestial performance, that some peasants had harboured terrorists and that a 'demonstration' was necessary, was entirely unconvincing. Implacable hatred and a passionate desire for revenge were created.

The outward calm which followed could deceive none but the wilfully blind. U.N.D.O. decided to adopt a conciliatory attitude. In 1935 an agreement was made with the Government by which U.N.D.O. supported it in the elections, and was rewarded with 18 seats in Parliament and a promise of more Ukrainian schools, concessions for Ukrainians in the universities, and places in the civil service for Ukrainians. The promises remained on paper. In 1938, during the Czecho-slovak crisis, U.N.D.O. suddenly announced that the Govern-ment had not carried out the terms of the agreement, and that it considered its experiment in collaboration to have been proved a failure. In December, encouraged by the Munich Agreement and by the creation of an autonomous Ruthenia in Rump Czechoslovakia, Dr Mudrij, one of the nationalist leaders, openly demanded in the Sejm the creation of an autonomous Polish Ukraine, with its own Diet, control of its finances, Justice and Education, a separate military establish-ment, and a Cabinet of its own, some of whose members should also be members of the Polish Government. The re-semblance to Henlein's demands was ominous. It was clear that if Poland should become involved in war, she could not count on the loyalty of her Ukrainian subjects.

The Ukrainians of Bukovina were in a position somewhat similar to that of their kinsmen in Galicia. They had been closely connected with the Galicians in Austrian days. They had enjoyed the benefits of a civilised bureaucracy, and the peasantry had, like that of Galicia, attained an economic and cultural level comparatively high for Eastern Europe. The Roumanian annexation not only put their Roumanian neigh-bours in the province itself, with whom they had enjoyed equality under Austria, in a position of superiority over them, but brought a flood of Roumanian officials from the Old King-dom. These were less brutal and more corrupt than the Polish officials in Galicia. Life was tolerable but unpleasant. The twenty years of Roumanian rule were marked by a general economic, political and cultural decay, for which part of the responsibility lies with Bucarest and part with world condi-tions. The Bukovina Ukrainians remained in opposition, and their political development followed approximately that of Galicia, with which they maintained connections.

The majority of Roumanian Ukrainians were in Bessarabia. This province was perhaps the most misgoverned in Europe. Formerly the vineyard of the great Russian Empire, and one of its richest grain-bearing districts, it simply went to rack and ruin. Trade with Russia came to an end. Roumania is itself a wine-producing country, and could not provide a market for Bessarabian wine. No interest was taken in the magnificent fruit of the Dniestr valley. No roads were built. The Roumanians, whose nationalists spoke with such indignation of the backward condition in which St Petersburg had kept the country, did nothing to improve communications—on the ground that it was a frontier province, and an enemy invasion would be assisted by good roads.

The Land Reform gave the peasants the land, but Bucarest immediately disinterested itself in the peasants after the execution of the Reform. The peasants of Bessarabia were the most primitive and the worst equipped of Roumania. They did not know what to do with their land. Production was disorganised. This natural granary suffered from grain shortages. People died of starvation, and food had to be rushed in from Wallachia. The birth-rate was enormously high, and the subdivision of holdings proceeded rapidly. Relative overpopulation was more severe than would appear from the statistics of density of population, as agricultural methods were so much more backward than anywhere else in Roumania. A rural proletariat formed as elsewhere in Eastern Europe, with a standard of life lower than anywhere except perhaps Polesia. Political conditions were terrible. Officials came from the Old Kingdom simply to plunder the province. It was a colony to be exploited. Anyone who complained of the outrages of the officials was a 'Bolshevik', and treated as such. He was lucky if he got off with a mere beating. These conditions affected Bessarabian Roumanians and Ukrainians alike. The change from the peacefully brutish and stagnant existence of Russia to the horrors of Great Roumania seemed to point only one lesson. The Old Kingdom was responsible for all their ills. And so for Ukrainians and Roumanians alike the only desire was to break away from Bucarest. And to people with their limited horizon there was only one quarter from which salvation could come—across the river. Ties of race and language, memories of a better past, devotion of old people to an Orthodox Tsar whom they could not believe no longer existed, or enthusiasm of young people for a new world in which they believed that justice, security and dignity would be theirs— these factors combined in greater or lesser degree to draw both Ukrainians and Roumanians of Bessarabia to Moscow. When the Red Army entered Bessarabia in June 1940 all but a small number of intellectuals identified with the Bucarest regime and a larger number of Old Kingdom officials settled in Bessarabia since 1918 genuinely welcomed the change.

The future of the former Polish provinces of Ukrainian population depends on the future of the Ukrainian people as a whole. The war has brought violent changes to the Ukrainians. First the Polish then the Roumanian regions were brought under Soviet rule. A year after the annexation of Bessarabia the Germans began their attack on the Soviet Union, and from 1941 to 1944 all Ukrainian territories were under German rule. For some years before the war the relations of Berlin with the Ukrainian nationalists had been very close. Not only the extremist groups in exile with conspiratorial organisations in the country, but the respectable leaders of the Galician movement, had begun to see in the Germans their best hope. The Soviet annexation could not be welcome to men brought up in conservative nationalist ideas coloured by Austrian romanticism. Some nationalist leaders were imprisoned or deported by the Soviet authorities, others took refuge in the German portion of Poland, waiting for the German Army to achieve their dreams for them. When the Germans conquered the Ukraine, there was nothing to show that their Ukrainian nationalist admirers were able to raise much enthusiasm among the Ukrainian people, or even that the German conquerors had much respect for Ukrainian national aspirations. The speeches of Rosenberg suggest that the plan sketched in *Mein Kampf*, of conquering land in the east for the German farmer, land to be owned by Germans served by slave peoples, was to be put into practice.

A minority of Ukrainian nationalist intellectuals remained under Polish rule faithful to the idea of Petliura, that Ukrainian independence should be achieved by Polish help, and that Poles and Ukrainians should collaborate against Russia. A group of intellectuals known by the name of Prometheus devised the most elaborate schemes for the dismemberment of the Soviet Union. All brands of *émigrés* from Russia except ethnical Russians, and many foreign Governments, showed mild interest in these schemes. Caucasians, Azerbaidjanian Turks, Ukrainians, Finns, Poles and Japanese were especially interested. Polono-Finnish frontiers in the Urals and Caucaso-

Ukrainian frontiers in the Crimea were planned with great seriousness by erudite intellectuals at Warsaw coffee-house tables. Most of these exotic *émigrés* were shrewd enough to see that Berlin was a better place to take their plans to than Warsaw, but some continued to trust in the power of a neo-Jagiellonian Empire, to be created by the simultaneous destruction of Germany and Russia. The German-Soviet Pact and the entry of the Western Powers into war with Germany seemed to confirm their hopes. In the Polish emigration in the first winter of the war the dark evenings were wiled away in visions of a Poland from the Rhine to the Urals, or at least from the Elbe to the Volga. Now these brilliant dreams have faded. Although there are probably still Polish nationalists who think in some such terms, it seems likely that the Polish people in Poland approves this new attitude. It may be hoped that the Poles wish understanding and friendship with the Russians in a new Europe, provided that Russia recognises Poland's rights.

The history of Polish-Russian relations since the sixteenth century is a gloomy record of aggression and oppression, first by Poles of Russians and then by Russians of Poles. Yet Russians and Poles as individuals generally like each other. There is a mutual attraction entirely lacking in individual as well as in collective relationships between Poles and Germans. Conflicts between Poland and Russia, at least until the Partitions, were conflicts between Empires, dynasties or Churches. Conflicts between Poles and Germans have for a thousand years been conflicts between two nations bitterly conscious that they are enemies unto death. Russia has done great wrongs to Poland. The last case took place only five years ago, and brought great hardship to thousands of Poles. But the Germans are threatening the whole Polish people with physical extermination. They will fail, but their defeat in this war will not mean that the German menace to Poland is destroyed for ever. In face of the possible recurrence of this most frightful of all dangers, can the Polish people afford to remain in lasting enmity with the Russian people? The German threat to Russia is less than that to Poland, but the losses and sufferings sustained by the Russian people show that it is sufficiently terrible. Can the Russians in the long run afford to antagonise the Poles, whose passionate patriotism will never allow them to accept any foreign domination, but who can be loyal and most valiant friends?

Every friend of Poland must wish for a sincere and lasting settlement between Poland and Russia. But no good is done by underestimating the difficulty. The points of view hitherto maintained by Polish, Ukrainian and Russian nationalists are irreconcilable, and although the Soviet Union is not a Nationalist State, neither Poles nor Ukrainians are entirely convinced that Soviet policy is purified of all nationalism. It would seem that the Ukrainians of the Soviet Ukraine wish to remain united with the other nations of the Soviet Union. Although they were by no means always satisfied with their condition under Soviet rule, their wishes could be met, partly by greater prosperity, which is bound to follow greater development of the economic resources of the Soviet Union, partly by decentralisation and more genuine political freedom. Their kinsmen in Polish Volhynia may be expected to desire incorporation in the Soviet Union. The same is probably the case with the mixed Ukrainian and White Russian region of Polesia, and with the north-eastern provinces up to the neighbourhood of Vilna. If the wishes of the population are to be met, the Russo-Polish frontier will have to be drawn considerably to the west of that of 1921.

The case of Galicia is more difficult. The intimate connection between the Poles and Ukrainians of Galicia would be a strong argument in favour of the inclusion of this region in Poland, were it not that the policy of Warsaw for twenty years, and especially the events of 1930, created a deep gulf between the two peoples. Even so, the differences between the Galicians and the other Ukrainians, in both the religious and the political field, are great. Eastern Galicia had never formed part of the Russian State before 1939. It is doubtful whether the mentality formed in the nationalist movement in Ukrainian Galicia in the past hundred years could easily adapt itself to the conditions of the Soviet Union. Moreover, the claim of Poland to Lwow on national and cultural grounds must be recognised as extremely strong. The truth is that no solution of this question can be entirely satisfactory.

Whatever the future settlement, it will probably involve territorial loss in the east for Poland. Yet the territories ceded are miserably poor, and inhabited by people who are not Poles, will never become Poles, and will always be a source of unrest if they are forcibly incorporated in Poland against their will. Such unrest could not strengthen Poland or contribute to the prosperity of her people. The only elements that would have cause to complain of their loss are the big land-owners and the romantic nationalist intellectuals who are too enamoured of a distorted picture of the past to pay attention to the problems of the present.

Realistic and patriotic Poles would not need greatly to regret the loss if Polish interests are guaranteed in other directions. Such guarantees would include the occupation, temporary or permanent, of East Prussia; the improvement of the Polish frontier in Silesia; the protection of Polish trade connections through the Baltic with the outer world by some treaty between Britain, the Soviet Union, Poland, Sweden and Denmark ensuring joint military control of the Danish Straits; and the creation of a close system of Alliances of Poland with Czechoslovakia and the Danubian States. Such gains are not to be despised. They would be accompanied by large-scale material help in economic reconstruction and social policy by the Western Powers, and by the possibility of sincere friendship with Russia. They would give Poland far better prospects of security, peace, prosperity and greatness than she ever enjoyed at any time between 1918 and 1939.

It is to be hoped that the new rulers of Poland, whoever they may be, will turn their backs on the sterile imperialism and romantic illusions of the past and will give their people the opportunity to play a constructive part as one of the most energetic and promising of the secondary nations of Europe.

HUNGARIAN IMPERIALISM

The second 'Historical Nation' of Eastern Europe is the Hungarian. Like Poland, Hungary was never during its long history a national State, and until very recent times its rulers were not nationalists. 'Unius linguae uniusque moris regnum imbecille et fragile est' are the words attributed to the founder of the medieval Hungarian State, St Stephen. They have been interpreted in different ways at different times, but they have always been applied to this extent, that Hungarian policy has aimed at the defence of a territory which was always admitted to be greater than that occupied by people of Hungarian speech. Within this territory all citizens, of whatever language, were recognised as Hungarians, provided that they showed themselves loyal to the Hungarian State. The territory itself was sacred and inviolable. It comprised the Lands of St Stephen's Crown.

The Crown of St Stephen has for most Hungarians a peculiar, almost mystical, significance. The educational system of Hungary has for generations brought up children to believe that St Stephen's frontiers are something finally and eternally good, something that does not need rational arguments to justify it. All but those who consciously rebel against the traditions and ideas of the ruling class accept this point of view. For the benefit of non-Hungarians rational arguments are also used to justify the old frontiers, some of which have a certain weight. It is pointed out that the Kingdom of St Stephen was for centuries a centre of western, Catholic culture, and that the educated class of Hungary is still intellectually superior to that of neighbouring countries, at least to the south and east. It is recalled that the administration of Hungary enjoyed a fairly good reputation for honesty and efficiency. People of non-Magyar origin who accepted the Magyar language and Hungarian culture were able to rise to the highest positions in the Hungarian State. This State had excellent natural frontiers on three sides, and had developed a fairly balanced economy, in which each part had its function to fulfil and Budapest formed the centre and foundation of the whole.[1]

These are all useful debating arguments, and help to show that the old Hungary was not at all so bad a place as some of its wildest detractors have claimed. But they cannot alter the historical fact, which we may approve or deplore as we choose, that the non-Magyar nations of Hungary were not satisfied with their condition, but developed in the nineteenth century national movements of their own, which, whatever their original intentions, ended by aiming at separation from Hungary in order either to unite with kinsmen across the frontier or to set up independent States of their own. This process came to an end in 1918, when the Austro-Hungarian Monarchy broke up from within, and new national States came

[1] See Macartney, *op. cit.*

into existence. These States passed through various vicissitudes, but, as Mr Macartney observes, there was no evidence during the inter-war period to suppose that Slovaks, Croats, Serbs or Roumanians wished to return to Hungary. As for the remaining subject-nation of the old Hungary, the Ruthenes, they were so primitive and inarticulate that it was hard to say where their preferences lay, but the events of 1938–39 would seem to show fairly conclusively that they too were unwilling to become Hungarian citizens again.

The Treaty of Trianon was undoubtedly severe. The losses of territory were enormous, and, for any Hungarian nationalist, believing in the sanctity of St Stephen's frontiers, iniquitous. Even those who do not admit in principle the right of Hungarians to rule other nations within their historical frontiers must in fairness admit that the number of pure Magyars placed by the Treaty under Czechoslovak, Roumanian and Jugoslav rule was so large as to cause legitimate bitterness to any Hungarian. This number was certainly over two and a half million, and quite possibly over three million. The number of Hungarians left in Trianon Hungary was less than eight million. Thus more than a third of the total number of Hungarians in the world became alien minorities in other States.

The statistics of Hungary and of the Succession States give different figures for the number of Magyars acquired by the latter under the Treaty. In Slovakia the Hungarian census of 1910 showed 894,000 Magyars and the Czechoslovak census of 1921 showed 635,000. The respective figures for Ruthenia were 169,000 and 104,000. For the Vojvodina (Bačka and Banat) the Hungarian census of 1910 showed 442,000 and the Jugoslav census of 1921 showed 382,000. The number of Hungarians in Croatia was given by the 1921 census as 71,000. For Transylvania the Hungarian census of 1910 showed 918,000 while the Roumanian census of 1930 (note that twenty years should have brought a considerable increase of population) showed 827,000. For the whole area ceded by Hungary to Roumania the Roumanian census gave 1,354,000. Hungarian publicists claim as many as 1,900,000.

The Transylvanian Question has already been discussed. It has been shown that, owing to their separate historical traditions and the distance between a part of them and the Hungarian Kingdom, the Transylvanian Hungarians have

developed a special outlook of their own, which involves certain
reserves towards Budapest, although it in no way reduces
their sense of Hungarian nationhood or their unwillingness
to be ruled by Roumanians.

The Magyars of Vojvodina and Slovakia had no such
separate traditions. The Vojvodina had for several hundred
years been separated from Hungary, first under Turkish rule
and then as the military frontier ruled from Vienna, but its Hungarian population, which had increased during the nineteenth
century by immigration, had never had any special independence. As for the Magyars of Slovakia, they had not been
separated from the Kingdom of Hungary since the Magyars
entered the Danubian Basin. The loyalties of the Hungarians
of these regions therefore remained centred on Budapest.

The condition of the Hungarians in Czechoslovakia and
in Jugoslavia differed widely. In both States there were the
usual complaints, often justified, about insufficient educational
facilities, impossibility of entering the civil service, and tactless
behaviour of officials of the majority nation in purely Magyar districts. In all these respects the Hungarians fared
better in Czechoslovakia than in Jugoslavia. Educational
facilities in the former country were in fact generous, except
for the fact, which caused understandable bitterness, that the
University of Bratislava (Pozsony, Pressburg) was completely
de-Magyarised and Hungarian subjects excluded almost entirely from its curriculum. In Jugoslavia the Magyars had
more cause for complaint, and their schools, both primary
and secondary, were closed, though two of them were
eventually re-opened. That Czechoslovak and Jugoslav officials
behaved tactlessly is true. The latter even behaved brutally.
The worst case was the summary expulsion of Magyars
from the Vojvodina following the assassination of King
Alexander. Yet it must be remembered that it had been
abundantly proved that the assassins had received help from
the Hungarian Government, and, though that is hardly a
reason for victimising the innocent local population, the
feelings of the hot-headed Serbs can be understood.

In the social field the difference between the Hungarian
populations of Czechoslovakia and Jugoslavia was most
striking. In the former country the peasants and workers
enjoyed the benefits of democratic social institutions and

political liberty. These were particularly appreciated by the Left, which was powerless in Hungary itself, but had full scope for its energies in Czechoslovakia. The Land Reform benefited some, if not very many, Magyar peasants. Moreover, the tariff policy of Czechoslovakia was of considerable advantage to the middle class, and even small holders, among the Magyar peasantry. The agricultural protection introduced in 1930 favoured the Hungarian farmers of the plainlands on the frontier, by protecting them from competition from within Hungary proper, at the expense of the Slovaks of the mountain regions. The advantage of this policy to them was best appreciated after the return of Southern Slovakia to Hungary in 1938, when the prices of their products and their general standard of living began to fall.

The social conditions of the Magyars of Vojvodina were very much worse. The greater part of the Hungarian population were landless labourers, workers on the great estates of the Hungarian landlords. The Serbs and Germans of Vojvodina were prosperous farmers. The Jugoslav Land Reform took away much of the Hungarian landed property, but it did not give this to the landless Magyars, but partly to the smaller number of Slav (Serb, Bunjevac, etc.) labourers, partly to the Serbian peasants who already had land, and partly to war volunteers brought in to be 'colonists' on the frontier. The Magyar labourers therefore remained landless, but had much less means of livelihood, since, the estates being divided between Serbian or other Slav families, their labour was no longer needed to the same extent. If their condition had been bad under Hungary, it became desperate under Jugoslavia.

As for the other classes of the Vojvodina Hungarian population, they did not suffer materially to the same extent, but they were thoroughly discontented. Dispossessed landlords, dismissed civil servants, and impoverished tradesmen stored up hatred against the Jugoslav State. They could never resign themselves to their new situation, and the Jugoslav authorities knew this and disliked them for it. After 1929 political conditions notably deteriorated, and the brutality of the administration, from which Serbs, Croats and Slovenes suffered, fell with perhaps special severity on the Magyars.

Neither in Slovakia nor in Vojvodina could it be expected

that the Magyars would renounce their hope of return to Hungary. The support given by many Hungarian voters to various Czechoslovak parties, and the existence of a group of Vojvodina Hungarians advocating collaboration with the Jugoslav Government, were no proof to the contrary. For nearly twenty years return to Hungary was not a practical possibility. The Hungarians of the two countries were in fact divided into three groups. The first group were those who preferred to remain where they were as long as Hungary remained a reactionary State, since they enjoyed greater liberties than she could offer them. This group really existed only in Czechoslovakia. The second and third groups which were found also in Jugoslavia both wished to return to Hungary as she was, even if some of them would have preferred to see her reformed. These two groups differed only to this extent, that the one openly admitted its intransigence while the other believed in making the best of things for the time being by collaborating with the authorities, and some of the political parties, of the new State.

The Governments in Budapest had three possible aims. The first, and least, was to secure better treatment for the Hungarian minorities in the three neighbouring States. This policy the Hungarian rulers adopted when they felt themselves weak, and in addressing themselves to the Liberal opinion of Western Europe. Hungarian delegates raised the Minorities Question at the League of Nations, and Hungarian speakers in Britain, France and America spoke of the sufferings of the Hungarian minorities. The second aim, advanced when circumstances seemed more favourable, was the revision of frontiers to restore certain purely Hungarian districts to Hungary. Such districts were the Schütt Island in the Danube east of Bratislava, the northern part of Bačka, the corner of Baranya between Drava and Danube, and the northern part of the Crişana plain. The third aim, seldom openly avowed outside Hungary itself, and never raised officially by Hungarian delegates abroad, but always present in the minds of the Budapest ruling class, was the integral restoration of the frontiers of St Stephen. The first two aims were based on the principle of national self-determination, whereas the third was openly imperialist.

During the first ten years after 1920 Hungarian efforts were devoted to convincing public opinion in the west, and especially in Great Britain, of the need to revise the Treaty. Great sums were spent on revisionist propaganda, and the Revisionist League was exceedingly active. A big success was obtained by the enlistment of Lord Rothermere. But in the end the results were disappointing. The *Daily Mail* failed to persuade the apathetic British public that Hungary's woes were worth its attention. More effective was the attempt to interest Italy. From 1928 onwards Mussolini, anxious for assistance in his anti-Jugoslav policy, declared himself for Revision, and paid great attention to Hungary.

But it was not until Hitler won the diplomatic leadership of Europe, by the help of the British and French Governments, in 1938, that Hungary obtained practical satisfaction. When Czechoslovakia was partitioned, the Vienna 'Arbitration' gave Hungary a slice of Slovakia, mainly inhabited by Hungarians, and in the following March, independently of the Reich and with Polish support, Ruthenia was annexed. Half of Transylvania followed in August 1940, and in April 1941 the reward for a treacherous attack on Jugoslavia, with which she had recently signed a Pact of Friendship, gave the Bačka to Hungary. Yet the Hungarian ruling class is still unsatisfied. The frontiers of St Stephen are not yet restored. It does not look as if Hitler would restore them. He needs the remnants of Slovak, Croatian and Roumanian goodwill. Hungary has not been so much more useful to him than her neighbours that he should put her in the position of 'Herrenvolk No. 2' in Central Europe. On the other hand, an Allied victory is still less likely to be helpful, since Czechoslovakia and Jugoslavia are both Allies of Britain, Russia and America.

Yet the Hungarian ruling class still clings to the historical imperialism of St Stephen's Crown. It will never abandon this idea. As long as it holds power in Hungary, relations of friendship with neighbouring States will be impossible, for the Hungarian rulers will always consider themselves a nation superior to others in Eastern Europe. They will be prepared to treat the other nations with tolerance, on condition that they accept their hegemony, but they will never associate with them on equal terms. This ruling class not only can never bring Hungary friendship with her neighbours, but has a bad record in its policy towards internal problems. Under it the social condition of the Hungarian peasants has remained wretched. By its selfish social policy it obliged large numbers of Hungarians to emigrate. Thousands of men and women have been lost to Hungary and gained by countries overseas. Among the middle class of peasants the introduction of the one-child system, due to the desire not to lower a fairly good standard of living by dividing among several children a holding which it is impossible to enlarge by the acquisition of land from the big estates, has further terribly weakened the Hungarian nation.

During the last fifty years the encroachments of neighbouring peoples on Hungarian territory have steadily increased. Upper Hungary became more Slovak, Southern Hungary more Serbian, Transylvania more Roumanian for several decades before the Treaty of Trianon gave these territories to neighbouring States. The loss of territory by the Hungarian people due to population decline did not cease even in 1920. During the last twenty years the pressure of the German population within Trianon Hungary, in the region west of the Danube, has grown stronger. Villages formerly Hungarian have become German, Hungarian peasant families have died out, and their land has been acquired by Germans.[1]

This process would have been dangerous to the Hungarian people even if no aggressive regime had been in power in Berlin, and even if Austria had remained independent. Now the future of the whole nation is in deadly danger. And this situation has been caused by the policy of that same Hungarian ruling class which insists on maintaining and propagating an antiquated if picturesque Imperialism which no longer corresponds to the demographic, political or economic realities of Europe. This class has since 1867 simultaneously undermined the strength of the Hungarian people and clung in its foreign policy to romantic illusions which are bound to poison the relations of Hungary with her neighbours.

It is time that this class gave up the power to people more capable of understanding the needs of the modern world. Hungary cannot be a healthy or happy country until she is ruled by the representatives of the peasants and workers in their interests. As the peasants have been for centuries denied political education and experience, and as the industrial

[1] Kovács, *A néma forradalom*.

workers do not form a very large proportion of the population, it is inevitable that during the next generation an important part should be played by the intellectual class. There
are progressive elements in this class. Not all are enamoured
of the past to the exclusion of the present. It is not true that
all Liberal and socially progressive intellectuals in Hungary
are Jews. There are many such of pure Magyar origin, who,
by reforming Hungary and giving freedom and education to
the peasants, could put the country on the way to a happy
future. If new people and new classes come to power, turn
their backs on the past, and decide to collaborate on equal
terms with neighbouring nations, Hungary can hope to play
a constructive part in the new Europe.

If Hungary renounces her old Imperialism, she has a right
to expect honourable treatment in the future. The frontiers
of Trianon were not ideal, and there seems no reason why they
should be regarded as sacred for all time. The frontier between
Hungary and Slovakia could be drawn on lines more generous
to Hungary than 1920 while less unfair to the Slovaks than
1938. In the south the Medjumurje and Prekomurje should
certainly be returned to Jugoslavia, as they have Jugoslav
majorities. The question of the Bačka is more difficult. By
her treacherous attack on Jugoslavia, and by the atrocities
which her armies and police have since committed, Hungary
has incurred the hatred of our Jugoslav Allies. The least that
can be expected is that the guilty should be punished, and that
Hungary should make some sort of restitution for the wrongs
done to Jugoslav citizens. It is probable that in the areas
where outrages were committed there will be spontaneous acts.
of revenge. But when the first wave of violence, inevitable in
revolutionary upheavals of national or social nature, is over,
and the problems of the future come up for consideration, it
may well be considered that it would be a source not of
strength but of weakness for the new Jugoslav State to incor-
porate against their will some hundreds of thousands of
Hungarians within its frontiers. It might be found desirable
and possible to draw a frontier somewhat to the south of
that of 1920, thus returning to Hungary the most purely
Magyar areas of the Bačka. The frontier with Roumania
should certainly be different from that of 1920. The plainland from Oradea-Nagyvárad to the Ruthenian frontier

has a Hungarian majority, and should be retained by Hungary.

There remains the question of Ruthenia. This province is economically connected with Hungary, and is bound to suffer as long as it is separated by tariff barriers from the Hungarian market. On the other hand, its population is mainly Slav, approximating more closely to the Ukrainians than to any other branch of the Slav family. Although before 1914 the Ruthenes were reasonably contented, and had hardly any national feeling, it appears that the last twenty years have brought a change. The Hungarian occupation in 1939 was resisted with arms, and followed by bloody repression. Nor is there any evidence that the Hungarian administration has since been able to win the sympathy of the population. Under the Governorship of the notorious Kozma acts of injustice and violence continued. Sympathy for the Soviet Union, on grounds both of race and of ideas, increased, and is probably now stronger than ever. Direct incorporation in Hungary would therefore appear undesirable.

Another possibility is incorporation, together with the whole Ukraine, in the Soviet Union. This might be a popular solution in Ruthenia, but would give rise to many difficult problems, for the establishment of a Russian foothold on the west side of the Carpathians would imply an extension of the Russian sphere of influence involving responsibilities which Moscow might well hesitate to undertake. The third solution, which seems the most likely to be realised, is that Ruthenia should return to Czechoslovakia. Despite its economic links with Hungary and the ethnical affinity of its people with that of Galicia and the Ukraine, it is probably most convenient that Ruthenia should be reunited with Slovakia and the Czech Lands. There is no doubt that Ruthenia benefited considerably from Czechoslovak rule, and that the unfortunate experience of Hungary since 1939 has made the Ruthenes less likely to grumble at the much smaller faults of the Czechs and Slovaks. The Czechoslovak solution would prove satisfactory provided that full account were taken of the dependence of Ruthenia on the Hungarian market, and that the normal exchange of goods were not prevented by high tariff barriers.

The details will be decided by the peacemakers. It is hoped that this survey has made clear the fundamental features of the international problem presented by Hungary, and the alternative lines along which solutions can be sought. If these fundamental features are ignored in the settlement, the settlement will be bad.

The Hungarian nation is a fact, which no chauvinist rhetoric will conjure out of existence. Hungary has twice in thirty years fought on the opposite side from Britain, and has done great harm to Britain's Allies. Yet it should not be forgotten that Hungary is a semi-feudal State, in which the greater part of the people has had no chance for a thousand years to influence policy, and that the aristocratic leaders of Hungary who are now helping our enemies had previously enjoyed keen sympathy in influential circles in Allied countries. It is even arguable that their knowledge of that sympathy encouraged them to set out boldly on the course that they have since pursued. The Hungarian people is less responsible than most for the sins of its rulers. These rulers will go, and a new Hungary will come into being. This new Hungary should receive common justice. No wild schemes of Partition can do anything but harm. When this nation, which occupies the central position in the region between Germany and Russia, has received, not privileges but internal reforms and international equality, Eastern Europe can begin to hope for stability and peace.

BALKAN IMPERIALISMS

The Balkan Peninsula is the scene of Imperialisms less continuously upheld and less firmly rooted in public opinion than those of Poland or Hungary, but in no way inferior to them in violence and extravagance.

The Imperialism of the modern Greek State is based on sea-power. The Greeks have always been skilled sailors and merchants. In classical times Greek commerce dominated the Aegean and most of the Mediterranean. In the Middle Ages first Arab and then Italian sea-power challenged that of Greece, but the Greeks were always active in the Aegean. During the decline of the Ottoman Empire its Greek subjects regained their position in maritime trade. Greek colonies and the Greek language are found to-day on the coast of Asia Minor, in Syria and Egypt and even up the Nile valley to Khartoum and down the east coast of Africa. It was natural that the most imaginative minds of liberated Greece should dream of the restoration of a Hellenic Empire round the Aegean, and should even cast their eyes on the greatest political centre of Greek History, Constantinople. Moreover such was the spell of the personality of Eleutheros Venizelos that he won in the First World War the Allied statesmen for his idea. The Great Idea was brought to nothing by the tragedy of Anatolia, and the Greek communities of Smyrna and the Aegean coast were expelled to make room for the fierce Turkish nationalism of Kemal. Greek Imperialism was driven from Asia, and could find compensation only by continental expansion, in Macedonia and Epirus. Here it is confronted by other peoples, little known to the Greeks, regarded vaguely as barbarians and intruders, the Slavs and Albanians.

Bulgarian Imperialism cannot boast a past comparable to that of Greece. The enthusiasts of Sofia can call only on the blurred memory of the medieval chieftains Boris and Simeon. Yet Bulgarian ambitions are far from modest. The basis of their appetites is the 1878 Treaty of San Stefano. This treaty was drawn up by the Russians, who wished to create in the Balkans a powerful Slav State. Since at that time the distinction between Serb and Bulgar was not very clear, least of all in Macedonia, and since Serbia was a small principality under the influence of Austria-Hungary, whom the Tsar did not wish to offend, it was thought that Russian aims could best be achieved by the creation of a Great Bulgaria. The treaty gave Bulgaria Macedonia as far west as Ohrid, the Thracian coast up to Chalcidice and stretched northwards to the vicinity of Niš. The realisation of this treaty was prevented by the intervention of Britain, which feared Russia and supported the Ottoman Empire, a fact which is always noted to the discredit of Britain by Bulgarian nationalists. The German partition of Jugoslavia has now given Bulgaria approximately the San Stefano frontiers, but this does not satisfy the more energetic imperialists. They demand Salonica, Turkish Thrace and even Istanbul itself. For if Bulgaria is to be the greatest State in the Balkans, should she not also possess the historic capital of the Balkans, the imperial city on the Bosphorus once unsuccessfully besieged by Krum the Mongol Khan of the nomad Bulgars?

Serbian Imperialists are more modest than their Bulgarian rivals. They aspire to Salonica, the outlet for all trade passing from Central Europe down the Vardar valley to the Mediterranean, and they would like to round off their frontiers by extending them from the Lake of Ohrid through Northern Albania to the Adriatic. Otherwise they are contented with the territories formerly constituting Jugoslavia. Moreover, it should be emphasised that these Imperialists are in normal times neither very numerous nor very influential. Having been a 'satisfied' State in 1918, and having enough trouble to cope with the problems of her northern provinces, Jugoslavia showed little desire for expansion to the south. Nevertheless these Imperialist aims were seriously entertained by some, and may conceivably become topical again. No survey of the Balkans could be complete which did not mention them.

Two essentially non-Balkan States are vitally affected in their policy and strategy by the Balkans. These are Turkey and Italy.

Turkey was once the greatest Imperialist Power in South-Eastern Europe. Now the Turks have abandoned their European Imperialism, turned their backs on the imperial city and concentrated on building up a new life in their Anatolian homelands. Yet, even though despised, Istanbul is the gateway between the Mediterranean and the Black Sea. Its possession is necessary for Turkish security, and Turkish policy must therefore be concerned to prevent the rise of a dangerously strong Power on the Balkan mainland.

Italy's interest in the Balkan Peninsula has been since her rise to Great Power status mainly aggressive. Albania, the eastern shore of the narrowest part of the Adriatic, is of importance for Italian control of that sea, while the possession of the Dodecanese Islands has for thirty years assured Italy a strong position in the Aegean.

Such are the ambitions and fears underlying the modern struggle for power in the Balkans. Although of interest only to small numbers in each country, they have determined the policies of States and decided the lives of peaceful citizens. On the removal of extravagant Imperialist dreams and the smoothing out of vital conflicts depends the hope of future security and progress for the Balkan peoples.

The fundamental problem is the relationship of Serbs and Bulgarians. These nations have fought each other four times in the last sixty years, and even in the periods of peace outrages have been frequently committed by extremists on each side against the other. Yet there is no doubt that a great number, perhaps the majority, of Serbs and Bulgarians deplore these past quarrels, which they regard as fratricidal. The two nations have very much in common, and of this both are well aware. The conception of separate Serbian and Bulgarian nations is a recent one. The Bulgarian and Serbian Empires of the Middle Ages were not national States. Their frontiers overlapped at different times, and their population consisted of Slavs speaking an undetermined and primitive tongue. Under Ottoman rule the people of Serbia and Bulgaria thought of themselves as Christians and Slavs rather than as Serbs or Bulgarians. It was the accidents of Great Power diplomacy and the creation of separate princely dynasties that led to the development of separate modern nationalisms.

There are Serbs and Bulgarians who consider that this was a tragic mistake, and that there should be one single Southern Slav nation. They are bound to admit that the literary languages of Serbia and Bulgaria are now too distinct from each other in grammar, pronunciation and word-forms for it to be possible to impose one single 'South Slav language' on both. But they believe that the two nations are so closely related that they should regard themselves as brothers, and should live together within one great State. This idea was very strong in both countries before the war of 1941, and it is probable that even the renewed bitterness caused by the Bulgarian attack on Jugoslavia and the subsequent annexation of Macedonia has not destroyed it.

It is probably stronger to-day among Bulgarians than among Serbs, for apart from the Agrarians and Velchev group, who have always advocated friendship with the Jugoslavs, there are others who, unconvinced that the Axis will win the war, would like to 'reinsure' themselves by friendship with the Serbs, and who hope by offering Belgrade a powerful Southern Slav State to separate Jugoslavs from Greeks, and to protect themselves from the fury of the latter. These Bulgarians, both the more and the less sincere, would willingly sacrifice the Macedonians if they could come to terms over their heads with the Serbs, preferably on the basis of a partition of Macedonia that would leave Bulgaria rather more than she had in 1918. The only opponents of an agreement with the Serbs are the die-hard Bulgarian Imperialists and the section of the Macedonians which supports them. And this group is less powerful in Bulgaria than might at first sight appear. On the Serbian side it may be expected that there would be less enthusiasm, as a large part of the Serbian people is now suffering from Bulgarian occupation. Yet there are strong indications that the idea of Southern Slav unity, taken to include the Bulgarians also, is still widespread among both Serbs and Croats in occupied Jugoslavia. As for the Croats, it should be emphasised that all the democratic leaders of the Croatian Peasant Movement, beginning with the Radić brothers, have supported the idea of South Slav Unity. The realisation of this aim of course depends not only on the willingness of the Southern Slavs themselves, but also on the approval of Greece.

Greece is not a continental State in the same sense as Jugoslavia or Bulgaria. The heart and brain of Greece are at the south of a narrow peninsula surrounded by the Mediterranean. The interior of the country consists of sparsely inhabited mountains. The people of Greece are primarily seafarers and traders. They are more interested in the Mediterranean, or even in the great world beyond Suez and Gibraltar, than in the Balkan Peninsula or Eastern Europe. Yet Greece cannot afford to turn her back on the Continent, for she possesses territories which geographically belong to the Continent and bind her to the problems of the Continent. These are Macedonia, Thrace and Epirus.

The Bulgarians have for the last twenty years resented the fact that they were cut off from the Aegean. In 1913 they had been given Dedeagach (Alexandroupolis), but in 1918 this was taken away from them. From the tops of the Rhodope mountains the Bulgarian shepherds could see the sea, but Bulgaria had no port on its coast. Between Chalcidice and the Maritsa a thin strip of Greek territory, in places only twenty or thirty miles broad, held her back. The Bulgarians regarded this as sheer vindictiveness. The Greeks had so many ports, why should they grudge Bulgaria one? On the other hand, the Greeks claimed that the coastal population was Greek, and pointed out that they had made several offers for special facilities for Bulgarian trade in Greek ports, which Bulgarian Governments had refused. Relations remained bad on both sides, and even road and railway communications between the two countries were left incomplete.

Jugoslavia was less immediately interested than Bulgaria, but was not satisfied with the opportunities offered her for the use of Salonica port. This remained a source of disputes for some years, until settled by the treaty of 1929, made by the Government of Venizelos, which gave Jugoslavia a Free Zone, promised help for transit trade, and included Jugoslav renunciation of any 'pretensions touching Greek sovereignty'. Yet the facts remain that Greece feared Slav expansion towards the Aegean, that the Bulgarians felt themselves selfishly and arbitrarily excluded from Mediterranean trade, and that many Jugoslavs sympathised in this matter with the Bulgarians. On an objective view, it seems that it would be equally unjust to give Greek towns to Slavs, or to exclude Slavs from the sea by arbitrary frontiers defended with tariff barriers. Moreover, even if the trade policy of a Greece holding the whole coast-line were extremely liberal, this would not finally satisfy the Slavs, for they would fear that the Government, and with it the policy, might change.

The best solution of the difficulty would seem to be that such a state of affairs should be created that all Greeks, Bulgarians and Jugoslavs could have equal access to the Aegean, Adriatic, Black and Mediterranean Seas. This would be the case if a Balkan Federation were created to include the former territories of Jugoslavia, Bulgaria and Greece. In this case the towns of the Aegean coast would remain Greek in population, and the principal language of administration would be Greek, but Bulgarian citizens and goods would have perfectly free use of them. This solution would substitute for the dangerous idea of a South Slav Union the more comprehensive notion of a Federation of all Balkan peoples. A South Slav Union, even if effected with the most peaceful intentions, could not fail to provoke Greek, and probably Turkish, suspicions, and the reaction to these suspicions would in turn be an increase of emphasis on the Slav character of the Union, and a tendency towards Pan-Slav Imperialism. This would be avoided if Greece could join the other Balkan peoples in one Federation. This would, however, imply a certain revision of the habits of thought of the Greeks, especially a greater willingness to take an interest in the problems of Eastern Europe and to become acquainted with the Southern Slav peoples. It might be argued that this would be a small price to pay for external security and the prospect of material and cultural progress.

The problem of Albania has caused a good deal of trouble in the last twenty years. The Albanian people is numerically small, and both politically and economically backward. The Albanian coast is near to Italy, and communications between it and the Balkan hinterland are not good. Consequently the country is exposed to Italian aggression. The weakness of Albania is a danger to the independence of the other Balkan nations. If on the expulsion of the Italians an independent sovereign State of Albania were created, it is unlikely that it could long defend itself when, as is to be expected, Italy should have recovered the status of a Great Power. For these reasons Serbian and Greek nationalists have for many years past desired to partition Albania. This project seems highly unsatisfactory. The appetites of Balkan Imperialists are not easily sated. When they had destroyed Albania, the Serbian and Greek chauvinists would only squabble with each other. Moreover, the existence of a disaffected Albanian population would be a permanent cause of weakness to the partitionary States and a permanent incitement to Italy. And in any case, why should the Albanians have less right to freedom than other nations?

The only sound solution would appear to be that Albania should form one of the autonomous units of the projected Balkan Federation. In fact the backward condition of the country would inevitably make it the weakest member of the Federation. Considerable investments over a period of years would be necessary in order to raise the standard of living and the education of the Albanians. Moreover, the needs of defence of this very vulnerable area would necessitate the presence on the Albanian coast-line, at least until relations with Italy had been settled on a satisfactory and permanent basis, of military forces which could not be exclusively composed of Albanians. But with goodwill on all sides difficulties of this sort could be met. The essential point is that within

Albania the bureaucracy, schools, courts, etc. should be run by Albanians, that the Albanian language should be used, and that Albanians should enjoy in all parts of the territory of the Federation equal rights with all other citizens.

The question of Albania's frontiers is one for the peace-makers. It should, however, be mentioned here that the frontiers of 1918–39 did not coincide with the limits of the territory occupied by Albanians in Europe. An Albanian minority whose numbers are variously estimated between 400,000 and 700,000, was included in Jugoslavia, inhabiting the plain of Kosovo and Western Macedonia. A smaller Albanian minority was incorporated in Greece, in the district known as Chamuriya. Many of these Albanians are of Orthodox religion, and as such were counted in Greek census returns as Greeks. The true number is therefore impossible to determine. The exchange of populations between Greece and Turkey was based on an identification of Moslems and Turks. Consequently many Moslem Albanians from Greek Epirus were sent to Turkey, where they were obliged either to accept Turkish nationality or to find their own way to Albania. As many were too poor to pay the expenses of the journey, they remained in Turkey. The Albanian Government made attempts to repatriate them, but many were lost to Albania. The result was, of course, a notable decrease of the number of Albanians in Greece. At the same time, there is a Greek minority in Albania, of unknown numbers, in the region of Argyrokastro and Korcha, occupied by the Greek army in the 1940–41 winter campaign.

The decisions of the peace regarding these minorities on the Albanian frontiers will depend on whether the Greek and Jugoslav leaders are more interested in increasing their prestige or in ensuring the loyalty of their subjects. In any case if, in a Balkan Federation, a substantial minority of Albanians is left outside the Albanian unit, it is essential that these should enjoy full cultural and political rights. If this is not ensured, the whole purpose of the Federation will have been distorted and its chances of survival will be poor.

It can be assumed that the Italians will be driven out of the Balkan Peninsula and the Aegean. The future of the Dodecanese will no doubt be decided between the Turkish and Greek representatives. Albania must be completely cleared of

Italians. The Albanians of to-morrow will profit from the roads and other public works performed by the Italians, but will certainly refuse to allow themselves to be ruled by foreign conquerors. In Dalmatia the Italians must not only give up the territory acquired in 1941, but must abandon Zara, for twenty years a thorn in the flesh of Jugoslavia, and the islands off the coast awarded to Italy in 1918. Finally, the areas of Slav population in Istria and Gorizia must be ceded to Croatia and Slovenia. Italy in 1922 acquired well over half a million Slavs, who for twenty years of Fascist rule suffered great hardships and oppression. In 1941 the Italians annexed a part of Jugoslav Slovenia, and have committed acts of cruelty against the Slovene people. The least that can be expected in restitution is that defeated Italy should cede to our Jugoslav allies lands which she should never have received, which are passionately desired by the Slovenes and Croats, and which are of no value to a great State such as Italy.

The chief concern of Turkey in the Balkans is to preserve her position in Thrace and to guard the Straits. Up to the First World War the chief threat to the Straits came from Russia. Russo-Turkish relations were usually uneasy and from time to time broke out in war. During the first years of the Turkish Republic relations with Russia improved, for the Soviet Government gave diplomatic and material help to Turkey, and renounced the imperialistic policy of the Tsardom. Good relations continued until the present war, when the Soviet Union took up a somewhat arrogant attitude towards Turkey. German propaganda has made the most of the tactlessness of Moscow in 1939 and 1940, and has attempted to convince Ankara that Germany is its protector from the 'Russian menace'. This has not deceived the greater part of Turkish public opinion, if one may judge by the Turkish Press. Although some intellectuals play with the idea of a Great Turkish State, to be built on the ruins of a dismembered Russia, the majority of Turkish writers have resisted German blandishments. The well-known journalist Yalchin welcomed the Anglo-Soviet Treaty as a sign that the isolation of Russia was over and that she would in future play that part in world affairs which her own greatness and the stability of Europe alike demanded.

The friendship of Britain and Turkey is traditional, and if

Turkey maintains her friendly neutrality to the end of the war Britain will have much reason to be grateful to her. It is therefore natural that Britain, regarding Turkey as one of the bastions of peace and security in the Middle East, should wish to see her strategical position guaranteed. This does not mean, however, that Britain can allow Turkey to play off Russia against her, or that the Straits Question can be suffered as in the past to poison Anglo-Russian relations. Friendship with the Soviet Union will be for Britain after the war even more important than friendship with Turkey, with which it is in no way incompatible. There is no reason why an agreement should not be made between the three States, protecting the rights of Turkey and satisfying the wishes of the two Great Powers.

If the relations of Turkey to Russia could be put on a sound basis, the Balkan Question would be much less important for her. Yet Turkey's interests in Thrace demand close relations between her and the Balkan States, while her common interest in peace in the Aegean necessitates collaboration with Greece. If a Balkan Federation were created, Turkey could hardly join it. Turkey has a special geographical position, set between Europe, Asia and Africa. She is bound quite as much to the Moslem world as to Europe, and she has interests on the boundaries of Syria, Persia and Mesopotamia which do not even remotely concern the Balkan peoples. It is of the greatest importance, however, that Turkey should maintain friendly relations with any Balkan Alliance or Federation. Indeed, without such friendly relations neither Turkey nor the Balkans could enjoy security and peace.

Under no circumstances must Turkey be given reason to think that a Balkan Federation is directed against her, nor must the Balkan peoples be led to believe that Turkish policy is dictated by any Great Power hostile to their aspirations. There is no reason why these dangers should not be averted. There is no reason why Greece should not at the same time be a member of a Balkan Federation and yet maintain especially close relations with Turkey and with Great Britain and other Mediterranean Powers. These close relations would not be hostile to the interests of the other members of the Federation, but would be of less direct interest to them. At the same time the territories formerly comprising Jugoslavia, which it is anticipated would be included in such a Federation, would have interests in the Danubian Basin which would hardly concern Greece.

The advantage of a Balkan Federation of this kind is that it would have a better chance of eliminating old and sterile imperialisms, and of creating durable relations between peoples who have spent too long wasting their energies in fighting each other, and would all gain far more from uniting on a basis of common interests. It is possible that, if such a Federation came into being, and proved a success, even such thorny problems as Macedonian Autonomy and Albanian Minorities might one day find a just solution.

The success of a Balkan Federation depends, however, on two conditions. Social reforms must be carried out, and maintained, on similar lines throughout all parts of the territory of the Federation, and international peace and security must be guaranteed by an unshakable external force for at least a generation. Without these conditions no Balkan Federation can prosper, and the peoples of the Balkans can face the future only with despair.

The problems mentioned in the last two chapters can best be illustrated by a brief summary of the history of the relations between the States of Eastern Europe during the last twenty years.

This summary will show not only the influence of territorial disputes and Small-Power Imperialisms on the policy of the Eastern European States, but the effect on Eastern Europe as a whole of the plans and intrigues of the Great Powers.

CHAPTER NINE

INTERNATIONAL EXPERIENCE, 1918–41

THE FRENCH SYSTEM OF ALLIANCES

THE fundamental purpose of the 1919 Peace Settlement in Eastern Europe was to create a *cordon sanitaire* of new States between the two dangerous Great Powers, Germany and Russia. Although only Germany had been the enemy of the Entente during the war, there was little less fear and distrust of Russia. The Bolshevik Revolution was a threat to the established order, and Russia had a number of territorial grievances which ensured her opposition to the Versailles system. The permanent nightmare of Western statesmen during the first decade after the Armistice was an alliance of Germany with Russia. This nightmare was made the more probable by the strength of the Left in the German Republic. The German-Russian Treaty of Rapallo of 1922 seemed to give these fears confirmation. The chain of medium or small States from the Baltic to the Balkans had therefore an important part to play in Allied, and especially in French, strategy, by keeping the two dissatisfied Powers apart and giving France help if necessary against Germany.

For the first ten years Germany was hardly dangerous. Disarmament, Allied military occupation, reparations and inflation reduced her to comparative impotence. The task of keeping her down was in the efficient hands of M. Poincaré, and the Eastern European States had no cause for alarm. Most of them had coldly correct relations with Germany. The German nationalist Press published periodical attacks on neighbouring countries, particularly on Poland, which were repaid with polemics in the same style, but these had little political importance. Germany was unreconciled, and her small neighbours knew it, but they trusted France to handle the situation.

Greater fears were entertained with regard to Russia. The Soviet invasion of Poland, provoked by Pilsudski's Ukrainian adventure, was repelled in 1920, and was followed by treaties between the Soviet Union and her Baltic neighbours. The independence of Estonia, Lithuania and Latvia was recognised and their frontiers were determined. The Polish frontier, which included within Poland large numbers of White Russians and

Ukrainians, was fixed by the Treaty of Riga between Poland and the Soviet Union in 1921. The relations of the Baltic States and of Poland with their large neighbour remained correct but not friendly for the following ten years. Roumano-Soviet relations were complicated by the refusal of the Soviet Union to recognise the annexation of Bessarabia by Roumania. Consequently Roumania did not recognise the Soviet Government until 1934. Few attempts were made on either side to improve the situation. Strangely enough, of all Roumanian politicians the one who made the most serious attempt to liquidate the dispute was the reactionary Vaida-Voevod who tried once in 1919 and again in 1932, being prevented in the first case by King Ferdinand and in the second by a change of Government in Bucarest. Until Titulescu became Foreign Minister Roumania adopted an arrogant attitude towards the Soviet Union, being encouraged to believe that in any dispute she could always count on the support of the Western Powers. In 1921 an alliance was signed between Poland and Roumania for defence against Russian attack.

In actual fact Russia was too occupied in healing her own wounds, and in carrying out her plans of social reconstruction, to think of foreign adventures. Once the first enthusiasm of revolutionary expansion had died down, and it became obvious that Europe was not going to go Communist, Moscow adopted a purely defensive policy. Russian participation in the discussions on the Kellogg Pact in 1928–29 and in the Disarmament Conference of 1932–33 were a sign of a desire for a slightly more active policy, but it was not until its entry into the League of Nations in 1933 and the signature of the Franco-Soviet Pact in 1935 that the Soviet Union became an important factor in European politics. As long as the possibility of Russian military intervention in Europe was remote, the small Eastern European States could afford to ignore the existence of the Soviet Union, and in fact did so.

In the first part of the inter-war period the main obstacle to the creation of an Eastern European united block between Germany and Russia, the aim of French policy, was the discontent of the defeated countries of Eastern Europe, Hungary and Bulgaria. Having lost more than half her territory, Hungary could hardly be expected to accept a subsidiary role in an international system created at her expense. This was all the more improbable as the restored regime in Budapest was led by men devoted to the memory of the past, who could never recognise the right of the nationalities of Historical Hungary to States of their own, and who were able to offer their own people, as compensation for the social reforms which they would not grant it, only the prospect of revenge in the international field. Bulgaria had had far smaller losses, but her nationalists were no less incapable of resigning themselves to the frustration of their Macedonian and Thracian ambitions.

While Stamboliiski was in power in Sofia, Bulgarian policy was conciliatory, but Hungary from the first adopted a truculent attitude. The two attempts of ex-King Charles to return to Hungary caused profound alarm in the neighbouring countries, where the Habsburg Dynasty was regarded as the symbol of all that was most hateful in the old system. It was this alarm which brought into being the Little Entente. In August 1920 was signed the Czechoslovak-Jugoslav Treaty, followed in April 1921 by the Czechoslovak-Roumanian and in June 1921 by the Roumanian-Jugoslav. The last had provisions concerning attack by Bulgaria, which Czechoslovakia did not accept. All three treaties provided for common defence against Hungarian aggression. No mention was made, however, of the three Great Powers which threatened respectively Jugoslavia, Czechoslovakia and Roumania, namely Italy, Germany and Russia.

Relations between the Little Entente and Poland were somewhat uneasy. Polish-Roumanian relations were determined by the treaty of 1921 against Russia. They remained correct until the end, but were never intimate or friendly. Jugoslavia was too far distant to have important relations with Poland. Czechoslovakia was obliged to take account of her northern neighbour, but the relations of the two Republics were seldom satisfactory. They started badly with the Teschen Dispute. The Teschen district of Silesia was one of the richest industrial areas of Austria-Hungary. It was claimed on historical grounds by the Czechs, but for ethnical reasons by the Poles. An ethnical delimitation was proposed by the Powers in 1918, but this satisfied neither party. In July 1920 the Conference of Ambassadors decided the issue, and the frontier adopted by it gave Czechoslovakia a larger share than had been intended, with a population of 80,000 Poles. Resentment against the Czechs in Poland was increased by the refusal of the Czechoslovak Government to allow the passage of arms through Czechoslovak territory to help the armies of Pilsudski against the Soviet invaders. This attitude was dictated by the sympathies of the Czechoslovak railway workers.

Friendship between the two Republics was made difficult by the difference in mentality of the two ruling classes. That of Poland was dominated by the Conservative, romantic gentry ('szlachta'), that of Czechoslovakia by the Liberal bourgeoisie. Nevertheless a Treaty of Friendship was signed in 1921, by which each side agreed to refrain from intervention in the internal affairs of the other. Slovakia and Eastern Galicia were explicitly mentioned. The treaty was, however, never ratified. In 1923 the Polish Foreign Minister proposed that the Little Entente be extended to include Poland, but nothing came of the proposal. In 1925 apprehension at the implications of the Locarno Pact brought the two governments together again. An arbitration agreement was signed in that year, for non-territorial disputes only. In the following year the Polish Foreign Minister visited Prague to propose a full alliance. The Czechoslovak Government hesitated, and shortly afterwards the Pilsudski *coup d'état* overthrew the Government that had made the offer. For the following years Polish-Czechoslovak relations continued to be coldly correct. Under the Pilsudski regime the differences between the two States were accentuated, and the attempt to create intimate relations was abandoned.

For the first years after the Armistice France was universally considered to be the strongest Power on the Continent. Her prestige stood higher than ever since the days of Napoleon I. None doubted her will and ability to maintain the Settlement of 1919. The beneficiaries of that system sought the closest possible relations with her. In 1925 the Locarno Pact, which alarmed Eastern Europe by its possibility of allowing the recovery of Germany, was accompanied by Franco-Polish and Franco-Czechoslovak military alliances. These alliances, together with the Little Entente, remained fundamental features of the Eastern European political situation until the rise of Hitler.

ITALIAN POLICY IN EASTERN EUROPE

The First World War had destroyed the two Eastern Empires of Austria-Hungary and Russia, and the Peace Treaties had for the time being crushed Germany. The disappearance of these Great Powers had left a vacuum in Eastern Europe. France, we have seen, inspired the Peace Treaties, and intended to play the chief part on the Continent. But there was one other Great Power more favourably placed by geography for intervention in Eastern Europe than France; this was Italy.

Italy had been on the victorious side in the war, but had got very little at the Peace. The Revolution of Kemal Atatürk had thwarted her ambitions in Asia Minor, and the Secret Treaty of London, which had promised her large parts of Dalmatia, had been disowned by President Wilson. Having come into the war less from necessity than from the hope of territorial aggrandisement, Italy felt cheated. The internal difficulties of the first few years, during which the revolutionary working-class movement nearly obtained power, prevented vigorous action in the international field. The advent of Fascism, however, made possible a more enterprising foreign policy. Internal opposition to Mussolini was soon suppressed, and the elements of the middle class and of the younger generation whose support had brought the Fascists to power, demanded something sensational from their leader.

Italian interest in Eastern Europe before 1914 was determined by her relations with Austria-Hungary. The most important issue between the two States was that of Trieste and the Trentino, regions of Italian population occupied by Austria-Hungary. But behind this particular question lay the whole problem of supremacy in the Adriatic. As long as the eastern coast was in the hands òf a potentially Great Power Italy felt threatened.

The removal of this Great Power might have been expected to solve this problem, but Italy was not satisfied. An united Jugoslav State could be dangerous if supported either by France or by Russia. Russia was for the time being out of the picture, but the Slav sympathies of the Jugoslavs were a permanent factor. As for France, she was apparently stronger than ever, and entertained the closest relations with Jugoslavia and with her Allies of the Little Entente. The conquest of Libya in 1911 had increased Italy's status as an African Colonial Power, and her designs on Tunisia went back to the eighties. In view of the possibilities of conflict with France, the neighbourhood of a strong Jugoslavia was highly inconvenient. For these reasons Italy wished to guarantee herself against attack from behind by establishing a foothold on the eastern shore of the Adriatic, such as would make that sea in practice an Italian lake.

These considerations were bound to influence any Italian nationalist Government. The advent of Fascism made them more urgent, for Mussolini had never concealed the fact that he was not content with the status of junior Great Power. Even supremacy in the Adriatic and aspirations in Tunisia were not enough for him. He aimed at control of the whole Mediterranean and the restoration of the Roman Empire. These grandiose plans could not be realised without challenging the might of Britain and France. For the time being this was unthinkable, but until powerful Allies could be found steps could at least be taken to strengthen Italy's position in the Eastern Mediterranean.

Italy had already valuable Aegean bases in the shape of the Dodecanese, taken in 1911 from Turkey. Separated by a narrow strip of land from the northern coast of the Aegean was defeated and dissatisfied Bulgaria. Opposite Southern Italy, at the narrowest point of the Adriatic, was the new and unstable State of Albania. Albania and Bulgaria were separated by Jugoslav Macedonia, to parts of which each advanced claims on ethnical grounds. From Durazzo to Salonica, across Albanian, Jugoslav and Greek territory, had once gone the 'Via Egnatia', highway of Imperial Rome for the domination of the Balkan Peninsula. Again to the north of Jugoslavia was defeated and dissatisfied Hungary, which had not renounced the fertile lands of Banat and Bačka, and hoped that the discontent of the Croats with Belgrade might induce them to return to their former union with Budapest.

Italian policy in Eastern Europe between the Peace Conference and the rise of Hitler was based on fear of Jugoslavia, opposition to the diplomatic activity of France, and desire to prepare positions in the Eastern Mediterranean for the ultimate conflict with the Western Powers. These motives induced Italy to support Hungarian and Bulgarian revisionism, to give material assistance to Croatian and Macedonian terrorists, to develop a stranglehold in Albania, to intrigue for the break-up of the Little Entente, and when that failed to create a rival block of States in Central Europe under Italian influence. This policy is easily intelligible from the point of view of Italian nationalist interests. It was pursued with much greater skill than was the opposite policy of France. It succeeded in keeping alive and even intensifying existing hatreds between Eastern European States, and maintained all Eastern Europe in a condition of unrest and tension until Germany, the only real Great Power besides Russia, was ready to play the leading part in mischief-making. The importance of Mussolini's Eastern European policy from 1922 to 1936 cannot therefore be overestimated. If it ended to the advantage not of Italy but of Germany, that cannot detract from the Duce's diplomatic skill.

The first diplomatic crisis connected with the Adriatic was caused by the status of the town of Fiume. This had been the one port of the Hungarian half of the Habsburg Monarchy, the piece of coast to the south of it being known as the 'Croatian coast', as contrasted with Dalmatia proper, which was under Austrian rule and began farther south. The Secret Treaty of London of 1915, which induced Italy to throw in her lot with the Entente, had promised most of Dalmatia to Italy, but had left Fiume to Croatia, the status of which had not then been fully considered. When it became obvious at the Peace Conference that Wilson would not recognise the Secret Treaty, the Italian representatives demanded that Italy should receive Fiume. Jugoslavia objected to this, and advanced a counterclaim on ethnical grounds to the peninsula of Istria, at the north-eastern corner of the Adriatic, between Trieste and Fiume. This peninsula had a partly Slovene, partly Croatian population, the Italians being definitely in the minority. Even Trieste itself, although predominantly Italian, had a large Slav population, and its hinterland and the region of Gorizia were mostly inhabited by Slovenes.

While the arguments between Jugoslavia and Italy continued, the Italian poet Gabriele d'Annunzio brought off a theatrical exploit by seizing Fiume with a few enthusiasts, on 12 September 1919. In the following year he proclaimed the independence of the city under his Government, which he called the 'Reggenza del Carnaro'. Meanwhile Italo-Jugoslav negotiations continued, and in November 1920 the Treaty of Rapallo settled the frontiers, giving Italy Istria, the Dalmatian city of Zara and four islands, creating a Free State of Fiume and leaving the rest of the eastern coast, as far as the Albanian frontier, to Jugoslavia, on the understanding that Italian minorities would be protected. D'Annunzio at first refused to accept this treaty on the grounds that he should have been consulted, but gave in after force had been threatened. In 1921–22 fights between 'autonomists' and Fascists in Fiume, and attacks by armed Fascist bands on Slovene villages in Istria caused tension between Jugoslavia and Italy. Once in power Mussolini demanded the incorporation of Fiume in Italy, which took place, after half-hearted protests by Jugoslavia and by the Fiume 'Government', in September 1923. There was little that Belgrade could do. The Jugoslav Foreign Minister, the Radical Momčilo Ninčić, was keen to effect a reconciliation with Italy, and adopted a friendly attitude. In January 1924 a Pact was signed by Mussolini, Ninčić and Pašić in Rome, by which Jugoslavia finally recognised Italian sovereignty over Fiume.

More serious was the Albanian Question. The Albanians, the last of the European subject-nations of the Ottoman Empire, had become nominally independent in November 1912, and had accepted as ruler two years later Prince William of Wied. The prince, however, left the country on the outbreak of war, and during the following four years various parts of the country were occupied by Austrian, Greek and Italian troops, while the outlying regions were ruled, as in the past, by local tribal chiefs. At the Peace Settlement it had to be decided whether Albania should be independent or should become an Italian Protectorate. There was considerable opposition in Albania to the second idea, and in 1918 a Conference at Lushniya expressly repudiated it, and set up a Government of four Regents, of which two were Moslems, one Orthodox and one Catholic. The Italian Government was impressed by the determination of the Albanian leaders, and, being faced with an uncertain internal situation in Italy, decided to seek satisfaction of its aims by supporting Albanian independence and maintaining close relations with the young State. Italian troops were withdrawn from all Albanian territory save the island of Saseno, off Valona harbour.

In 1921 a Declaration of the Conference of Ambassadors provided that, if the territorial or economic integrity or independence of Albania should be threatened, then, whether or not the Albanian Government asked for help, the four Great Powers, Great Britain, France, Italy and Japan would advise the League of Nations to intervene, and to entrust such intervention to Italy. The Declaration was motivated by the statement that any modification of Albania's frontiers would constitute a threat to the security of Italy. At the same time the Powers demanded that all Jugoslav troops should be withdrawn from Northern Albania. Belgrade thereupon abandoned its support of a revolt of the Catholic Mirdite tribe, and Italy had secured a diplomatic victory.

The internal affairs of Albania were turbulent, and gave opportunities to both sides to meddle. In 1923 the Prime Minister, Ahmed Zogu, lost the elections, and his device of resigning and putting his fiancée's father, Shevket Bey Vrlaci, a big landowner, in power only led to a revolt. Zogu fled to Jugoslavia, accompanied by both the Moslem Regents. The Orthodox Regent then appointed as Prime Minister the Bishop of Durazzo, Monsignor Fan Noli, a distinguished scholar. The new Premier maintained good relations with Italy, and determined to carry out a Land Reform. This won him the hostility of the Beys, who prepared a revolt. In 1924, simultaneously with the Pact of Rome concerning Fiume, Jugoslavia and Italy signed an agreement not to interfere in the internal affairs of Albania. Nevertheless, a few months later, the Jugoslavs provided Zogu with a mixed Serbian and Russian *émigré* force, with which he entered Albania, and, helped by the Beys, turned out Fan Noli. He then summoned a carefully 'elected' Constituent Assembly, which abolished the old Regency system and substituted a Republic. Zogu became President. In 1926 a serious rebellion broke out in the north, threatening Scutari. Zogu won, however, and his police chief Yuka thoroughly repressed the revolt. Until the Italian conquest in 1939 Zogu's supremacy was not seriously threatened.

Once firmly established, Zogu forgot his old friends in Belgrade, and made advances to Italy. In 1925 an Albanian National Bank was founded with 53 % Italian capital. In

1926 was created a Society for the Development of the Economic Resources of Albania, controlled by the bank. In return for the loans made by this society, Albania promised for forty years to take no action which might prejudice her revenues without first consulting Italy. About the same time petrol was discovered near Valona, and, as French and British companies were not interested in an enterprise promising quite small profits, the concession was given to Italy.

In November 1926 an Italo-Albanian Pact was signed. It expressed the common interest of both parties in the preservation of the political, juridical and territorial *status quo* of Albania, and engaged them to afford each other 'mutual support and cordial collaboration'. Neither would conclude any political or military agreement with a third party prejudicial to the interests of the other. In the hope of allaying the suspicions of Jugoslavia, a letter from the Italian Minister in Tirana was simultaneously published, which said that the 'cordial collaboration' referred only to proposals from one party freely accepted by the other. This entirely failed to reduce the indignation of Belgrade. It was pointed out that Italy had guaranteed the Zogu Government against all internal opposition, and that any Jugoslav-Albanian agreement was made impossible by the last clause. The consternation of the Jugoslavs was increased by the belief that the Pact had the full support of Britain. Before accepting it, President Zogu had asked the advice of the British Minister in Tirana, Mr O'Reilly, who had given his sincere opinion that such a Pact was incompatible with Albanian independence. This induced Zogu to hesitate for a time. Shortly afterwards Sir Austen Chamberlain, British Foreign Secretary, on a cruise in the Mediterranean, was visited by his close friend Signor Mussolini, who complained bitterly of the Minister's advice. Sir Austen decided that it was an offence for a British diplomat to oppose the will of the Duce. Mr O'Reilly was removed from his post, and the Pact was signed. It was hardly surprising that these circumstances should cause Belgrade to believe that the British Government had given Italy a free hand in the Balkans.[1]

The reaction of Jugoslavia was to speed up the negotiations

[1] For further details of the O'Reilly incident, see Robinson, *Albania's Road to Freedom*, 1941.

for a Franco-Jugoslav Treaty. This was signed on 11 November 1927. It was a comparatively harmless document, and did not contain military clauses, but it roused great fury in Italy, and was followed eleven days later by the publication of a formal military alliance between Italy and Albania. In the following year Zogu declared himself king. His title, 'King Zog I of the Albanians', caused further resentment in Belgrade, as it implied an interest in the numerous Albanian minority in Jugoslavia. The Italians strengthened their hold in the following years over the Albanian Army and the economic life of the country. There was nothing that Jugoslavia could do except watch and get angry. Italo-Jugoslav relations remained diplomatically correct, but there could be no sincerity on either side as long as Italy financially supported I.M.R.O. and thus held Jugoslav Macedonia in pincers.

Italian relations with Greece were at first unsatisfactory. The Italian refusal to give up the Dodecanese caused great indignation, which was increased by what was regarded as a treacherous attitude during the Anatolian War, when Italy hastened to abandon her plans in the Adalia region, and to come to terms with Kemal Atatürk at the expense of the Greeks. In 1923 the murder of General Tellini, the President of the Albano-Greek Frontier Delimitation Commission, gave Italy an excuse to occupy Corfu, which was only evacuated on the payment of a Greek indemnity of fifteen million lire. Italy encouraged Bulgarian terrorists to make themselves a nuisance to Greece as well as to Jugoslavia. They met their match in the Greek Dictator General Pangalos, who in 1925 used a frontier incident as an excuse to raid Bulgarian territory in force. He was obliged to retire by pressure from the League of Nations. In 1928 Venizelos again became Prime Minister of Greece, and at once attempted a reconciliation with Italy. In the same year a Treaty of Friendship was signed by the two countries, and Venizelos declared that the Dodecanese Question was settled. This won the Premier some unpopularity in Greece, but did not solve the problems of Italo-Greek relations. Mistrust of Italy's known imperialistic intentions remained firmly rooted in Greece.

Fear of Italian designs and impatience with Bulgarian terrorism brought the Balkan nations closer together. From 1930 onwards Balkan conferences on non-political subjects were held. The ideas of Balkan unity, and 'the Balkans for the Balkan peoples' were discussed with increasing interest by the intellectuals of these countries. Modest results of the conferences were the Balkan Chamber of Commerce and Industry set up at Istanbul in 1931, and the Oriental Tobacco Office set up with Greek, Bulgarian and Turkish representatives in 1933. At the same time the idea of closer political relations made progress. A leading part was taken by Turkish diplomacy. Kemal Atatürk had signed an agreement with Greek Premier Venizelos in November 1930, and this was the beginning of the Greco-Turkish friendship which later became one of the fundamental features of the Balkan international system. Turkey had reasons as strong as those of Greece for fearing the expansion of Italian power in the Eastern Mediterranean. Jugoslavia needed any support she could get in view of the threats to Dalmatia and Macedonia. Roumania, less interested in Balkan affairs, feared Bulgarian ambitions and was eager to maintain close relations with Turkey, on whose good will depended all her sea-borne trade. The result of these discussions and considerations was the Balkan Entente, which came into being in February 1934. Bulgaria and Albania were not invited, but the text of the Treaty expressly stated that other Balkan States were free to join.

The main preoccupation of Roumania and of Greece was defence against Bulgaria. Jugoslavia was also interested in the question of Italian aggression, but did not insist. Although not a party to the Alliance, Czechoslovakia had taken great interest in it, and hoped that it would be not a mere anti-Bulgarian alliance, but a diplomatic front of all the Balkan States against outside interference. In this Czechoslovak and Turkish aims were identical. This wider conception led to the inclusion of a 'secret clause', communicated to the British, French and Italian Ministers in Athens, to the effect that if a signatory were attacked by a non-Balkan Power, and the latter were joined by a Balkan Power, the other signatories would go to war with the aggressor Balkan Power. The implications of this clause, however, so alarmed the signatories that Turkey required Roumania to give a specific undertaking that she would not expect Turkish assistance against Russian attack, and Greece declared that she would not be drawn into war with any Great Power.

As for the other Balkan States, it was obvious that Albania, utterly dependent on Italy, would not join. Bulgaria adopted a much more friendly attitude after the Velchev-Georgiev *coup d'état* of 19 May. If this Government had remained longer in power, it is possible that Bulgaria might have joined, at least if a few minor territorial adjustments had been made. But the overthrow of Georgiev by King Boris made this impossible. Thus the Balkan Entente, of which much had been hoped, was never able to play an important part. It remained an Alliance directed against Bulgaria, with which any one of the signatories could have dealt alone without difficulty.

Italian policy in the Danubian Basin was based on the same principles of opposition to French diplomacy and encirclement of Jugoslavia. At first Italian diplomatic activity seemed harmless enough. Treaties of Friendship were concluded by Italy with Czechoslovakia in 1924 and with Roumania in 1926. Both countries wished to maintain friendly relations with Rome, the former being bound by the memory of the comradeship-in-arms of Czechoslovak Legionaries on the Italian front, the latter by likeness of language and culture. But both had important common interests with Jugoslavia and close friendship with France. Italian attempts to win Averescu from the Little Entente led to nothing, and Beneš remained loyal to his Slav Ally. Mussolini, therefore, in 1927 concluded a Pact of Friendship with Hungary, the Italian Press began to talk about the historical friendship of the two nations and their common struggles in 1848, and in 1928 the Duce made a speech in favour of Treaty Revision, enthusiastically received in Budapest. From this time the relations of Italy with the Little Entente cooled rapidly, while Italo-Hungarian friendship strengthened.

The World Economic Depression brought a deterioration of political relations in the Danubian Basin. The Successor States raised their tariffs to bring immediate relief to domestic interests. The Czechoslovak denunciation of a Trade Treaty with Hungary in 1930 was a severe blow to the latter country. At the same time Austria, faced with ruin by the collapse of the Vienna Bank, the Kredit-Anstalt, proposed to conclude a customs union with Germany. This plan had to be abandoned owing to the fierce opposition of France and the Little Entente. In the following year, however, a conference was held at

Stresa, on the initiative of the French Prime Minister, André Tardieu, to consider means of relieving the Danubian economic situation. A plan for the creation of a Danubian customs union was thwarted by the opposition of Germany and Italy, who not only feared that their important trade interests in the area would suffer, but were concerned to prevent any consolidation of the situation in Eastern Europe which would make it less easy for them to intrigue and interfere. They could rely on the support of Austria and Hungary, and the whole work of the conference was brought to nothing.

In February 1933 the Little Entente was strengthened. A Permanent Council of the Little Entente, consisting of representatives of the three countries, was created, which was to meet at least three times a year. The possibilities of extending mutual trade were examined. Foreign Minister Beneš, the moving spirit of Little Entente policy ever since its foundation, hoped to make the Alliance the basis of fuller collaboration between all Danubian Powers. So long, however, as none of Hungary's demands were satisfied, and so long as these demands enjoyed the support of one or more Great Powers, this broad aim was bound to remain unattainable.

In March 1933 Mussolini proposed to the British Prime Minister the conclusion of a Four-Power Pact of Britain, France, Italy and Germany. It was clear from the Duce's public statements on the subject that the Pact was intended to give these Powers a sort of Directorate of European Affairs, and that their policy was to include territorial revision. The proposal met, not unexpectedly, with violent opposition from the Little Entente and Poland. This opposition caused France to demand emendations in the Pact, which, when finally signed, lacked practical value.

Mussolini, disappointed in his aims and forced for the time being to recognise the greater strength in Eastern Europe of the French system of Alliances, fell back on the more modest plan of organising an Italian block in the Danubian Basin. In March 1934 were signed the Rome Protocols which provided for consultations on matters of policy between Italy, Hungary and Austria. The Protocols laid special stress on the economic factor, expressed the hope that markets would be found for Austrian manufactures and Hungarian agricultural produce in Italy, and promised to facilitate the use of Trieste for Hungarian and Austrian export trade.

In 1934 Italian influence in Austria reached its height. Ever since the 'Hirtenberg affair' when Austrian workers had exposed the smuggling of Italian arms into Hungary, Mussolini had been determined to settle accounts with Austrian Social Democracy. Austria had been ruled since 1922 by the Catholic Christian Social Party. This party's policy had been definitely conservative, but had respected the forms of Democracy. It relied on the support of the Catholic peasantry and the bourgeoisie. Since 1931 the increasing misery of the working class, and the fear of Socialism displayed by the Viennese bourgeoisie and the provinces, caused increasing bitterness on Right and Left. A Fascist military organisation, the Heimwehr, led by Prince Starhemberg, openly prepared for Civil War. In March 1933 the Christian Social leader, Dollfuss, proclaimed a Dictatorship. A new Constitution was produced, based on the Papal Encyclical 'Quadragesimo Anno'. The regime cultivated the closest relations with Italy, and was encouraged to put into practice the Christian principles which it announced, by exterminating the Socialists.

Throughout the year the situation grew more tense, and in February 1934 the Social Democratic leaders, faced with inevitable destruction, called a last desperate rising. After a few days of civil war the Government won. Its victory was followed by mass arrests of Socialists, many severe sentences of imprisonment and an unknown number of executions. All expression of oppositional opinions, in word or print, was forbidden, and Austria became a Fascist State.

Now, having, with the help of the Duce, made mortal enemies of one-third of the nation, the Government had to face a new threat. As long as Brüning was in power in Germany, the Austrian Clericals had favoured Union with the Reich (Anschluss). Now that the heathen Hitler had taken his place their enthusiasm for their northern brothers rapidly waned. Moreover, for Mussolini's designs against Jugoslavia, a link with Hungary through Austria was essential. Loss of Italian supremacy in Vienna would mean an end to all Italian plans in the Danubian Basin. Therefore the Duce supported Dollfuss as resolutely against the Nazis as against the Socialists.

Outside help could not, however, prevent the regime from

being hated in Austria. A large part of the Austrian bourgeoisie and intelligentsia were connected by commercial or
sentimental ties with the Third Reich. Many of them were
strongly anti-Clerical. Anti-Semitism was very old in Vienna,
and was used by Nazi supporters against the Dollfuss Government, which showed tolerance to the Jews. Finally a part of
the working class, especially the unemployed, having lost
sympathy with the Trade Unions who could do nothing for
them, turned in despair and hatred to Nazism.

The climax came on 25 July 1934 when a band of Nazis
captured the Ministry on the Vienna Ballhausplatz and
murdered the Chancellor, Dr Dollfuss. The rebellion was, however, quickly suppressed by the Government, and Mussolini
ostentatiously mobilised on the Brenner. As Hitler was not
yet ready to risk war, the Anschluss plan was dropped for
three years.[1]

Italian policy in Austria provoked great distrust in Jugoslavia. The rebels of July 1934 fled across the Carinthian
frontier to Slovenia, where the authorities received them
kindly. Jugoslavia made it clear that she preferred the Anschluss to a restoration of the Habsburg Dynasty, of which the
Vienna regime talked a good deal both before and after the
murder. The implacable opposition to the Habsburgs was
shared by Roumania and to a lesser extent by Czechoslovakia,
even though the latter was obviously more directly threatened
by an extension of the frontiers of the Reich. The events of
July caused a deterioration of Italo-Jugoslav relations, which
came to a climax with the murder in October of King Alexander
in Marseilles. There was no doubt that the organisers of the
murder had enjoyed for years the help of the Italian and
Hungarian Governments. The French Government, however,
wished at all costs to secure an agreement with Italy against
the rising German menace, and therefore put pressure on
Jugoslavia to say nothing about the Italian share in the crime,
while inducing Italy to persuade Hungary to adopt a conciliatory attitude. Thus the 'solution' of the Marseilles incident,
acclaimed by many well-meaning people as a 'triumph of

---

[1] For a full account of the Austrian tragedy from the Peace to 1938, see
G. E. R. Gedye, *Fallen Bastions*, 1939. Mr Gedye, as a correspondent in Vienna
for thirteen years, has unrivalled knowledge of the subject. Another interesting
book is F. Borkenau, *Austria and After*, 1938, which summarises the most
important factors in the collapse of Austria.

the League of Nations', was in point of fact a peculiarly discreditable piece of 'secret diplomacy'.

The death of King Alexander was undoubtedly an international disaster. The king had always been true to the French political system in foreign policy. His successors, frightened of Italy and disgusted with the French attitude to the murder, began to listen to the sweet blandishments of the Third Reich. Meanwhile the Franco-Italian negotiations led to the Mussolini-Laval Agreement of January 1935, and in April the announcement of the introduction of conscription in Germany was met by a not very convincing 'Stresa Front' of Britain, France and Italy, whose representatives solemnly met—to protest. In the summer of 1935 the Abyssinian crisis developed, and the labours of Pierre Laval were undone by the outburst of popular indignation in Britain which led to the imposition of sanctions on Italy by the League of Nations. The results were the conquest of Abyssinia, and the appearance, on the outbreak of the Spanish War in 1936, of a new diplomatic constellation, the 'Berlin-Rome Axis'.

ITALY BETWEEN THE WESTERN POWERS AND GERMANY

From the summer of 1936 onwards the place of Italy as the chief disturber of the peace in Eastern Europe was taken by Germany. Italy had done a good job by keeping the wounds open for sixteen years and by turning the knife from time to time. Now she had to resign herself to second place.

Ever since 1870, when Italy achieved unity and the Prussian victories transformed the balance of power in Europe, there had been only two policies for Italy.

She could regard Germany as her principal enemy. Such a view would have plenty of historical justification, for ever since the Saxon Emperor Otto I Northern Italy had been the object of German greed. The last of the German rulers of Northern Italy had been the Habsburgs, who had not been driven out of Lombardy and Venetia until 1859 and 1866. Even after 1870 Austria-Hungary, which fell as the years passed increasingly under the influence of the new German Empire, had retained at Trieste a great port on the Adriatic coast. There were grounds enough for fearing Germany. But

Italy alone could not resist a State whose population was nearly twice her own, and whose economic resources were immensely superior. If Italy was to resist Germany, she must maintain friendly relations with Great Britain and France. But in this case she must abandon such ambitions as conflicted with British and French security in the Mediterranean and in Africa. She must be content with a status of theoretical equality but practical inferiority as one of three Western Powers.

Alternatively, Italy could decide to carve herself an Empire at the expense of Britain and France. In this case she must rely on the help of Germany. She would risk losing her independence, for it was hardly to be supposed that a powerful Germany would allow an artificially independent Austria to survive, or, having swallowed little Austria, that she would long consent to be separated by a narrow Italo-Slovene corridor from the sea. And the presence of a Germany of 80,000,000 citizens on the Adriatic would be a greater threat than that of a feeble Austria-Hungary.

Italian policy has no escape from this dilemma. All Italian statesmen realise the fundamental community of interest of Italy with the Western Powers against the German colossus. But at the same time Italian nationalists resent the superior attitude adopted towards their country by Britain and France. Italy has as old a history as any European country, save Greece. Of all the factors that have made up modern European civilisation the contribution of medieval Italy is perhaps the greatest. But centuries of foreign rule and internal division deprived Italy of a share in the spoils of the expansion of Europe. Britain, France, Spain, Holland and Portugal grabbed what they could while Italy was powerless. The Italian nation of to-day is young and vigorous. The population trend of Italy resembles that of Eastern Europe rather than that of the West or of Germany. Italy is a poor country, and suffers from an overpopulation problem comparable to that of the Balkans, Poland and Roumania. Italian nationalists observed the selfish commercial and immigration policy of the Western European and American States. Foreign markets were closed to Italian goods and foreign countries to Italian men and women. Italian prestige was not humoured by the grant of colonies. France, with her high standard of living, falling population and empty country, aggressively asserted her superiority and treated Italy as a poor relation. Britain dominated the sea that washes the shores of the Italian peninsula. The distribution of prestige and wealth between the three Western Powers did not correspond with the needs of the three peoples or the trends of the three populations. Collaboration with the west might be in the lasting interest of Italy, but Italy could not accept it unless Britain and France were prepared seriously to alter the balance of power to the advantage of Italy. As there was no sign of such willingness, a strong current of opinion in Italy favoured the policy of resisting Britain and France, using such help as could be found—if need be, that of Germany. They no doubt believed that the time would come when, having with German help forced the Western Powers, by 'persuasion' or by force, to disgorge some of their possessions, Italy could turn about and join the weakened and chastened, but still strong, Western Powers, against the too dangerous Germany.

There were strong arguments on either side, but Italy could not and cannot avoid the choice. Either Imperialist Expansion at the expense of National Independence, by joining Germany against the west, or a somewhat drab independence maintained, at the expense of imperial ambitions, by joining the west against Germany. The first policy was more likely to bring Glory, the latter Security.

Mussolini never hesitated. He had come to power on a programme of extreme nationalism, contrasted with the pacifism of his adversaries of the Left. He himself had always been more interested in foreign policy than in anything else. He was determined to be a Great Man, to throw his weight about and to seize any territory he could find in any continent. For the first fourteen years he had a clear field in Eastern Europe as both Germany and Russia were absent. It is true that he did not achieve much, for he could not afford a conflict in the Mediterranean with the Western Powers. But he made the preparations for the catastrophe. When Germany became a Great Power again, he had to make the choice. There could be no doubt as to his decision. Committed to a policy of Imperialism, he was bound to go against the west. Austria may have stuck in his throat, but he chose Germany.

This decision became clear after the Abyssinian War, but it is a ridiculous mistake to believe that it was caused by it.

That the policy of Britain and France in the Abyssinian War was the worst possible, need hardly be proved. It is one of the few things on which Left and Right are agreed. But if Britain and France had politely handed Mussolini Abyssinia, they would not have won his gratitude. That public opinion in Italy was annoyed by the British attitude is true, but hardly important. Mussolini was out for control of the Mediterranean, for Tunisia, Corsica, Somaliland, Kenya, Egypt and as much more as he could get. And as none of this would have been surrendered by Britain or France, he was bound to join with Germany. The fault of British and French policy—and here Right and Left are no longer in agreement—was not that it did not help the Duce to Addis Ababa, but that it did not break him when the chance was offered, before Germany was yet strong. And this fault is only a part of the supreme fault, in which the British Conservative Party should have the chief blame, but for which the whole British people is largely responsible—the failure to keep Britain armed.

From 1936 onwards, then, Italy and Germany marched together. Italy had to cut her losses in Eastern Europe. And the losses were not heavy. The real importance of Austria to Italy had been as a link connecting her with Hungary, which latter was necessary to her as a means of pressure on Jugoslavia. The same end could be served far more effectively by alliance with the Reich. German pressure on Jugoslavia was a much better means of inducing that country to abandon her Francophile policy than was the pressure of Hungary alone. If Jugoslavia should prove unwilling, she could be partitioned, Italy taking part of Slovenia and Dalmatia, Germany and the smaller neighbours the rest. There was no reason to suppose that a scheme of partition of the Balkan Peninsula into German and Italian spheres of influence was not possible. Germany need not interfere with Italian aims in the Adriatic, Macedonia and the Aegean. And if the prize of collaboration with Germany was control of the whole Mediterranean, the final goal towards which Italy's Balkan ambitions were mere stepping-stones, there was little ground for apprehension. The threat to Trieste would remain, but much would have been gained. And in fact Hitler was so anxious for Italian friendship that he was prepared to be generous. His conviction that

Germany needs Italy as an Ally can be found in *Mein Kampf*, and it has not changed with the passing of years. This sympathy of the Führer for Italy, so unusual in Austrians, has never been satisfactorily explained. It stood the Duce in good stead.

Italy, therefore, threw herself wholeheartedly into alliance with Germany. As long as her political structure was Fascist, and her foreign policy was Imperialist, there was no other possibility. Mussolini finally took this decision during the Abyssinian War, and he never looked back. Rumours of Germano-Italian dissension, however, were cleverly circulated from time to time. During the immediate pre-war period Führer and Duce took turns in truculence and politeness. While the one would demand a concession, the other would blandly offer his 'mediation' at a price. A few months after one crisis was 'solved' to the advantage of one partner, another would be started by the other. The manœuvre was often repeated, and invariably succeeded. So cleverly was the game played that not only men like Mr Chamberlain and his friends, totally ignorant of the past or present state of Europe, or Balkan politicians, pleased to regard themselves as Machiavellian geniuses brilliantly playing off their two great neighbours against each other, but even learned and experienced Western diplomats and journalists were deceived.

AIM AND METHODS OF GERMAN POLICY

German policy in Eastern Europe was aimed, as everyone now sees, and many have realised for years past, at full political, economic and military control of the whole space between Germany and Russia, in order to be able to strike, according to circumstances, either at the Soviet Union or at the Western Powers.

This control was prepared by a long, and brilliantly conducted, diplomatic battle. The whole area was not ultimately occupied without the use of force, but victory was assured beforehand by the Diplomatic War of 1936–39.

It is impossible without a mixture of disgust and anguish to recall the nonsense written during those years about the 'stupidity' and 'tactlessness' of German Diplomacy. The ignorant complacency of British newspapers and public speakers caused consternation even among the friends of Britain in Europe, and the historian of the future will certainly see in this one of the least edifying pages of our nation's history. German Diplomacy did not consist merely in politeness to crowned heads or prime ministers—although it could rival its opponents in this field when necessary—but used every weapon, open or secret, fair or foul, that was available. It was based on careful study of the history, economy, politics, social structure and psychology of each nation with which it had to deal, made possible by innumerable contacts of individual Germans with people of every class and origin in every country. The 'vulgar champagne-seller' von Ribbentrop outclassed the elegantly languid gentlemen opposed to him from the very start.

Perhaps the most important weapon of German Diplomacy was economic. The World Depression, followed by the fall of world prices and the closing of world markets, had reduced the States of Eastern Europe to a lamentable condition. Germany stepped into the breach. Indifferent to considerations of profit and loss, concerned only to accumulate the raw materials of war and reserves of foodstuffs, eager as far as possible to obtain these in markets where payment need not be made in strong currencies, the Third Reich had every interest in extending her trade with Eastern Europe.

The system by which Dr Schacht pushed German trade in these countries has been too often described in detail to need much treatment here.[1] Germany ordered large quantities of Eastern European products and then forced the Eastern European States individually to buy more from her in order to pay back the debt. She used her powerful position to compel them to accept goods of little value to them—large consignments of fountain-pens, mouth-organs, typewriters and binoculars. She paid for her imports prices well above the world-market level, but she repeatedly forced her partners to raise the exchange rate of the Reichsmark with their currency. The high prices offered by Germany affected the general internal price level of the Eastern European countries, and made all their exports so expensive that other countries became less willing than ever to buy their goods, thus in-

[1] See Graham Hutton, *Danubian Destiny*, the numerous works of Dr Paul Einzig and the back numbers of *The Economist*.

creasing still further their dependence on Germany. The more industrial equipment and machines the Eastern European countries bought, the more they depended on Germany for spare parts and replacements.

Gradually Germany acquired the whip hand. At any moment she could threaten to divert her trade elsewhere. The loss to Germany would be comparatively unimportant, for her trade with Eastern Europe made up a fairly small percentage of her total foreign trade. But for the small States it would mean ruin, a relapse into the swamp from which they had just begun to emerge, with concomitant political dangers which the Governments could not face. The economic stranglehold once established, Germany could use it for other than economic ends. Commercial and technical missions could provide useful cover for political and military espionage, and German buyers could use opportunities for political propaganda among the peasantry.

These evils did not escape the notice of the Eastern European Governments, but there was little that they could do to protect themselves. It was quite impossible to interest British, French or American business men, exclusively concerned with profits and in any case largely committed to trade with their Empires. Germany was able to offer Eastern Europe many industrial products which it dearly needed, and did not demand payment in dollars or sterling. The prices offered for their products were good, and the fact that quantities to be bought were fixed beforehand made possible preliminary planning of production, thus reducing the harm to be feared from future fluctuations of the trade cycle. Although the German interest in selling industrial products conflicted to a considerable extent with the nascent industry of Eastern Europe, there were many branches of industry which were not so threatened, and one school of thought argued plausibly that German help would be invaluable in the planning of an industrialisation which would take account of the interest of the Eastern European economy as a whole. In any case any Government which refused the material benefits offered by German trade would have risked severe unpopularity and ultimate overthrow.

A second weapon of German Diplomacy was anti-Semitism. It has not yet been generally understood that Nazi persecution of the Jews served not only to find a scapegoat for popular discontent within Germany, but to win the Third Reich popularity abroad. The young men of the Roumanian, Hungarian and Polish bourgeoisies aspiring to seize the jobs of the Jews in industry and trade came to regard Germany as a Promised Land of Social Justice, fighting for the rights of the oppressed victims of the World Jewish Plot. Anti-Semitic movements such as the Iron Guard received money from Berlin, and made their influence felt in the highest places.

A third weapon was anti-Bolshevik propaganda. Nazi spokesmen took great pains to convince the Eastern European despots that the Third Reich was the only barrier protecting them from the Bolshevik flood. The Bolshevik obsession had, we have seen, dominated the Eastern European ruling classes ever since 1918, and the German argument was strengthened when in 1935 France, their traditional protector, made an alliance with the Soviet Union. German and Italian 'non-intervention' in the Spanish War raised the prestige of Hitler in Conservative, and especially Catholic, circles, which were little disturbed by the persecution of the Church in Germany. The existence of the aggressive German Dictatorship, ready to 'non-intervene' whenever necessary to strike down the Red Monster, was a source of comfort to all the little Dictatorships, which felt relieved of the necessity to make concessions to popular discontent. Germany encouraged them in their intransigence, knowing that such a policy would demoralise the peoples and undermine the powers of resistance of the States.

A fourth weapon, used simultaneously and in the same places as the Bolshevik bogey, was social revolutionary propaganda. Germany posed as the defender of the oppressed peasantry against Jews and landowners. In Hungary and Roumania German agents simultaneously frightened landowners and capitalists with the spectre of the hungry, disinherited masses and excited the masses against the landlords. That the Nazis were using both arguments was no secret, and it is a tribute to the skilful demagogy of Hitler and to the powers of self-deception of the Eastern Europeans that the manœuvre invariably succeeded. As usual, those who proved most sorely deceived were the peasantry. Germany's propagandists offered Social Justice to the peasants up till 1940, but once her strategic aims in the Danubian Basin had been achieved, she dropped the idea, and gave full support to the big landowners, on whose more efficient methods of production she relied for her war-time food supply. But the revolutionary agitation of 1936–40 had paved the way to her success.

But the most important cause of German success lay in the diplomatic victories won over the Western Powers. Not only were the peoples of Eastern Europe, longing for simple civil liberties and social reforms, which are elementary principles of Democratic Government and are threatened by Dictatorships, the natural allies of the Western Powers against the expansion of Germany, their eternal historical enemy; the ruling classes too infinitely preferred Anglo-French supremacy in Europe to German. Educated men and women in all Eastern Europe except Hungary regarded France as their spiritual home, and all, Hungarians included, considered Britain the greatest World Power and respected her as a just and honourable influence in Europe, where she was, they believed, sufficiently disinterested to be fair. But France and Britain cared neither for the peoples nor for the rulers of Eastern Europe. And as Hitler scored one success after another—Saar, Conscription, Remilitarisation of the Rhineland, Spain, Austria, Czechoslovakia, Memel—the immense capital of good will and esteem for the Western Powers was frittered away. When the creators of the 1919 Settlement denounced their own work, and pleasantly shook hands with the robber chiefs, it was not astonishing if the small men crawled into their own holes, and tried to make the best terms with the new victors.

Polish Policy

The first of the Eastern European Powers to break away was Poland. The first fifteen years after the Peace had been a fortunate period for the Poles, since the weakness of their two great neighbours had relieved them of immediate danger. The gradual recovery of Russia and the advent of Hitler to power in Germany changed this situation. The loudly proclaimed hatred of Hitler against the Soviet Union raised the spectre of a German-Russian War across Polish territory. Soviet help against Germany could not be attractive to the Pilsudski regime, which was based on repression by force of all popular discontent, and in which since 1926 the influence of landowners and industrialists had notably increased. Poland had signed in 1932 a Non-Aggression Pact with the Soviet Union, but this was about as far as she was prepared to go. Before the new German danger the most natural place to seek help was France. Pilsudski consulted the Paris Government about the possibility of joint preventive action against Hitler, but received an evasive reply. The Four-Power Pact of 1933 caused anger and alarm in Warsaw, both as a blow to the prestige of Poland, which liked to consider itself a Great Power, and as a sign that Western Powers were willing to go far towards concession to Germany, and even to favour territorial revision. Pilsudski convinced himself that little was to be expected from France. At the same time Hitler, still completely isolated, was looking round for a friend. After some months of secret negotiations Germany and Poland on 26 January 1934 surprised the world by the announcement of a Ten Years' Pact of Non-Aggression.

Her prestige and independence superficially strengthened by this Pact, Poland was now able to take an arrogant attitude towards France and her small neighbours. She refused to take part in the negotiations for an 'Eastern Locarno' in the spring of 1935. The conclusion of the Franco-Soviet Pact in May further alienated Poland from France, whom German propaganda now began to make out as the handmaid of the Bolsheviks. The death of the Marshal in the same month removed a possible restraint on Colonel Josef Beck, since 1932 Foreign Minister in succession to the Francophile August Zaleski.

Beck's policy has been the subject of much controversy ever since 1934. In retrospect it is perhaps possible to see it more clearly. It cannot strictly be described as 'Germanophile'. Beck undoubtedly put first and last the interest of Poland, as interpreted by himself. It was the difficult task of Polish policy to balance between Germany and Russia, both of which were regarded as the eternal enemies of Poland. Beck had no love for Germany, and no desire to serve German Imperialism. He well knew the hatred of the Polish people for the Germans. This hatred is in fact far more deeply rooted in the average Pole than hatred of Russia. There is great similarity of character between Russians and Poles. Individuals of the two nations usually like each other. Russo-Polish hatred is essentially political, based on unhappy memories of the misdoings of Russian bureaucrats and Polish landlords. The feeling of

the Pole towards the German is quite different. It is both
political and personal hatred, based on complete lack of
mutual understanding, unbridgeable difference of mentality
and a far longer history of war and oppression than in the
case of Russia.

All this Beck knew, and understood that Polish policy could
never be subordinated to German interests. There could be
no doubt that if Germany threatened vital Polish interests,
Poland would fight. Yet the fact remains that, despite his
intentions, Beck did become a tool of German Imperialism.
The 1934 Pact was more than a mutual renunciation of
aggression. It marked the beginning of German-Polish active
collaboration in an aggressive policy in Eastern Europe.

The repeated visits of General Goering to the Radziwill
estates were not simple hunting trips. Poland not only hoped
that German expansion to the east would take the southern
route, through Austria and Czechoslovakia to Roumania and
the Ukraine; she actively helped Germany in this direction.
The small Polish minority in Teschen was instructed to follow
Henlein's lead in making trouble for Czechoslovakia. Father
Hlinka's ambitious assistant Sidor received moral and material
help from Warsaw, and great hopes were held of trouble in
Slovakia. In Roumania Polish agents had close relations with
the Iron Guard, while Polish diplomacy worked on parallel
lines with that of the Reich to induce King Carol to abandon
his ties with Czechoslovakia. The relations between Poland
and Hungary became steadily more intimate, and Polish
spokesmen expressed open sympathy for the revisionist aims
of General Gömbös.

The aim of this policy was the destruction of Czechoslovakia
and the deflection of German expansion towards the south-
east. It was hoped that thus Polish territory would not be
needed for the German advance, which, the attitude of the
Western Powers being what it was, there seemed no possibility
of stopping. The end, so the Warsaw politicians calculated,
would be the destruction by Germany of Bolshevik Russia.
The danger of Revolution would be removed, the Colonels'
regime would be saved from any internal threat, and Germany
in her gratitude for Polish diplomatic help would give Poland
a few chunks of Russian territory. Then later, if a strengthened
Germany should prove troublesome, Poland could hope that

the Western Powers, at last alive to the danger, would give her assistance, or, better still, that Germany could be again diverted from Poland, this time against the Western Powers, which would ultimately beat her while Poland remained prosperously and comfortably neutral.

The basis of Polish policy, then, was not love of Germany, but a combination of territorial greed, fear of revolution on the part of the landowners and colonels, mistrust of the strength and will to resistance of the Western Powers, and the supreme confidence of Colonel Beck in his own Machiavellian genius. This policy played an extremely important part in the preparation of German plans for Eastern Europe.

THE BREAK-UP OF THE FRENCH SYSTEM

The second of the gainers of 1918 to seek friendship with Germany was Jugoslavia. The new policy is associated with the name of Dr Milan Stojadinović, but it could not have been carried on without the approval of the Regent Prince Paul, who was the real ruler of the country, and who had always been more interested in foreign policy than in internal affairs. Paul was exceptionally accessible to the Bolshevik bogey argument, and he was encouraged to seek closer relations with Germany by the attitude of the Western Powers, particularly by that of Britain. The British Minister had during the last few years of the reign of Alexander occupied a special position in Belgrade, and this continued to be the case under Paul, who had received his education in England, and was regarded as a staunch Anglophile. The inclination of Jugoslav policy towards Germany was exceedingly unpopular in the country, and was not made more acceptable by the circulation of 'semi-official' rumours by Government agents, to the effect that the policy had the full support of Britain, and had even been undertaken on British advice. These rumours, which were widely believed in Jugoslavia, did not reduce the deep-seated antipathy of the Jugoslavs to Germany, but they succeeded in creating a large measure of distrust of Britain.

The German approach to Jugoslavia began through Bulgaria. The Germans, accurately informed by their representatives of the state of feeling in the Balkans, noted the desire of the Serbian and Bulgarian peoples for more friendly relations, and decided to use this for their own ends. This desire originated in the two peoples, and was for a long time resisted by their rulers. It was combined with the desire for free Government and Balkan Peace. These last two ideas were not at all to the liking of the Germans. The Velchev *coup d'état* gave expression to the desire of the Bulgarian people for friendship with Jugoslavia, and was at the same time directed against Italy and Germany, and towards understanding with France. The overthrow of Velchev and Georgiev by King Boris removed the threat to Germany and Italy. The Royal Dictatorship cultivated good relations with the Axis, and the German economic stranglehold on Bulgaria was tightened.

Germany now persuaded her Italian Ally that the old policy of open support for Macedonian terrorism against Jugoslavia was no longer useful. Bulgaria was cast for a new role in Axis strategy. Boris was urged to keep up the appearance of friendship for Jugoslavia. The foreign policy of Velchev was to be continued, and Bulgaria was to be used as a means of seducing Jugoslavia from her obligations first to the Balkan and then to the Little Entente. In January 1937 a Pact of Eternal Friendship was signed between Jugoslavia and Bulgaria. The Pact gave official expression to the genuine wish of the two peoples, but it was entirely insincere. The Stojadinović and Kiosseivanov Governments were unpopular Dictatorships, fearing and hated by their peoples, and each prepared to do the other down when the occasion should arise. The Pact was merely one more move in the game of Berlin.

Roumania showed more resistance to German pressure. Carol II lived in perpetual fear of 'Bolshevism', the danger of which was made more real by the unsettled Bessarabian Question. French influence was still the strongest in Bucarest, and in 1934–36 it was used in favour of a Roumano-Russian reconciliation. The Franco-Czechoslovak and Soviet-Czechoslovak Pacts could only come into effect if Soviet troops were able to pass through Poland or Roumania. The intransigent attitude of Poland made Paris concentrate its efforts on Roumania. The presence of the Red Army was no less feared by Roumania than by Poland.

As long as Titulescu, the champion in Roumania of the League of Nations, remained Foreign Minister, France felt confident of Roumanian support. In 1936, however, he was dismissed by the king. For the next two years at the conferences of the Little Entente Roumania was torn between Jugoslavia, which had no diplomatic relations with the Soviet Union and was moving steadily into the German orbit, and Czechoslovakia, which urged a speedy settlement with the Russians. Carol attempted to steer between the two extremes. He assured Czechoslovakia and France of his loyalty, and he pushed forward the building of the Bukovina-Transylvania railway, by which, when completed, Soviet troops would be able to pass through the north of Roumania to Czechoslovakia. But he held the Russians at arm's length and took great care to give no offence to Berlin. His aim was undoubtedly the independence of his country, and he was fully aware of the German danger. But the nation's powers of resistance were undermined by his internal policy. Like Schuschnigg in Austria, he tolerated the activities of the Germanophiles, and savagely repressed not only the extreme Left but moderate Democrats.

Alone of the Eastern European States Czechoslovakia stood up to German pressure. The strategic position of Bohemia-Moravia, surrounded by mountains, was of capital importance. As Bismarck had once said, he who holds Bohemia, holds Europe. Czechoslovakia remained a democratic State, and gave shelter to the enemies of Nazism. She lay half-way between France and Russia, the value of whose Alliance depended on her preservation. She had a magnificent armaments industry, and her army was believed to be efficient. She was wedged between Saxony and Prussia on the one side and Bavaria and Austria on the other. She was, as Dr Goebbels often pointed out, a dagger pointed at the heart of Germany.

Hitler was concerned above all to remove this threat. He must have all Eastern Europe under his influence in order to be able to attack Russia or France, but he could not control Eastern Europe unless Czechoslovakia would change her policy. It is unquestionable that public opinion in Germany was interested in the fate of the three million Germans of Czechoslovakia, and that indignation was created by the campaign of lies about their 'oppression' by the Czechs. It is also true that Hitler aimed always at the incorporation in his Reich of the German communities beyond its frontiers. But these were secondary considerations. The pressing need was to 'neutralise' Czechoslovakia. If Beneš had been willing to follow the examples of Beck and Stojadinović, Hitler would have been content to leave the 'Sudeten Germans' where they were.

Offers were several times made to Prague. Abandonment of the Franco-Russian orientation would have won Czechoslovakia favourable terms. But neither Masaryk nor Beneš would accept such terms. They were devoted to the cause of Democracy. They knew that an increase of the power of the Third Reich would mean the end of the civil liberties and social institutions of the Czech people. And they believed that France and Britain would support them. Up till the summer of 1938 all French Governments protested their devotion to the Alliance, and the attitude of British public opinion in the Abyssinian crisis was considered proof that Britain would not abandon Czechoslovakia to her fate. And so Hitler, seeing that he could not win over the Republic, decided to destroy it.

During 1936 and 1937 there was much talk in Central Europe of a Vienna-Prague-Budapest 'Triangle' for the defence of the Danubian Basin against external Imperialism. It was favoured by such men as Milan Hodža, the Slovak leader and later Czechoslovak Prime Minister, and the Hungarian politician Tibor Eckhardt. The plan never took concrete form.

The Hungarians feared Germany, the traditional enemy of their country, but the Budapest Government could not accept collaboration with Czechoslovakia unless the latter were willing to make some territorial concessions. This some Czech leaders might have been prepared to do, but opposition in Slovakia to the slightest change was overwhelming, and particularly among those political groups who were most hostile to the Czechs and most willing to listen to the blandishments of Berlin and Warsaw. Moreover Jugoslavia and Roumania, although hesitant enough when it was a question of supporting Czechoslovakia against Germany, were insistent that no revision should be made, which would set a precedent for similar concessions by themselves.

Austria was more directly threatened than Hungary by German expansion, but she too was unwilling to collaborate with Czechoslovakia. The best friends of the Czechs in Austria, the Social Democrats, had had no influence on policy since

1934. Schuschnigg, the successor of Dollfuss, was determined to prevent absorption of his country in Nazi Germany, but he was no less determined to keep the Left suppressed. Among the Austrian bourgeoisie Nazi ideas were constantly spreading, and many members of Schuschnigg's monopolist political organisation, the 'Vaterländische Front', who were outwardly good Catholics and loyal servants of the regime, were secretly working for the Nazis. Business, the bureaucracy and the police were full of agents of Hitler, who denounced Austrian patriots, whatever their views, as 'Reds', and systematically undermined the authority of the Government.

Schuschnigg, following Dollfuss' foreign policy, relied on Italian friendship. Italian advice was to seek better relations with the Third Reich, to make further concessions to Hitler, and to trust 'Uncle Benito' to see to it that Austria would remain independent. Schuschnigg devotedly obeyed his master's instructions, and avoided contact with either France or Czechoslovakia. Many Austrians—not only of the Left—saw clearly that this could only end one way, but their counsels were not heeded, and they had no means of influencing events.

In February 1938 Schuschnigg was summoned to Berchtesgaden to hear Hitler's terms. A month later the German army was in Vienna. At the last moment the unfortunate Chancellor attempted to resist. He appealed to the people to defend their country, allowed the old Socialist leaders to hold meetings, begged for help in Prague and Paris. Then, when the underground leaders of the Left had had just enough time to expose themselves to Hitler's spies, Schuschnigg capitulated. And while the Gestapo tortured and murdered Austrian Democrats, Socialists and Jews, Cardinal Innitzer had the Swastika flown from the graceful spire of St Stephen's Cathedral, and the Archbishop of Canterbury (now Lord Lang) read in the House of Lords a letter received from a friend in Vienna describing how wonderful the New Order was.

The Anschluss placed Czechoslovakia in mortal danger. Even now perhaps Prague could have obtained good terms by adapting its foreign policy to the needs of Berlin. But France protested her loyalty, Russia stuck to the commitments of the Pact and British statesmen had repeatedly stressed the absolute unity of policy of London and Paris. In those days the word of Englishmen and Frenchmen still

commanded profound respect, and Beneš maintained his attitude. He was willing to make every reasonable concession
to the German minority, but he refused to change the frontiers
of the State or to give up his foreign commitments. Meanwhile his small Allies of the Little and Balkan Ententes grew
ever more timorous. The meeting of the Little Entente in the
summer revealed wide differences of opinion. While about a
hundred thousand Jugoslavs offered their services to the
Czechoslovak Legation and Consulates for the event of war,
Stojadinović drew closer his relations with Berlin. In July
was held in Prague the last great festival of the national
gymnastic association—the Sokols. It was a tremendous
demonstration of national solidarity and of confidence in the
Government. Thousands of Jugoslav, Roumanian and Bulgarian delegates were cheered by the crowds in the streets of
Prague. In Poland the Peasant Party and the Socialists held
meetings in favour of Czechoslovakia while Colonel Beck
plotted his share in her dismemberment. Even in Hungary
a large part of public opinion hoped that Czechoslovak resistance would be successful.

It was the test case, watched by all Europe. The results
were the sudden visits of Chamberlain to Germany, the mid-
night ultimatum to Czechoslovakia from her former Allies,
the delirious enthusiasm of the representatives of Britain's
Democracy at the news of the Duce's 'invitation' to Munich,
and the frantic cheers evoked by the scrap of paper waved at
the aerodrome as a proof that there would now be 'Peace
for Our Time'. In Prague the people assembled in Wenceslas
Square and demanded the resignation of the Government and
a war of desperation. Demonstrations against France and
Britain filled the cities of the Republic. Hodža was replaced
by General Sirovy, who, though acclaimed as the strong man
and saviour of the country, executed the Munich terms. For
five months the Government of the Rump Republic, led by
the Agrarian leader Beran, used the popular fury against the
Western Powers to further collaboration with the Third Reich,
the only course left. But Hitler soon decided that he could
not trust the Czechs, and that they were incapable of becoming
real friends of Germany. The newly created autonomous
Government of Slovakia and the Central Government of Prague
were easily played off against each other, and on 15 March

1939 Hitler marched into Prague. Slovakia received her 'Independence' under the Christian paladin Monsignor Tiso. The most immediate sufferer from Munich was Poland.

The Munich settlement had given to Ruthenia, the third province of the rump Czechoslovakia, an autonomous Government, nominally subordinate to Prague, presided over by the Uniate priest Monsignor Voloshin. This tiny province was made the centre of a large and expensive Ukrainian propaganda organisation. Quantities of fanatical young men, trained in the school of up-to-date Nationalism and Fascism in Berlin, poured into the wretched village of Hust to give lectures on the Great Ukrainian Fatherland to audiences of dazed peasants from the mountains, who hardly understood one word in ten. A Storm Trooper organisation known as the 'Sich' was also organised. The whole ridiculous comedy, with its bombastic braying about making a 'Piedmont' of the most miserable hole in Eastern Europe, had only one purpose—to excite the Ukrainian population of Poland, and if possible also of the Soviet Union, to help the future German invasion. The Poles did not like the idea, and the Hungarians had their eyes on Ruthenia.

In March 1939 Hitler suddenly dropped the whole scheme. By forcing the dismemberment of Czechoslovakia, he left Ruthenia to the mercies of the Hungarians. The adolescents of the Sich were the only people who worried much about it. They resisted the Hungarian army and were mercilessly mown down. With much blaring of trumpets in Warsaw, and rather less in Budapest, the common frontier of Poland and Hungary was established.

There were people in both capitals, of strong anti-German feelings, whom hatred of Czechoslovakia had so blinded that they genuinely believed that the destruction of the Republic and the erection over its corpse of a Hungaro-Polish frontier would form a strong barrier to German expansion towards the east. Now that the modern fortifications of the Bohemian mountain fastnesses and the Škoda armament works were in German hands, an impregnable line of defence was to be created from nothing across the plains of Pannonia and Galicia.

The illusion died quickly. Hungaro-Polish friendship was essentially a relationship of two aristocracies. The Polish and Hungarian peoples were ignorant and indifferent towards each other. The Hungarian Government took a more realistic view of the situation than the Polish. It sympathised with its neighbour, but it could do little to help it. So now Poland was surrounded on three sides by Germany or German Protectorates. The acquisition of 80,000 Poles and 250,000 Czechs in Teschen and the creation of a short frontier with a helpless small Power were small consolation for the horrible reality. In the words of Goethe,

> Die ich rief, die Geister
> Werd' ich nun nicht los.

It is not yet possible to give a verdict on the Munich Agreement. Whether the months between the Anschluss and the Sudeten crisis could have been used by the British Government as effectively as the almost exactly equal period between the fall of Prague and the invasion of Poland was used in the following year for the preparation of public opinion for the necessity of war; whether the Pacifism of British policy in 1938 was mainly due to the mood of the British people or to the intention of the British Government; whether the twenty months between the Munich Agreement and the invasion of the Low Countries were used fully to improve Allied armaments; whether the superiority of German military and air power over that of the Allies was greater in September 1938 than in September 1939 or May 1940—these questions, on which the merits of the Munich Agreement depend, can only be answered when the Official Secrets of to-day are made known to the historians of the future. And perhaps Whitehall will never disgorge them.

What can be said with certainty is that Munich was the greatest defeat and the greatest blow to prestige suffered by Britain since the loss of the American colonies. All over Europe it was assumed, with anguish and horror, that Britain had handed the Continent to the Axis. Many decided, against their natural sympathies, that they must now throw in their lot with Germany. Uncompromising Democrats—of whom there were many—could not do this. Despair and ruin stared them in the face. In their impotent rage they cursed the name of Chamberlain, the symbol to some of capitalist Reaction and to all of the unforgivable faults of the whole British nation—ignorance of Europe, military unreadiness and belief that words could conjure evil spirits or the methods of the Board Room appease ravening wolves.

The Munich Agreement had excluded the Soviet Union from the company of European Great Powers, and had removed the strategic basis of the Franco-Soviet Pact. The negotiations in the summer of 1939 between the Western Powers and the Soviet Union were not sincere on either side. Russia had no reason to endanger her existence for the sake of two Powers who had abundantly proved their hatred of her, and who were not in a position to give her any military assistance in the event of a war, of which she would have to bear the brunt. The Polish Government, confident, if official and semi-official utterances may be believed, that the Polish Army would quickly occupy Berlin, would not consider 'allowing' the Red Army to come to its aid. Distinguished British journalists declared that an alliance with the Soviet Union would only be a hindrance to the Allies. Thus, although the conclusion of the German-Soviet Pact of August was a shock to world opinion, it need not really have surprised anyone.

THE CONQUEST OF EASTERN EUROPE

The Eastern European State most immediately threatened by the outbreak of war and the partition of Poland was Roumania. Germany now had several means of pressure on Carol.

One was the illegal but still existent Iron Guard. Two years of persecution and changing international circumstances had weakened the Guard. From a mass movement for popular revolution, it had become a small, disciplined murder-gang, its only aim revenge on those responsible for Codreanu's death. On 20 September Prime Minister Armand Călinescu was murdered. His death was a great loss to Roumania, for he was the only resolute and courageous man among Carol's advisers, and firmly devoted to the cause of the Western Allies. The murder was followed by mass executions of Guardists in every province. All Prefects received orders to shoot three local Guardists. Some chose their men conscientiously, others, afraid of Guardist revenge, did not touch the local Iron Guard, but executed madmen or criminals from the State prison. The massacre caused more hatred against the Government, and did not improve the situation.

FRONTIERS OF HITLER'S EUROPE

The second German means of pressure was Hungarian Revisionism. This danger had become more acute since the occupation of Prague in March. On this occasion the Germans had used the Hungarian threat to obtain from Roumania an extremely far-reaching Trade Treaty, which amounted to a promise of permanent joint planning of the Roumanian economy. At the same time Carol had urgently asked for some sort of help in the west, and had obtained a guarantee from Mr Chamberlain which did not commit Roumania to help the Allies. From March onwards a large part of the Roumanian Army had been kept mobilised on the western frontier.

The third means of pressure of Berlin was the Russian threat. To seek a way out by appealing direct to Russia for a settlement of outstanding questions was hardly possible. Carol's personal antipathy to the Soviet regime made such action difficult at the best of times. Russia and Germany appeared to be working so closely together that no manœuvre by a small Power could separate them. The Allies were now on the worst possible terms with the Soviet Union, and would certainly not encourage any Roumanian *rapprochement* with it. The French newspapers, widely sold in Bucarest, were full of virulent attacks on Russia and hardly mentioned the fact that France was at war with Germany. A large number of distinguished British and French political personalities were clamouring for war with the Soviets. Thus, if he had made overtures to Moscow Carol would only have estranged the Western Powers and annoyed Germany. Moreover, it is unlikely that Moscow would have been willing to give him tolerable terms. The Baltic States provided an example far from encouraging.

So Carol increased the mobilisation, keeping large forces on both the northern and the western frontiers. The burden of the mobilisation on the population was severe. Taxes were mercilessly exacted, agriculture was disorganised by the removal of able-bodied men for the army, and food prices rose rapidly. Financial help from the Allies, such as was received by Turkey, would have helped the situation, but this could not be accepted without impairing Roumanian neutrality. One school of thought favoured the linking of Roumanian policy to that of Italy, but the 'Non-Belligerency' of the Duce appeared every month more clearly in its true light. There was little that Carol could do except wait and hope. He undoubtedly preferred the Western Powers to Germany, but events were against him. And his oppressive and inefficient regime deprived him in the emergency of the support of his people.

The collapse of France was followed by a last-moment attempt to throw Roumania into the arms of the Axis. On 27 June came the Soviet ultimatum for the cession of Northern Bukovina and all Bessarabia. Britain was clearly in no position to help, and the Axis remained silent. The loss of Bessarabia was extremely useful to the Axis. It created among a large number of Roumanian nationalists who had favoured an understanding with the Soviet Union, a great disillusionment. Such people were not very numerous, but they counted. The mass of the Roumanian people were indifferent, and the ruling clique cared little for the loss of a backward province that had only been a burden to the country. But a grievance was created among some of the decent elements of the Roumanian bourgeoisie, which was found useful a year later when the Axis needed Roumanian help against the Soviet Union.

It was on the whole to the advantage of the Axis that Bessarabia should be taken, but it was extremely important that it should be taken without fighting. If Roumania had declared war on Russia, Russian planes would have bombed the Roumanian oil wells, and the Russian army might have arrived in Ploeşti before the Germans or their Hungarian vassals could have got there. The destruction of Roumanian oil was one fatal blow that Germany must avoid at all costs. Therefore Germany, whose agents cursed Carol—who had for months past been braying about a 'Wall of fire, steel and cement' round Roumania's impregnable frontiers—for his ignominious surrender, instructed her diplomats to press the king to yield.

The double gain of the Axis from this affair was hardly compensated by the Russian gain. The Soviets had a claim of long standing to Bessarabia, and it is not surprising that they should have seized the opportunity to enforce it. Moreover, to advance to the mouth of the Danube was in keeping with their general plan of occupying strategic positions as far to the west as possible in preparation for the inevitable conflict with Germany. But when war came a year later the Bessarabian advanced position was soon lost. Although even if the Soviets had been generous to Roumania this could not have prevented Antonescu and his band from joining the German attack on Russia, at least he would have lacked any plausible propagandist argument to work up enthusiasm among the perplexed Roumanian peasant soldiers.

The Bessarabian crisis shook Carol; he was overthrown by the Transylvanian tragedy. From the beginning of July onwards the Hungarians and Bulgarians pressed for satisfaction on their claims. On German advice the Roumanian Government opened conversations with the former at Turnu Severin and with the latter at Craiova.

There was no doubt from the first that Southern Dobrudja would be ceded to Bulgaria. Few Roumanians cared about it. It had a predominantly Turkish and Bulgarian population. The Roumanians were newcomers, mostly Macedonian Vlachs colonised in this sparsely populated region with the double intention of developing its economic resources and of making the sea coast Roumanian. After feeble attempts to save a few scraps, the whole territory was handed over.

Transylvania was quite another matter. A very large number of Roumanians, including peasants and workers as well as intellectuals, felt strongly about this province, the 'cradle of the Roumanian race'. There was a strong popular movement for resistance, especially strong in Transylvania itself, but important throughout the country. The conversations at Turnu Severin broke down, and the Axis decided to 'mediate'. The Foreign Minister, Mihail Manoilescu, a conceited charlatan who fancied himself a great political thinker and had had his works translated even into Portuguese, a devoted admirer of Hitler and Mussolini, was summoned to Vienna. He arrived with a large staff of well-qualified experts, prepared for long discussions. Ribbentrop presented him with a map. He rang up the king. 'Mr Ribbentrop wants an answer at once. He can only wait a few hours unfortunately, as he has a pressing engagement elsewhere.'

Carol never needed honest advice so much as in that moment. But he had no one to turn to except the sycophants whom he had nominated to his 'Royal Council'. A few outside opinions were asked, including those of Maniu, Mihalache and

Constantin Bratianu. These gentlemen, who during the preceding two months had done nothing to force the hand of the Government, who had refused to put themselves at the head of the national movement for resistance, now declared their implacable opposition to surrender—and thanked God that they were not in Carol's place.

Carol had one trump card, not available to his Hungarian adversaries—the oil wells. He might have said, 'We will fight rather than accept this dismemberment. You may invade and conquer our country, but when you reach Ploeşti the refineries will be in ruins and the wells will be out of action for a year.' It is doubtful whether Hitler would then have insisted. But Carol was surrounded by weak men and German agents. He had no Călinescu to back him up. He lost his head. A rumour put round by Axis agents to the effect that the Russians were about to invade Moldavia, and that only Axis help could save Roumania from 'Bolshevism'—a pure invention—threw him and his friends into a panic. He surrendered.

Roumania in the late summer of 1940 presented a strange spectacle. The timid suggestions of British statesmen a year earlier that Roumania should consider slight concessions to Bulgaria in order to create an Eastern European block against Germany, had been indignantly rejected as an insult to Roumanian national honour. Now the whole area claimed by Bulgaria, and more than half Transylvania, with over a million Roumanians, were handed over without a murmur. The people cursed Carol for the disaster, but the hated king's successors organised green-shirted bands who danced the national dance in the Calea Victoriei, and greeted the events of August and September as a glorious victory. A month later troops of the Power which had mutilated their country were walking down the same street, and eight months after that Roumanian soldiers were dying to further the ambitions of their nation's enemy.

In the autumn of 1940, with his troops in Roumania and with Hungary willing, with some reservations, to play his game, Hitler could choose one of three directions for further expansion—south-east down the Black Sea coast to the Straits, north-east into the Ukraine, or south to the Aegean.

The attitude of Turkey was a vital factor from now onwards.

Since the Montreux Conference of July 1936 Turkey had had the right to fortify the Straits, and her barren Anatolian hills linked the Balkans with the Middle East. Before the war she had been courted by both sides, each of which had offered her important economic and financial benefits. True to the principles of the founder of the Republic, who died a year before the outbreak of war, she had favoured the Allies rather than Germany. In December 1939 the Anglo-Franco-Turkish Treaty was signed. When Italy entered the war, Turkey declared herself 'non-belligerent', and the collapse of France did not weaken her loyalty to Britain. In the summer and autumn of 1940 the Turkish Press was full of Allied news items and opinions, and Turkish officials stressed their country's devotion to her Ally.

During the first months of the war Turkey had had more to fear from Russia than from Germany. The traditional friendship between the Turkish Republic and the Soviet Union was somewhat shaken when in the winter of 1939 Foreign Minister Sarajoglu was peremptorily summoned to Moscow. But after some weeks of waiting and talking he returned to Ankara without having made any dangerous concessions. After the occupation of Roumania a direct German threat was added to the Russian danger. But Turkey stood up well to the war of nerves. False rumours spread by Axis agents of a German-Russian partition of Turkey brought no results. The Axis looked for easier game.

Greece had been a Monarchy since 1935. The Venizelos Government of 1928–32 had been succeeded by a series of Ministries. The tension between friends and opponents of Venizelos had grown, sharpened by the discontent due to the economic crisis. In 1935 the Venizelists made a rising, which was suppressed by General Kondylis, who in November restored King George II, the son of ex-King Constantine. George began his reign by an amnesty to political prisoners, and the exiled Venizelos ordered his followers to serve the king loyally. The political situation however remained difficult. The leaders of the main parties all died one after the other, and the formation of a satisfactory government became more difficult than ever. The king entrusted the Premiership to General Metaxas, the head of a group of nine Deputies in the Parliament. In August 1936, impressed by the danger of 'Communism' represented by a strike in the Kavala tobacco industry, George II authorised the general to proclaim a Dictatorship.

General Metaxas had the reputation of being pro-German. He had received part of his training in Germany, and admired the German army. In 1915 he made a plan for the occupation of the Dardanelles, which he offered to the British General Staff. Metaxas was a good officer, and the plan was probably a good one. With incredible tactlessness the British returned the plan without thanks, according to one version without even opening the envelope. It is not surprising that the general's feelings about the British should have changed for the worse. Metaxas introduced the outward forms of totalitarian Government. The Press was heavily censored, several political leaders were interned on the islands, a Youth Movement based on the Hitler Jugend was created. During these years German economic penetration made rapid progress. Germany became the best market for Greek tobacco, and German firms took an interest in the development of Greek resources. German political influence correspondingly grew.

In April 1939 Mussolini seized Albania. For several years previously King Zog had shown reluctance to accept Italian tutorship. He had been either unable or unwilling to repay loans, and had refused some demands for concessions. As the hour of crisis approached in Europe, Mussolini decided to make sure of his position on the eastern shore of the Adriatic, and on Good Friday his troops landed.

The occupation caused alarm in both Jugoslavia and Greece. It led to a British guarantee to Greece which, like the simultaneous one offered to Roumania, involved no obligation to assist Britain in case of war. The guarantee annoyed Italy, and, although Italo-Greek relations remained outwardly correct, the Italian Press began to agitate about the 'sufferings' of Albanians in Greek Epirus and to take a generally arrogant attitude to Greece.

Mussolini expressly mentioned Greece as a country with which he wished to maintain friendly relations in his speech announcing the declaration of war on Britain and France, but in the summer of 1940 Italian activity gave rise to fears in Greece. The shooting of an Albanian bandit in the frontier region was made the occasion for an Italian Press polemic, and on 15 August the Greek warship *Helle* was sunk by 'an unknown submarine' during the celebrations of the national Greek holiday. The Axis began to accuse Greece of plotting with Britain. On 28 October the Italian Minister presented a note containing impossible demands, and was met by Metaxas with a declaration of war. Whatever may have been Metaxas' ideological sympathies, his patriotism showed itself in the moment of crisis, and his years of careful training of the army produced their result in the magnificent resistance to the Italian invader.

Germany had not participated in the attack on Greece, as it was expected that Italy would quickly crush all resistance. But when the Greek army pushed the Italians back into Albania, Hitler had to do something. Pressure was exerted on Bulgaria. King Boris would no doubt have preferred to remain neutral. But Britain was not able to help him; he feared Germany far less than Russia, which he believed would dominate the Balkans if Germany were defeated; he was himself a German prince; and he could expect substantial rewards on the Aegean coast and in Macedonia for any help rendered to the Axis. After a period of hesitation, during which American as well as British influence was used to hold him back, the Soviet Union published a statement that Moscow did not approve of the entry of foreign troops into Bulgaria, and Bulgarian Democrats led by ex-Premier Mushanov protested against such a policy. Boris nevertheless yielded. At the end of February 1941 German troops poured from Roumania across hastily constructed Danube bridges into Bulgaria.

Jugoslavia, which had hitherto protected her neutrality, was now faced with a crisis. The overwhelming majority of Serbs and Slovenes, and most Croats, sympathised with Britain. The young generation of Serbs of the Left had at first allowed their hatred of Chamberlain to cloud their judgment, and German propaganda had exploited the German-Soviet Pact, not to create sympathy for Germany—that was quite impossible—but to increase mistrust of 'Anglo-French Imperialism'. The collapse of France and the courageous determination of Britain to fight on alone, the failure of German air attacks to break British morale and the success of the Greeks against Italy, restored universal sympathy for the Allied cause.

The task of the Government, however, was no easy one. Prince Paul himself sympathised with Britain, but feared war, both on account of the destruction involved and because the consequent poverty and despair might lead to social revolution. Premier Cvetković was a mere tool of the prince, a small-town politician who had little liking for the Axis Powers, but was prepared to carry out any instructions. Korošec used his personal influence over the Prince Regent to increase concessions to the Axis. He talked of neutrality, but his sympathies were on the side of the Fascists.

The Croatian Ministers were anxious to avoid war, for they knew that Croatia, being quite open to attack from north and east, could be overrun, that the fighting would be done in Serbian territory and their own country would be occupied. Moreover, they feared the activity of the pro-Fascist elements, both within and without the Croatian Peasant Party, who would sabotage the war effort and would be favoured by the Axis after occupation. Dr Maček was a firm believer in Democracy and in Southern Slav unity. He never swerved from this belief. But he was convinced of the necessity of peace, both for Croatia, the problems of whose newly received autonomy were still far from solution, and for Jugoslavia as a whole. He therefore favoured every concession to the Axis which would leave some independence to the country. He was convinced that Britain and America would win the war, but he did not see that their victory could be appreciably helped by the entry of weak Jugoslavia. He hoped that the country could remain at peace, and the three nations be kept together, until the Allied victory restored Democracy and Security to Europe.

Lastly, there were three Serbian Ministers in the Government who urged a more resolute attitude to Axis demands. Like Maček, they believed in Allied victory, but they were more concerned than he to see that no action of Jugoslavia could be interpreted as help to the Axis. These were Professor Konstantinović, one of the technicians of the August 1939 Agreement and now Minister of Justice, the object of constant attacks in the Axis Press as a 'Freemason, Communist and British Paid Agent'; Budisavljević, Minister of Social Welfare, of the Independent Democratic Party, a staunch Democrat and an old enemy of the Germans; and the Minister of Agriculture, the representative of the Serbian Agrarian Party, the Bosnian Ćubrilović.

The Greek war made the position of Jugoslavia most delicate. In November Italian planes bombed Bitolj, the second town of Jugoslav Macedonia, causing a number of deaths and considerable damage. One school of thought urged that Jugoslavia should provoke war by attacking Bulgaria before the German troops entered. The death of Korošec in December helped the party of strong action, but more prudent counsels ultimately prevailed. From the beginning of March the policy of the Axis grew more menacing. The equivocal attitude of Jugoslavia was a nuisance to Hitler, and had to be cleared up before the Greek affair could be concluded. The Belgrade Government tried to postpone decision. Poor Cvetković imagined to the end that he, the Balkan Machiavelli, could exploit the 'conflict of interest' between Hitler and Mussolini to play them off against each other. But Axis pressure was relentless. On 25 March Cvetković and the Foreign Minister Cincar Marković left Belgrade for Vienna, where they signed the Three-Power Pact. It was hoped that Britain would be satisfied with the facts that no military commitments had been undertaken, and that the transport of Axis troops and munitions through Jugoslavia was not required. The three democratic Serbian Ministers, mentioned above, at once resigned.

For the last weeks resolutions and exhortations had been pouring into Belgrade from individuals, groups and societies of many kinds in all the provinces, urging the Government not to surrender to the Axis, to put the honour and independence of Jugoslavia above all else. The signature of the Pact roused intense anger. The *coup d'état* of 27 March was carried out by a small number of daring officers, true heirs to the tradition of the great conspirator 'Apis' Dimitrijević. But they were only carrying out the will of the nation, which, with the romantic fanaticism peculiar to the Serbs—who had made of their great defeat of Kosovo the symbol of their national honour and the subject of their great epic poetry—preferred destruction to treachery.

A week after the Anglophile 'Quisling-malgré-lui', the hated Prince Paul, was bundled out of his country to a comfortable exile, the German planes descended on the unprepared open city of Belgrade. The preceding days had been filled with desperate attempts by the new Foreign Minister, the same Ninčić who had signed the Pact of Rome in 1924, to stave off disaster. The old game of 'inter-Axis rivalry' was played by the two Dictators to lull the Government into a false sense of security, and to induce it to postpone mobilisation. Thanks to the omissions of the Stojadinović regime, and the ill-founded last-minute optimism of the Simović Government, the country was quite unprepared for war, and the Germans had little difficulty in crushing the Jugoslav army. The potential threat to the Italian positions in Albania was removed, and the Axis armies thrust on down to Athens.

The real contribution of Jugoslavia to the Allied cause is threefold. In the first place the 27 March *coup d'état* was a moral gesture of a remarkable kind. It was the first slap in the face that Hitler had received. It showed him that there was one people at least in Europe that cared nothing for the benefits of his New Order, that would never be bribed into gilded slavery. Such a gesture a man of Hitler's breed could never forgive or forget. The savagery of the troops of occupation in conquered Jugoslavia is beyond doubt largely due to the Führer's personal rage. From 1934 onwards Germany had perhaps expended more diplomatic effort in Jugoslavia than anywhere else in Eastern Europe, and the result was this affront. The wild bravery of the action will stand in History as an encouragement to all generations of free men.

In the second place, Jugoslavia's action compelled Hitler to bring up additional troops for his Balkan campaign. The campaign took longer, and required more men, than had been anticipated. The consequent modification of plan and change of troop movements lost Hitler one valuable month of campaigning weather in Russia.

Thirdly, after the defeat of the main armies and the official capitulation, a large number of troops took to the forests and hills, with their equipment, and carried on a guerrilla war, which they never abandoned. The terror of the occupying forces drove still more, defenceless peasants and proscribed intellectuals, to join them. Thus was formed the people's army which for just under four years kept many Axis divisions occupied in Bosnia, Montenegro, Serbia, Dalmatia and Slovenia, and, since the fall of Italy, in most of Croatia also.

Thus Jugoslavia has made a contribution to the common cause which can be compared even with that of Greece. These two small States sacrificed everything for the principle of Freedom. They have suffered beyond anything which the people of Britain can imagine. Greece has lost thousands of her sons in war, and thousands more by famine, while the ordinary civil population is liable to summary arrest and execution. In Jugoslavia the casualties of war and deaths from hunger have been fewer, but this has been more than compensated by the frightful scale of the massacres carried out by Germans, Italians, Hungarians, Bulgarians and Croatian and Serbian Fascists. Now that victory has been won, Greeks and Jugoslavs have a sacred claim on the services of the British people.

Conclusions

Of the eight Eastern European States, five—Czechoslovakia, Albania, Poland, Greece and Jugoslavia—were in the spring of 1944 still under enemy occupation; two—Hungary and Roumania—were fighting Hitler's battle in Russia; and one—Bulgaria—was in the happy position of having gained large increases of territory with Axis help and of having to do no more in return than make a Platonic declaration of war on Britain and America.

The plight of the occupied countries is the worst, but the 'Axis Allies' are not in an enviable situation.

Roumania handed herself over without reserve to the Axis in 1940. While Antonescu's clique throw quickly earned money about, the Roumanian people served as a source of cannon fodder and an object of constant economic exploitation.

Hungary put up more resistance. Teleki even made a Pact of 'Eternal Friendship' with Jugoslavia in December 1940 in the short-lived hope of loosening the Axis grip. When the German demand came for passage of troops, his own General Staff turned against him, and the Regent Horthy, who not long before had made a great show of his hostility to the Germans, betrayed him. He killed himself, and Hungarian troops marched into Jugoslavia with German, to be rewarded with the Bačka and the honour of acting as Hitler's policemen in part of the Balkans. When the time came for war with Russia, Hungary had to join in, and was compelled by in-

creasing pressure to give greater quantities of men for her
master's war.

Bulgaria escaped this unpleasant duty mainly because even
Hitler understood that the love of the Bulgarians for Russia is
such that they would probably desert to the enemy. He wisely
hesitated to use them against Turkey.

The two 'Quisling States' created by the Axis, Slovakia
and Croatia, also made their contributions to the 'Crusade'.
The murderer Pavelić obediently handed over Dalmatia to the
Duce, and attempted to convince his masters that he should
be taken seriously by the energy with which he massacred un-
numbered thousands of Serbian men, women and children in
Lika, Slavonia and Bosnia. However, he never subdued resistance in his 'Independent State'. First the Serbian population rose in arms, then they were joined by their Croatian
kinsmen. Despite the massacres, Serbs and Croats were united
in struggle against a common enemy by Tito, whose policy of
Jugoslav solidarity has already done much to overcome old
national feuds.

As for the Slovak leaders, the ridiculous Tiso and the renegade Hungarian Tuka, who learned Slovak when he was
approaching middle age, they were the laughing-stock of their
people and of Europe. The true feelings of the Slovak people
were shown first by desertions on the Russian Front, and
finally by the National Rising of September 1944.

The only State in our area which preserved its independence
and neutrality was Turkey, an Asiatic Power with a foothold
on European soil. During April 1941 bitterness was felt in the
Balkans that Turkey had not come to the aid of her friends
of the Balkan Entente. But looking back it is easy to see that
Turkey's attitude benefited the Allied cause. If she had
entered the war when Syria was still in Vichy hands, the
German armies could have swept through Anatolia and down
the coast into Egypt, taking the then sorely pressed armies
of Wavell in the rear. Turkish neutrality was until the spring
of 1943 a bulwark of the British strategic position in the
Middle East. If after that it became an obstacle, it is still only
fair to give credit to the Turks for resisting German blandishments in the earlier war years.

The *cordon sanitaire* erected in 1919 broke down. Some
States remained true to their old friends, and have suffered.

Others have given invaluable military assistance to the enemy. Hungary and Roumania between them provided a million men. These two armies, which some British military critics dismissed as of no interest or importance, equipped with German arms and generally supervised by German senior officers, played a decisive part in the battles on the Don. These armies should have fought on our side.

Several reasons explain the collapse of the 1919 settlement. The rotten internal system of oppression, corruption, ignorance and brutality morally disarmed the Eastern European peoples. Social tension led to political hatred, political hatred to Police Dictatorships. The Governments, terrified of 'Bolshevism' in their peoples, fell a prey to German propaganda. They allowed the Germans to build a Fifth Column in business, the bureaucracy, the Press and even the army. This Fifth Column used every direct and indirect means of disruption, and in six years it did its work well.

Secondly, the Eastern European States never made a serious attempt to collaborate. They remained divided into victors and vanquished, the former proudly rejecting all proposals for change, the latter unwilling to abandon their maximum demands. When in one country there appeared a statesman ready to negotiate with understanding, he met with no response on the other side.

Thirdly, mistrust of the small Revisionist Powers blinded the small Victor States to the greater dangers from the Great Powers. Both the Little Entente and the Balkan Entente were misdirected. They never served the purposes intended for them by such far-sighted statesmen as Beneš and Atatürk, but were no more than limited alliances against small States which represented no danger.

Fourthly, unnecessary ill-feeling between the Eastern European States was caused by high tariffs and by persecution of national minorities. These were only the inevitable consequence of the doctrines of Nationalism, applied in the cultural and economic fields. Nationalism was itself a consequence of the division of the peoples into a small, grasping and ambitious semi-bourgeois or aristocratic class and a helpless mass of backward peasants. The country which suffered least from these evils, which most consistently defended a foreign policy based on Democracy, which most sincerely worked for solidarity of Eastern European nations, which treated its national minorities most humanely, Czechoslovakia, was also the country with the most balanced social structure. Yet it must not be imagined that even Czechoslovakia was free from these faults.

But the fundamental cause of the collapse lies not in the faults of the Eastern European States, but in the policy of the Great Powers of the West. It is quite useless to discuss whether France or Britain was more to blame. Britain was as much responsible for Versailles as was France, and British interests were as much threatened as French by the rise of any one European Power to hegemony on the Continent. For years British policy treated Italian mischief-making in Eastern Europe with benevolent neutrality. When Germany became a menace again, it was Britain that pressed France to be 'fair' to the former enemy. That French Governments did not insist with sufficient force on repressive measures is unhappily true, but that does not exonerate Britain. British capital investments in Germany enabled Hitler to begin his rearmament. British and French business men regarded Hitler for years as a useful bulwark against the 'Reds'. Above all, British Governments, for eighteen years predominantly Conservative in composition and for three Labour, failed to maintain the armed strength of Britain.

APPENDIX

RACIAL AND RELIGIOUS STATISTICS

[These figures are, with one exception, copied from the official census figures of the respective countries. They are therefore not uniform in character, as the censuses are of course not always held in the same year, and as the test applied for ascertaining nationality varies very considerably. This derives from the practice which obtained in the old Austro-Hungarian Monarchy. At the Hungarian census of 1910 knowledge of the Magyar language was often taken as ground for classifying a non-Magyar as 'Magyar': while in the Austrian census of the same year the rubric 'Umgangssprache' (or 'language habitually spoken') weighed down the scale in favour of German. It will be obvious that the interpretation of the rubric 'Mother-tongue' lends itself to a great variety in practice.

The figures given here are thus only approximate, and critical commentary is deliberately withheld, as it would involve the addition of a long and highly contentious chapter. But it is hoped that these tables will in some degree make good the absence of a full-scale racial map of Eastern Europe.—R. W. S.-W.]

A. POLAND

	Census of 30 September 1921*		Census of 9 December 1931†	
Poles	18,814,239	69·2 %	21,993,400	68·9 %
Ukrainians (Ruthenes)	3,898,431	14·3	3,227,000	10·1
Jews	2,110,448	7·8	2,732,600	8·6
Germans	1,059,194	3·9	741,000	2·3
White Russians	1,060,237	3·9	989,900	3·1
Russians	56,239	0·2	138,700	0·4
Lithuanians	68,667	0·3	—	—
Czechs	30,628	0·1	—	—
Others	78,634	0·3	878,600	—
	27,176,717		31,915,800	

* *Commission statistique de la République Polonaise*, 1925–6, p. 26; and *Die Nationalitäten in den Staaten Europas*, p. 56.
† *Concise Statistical Yearbook of Poland*, 1937.

Religions

Roman Catholic	20,670,100	64·8 %
Greek Catholic	3,336,200	10·4
Orthodox	3,762,500	11·8
Jewish	3,113,900	9·8
Protestant	835,200	2·6
Others	197,900	0·6

B. CZECHOSLOVAKIA

	Census of 15 February 1921*		Census of 1 December 1930†	
Czechoslovaks‡	8,760,937	65·5 %	9,668,770	66·9 %
Germans	3,123,568	23·4	3,231,688	22·3
Magyars	745,431	5·6	691,923	4·7
Ruthenes (Ukrainians)	461,849	3·5	549,169	5·7
Poles	75,853	0·5	81,737	0·5
Jews	180,855	1·3	186,642	1·29
Roumanians	13,974	0·1	13,044	0·09
Gypsies	—	—	52,209	0·2
Others	—	—	—	—
	13,374,364		14,729,536	

* *Czechoslovak Statistics*, vol. 9, pp. 65–6; see also *Die Nationalitäten in den Staaten Europas*, pp. 172 sqq.
† *Statesman's Yearbook*, 1944.
‡ Czechs and Slovaks are not returned separately. A rough estimate places them at 6,800,000 and 2,000,000 respectively. The census of 15 December 1940 in 'independent' Slovakia showed a population of 2,653,564.

Religions

Roman Catholic	10,831,096	Orthodox	145,598
Greek and Armenian	584,041	Jewish	356,830
Catholics		Old Catholic	22,712
Protestant	1,129,758	'Konfessionslos'	854,638
Czechoslovak Church	793,385	Others	9,878

C. HUNGARY

	Census of 31 December 1920*		Census of 31 January 1941†
Magyars	7,147,053	89·6 %	11,017,170
Germans	551,211	6·9	865,530
Slovaks	141,882	1·8	308,070
Roumanians	23,760	0·3	1,144,260
Ruthenes (Ukrainians)	1,500	—	586,800
Croats	36,858	0·5	Serbs and
Serbs	17,131	0·2	Croats
Bunjevci and Šokci	23,017	—	513,450
Slovenes	6,087	—	
[Total of Jugoslavs	83,093]	—	Jews‡ 161,370
Others	31,744	0·4	73,350
	7,980,143		14,679,573

* *Recensement de la Population en 1920*, vi, p. 64; *Die Nationalitäten*, p. 331.
† *Statesman's Yearbook*, 1944.
‡ Not previously returned as a nationality in Hungary.

It will be noted that the census of 1941 was subsequent to the re-incorporation of Slovak and Ruthene territory under the first Award of Vienna in November 1938, and of Roumanian territory under the second Award of August 1940.

Religions (from the census of 1941)

Roman Catholic	5,634,003	Orthodox (Greek	39,839
Greek Catholic	201,013	Oriental)	
Calvinist	1,813,162	Unitarian	6,266
Lutheran	534,165	Jewish	444,567
[Protestant total	2,347,327]		

D. ROUMANIA

	An earlier estimate*		*Census of 29 December 1930†*
Roumanians	11,545,311	71·9 %	12,980,033
Magyars	1,463,573	9·1	1,426,178
Jews	778,094	4·9	725,318
Germans	713,564	4·5	740,169
Ukrainians	500,484	3·1	577,693
Bulgarians	351,328	2·2	361,058
Turks and Tatars	222,375	1·4	288,793
Russians	174,393	1·1	415,217
Gypsies	133,075	0·8	278,793
Serbs	52,570	0·3	—
Poles	35,433	0·2	—
Slovaks	26,884	0·2	—
Others	46,704	—	—
	16,050,239		17,793,252

* *Statistisches Handbuch der Europäischen Nationalitäten*, p. 228; see also *Die Nationalitäten*, p. 282.
† *Statesman's Yearbook*, 1944.

Religions (in round figures)

Orthodox	13,200,000	Unitarian	75,000
Uniate	1,426,000	Jewish	1,500,000
Roman Catholic	1,200,000	Moslem	260,000
Calvinist	720,000	Others	140,000
Lutheran	400,000		

E. JUGOSLAVIA

	Census of 31 January 1921		Census of March 1931	
Serbs and Croats	8,911,509	74·3 %	Serbs	5,953,000
			Croats	3,221,000
Slovenes	1,019,907	8·5	Slovenes	1,134,000
			Bosnian Moslems	729,000
[Total of Jugoslavs	9,931,416]	82·8		11,037,000
Other Slavs (a)	176,479	—		153,000
Magyars	467,652	3·9		467,000
Germans	505,790	3·9		499,000
Albanians	439,657	3·6		
Roumanians	231,068	1·9		
Italians	12,533	0·1		
·Others	220,200	1·8		
	11,894,911			

Religions (census of 1931)

Orthodox	6,785,501	48·7 %
Roman Catholic	5,217,910	37·4
Greek Catholic	44,671	0·3
Protestant	231,169	1·6
Moslem	1,561,166	11·2
Jewish	68,405	0·4
Others	18,006	0·1

(a) This rubric includes Ruthenes, Slovaks and Czechs.

F. BULGARIA

Census of 1934

Races		Religions	
Bulgars	5,274,854	Orthodox	5,128,890
Turks and Tatars	618,268	Roman Catholic	45,704
Gypsies	80,532	Moslem	821,298
Jews	28,126	Jewish	48,398
Armenians	23,045	Armenian	23,476
Roumanians	16,405	Protestant	8,371
Russians	11,928		
	6,077,939		

G. AUSTRIA

Census of 7 March 1923

Germans	6,272,892	Slovenes	43,383
Czechs	93,533	Magyars	25,071
Slovaks	5,170	Others	47,943
Serbs and Croats	46,771		

H. ITALY

The census of 1 December 1921 returns the following racial minorities:

A. In Venezia Tridentina (i.e. Trentino), in a total of 647,703:

> 426,638 Italians and Ladines
> 195,650 Germans

B. In Venezia Giulia*, in a total of 919,897:

> 531,824 Italians
> 258,944 Slovenes ⎫
> 92,800 Croats ⎬ 351,744 Jugoslavs
>   ⎭
> 4,185 Germans

> * Including Zara, but excluding Fiume.

There is no longer any sign of the 56,916 Slovenes inside Trieste returned under the Austrian census of 1910. In *Die Nationalitäten*, pp. 473–4, it is claimed that there were not less than 600,000 Slovenes and Croats in the Kingdom of Italy after 1918.

As the Hungarian arguments in all disputed questions are based upon the Census of 1910—the last held in the old Austria-Hungary—the following official tables of nationality and religion in the then Kingdom of Hungary are here added.

(a) *In Hungary proper.*

Magyar	9,944,627	54·5%	Roman Catholic	9,010,305	49·3%
German	1,903,357	10·4	Uniate (Greek		
Slovak	1,946,357	10·7	Catholic)	2,007,916	11·0
Roumanian	2,948,146	16·1	Calvinistic	2,603,381	14·3
Ruthene	464,270	2·5	Lutheran	1,306,384	7·1
Croat	194,808	1·1	Orthodox	2,233,979	12·8
Serb	462,516	2·5	Unitarian	74,275	0·4
Other	401,412	2·2	Jewish	911,227	5·0
	18,265,493				

(b) *In Croatia-Slavonia.*

Croat	1,638,354	62·5	Roman Catholic	1,877,833
Serb	644,955	24·6	Orthodox	653,184
Magyar	105,948	4·1	Uniate	17,592
German	134,078	5·1	Protestant	51,707
Other	98,619			
	2,621,954			

(c) Total population. In lands of Crown of St Stephen 20,886,487.

In some tables a few altogether insignificant racial fragments have been omitted, with the result that they do not add up correctly. In each case the aggregate and the single item are correct.

INDEX